Urban Sustainability Transitions

The world's population is currently undergoing a significant transition towards urbanisation, with the UN expecting that 70% of people globally will live in cities by 2050. Urbanisation has multiple political, cultural, environmental and economic dimensions that profoundly influence social development and innovation. This fundamental long-term transformation will involve the realignment of urban society's technologies and infrastructures, culture and lifestyles, as well as governance and institutional frameworks. Such structural systemic realignments can be referred to as urban sustainability transitions: fundamental and structural changes in urban systems through which persistent societal challenges are addressed, such as shifts towards urban farming, renewable decentralised energy systems, and social economies.

This book provides new insights into how sustainability transitions unfold in different types of cities across the world and explores possible strategies for governing urban transitions, emphasising the co-evolution of material and institutional transformations in socio-technical and socio-ecological systems. With case studies of mega-cities such as Seoul, Tokyo, New York and Adelaide, medium-sized cities such as Copenhagen, Cape Town and Portland, and nonmetropolitan cities such as Freiburg, Ghent and Brighton, the book provides an opportunity to reflect upon the comparability and transferability of theoretical/conceptual constructs and governance approaches across geographical contexts.

Urban Sustainability Transitions is key reading for students and scholars working in Environmental Sciences, Geography, Urban Studies, Urban Policy and Planning.

Niki Frantzeskaki is Associate Professor of Sustainability Transitions Governance at the Dutch Research Institute For Transitions (DRIFT), Erasmus University Rotterdam, The Netherlands.

Vanesa Castán Broto is Senior Lecturer at the Bartlett Development Planning Unit, University College London, UK.

Lars Coenen is City of Melbourne Chair in Resilient Cities at the Melbourne Sustainable Society Institute, Faculty of Architecture, Building and Planning, University of Melbourne, Australia.

Derk Loorbach is Professor of Socio-economic Transitions and Director of the Dutch Research Institute For Transitions (DRIFT), Erasmus University Rotterdam, The Netherlands.

Routledge Studies in Sustainability Transitions

Series editors: Johan Schot, John Grin and Jan Rotmans

Urban Sustainability Transitions

**Edited by Niki Frantzeskaki,
Vanesa Castán Broto, Lars Coenen
and Derk Loorbach**

LONDON AND NEW YORK

First published 2017 by Routledge

2 Park Square, Milton Park, Abingdon, Oxfordshire OX14 4RN
52 Vanderbilt Avenue, New York, NY 10017

Routledge is an imprint of the Taylor & Francis Group, an informa business

First issued in paperback 2019

British Library Cataloguing in Publication Data
A catalogue record for this book is available from the British Library

Library of Congress Cataloging in Publication Data
A catalog record for this book has been requested

ISBN: 978-0-415-78418-4 (hbk)
ISBN: 978-0-367-21908-6 (pbk)

Typeset in Times New Roman MT Std
by diacriTech, Chennai

Contents

INTERLUDE

PART II
Experimentation and Urban Sustainability Transitions

INTERLUDE

PART III
Politics of Urban Space and of Urban Sustainability Transitions

INTERLUDE

PART IV
Taking Stock and Connecting with Sustainability Transitions Studies

Figures

Tables

Boxes

Contributors

Tracey Arklay is a Research Fellow at the Institute for Social Science Research, University of Queensland, Australia. Her research interests include disaster management, Australian and State politics and policy capacity.

Flor Avelino has a background in political science and works as a transition researcher and lecturer at DRIFT, Erasmus University Rotterdam, The Netherlands. Her research is focused on the role of power and empowerment in sustainability transitions. As scientific coordinator of the Transformative Social Innovation (TranSIt) research project, she currently investigates how grassroots initiatives and transnational social movements challenge, alter or replace existing institutions. As the academic director of the Transition Academy, Flor strives to co-create new learning environments to challenge people to think and act for radical change.

Yvette Bettini is a Research Fellow in the Institute for Social Science Research, University of Queensland, Australia. She has a background in Human Geography and experience in community engagement and water/catchment management. Her research focuses on the social and capacity dimensions of environmental management, policy and governance.

Christian Binz is a post-doctoral scholar at the Department of Environmental Social Sciences, Eawag, Switzerland. His research focuses on the geography of transitions in infrastructure sectors. Working at the interface between evolutionary economic geography and transition studies, he aims at improving the understanding on how international and multi-scalar linkages shape innovation dynamics in clean-tech industries. Empirically he has analysed the emergence of a potable water reuse sector in California as well as of on-site water recycling industries in China and Europe. With his pronounced focus on innovation dynamics that co-evolve between industrialized and emerging economies he aims at adapting transition theory and related policy advice to the complex geography of today's globalizing knowledge economy.

Anne Katrine Braagaard Harders is a PhD Candidate at the Center for Design and Innovation for Sustainable Transition at University of Aalborg's Copenhagen Campus, Denmark. Anne Katrine has centred her research on urban development projects' role in urban sustainable transitions with a particular focus on urban mobility. In her research she in investigating how visions for sustainability is understood, interpreted and translated throughout the execution of urban development projects in the city as a diverse and conflictual assemblage of people, interests, objects, infrastructures, competencies and resources. Anne Katrine has taken part in various projects on sustainable urban transition and mobility as well as teaching and participation in networks.

Vanesa Castán Broto is Senior Lecturer at the Bartlett Development Planning Unit, University College London, UK. Her research is concerned with cities, development and climate change. She has done research on the role of knowledge in environmental conflicts; the role of experiments in reconfiguring governance; the possibilities and implications of participatory planning for climate change and most recently, the role of energy transitions in cities in the global south. She currently holds an ESRC Future Research Leaders Fellowship to study energy landscapes.

Sarah Burch is a Canada Research Chair in Sustainability Governance and Innovation, and Assistant Professor in the Department of Geography and Environmental Management at the University of Waterloo, Canada. Her most recent book is *Understanding Climate Change: Science Policy and Practice* and she has written numerous articles on the governance of urban sustainability transitions. She is a Coordinating Lead Author in the Assessment Report on Climate Change in Cities(ARC3-2), and North American coordinator of the Earth System Governance network of Research Fellows. She was a Contributing Author to the Fourth Assessment Report of the Intergovernmental Panel on Climate Change, and she teaches a Massive Open Online Course called 'Climate Literacy: Navigating Climate Change Conversations,' which reaches thousands of students around the world.

Federico Caprotti is Senior Lecturer in Cities and Sustainability at King's College London, UK. He works on eco-urbanism and the green economy, with a particular focus on China and Europe. He is the author of the recent book, *Cities and the Transition to Low Carbon Economies* (2015). Federico also runs the Masters programme in Sustainable Cities at King's, and leads an international, ESRC and NSFC funded research consortium investigating transitional 'smart and eco' cities in a comparative EU-China perspective. Federico holds a doctorate and bachelor's degrees from Oxford University.

Dr Lars Coenen is full professor and the inaugural 'City of Melbourne Chair of Resilient Cities', an initiative between the City of Melbourne and University of Melbourne aimed at improving the city's resilience to sustainability challenges. Working closely with the city's chief resilience officer, Lars seeks to strengthen Melbourne's role as a leader in knowledge based urban resilience, leverage opportunities to attract research funding and provide a new model for collaborative research. Lars is an interdisciplinary scholar cross-cutting the fields of innovation studies, economic geography and science and technology studies. His research interests converge around the geography of innovation: Why is it that some regions and cities in the world stand out in their ability to foster and diffuse novelty? What explains this spatial concentration of innovation in an era of globalization? How can regions and cities improve their capacity to innovate? In particular he is interested in addressing this broad set of questions on innovations related to pressing societal challenges such as climate change. His work has been published in leading international journals such as Research Policy, Environment and Planning A and Economic Geography. He is well-known for pioneering research on the geography of sustainability transitions. His paper 'Environmental Innovation and Sustainability Transitions in Regional Studies' has been awarded the 2013 best paper award in Regional Studies (co-authored with Bernhard Truffer).

Morten Elle is an associate professor with the Center for Design, Innovation and Sustainable Transition, Aalborg University, Denmark. She has been working with sustainable urban transition since the 1980s, with focus on the links between infrastructure and livability. He has contributed to several books, for instance: Alexander and Price's, *Managing Organizational Ecologies* (2012).

Nigel Forrest is a post-doctoral research associate in the Decision Center for a Desert City and Global Institute of Sustainability at Arizona State University, USA. Nigel's general research interest is in transformational sustainability solutions in which he currently focuses is on transformational water solutions for the Colorado River Basin. His prior research, also solution-oriented, has included urban sustainability processes and grassroots community sustainability transition initiatives. Nigel manages the Transformational Sustainability Research and Education lab at the School of Sustainability, actively coordinating and engaging students from multiple disciplines in sustainability experiments with community stakeholders. Nigel holds a Ph.D and Master's degree in Sustainability from Arizona State University, and a Bachelor's degree in geology from the University of Glasgow. He has taught sustainability at graduate, undergraduate, and high school levels.

Niki Frantzeskaki is Associate Professor of Sustainability Transitions Governance at DRIFT, Erasmus University Rotterdam, The Netherlands. She holds a PhD on 'Dynamics of Sustainability transitions' from Delft University of Technology. She has been working at DRIFT since 2010 where she researches contemporary sustainability transitions and their governance across Europe (UK, Greece, Italy, the Netherlands) and in developing countries like Vanuatu and Ghana. She is coordinating research on environmental governance, transition management and urban living labs for urban sustainability transitions by leading and being involved in a portfolio of research projects including: URBES, ARTS, IMPRESSIONS, GUST, RESILIENT EUROPE, and SUSTAIN.

C. F. Fratini is a Postdoc researcher in urban planning and governance for sustainability transitions. Her theoretical work focuses on complexity science, transition theories, Science and Technology Studies (STS), urban political ecology, urban, organizational and institutional studies. Her empirical work focuses on urban innovations, environmental and infrastructural management, public administration and business models for urban service delivery with a privileged focus on urban water governance and practices. She contributed to develop a tool for urban flood resilience (The 3-Point-Approach) combining engineering knowledge on flood risk management with a qualitative analysis of the contingency of values assigned to water in the urban space, considering the mutual interrelations existing among infrastructural development, social complexity and natural variability. In her latest work, she unfolds and discusses past and present transition dynamics characterising the innovation of Danish urban water management practices over the last century providing insides on how actor's networks, their contingent power and politics shapes innovation pathways in cities.

Lea Fuenfschilling is a postdoctoral researcher at CIRCLE, Lund University, Sweden, as well as a lecturer at the Department of Sociology, University of Lucerne, Switzerland. She holds a PhD in Sociology from the University of Basel. Her dissertation is entitled "A dynamic model of socio-technical change. Institutions, actors and technology in interaction" and was published in 2014. Her current research interests are centred on understanding the dynamics of socio-technical change and innovation in infrastructure sectors (e.g., water) by focusing on different aspects of institutions, actors and technology as well as their interrelatedness. Special attention is thereby devoted to the process of institutionalization of new, potentially more sustainable socio-technical configurations. Specifically, she currently investigates the role of urban living laboratories in facilitating transformative change in cities as well as the influence of the economic profession on the creation of water markets.

John Grin is a full professor of 'policy science, especially system innovation' at the Department of Political Science at the University of Amsterdam, The Netherlands. He is co-director (with Marlies Glasius) of the *Programme Group* Transnational Configurations, Conflicts and Governance of the Amsterdam Institute for Social Science Research (AISSR). A physicist by training (BSc, 1983; MSc, 1986), he obtained his PhD in 1990 at the VU University in Amsterdam on a thesis on technology assessment in the area of military technology and international security, he worked on these issues for another two years at VU University and Princeton University. In 1992 he joined the University of Amsterdam. The constant throughout his career has been an interest in the relationships between science, technology, society and politics. In addition to system innovations and transitions, his research interests include policy analysis and design (including technology assessment), policy implementation, policy learning and novel modes of democratic governance. Empirically, much of his work focuses on agrofood, health care and water management.

Annegret Haase is an urban researcher working on urban shrinkage and reurbanization, urban land use change, socio-spatial inequalities and urban governance; the regional focus is Europe. She leads a working group on urban land use change and urban ecosystem services within an integrated project on urban transformations towards sustainability at Helmholtz Centre for Environmental Research – UFZ, Leipzig, and has been part of several international projects including the coordination of the EU 7FP project Shrink Smart.

Dagmar Haase is a Professor and a land-use scientist and urban landscape ecologist working on land use scenario modelling and urban ecosystem services estimation in European cities. She leads a Lab at the Humboldt University in Berlin, Germany and is guest scientist at the Helmholtz Centre for Environmental Research – UFZ, Leipzig. Dagmar has been participating in leading EU projects on urban land use change/management and ecosystem services research (PLUREL, URBES, GREENSURGE).

Nichola Harmer is a Lecturer in Human Geography at Plymouth University, UK. She has worked on a range of topics in geography and international relations including sovereignty, ethics, identity and power in British Overseas Territories, resilience, responses to climate change, and eco-urbanism. Nichola holds a PhD in Geography from Plymouth University, an MA in Politics from the University of Exeter, and a Bachelor's degree from the University of Sussex.

Brian W. Head is Professorial Fellow in Public Policy and Sustainability Research, Institute for Social Science Research, University of Queensland, Australia. His experience includes senior roles in the Queensland Government. His current research includes evidence-based policy and governance to address major problems including water resources and climate change adaptation.

J. S. Jensen is a Postdoc researcher in the Department of Development and Planning, Aalborg University, Denmark. Coming from a background in philosophy and environmental planning his current research interests spans sectorial transformation processes, transitions of socio-technical systems, urban transformation and the relation between economic institutions and sociotechnical transitions. His research addresses empirical domains such as construction, the built environment, water and cities and the role of new public management reforms in system transitions. His theoretical interests include institutional theory, science and technology studies, transition theory and urban studies. Inspired by urban assemblages literature and writings on urban political ecology his latest work focuses on the urban as a productive context for transitions processes, due to the ongoing strategic work that goes into managing the ambiguities and tensions among the various systems and practices that characterise such contexts.

Braden Kay is a Sustainability Officer with the City of Orlando, Florida. He was a postdoctoral researcher at the Global Institute of Sustainability at Arizona State University managing community engagement, sustainability visioning, and strategy building efforts for Reinvent Phoenix, a federally funded long-term planning project in Phoenix, Arizona. Dr Kay holds a Ph.D.

in Sustainability from Arizona State University, and a Bachelor's degree in American Studies from Carleton College in Minnesota. He was a Teach for America Corps Member in St. Louis, Missouri as middle school special education teacher, and was on the founding team of KIPP LEAD Charter School in Gary, Indiana.

Kinga Krauze is an assistant professor in the European Regional Centre for Ecohydrology of Polish Academy of Sciences. Since 2007 she is the Vice-Chair of the European Long-Term Ecosystem Research Network and the deputy lead of its Expert Panel on Science Strategy. She is also a core member of the Science Committee and the Regional Representative of Central and Eastern Europe in the Global LTER Network. Since 2004 she has been a member of the Council of the International Network of Excellence ALTER-Net (Europe's biodiversity, ecosystem and ecosystem services research network). Her research interests focus on: fish ecology, river ecology, use of fish as indicators of river ecological status, implementation of ecohydrological measures at landscape scale for sustainability of river systems, socio-economic drivers of landscape transformation and biodiversity change, green infrastructure and ecosystem services, networking and capacity building for socio-ecological research. She is the author of 20 publications in international journals and books, over 10 international guidelines and reports, and 70 oral presentations at international conferences.

Jakub Kronenberg is an associate professor in the Department of International Economics at the University of Lodz, Poland. His research interests focus on economy–environment interactions, in particular from the perspective of ecological economics, and environmental and resource economics. His book *Ecological economics and industrial ecology* was published by Routledge in 2007. He gained international research experience while working in France, Sweden, Switzerland, the UK and the Kyrgyz Republic. In 2001–2003, he served as environmental management consultant to the UNDP Umbrella Project. Since 2009 he is member of the board of the Sendzimir Foundation that promotes sustainable development in Poland. While not working, he may be bird-watching or travelling. Website: www.economics-of-sustainability.com/jk

Anthony M. Levenda is a PhD candidate in the Toulan School of Urban Studies and Planning at Portland State University, USA. His research and publications lie at the intersection of urban geography, political economy, and sociology of technology. His dissertation project examines the governance of smart grid and smart city infrastructures.

Derk Loorbach is Professor of Socio-economic Transitions and Director the Dutch Research Institute For Transitions (DRIFT), Erasmus University Rotterdam, The Netherlands. In his PhD he developed the concept and approach of transition management as new governance perspective and experimental governance approach. He has been working at the interface of science and society ever since, combining cutting edge transitions research with close cooperation with policy and business to further sustainable development in practice. Currently, the focus of his research is on the dynamics of destabilisation and acceleration focusing on the changing role of (local) government and urban transitions.

Anne Maassen is an international development professional in the sustainable energy and climate change sector. Her expertise is in climate finance and market creation project design and evaluation for a range of multilateral development banks and agencies (e.g., IFC, EBRD, UNIDO, UNDP, the European Commission) in Central Asia, Africa, Southern and Eastern Europe, and the Middle East. She also works on the Science of Delivery agenda at the World Bank, which is concerned with datadriven and rigorous processes for understanding what works, under what conditions, why, and how. She holds a PhD in Geography (Durham University, UK), as well as an MSc in Environmental Monitoring, Modelling and Management (King's College London, UK).

Timon McPhearson is Assistant Professor of Urban Ecology at The New School's Environmental Studies program, Director of the Urban Ecology Lab, and research faculty at Tishman Environment and Design Center, where he works directly with designers, planners, and managers to foster sustainable and resilient cities. He investigates the ecology *in, of* and *for* cities and teaches urban resilience, systems thinking and urban ecology at the university. Dr McPhearson is a founding member of the ICLEI Urban Biosphere (URBIS) Initiative, a contributing author to the UN Convention on Biological Diversity's Cities Biodiversity Outlook, a member of the Urban Climate Change Research Network (UCCRN), and co-leads the Future Earth Urban Platform (FEUP). He is also Co-PI of the US National Science Foundation (NSF) $12 Million "Urban Resilience to Extreme Weather Related Events" Sustainability Research Network (UREx SRN, 2015-2020). His work is published widely including in scientific journals (*Nature, AMBIO, Urban Ecosystems, Landscape and Urban Planning, Ecosystem Services*), in books (*Sustainability in America's Cities, Second Assessment Report on Climate Change in Cities*) and popular press (*Revolve Magazine*, The Nature of Cities), and covered by the *New York Times, The Nation* and the *Chronicle of Higher Education*.

Thaddeus R. Miller is an Assistant Professor in the Toulan School of Urban Studies and Planning and Faculty Fellow in the Institute for Sustainable Solutions at Portland State University, USA. His research explores the social and political dimensions of science, technology and sustainability. His book, *Reconstructing Sustainability Science: Knowledge and Action for a Sustainable Future* (2015), discusses how scientific research can be aligned with more sustainable social and environmental outcomes.

Timothy Moss is Senior Researcher at the Integrative Research Institute on Transformations of Human-Environment Systems (IRI THESys) at the Humboldt University of Berlin. His research interests cover the governance of urban infrastructures in transition, the spatial organisation of water and energy management and institutional dimensions and dynamics of resource use in cities and regions.

Josephine Musango is a Senior Lecturer at the School of Public Leadership, Stellenbosch University, South Africa. She holds a Transdisciplinary Doctorate in Public and Development Management, and a Masters Degree in Agricultural Economics, both from Stellenbosch University. Her research interest is undertaking transdisciplinary research focused on integrating economics into sustainable resource management and solving complex social and policy related problems through application of economic analysis and system dynamics modelling. Her particular interests are on social, resource management and policy challenges including green economy, energy, water, land use, transport and waste management at an urban and country scale. She also has expertise in other modelling approaches including material flow analysis, agent based modelling, discrete event modelling, Bayesian networks and econometrics. She has published widely in peer reviewed journals and in international and local conferences.

Michael Ornetzeder is a Senior Scientist at the Institute of Technology Assessment at the Austrian Academy of Sciences, and a Lecturer at the University of Natural Resources and Life Sciences in Vienna and at the University of Applied Sciences Upper Austria. From 1990 to 1997 he was a project manager at the Centre of Appropriate Technology at the Technical University of Vienna. From 1998 to 2007 he worked as head of department at the Centre for Social Innovation (ZSI). In 2004 and 2005 he was a research fellow at the International Institute for Applied Systems Analysis (IIASA), Laxenburg. His current research is within science and technology studies, with a particular focus on sustainable energy technologies, user innovation and social learning.

Camaren Peter is a pure and applied scientist by training (physics and astrophysics). He obtained his PhD from the Graduate School of Business at the University of Cape Town in complexity-based modelling for sustainability, and now works as a writer and research consultant. Camaren has worked closely with local and global institutions on sustainability in developing world contexts (especially cities). He is an extra-ordinary senior lecturer in the School of Public Leadership in the Faculty of Economic and Management Sciences (Stellenbosch University). His first book *Lazarus in the Multiple: Awakening to the Era of Complexity* was released in January 2016.

Saska Petrova is a Lecturer at the School of Environment, Education and Development at the University of Manchester, UK. Her main research interests are in intra-community relations and vulnerabilities as they relate to natural resource management, energy flows, social justice and local governance. Saska has published extensively on these issues, including a forthcoming monograph titled *Communities in Transition* (2014). A distinct part of Saska's work focuses on the relationship between urban energy vulnerability and sustainability transitions. This is in part a result of, inter alia, her involvement in a number of interdisciplinary projects funded by the Royal Geographical Society, EPRSC, Cheshire Lehman Fund and Higher Education Academy. She also has an extensive professional background as a public advocate and consultant for a range of global government institutions and think tanks.

Dieter Rink is an urban sociologist working on sustainable urban development, urban land use change and urban ecology, shrinkage and urban governance; the regional focus is Europe. He has been participating in national and EU projects (URBS PANDENS, ALTER-Net) and was the coordinator of the EU 7FP Shrink Smart-project.

Blake Robinson is a researcher and project manager at the Sustainability Institute, and an Extraordinary Lecturer at the Stellenbosch University's School of Public Leadership, South Africa. He holds an M. Phil. in Sustainable Development from Stellenbosch University, and a B. Bus. Sci. (Marketing Honours) from the University of Cape Town. His research focuses on sustainable cities, with an emphasis on the use of spatial planning, infrastructure and other interventions to allow built environments to operate in a more resource efficient and environmentally restorative manner. He is particularly interested in how these interventions can be used to reduce inequality. Blake has worked on a number of South African and international reports on sustainable cities, including UNEP's *City-Level Decoupling* report, and UN-Habitat's *Urban Patterns for a Green Economy* guides.

Harald Rohracher has been Professor in Technology and Social Change at Linköping University, Sweden, since 2012. He was co-founder (1988) and director (1999-2007) of the Inter-University Research Centre for Technology, Work and Culture (IFZ), Graz, Austria. In 2009–10 he was Joseph A. Schumpeter Fellow at Harvard University and in Spring 2013 Simon Visiting Professor at Manchester University. In his research he is interested in the co-evolution of technology and society and the governance of socio-technical change towards greater sustainability, focusing, among others, on sustainable energy technologies, urban low-carbon transitions and the role of users and civil society in innovation processes. He is Associate Editor of the journal *Environmental Innovation and Societal Transitions* and co-editor of *Science, Technology and Innovation Studies* (*STI-Studies*) (*2005*).

Philipp Späth is Assistant Professor and part of the environmental governance group at the Institute of Environmental Social Sciences & Geography', Freiburg University, Germany. From 2003 to 2009 he was senior researcher at the Inter-University Research Centre for Technology, Work & Culture (IFZ) in Graz, Austria. Trained as a geographer and social scientist, he obtained a PhD in 'Science and Technology Studies' in 2009. From 1997–2003 he worked as a practitioner in promoting renewable energy and energy efficiency projects in Freiburg, Germany. His current research is in environmental governance, with a particular focus on the (multi-level) governance of socio-technical change, sustainability transitions, urban environmental governance, and local initiatives in support of strong sustainability.

Mark Swilling is Programme Coordinator: Sustainable Development in the School of Public Leadership, Stellenbosch University, South Africa, and Academic Director of the Sustainability Institute. He is also Project Leader of the TsamaHub, which delivers a transdisciplinary doctoral programme. Prof. Swilling obtained his Ph.D. from the University of Warwick in 1994 and has a BA and a BA (Honours) obtained through the Department of Political Studies at the University of the Witwatersrand. He has had 30 years' experience in urban development planning, sustainable city and human settlement projects, and has published 54 book chapters, 37 articles in refereed journals, 8 books and has compiled 22 Technical Reports. He has also written extensively for the popular media on a range of public policy issues, and delivered keynote addresses and papers at numerous international conferences. In 2007 he was invited to be a member of the International Resource Panel, established by UNEP.

Bernhard Truffer heads the Department of Environmental Social Sciences at Eawag, Switzerland, and is an Adjunct Professor at the Institute of Geography at the University of Bern. He has published widely on socio-technical transition, environmental innovation processes, Foresight and strategic planning. Empirical application domains are urban water management, energy and transport. One of his long standing research interests relate to the combination of insights from innovation studies and economic geography. This has recently resulted in several conceptual and empirical publications on the "geography of sustainability transitions".

Andrés Felipe Valderrama Pineda has been studying and working with sustainable urban development and the role of mobility. His work is based on a curiosity to understand the challenges of sustainable transition as more than a matter of the right intentions. There is no causal relation between people's intentions and actions – and thus no causal relation between visions and reality. Sustainable transition is a matter of practices.

Iwona Wagner is Assistant Professor in the Department of Applied Ecology at the University of Lodz, Poland. For several years, she was the Scientific Secretary of the Ecohydrology Project of the UNESCO's International Hydrological Programme and liaison for the International Environmental Technology Centre of the United Nations Environment Programme. Her research areas cover ecohydrology and urban ecohydrology, including stormwater management and planning strategies and city adaptation to global climate change, coordination and facilitation in multi-stakeholder platforms, and management and implementation of innovative trans-disciplinary projects. She is author of 16 publications in international journals, 15 chapters and co-editor of 6 international books and author of over 100 oral presentations at international conferences.

Arnim Wiek is an Associate Professor in the School of Sustainability at Arizona State University, USA. He is the head of the Sustainability Transition and Intervention Research Lab that conducts sustainability research on urban development, emerging technologies, resource governance, climate change and public health in the US, Canada, different European countries, Mexico, and Costa Rica. The group develops evidence-supported solutions to sustainability challenges and carries out this research in close collaboration with government, businesses, and community groups. Dr Wiek holds a PhD in environmental sciences from the Swiss Federal Institute of Technology Zurich, and a master's degree in philosophy from the Free University Berlin. He had research and teaching engagements at the Swiss Federal Institute of Technology Zurich, the University of British Columbia, Vancouver, and the University of Tokyo.

Katinka Wijsman is a PhD student at the Politics Department of the New School for Social Research (NSSR), USA. She works on global environmental politics broadly, and is specifically interested in the politics of measurement and data visualization as related to governance projects for just and sustainable land use. Her work is grounded in feminist studies of technoscience and political ecology. At the New School's Tishman Environment and Design Center she works on political ecology and sustainability transitions. Prior to coming to the New School, she was a researcher at Dutch Research Institute For Transitions (DRIFT) in Rotterdam and a lecturer at the University of Amsterdam. She holds an MSc in Political Science from the University of Amsterdam and an MSc in Industrial Ecology from Leiden University.

Julia Wittmayer works as senior researcher at DRIFT, the Dutch Research Institute For Transitions at the Erasmus University Rotterdam, The Netherlands. With a background in Social and Cultural Anthropology, her research focuses on social innovation and social sustainability in urban areas and on local scale. Theoretically, she is interested in the roles, social relations and interactions of actors involved in processes and initiatives aiming to contribute to sustainability transitions – with a specific interest for the role of research. Currently she coordinates the EU-FP7 funded TRANsformative Social Innovation Theory (TRANSIT) project.

Marc Wolfram is Associate Professor at the Department of Urban Planning and Engineering, Yonsei University, Seoul, South Korea. His work focuses on innovations in urban governance, policy and planning that enable and guide socio-technical and social-ecological system transitions. Recent key publications address research epistemologies for systemic urban change and urban transformative capacity.

1 Urban Sustainability Transitions

The Dynamics and Opportunities of Sustainability Transitions in Cities

Niki Frantzeskaki, Vanesa Castán Broto,
Lars Coenen and Derk Loorbach

Introduction

The agreement of a New Urban Agenda to put urban areas at the centre of achieving sustainable development for future generations was a key objective for Habitat III, the United Nations Conference on Housing and Sustainable Urban Development, which took place in Quito, in October 2016. Habitat III follows on from the inclusion of an urban goal among the Sustainable Development Goals adopted in New York in September 2015. The role of cities has been also recognised in other international frameworks such as the SENDAI Framework for Disaster Risk Reduction and the Paris Agreement on Climate Change. The New Urban Agenda emerges as a tool to harness 'the transformative power of urbanisation'. A massive demographic transformation is taking place, with the UN expecting that 70% of world population will be urban by 2050. However, the transformative power of urbanisation is not merely a demographic change. Urbanisation has multiple social, political, cultural, environmental and economic dimensions that will profoundly influence social development and innovation. This fundamental long-term transformation will involve the realignment of urban society, its technologies and infrastructures, urban cultures and lifestyles as well as governance and institutional frameworks. Such realignments are shockwise, nonlinear and complex processes of change, driven by deeper transformations but also by innovation and experimentation on the ground. Such structural systemic realignments within urban contexts can be referred to as urban sustainability transitions: fundamental and structural changes in urban systems through which persistent societal challenges are addressed. Examples range from shifts towards urban farming to renewable decentralised energy systems to sustainable urban mobility or social economies.

The need and drive for urban sustainability transitions is apparent (Tollefson, 2012). City governments are increasingly demonstrating what can be done in cities. Copenhagen in Denmark has pledged to be carbon neutral by 2025. Rio de Janeiro in Brazil has defended a model of environmental management that incorporates its poorest residents living in favelas. Cities like Singapore and Barcelona are experimenting with ICT to improve their service delivery. Increasingly, innovations are being developed and tested in cities all over the world. But city governments are only one actor in the context of urban sustainability transitions. The process of urbanisation that accompany land transformation and their manifestation in countries with different political systems questions the city and the city government as the central actor. The perspective of Urban sustainability transitions are processes of societal change and innovation with multiple causes, drivers and dynamics. A myriad of other actors have come to intervene in cities and urban areas with both punctual projects and initiatives to deliver impact at scale. Overall, the urban sustainability transition is a multi-actor process occurring simultaneously at different levels.

This volume seeks to contribute to this debate by interrogating two inter-related questions: what constraints and opportunities for sustainability transitions emerge within an urban context? To what extent can sustainability transitions be governed at the urban level and how? By exploring these two questions from different angles, this volume seeks to respond to a noticeable gap in the sustainability transitions literature. In a recent paper surveying the field of sustainability transitions, Markard et al. (2012) found that only 6% of transition studies have taken an urban perspective, compared to 38% adopting an explicitly national focus. Similarly, most theory in sustainability transitions has paid until very recently relatively little attention to the role of space and place in transitions which leaves it ill-prepared to understand and explain its geographically uneven development (Coenen et al., 2012). In spite of some exceptions (Bulkeley et al., 2011; Loorbach et al., 2016), there is a lack of insight on the possibilities and limitations in governing sustainability transitions at the level of the city. While important contributions have been made in the areas of mobility, food and energy (Geels et al., 2012; Spaargaren et al., 2012; Verbong and Loorbach, 2012), these studies have left unaddressed the specific questions about the dynamics of transitions that emerge in an urban context, and the active role that urban actors can play in instigating, starting or accelerating transitions.

In this context, the book makes two novel contributions. First, it shows how urban sustainability transitions are empirically and conceptually distinct from sector-specific transitions. Previous contributions on sustainability transitions have largely taken a domain-oriented approach (energy, water, food, etc.). By looking explicitly at urban transitions, this book foregrounds how multiple domain transitions intersect and are inter-related. Urban transitions are thus not distinct because they are observed at a different scale, but because they involve the alignment of resources and actor constellations across domains within a given geographical setting. Cities are thus 'natural' sites where the multiplicity of different dimensions concerning sustainability transitions comes together. To make sense of and govern this multiplicity requires city-specific analytical tools.

Secondly, the book shows that studying urban sustainability transitions identifies shortcomings in existing conceptual frameworks in transitions research, thus contributing to their further development. Moreover, urban sustainability transitions also invite us to engage with and reflect upon novel conceptual and methodological approaches beyond the usual models. The urban is not just a laboratory for policy and technological innovations: it is also a means for academics to develop new understandings of transitions to sustainability and why they matter. This volume aims to consolidate and extend the convergence points between transition studies and urban studies. Sustainable urban development and transformation, as an empirical field, has been studied by other approaches besides transitions theory such as urban studies, development planning and human geography (McKormick et al., 2013). Studying urban sustainability transitions thus invites for a potentially stimulating dialogue across different schools of thought in which the transitions perspective still needs to 'carve out' its specific value added. Cities have been and are likely to remain the seedbeds where major social and economic transformations in our societies are initiated and developed (Hall, 1998). Similarly, we know that urban agglomerations are highly conducive environments for novelty creation and disruptive innovation, not just in technological terms but also to foster policy, social and ethical innovations (Glaeser, 2000; Mieg and Topfer, 2013).

Overall, and following the research questions proposed above, this introduction provides an overview of the thinking that underpins the formulation of the book's objectives: (a) to provide new insights of how sustainability transitions unfold in different types of cities across the world and (b) to explore possible strategies for governing urban sustainability transitions. Following this, Section 2 outlines our contributions to studies of sustainability transitions and emphasises the implications of the book theme to their governance. Section 3 provides an overview of the structure of the book, and Section 4 outlines the five recommendations drawn from the book for developing and advancing research on urban sustainability transitions as a new pathway for sustainability transition studies.

Contributions of the Book

Contributing to Sustainability Transition Studies

The book taps into an emerging research current on urban sustainability transitions, as well as the geographies of sustainability transitions more generally, aiming to bring *new insights for transitions' theory and practice.* Following the Routledge Studies in Sustainability Transitions series, this book focuses on the co-evolution of material and institutional transformations, in socio-technical and socio-ecological systems. The book builds from empirical cases focusing on contemporary sustainability transitions in cities as grounds to examine distinct dimensions and patterns of transitions. These cases draw conclusions about theoretical concepts or frames that are required to better examine the complexity, distinct dynamics and politics of sustainability transitions in cities. As such the book engages with 'the here and now' of sustainability transitions, with cases distributed across very different geographical settings, with a pocketful of cases presenting historical analyses. The variety of urban sustainability transitions, brought together in this volume, provides a rich empirical basis to study and compare commonalities and differences in dimensions and patterns of transitions that hopefully allow the reader to see beyond the idiosyncrasies of the individual cases.

The book showcases, particularly, research that emphasises the multiscale dynamics of transitions beyond the multilevel frame of niches, regimes and landscapes. Hence, this book will contribute to the existing books in the series an explicit consideration of the scalar dimensions of sustainability transitions. This is akin to asking at what levels of social, economic and political exchange do sustainability transitions occur, including local to global interactions and interdependencies. In this way, the book also addresses the 'scale' and 'scaling' debate in sustainability transition studies building from contemporary cases.

Next to these, the book aims to create new conceptualisation(s) about urban sustainability transition processes building on evidence (empirical cases) from international cases on urban sustainability transitions beyond Europe. This book will extend the geographical scope of sustainability transitions by explicitly considering empirical evidence that goes beyond the areas that have traditionally received most of the attention in sustainability transitions debates (i.e., cities in North Western Europe). The book contains studies on sustainability transitions in mega-cities (e.g., Seoul, Shangai, New York, Adelaide), medium-sized metropolitan cities (e.g., Cape Town, Portland, Berlin, Copenhagen), and non-metropolitan cities (e.g., Freiburg). Opening up the geographical scope of the book provides an opportunity to reflect upon the comparability and transferability of theoretical/conceptual constructs and governance approaches of transitions theory across geographical contexts.

In the book, contributions bring different theoretical standpoints as analytical lenses to investigate transition dynamics: economic geography (Binz and Truffer), policy studies (Bettini et al.), governance theories (especially multilevel governance in Burch; Haase et al.; Pineda et al.), urban ecology (McPhearson and Wijsman; Kronenberg et al.) and sustainability science (Wiek et al.). Sometimes theoretical perspectives have been applied in conjunction with the usual suspects from transition research, including technological innovations systems (Binz and Truffer), the multilevel perspective (Caprotti and Hammer; Swilling et al.), transition management (Bettini et al.; Burch; Wiek et al.) and strategic niche management (Wolfram). This further justifies the need of theoretical plurality and integration for examining and consequently understanding contemporary urban sustainability transitions. The contributions that make up this book represent a large step forward in research for sustainability transitions in general and sustainability transitions in the urban context in particular. They advance new evidence on conceptual 'adaptations', 'alterations' and pointers on conceptual/theoretical extensions needed for examining urban transition dynamics. Overall, the contributions in this book emphasise urban sustainability transitions as consisting of multiple sub-transitions, deployed in multiple transition-scapes in cities and urban areas. They describe the urban sustainability transition as a political process in the making, permeated by conflicts and contradictions as well as alignment and cooperation.

Explaining the Governance of Urban Sustainability Transitions

Governance is the key question at the centre of this book. The governance of transitions refers to the multifaceted processes whereby persistent societal challenges are recognized, the potential for desirable transitions identified, and the dynamics that might guide and accelerate such a transition are stimulated. Governance is an often ill-described term that may be adopted with either an analytic or normative focus, often referring to multi-actor interaction processes. We did not prescribe a definition or approach to understanding the governance of sustainability transitions, but each contribution makes an effort to connect a case-specific understanding of urban transition dynamics with insights about how to bring about a sustainability transition in urban areas. For some authors such insights may have to do with specific processes of planning and managing the city. For others, however, governance processes are a means to overcome the challenges posed by a set of constraints.

Inspired by the contributions in this book and responding to the governance question, we hereby propose five governance insights that suggest what policy makers, civil society actors, and other practitioners need to consider for participating and being involved as active members, connectors, and change agents in urban sustainability transitions. Box 1.1 summarises the five governance implications that emerge from the comparative analysis of the cases presented in this book.

Indeed, more specific recommendations can be given in relation to each implication. Governance Implication #1 (Reflexively examine and invigorate stagnant transition dynamics and decelerated transition processes in spaces that persistent unsustainability prevails to exploit new types of lessons for reigniting transformations towards social, ecological and economic sustainabilities) directs attention to a need to reflect upon the social justice implications of sustainability initiatives and policies, as they can improve or worsen the vulnerabilities of social groups, such as energy poverty among young adults (Petrova). This governance implication is about opening up the problem frame to include considerations of external drivers, historicity and path dependencies in order to question the status quo. Depending on the standard of living within a city, sustainability transitions require different approaches: The core challenge of transitions in developing cities is how to create a *higher* standard of living – including new infrastructures, buildings, roads – that does not lock the city into resource dependency and negative climate impacts. On the contrary, the challenge for highly developed cities is how

Box 1.1 Governance implications from the combined analysis of the book chapters

---

Governance implication #1: Reflexively examine and invigorate stagnant transition dynamics and decelerated transition processes in spaces that persistent unsustainability prevails to exploit new types of lessons for reigniting transformations towards social, ecological and economic sustainabilities.

Governance implication #2: Provoke sustainability transitions' politics to instigate new relations, new understandings, new urban realities and ways of organising with and via urban transformative agency creation

Governance implication #3: Engage in politics and transformations of space for tipping urban transitions towards resilience, liveability and social, ecological and economic sustainabilities.

Governance implication #4: Nurture and foster experimental approaches from policy (top-down) and from communities (bottom-up) that connect processes of scaling with processes of local anchoring

Governance implication #5: The city is a droplet in a global pool of sustainability transition waves; meaning that cities can act as change agents and testing grounds that are shaped and shape global sustainability transitions and their dynamics.

---

to transform *existing* standards of living towards environmental sustainability without compromising the socioeconomic benefits that they provide (Peter et al.). These differences are not only manifest between different cities. Some examples in this book also emphasise how sustainability transitions unfold in the 'hotspots' within the city. These are places where transitions do not go 'according to a predetermined plan', but where understandings of sustainability conflict and are renegotiated. This conflict can disrupt existing plans and give a new direction to the urban sustainability transition (Rohracher and Späth).

In relation to the Governance Implication #2 (Provoke sustainability transitions' politics to instigate new relations, new understandings, new urban realities and ways of organising with and via urban transformative agency creation), the cases emphasise design policies and initiatives that can flexibly navigate the complexities of urban sustainability transitions. These complexities emerge as a multiplicity of actors with different visions advance transitions at different speeds in different parts of the city (Elle et al.). Rather than establishing add-on sustainability agendas, urban actors often find ways to creatively integrate sustainability agendas with other urban priorities such as climate change, livability and resilience. This can help to leverage synergies and show the multiple benefits that a sustainability agenda brings about connecting seemingly unrelated issues (Burch). Urban sustainability transitions follow processes that build and strengthen relationships between city administrators, civil society and business in times of tranquillity, to better withstand and recover from environmental crises, like droughts and flooding

(Bettini et al.; Wolfram). Measures such as attending conferences, workshops and events at the national and international level may be a practical way to learn from and connect with actors in other cities. These links can be mobilized to support, inform and resource urban sustainability transitions (Binz and Truffer). Equally, key to bring about an urban sustainability transition is to identify resourceful actors to be the intermediaries for anchoring new technological systems in cities is a key starting condition for urban transitions. Local networks of knowledge and expertise as well as political commitment play an important role (Binz and Truffer; Bettini; Burch; Wolfram). Governance Implication #2 is about acknowledging the inherent political nature of urban sustainability transitions and how they effect place and place identifies by actively (re)configuring new social relations.

In relation to the Governance Implication #3 (Engage in politics and transformations of space for tipping urban transitions towards resilience, liveability and social, ecological and economic sustainabilities) the cases emphasise the need to become aware and reflect upon power struggles and conflicts. These are inherent in urban sustainability transitions, as different actor groups struggle to define problems differently and promote their own solutions (Moss). Sustainability innovators often adopt an understanding of sustainability that takes account of the space-specific problems, histories and identities of a city. This helps to ground sustainability agendas and policies in the local realities of actors, as well as empowering them to creatively engage with these agendas. (Fratini and Jensen; Wolfram). For example, a key measure in urban areas is to creatively engage with vacant lots, such as brown fields, abandoned buildings and bare soil. These areas have found to be a source of biodiversity and ecosystem services in a city (McPhearson and Wijsman). Urbanisation is not always about growth. Cities that shrink in population and economic activity can employ, for example, the principles of land use perforation, that is, establishing loose patterns of build and open, green spaces in inner cities (Haase). Overall, transitions are not only processes of socio-technical change: changes are also socio-ecological because they bring about changes in the relationships between human and ecological systems in a city. Therefore, sustainability transitions require different planning considerations, such as a greater protection of green areas towards urban sprawl, consideration of a diversity of ecosystems other than forests and parks, or the importance to conduct modern ecosystem assessments to better understand the ecological diversity in the city (Kronenberg, Krauze and Wagner). Governance Implication #3 is about facilitating and engaging in and across new arenas for urban transitions in the making of politics and movements for livability, inclusion and resilience in cities.

In relation to Governance Implication #4 (Nurture and foster experimental approaches from policy (top-down) and from communities (bottom-up) that connect processes of scaling with processes of local anchoring), a key objective is to create spaces for initiatives to experiment with sustainability solutions, as this can help to raise awareness, demonstrate the feasibility and attractiveness of specific solutions as well as changing existing policies, cultures and discourses (Späth and Ornetzeder). Urban sustainability transition labs can be spaces for experiments to develop, test and implement sustainability interventions in cities or neighbourhoods. However, several factors need to be taken into account to successfully realise these labs, such as partnerships, capacity building, as well as monitoring and evaluation (Wiek et al.). Bottom-up and top-down transition processes require leadership by cities and local initiatives, shared visions of change, targeted empowerment, as well as governance intermediaries that create trust and translate perspectives between actors (Wolfram). Stemming from these, governance implication #4 is about creating physical, institutional and financial spaces for radical alternatives and experiments, resonating from the sustainability deficit.

Finally, Governance Implication #5 (The city is a droplet in a global pool of sustainability transition waves; meaning that cities can act as change agents and testing grounds that are shaped and shape global sustainability transitions and their dynamics) points towards the key role that urban sustainability transitions can play in global sustainability transitions, particularly when they are constituted as 'agents of change'. Messages and solutions proven in cities can be transferred and picked up globally (Fuenfschilling). For urban areas to lead action, however, there needs to be consideration of the actual capacity for intervention and the availability of resources. The emphasis on international organisations on national-led interventions as well as the difficulties to finance action in cities may limit the possibilities for local governments and other urban actors to lead transitions sustainability. Thus, it is important to also examine and track the impact imprint across spatial scales on the ways sustainability transitions shape and are shaped by ecological, geophysical, economic, political and cultural dynamics in the region and nation scales that they are embedded in (Caprotti and Harmer). Governance Implication #5 is about fostering and facilitating connections translocally: across urban places, communities and networks to mobilise and accelerate urban sustainability transitions.

Book Architecture and Chapter Contributions

The book contributes to transition studies by proposing a focus on urban context to empirically and theoretically understand sustainability transitions. Based on three distinguishing characteristics of the urban context as grounds to understand and explore (contemporary) sustainability transitions, we have structured the book as follows:

- Part I includes chapters that centre on characteristics that make urban sustainability transitions distinct from domain-based transitions.
- Part II includes chapters that centre on experimentation and its role in urban sustainability transitions.
- Part III includes chapters that centre on the politics of urban space, conflict and urban sustainability transitions.

Each part of the book includes an interlude chapter that summarises and distils lessons and governance implications from the collected chapters. Interlude chapters (Fuenfschilling, Miller and Levanda, Avelino and Wittmayer) are our 'lighthouse' chapters that take a reflective and meta-analytical perspective to address the objectives of the book and synthesise new messages and exiting findings.

Part I – Characteristics and Distinctiveness of Urban Transitions

The first collection of contributions helps explaining how urban sustainability transitions are distinct from domain-based sustainability transitions. The way actors, ideas, solutions and policy processes shape the conditions for comprehensive, domain-transcending sustainability transitions in cities are captured through the critical examination of the dynamic interconnections between those. At the same time, transitions in the urban context are products of interrelated change processes of different pace and magnitude. Cities experience fast pacing transitions in different systems of provision and stagnant processes in other ones, with governance processes bringing together otherwise unconnected actors. As Fuenfschilling (interlude chapter in this volume) argues "the particularities of urban spaces simultaneously provide opportunities and challenges for sustainability transitions".

Urban transition processes are driven by actors who are resourceful to propose and instigate local policy change and who are creative in localising ideas, institutions and solutions while enabling transformative capacities across connected networks. When examining closely the ways different actors establish conditions and enable agency creation for urban sustainability transitions, empirical results do not show a harmonious co-evolution towards 'a' common goal. Rather sustainability transitions entail processes of societal change away from perceived unsustainability. They are about contested visions, contradictions and ideas that require deliberation, a social arena for negotiating and reinvigorating all the dimensions of sustainability: social, ecological and economic. In this context, transition frameworks that centre around involving, empowering and mobilising agents of change such as transition management and strategic niche management are chosen and applied jointly with other theoretical perspectives. This theoretically promiscuous approach unravels the confluence between agency dynamics and transition processes in the making.

Binz and Truffer's case study of Chinese cities – Beijing, Shanghai and Xi'an – shows how urban actors mediate local and global resource flows by establishing urban niches. Specifically, they argue that local actors operate as intermediaries that couple local innovation processes and resource flows across scales coordinating the creation and survival of niches. They identify local actors that anchor processes in which external knowledge and practices are geographically embedded into local innovation systems and their institutions.

Bettini et al. take a closer look on how policy actors respond to change pressures and instigate transitions in urban infrastructure systems. They interlink the four dimensional framework of policy actions from transition management with policy studies to examine the way that how networking as an action diversifies interventions for enabling urban sustainability transformations. Looking at the transformational effects of creeping and sudden crises in Queensland, they cast an eye on the ways governance actions shift focus: from police to collaborative approaches, from short term to a mixed 'short-medium term' approaches in managing the urban water infrastructure. What the chapter points at is that "transition arenas have an active role to play in advocating for attention to issues in the absence of a perceived crisis", For such participatory interventions, planners should not underestimate the critical importance of creating and fostering collaborative arrangements and networks that can set a change agenda to enact transformative capacities.

Burch presents the journey of different policy actions and inter-tangled governance processes with the local dynamics for the championing city of Vancouver. She employs transition management and multilevel governance perspectives. While pointing at the importance of task descriptions and capacities within the local policy administration as catalytic for conditioning sustainability transitions, Burch also addresses the value of engaging with the business sector and of generating synergies between different actors and different visions. The Vancouver case also shows that despite a legacy of a frontrunner city and a well-versed collaborative approach with communities and businesses, there is a "growing inertia behind a political calculus that favours environmental risk-taking and leadership". To counterbalance this inertia, an urban narrative connects climate change agendas with sustainability visions.

McPhearson and Wijsman present an analysis that zooms out from actor-specific dynamics and looks instead to broader developments in the city, approaching urban sustainability transitions in the city of New York from a systems level. They employ urban ecology as their central theoretical perspective. From this perspective, they argue for knowledge of complex urban dynamics and interdependencies between technologies, infrastructures, urban ecosystem elements and social interests and actors. The case expores changing vacant lots in New York from areas that attract negative services (e.g., crime) to urban renewal spaces. The chapter shows that "a combined approach of urban ecology and sustainability transitions can provide insights into the functionalist components of the city (...) while addressing the social and political construction and meaning" of these relations and infrastructures.

Fratini and Jensen point to the insights that can be gained by focusing on the urban context for understanding conflicts in urban sustainability transitions. They focus on regime destabilisation in the urban water domain in Copenhagen. The chapter reveals the different framings and meanings that water as an urban element receives from different interest-scapes: from a place-making versus a sectorial approach. Instead of addressing this fluid understanding of urban elements as problematic, Fratini and Jensen note that ambivalence can result and stimulate transformations by simply allowing for conflict and redefinition of meanings that can in turn foster transformations.

Wolfram addresses the civil society constellations and their role in urban sustainability transitions by casting an eye on grassroots innovations in Seoul. In this chapter the focus is on unpacking what enables grassroots in cities looking at different governance conditions such as empowerment, involvement in urban governance and in experimentation, reconfiguration of social relations and reconfiguring the meanings of urban places. Articulation of visions and shared expectations, diversity of innovation and innovative practices by grassroots as well as social learning are among the intangible benefits and conditions for enabling grassroots' operations. The case of Seoul reveals that intermediaries at different levels and of different leadership (civil society–led and public sector–led as well as hybrid forms of those) play a crucial role in maintaining the transformative capacity and impact that urban grassroots have. In the case of Seoul, over time "the intermediation capacity has been steadily expanded, diversified and brought into proximity".

Caprotti and Harmer posit a space and place discussion of the governance of sustainability transitions with focusing on examples of eco-cities in China. They state that ecocities are spatial interventions of socio-technological nature that influence and 'support' socioeconomic, and socio-environmental processes and patterns. In this way, they shed light on cross-scale dynamics and effects of sustainability transition experiments. The Tianjin eco-city as a transition experiment shows that the space dimension in sustainability transitions is not another heuristic lens but a production of interactions and interrelations between spatially explicit interventions and the geopolitical, economic and technological contexts that are embedded in. Caprotti and Hammer propose approaches that can address politics, power and complexity of governance for examining and understanding urban sustainability transitions beyond the site specific and technology-bound approaches that dominate the field.

Part II – Experimentation and Urban Sustainability Transitions

Experimentation has become a key form of governance in urban environments. Bulkeley et al. (2014) describe experimentation as an open-ended process whereby different actors try to gain legitimacy for their proposals for intervention in the context of achieving a sustainable society. In this view, experimentation entails the implementation of projects with unknown impacts in concrete space, with the aim to render complex environmental problems such as climate change compelling and calculable. This form of experimentation is a key means through which urban sustainability transitions are reimagined and advanced. Thus, the second part of the book focuses on experimentation as the central governance processes in urban sustainability transitions.

The chapters in this section are not necessarily fine-cut examples of experimentation. Rather, they present a rich picture of the context of experimentation and its relevance to understand urban transitions. The focus is on the match between cities and experiments, why cities appear today to open up arenas for experimentation while simultaneously experiments drive urban opportunities for transitions. This section also reflects upon some of the limitations of experiment-thinking.

Overall, the chapters in the section offer a perspective on the extent to which different urban contexts open up or not the appropriate context of experimentation, and in those in which it happens, how experiments can lead to demonstrable sustainability improvements (such as in Malmo, Vienna and Freiburg). The question remains about the extent to which experimentation in specific settings can lead to broader reconfigurations beyond the specific locales in which experimentation occur. While local experiments appear to have greater demonstrable impact than donor-led programs, there are still challenges in demonstrating that local experiments can indeed have an impact beyond the specific context of operation. The examples show that processes of experimentation may lead to reconfigurations in adjacent or interrelated systems to those that experimentation focused upon such as in building codes (Vienna, Malmo), dissemination of institutional learning (Freiburg), trans-formation of relationships between the government and business (Malmo). In the case of Berlin, the city stayed as a repository for technology rediscovery, when the landscape became appropriate.

In all these examples experimentation, in contrast to top-down programs, can only be understood as a multi-actor, somewhat chaotic process. This is elegantly captured by the interlude chapter's reflection by Avelino and Wittmayer. They present a multilevel analysis of governance processes, which reflects upon the complex interactions between actors and the extent to which they can lead to transitions. They find that the government plays a key role either as a leading actor or as an obstruction for sustainability transitions. Their interlude delineates transitions as a profoundly political process, which is the key perspective developed in the following section.

Moss's historical analysis of waste-to-energy innovation in Berlin demon-strates the importance of temporal dimensions of technological experimen-tation. He shows that waste-to-energy technologies had already flourished in the 1930s Berlin, with both the technological and institutional means to enable its integration in urban infrastructure systems. It was an aversion to all things that resembled the Nazi regime that led to the condemnation of waste-to-energy technologies and their posterior rediscovery in the new millennium. Waste-to-energy technologies fitted Nazi narratives of modernity so well that they were rejected in the post-WWII period. The technology has been rediscovered due to external pressures, including national regulations, global environmental discourses and changing business landscapes. This example constitutes a challenge to linear narratives of socio-technical development emphasising instead the chaotic, temporally contingent and accidental nature of socio-technical innovation – a key perspective to understand the dynamics experimentation.

Maassen's account of climate aid in Eastern Europe, the Russian Federation and Central Asia provides an insight into how global policy may influence sustainable urbanisation at a regional level. Her regional account adopts a bird's-eye view on sustainable development in which the urban perspective seems to vanish. Maassen describes a process whereby climate aid comes to replace an ongoing investment shortfall. This climate aid supports actions which seem to advance the visions and strategies of donors, rather than of a collective assemblage of actors with a number of actions directed towards addressing political economy factors through capacity building and policy advice. There is no apparent role of urban actors – especially grassroots organizations – and little attempt to materially transform urban infrastructure. Despite the substantial resource investment, this is not a fertile broth for innovation. This is a context in which experimentation is the only alternative for any hope of action.

Späth and Ortnetzeder focus on studying initiatives that aim deliberately to break the car regime in Vienna and Freiburg explaining that, while the actors involved in these initiatives did not necessarily used the words 'regime' and 'niche', they explicitly sought to disturb the dominance of car as the main means of transport in the city by seeking to promote alternatives, in pretty much the way that is described in many transition studies. These are very positive examples that show that initiatives in a given local setting can have a positive and lasting impact, in this case, reducing local residents' dependency on cars. The authors find surprising that these experiments, which achieved their objectives, have not been replicated elsewhere in the country, even though they have become well-known examples of how the dominance of the car regime can be challenged through interventions in urban planning and architecture. In Vienna the project required changing building regulations prescribing the construction of car parking spaces. In Freiburg, a vision of a 'city of short distances' was coupled with new public transport projects and institutional development. Both cases show that success is not akin to replication, and that regime inertias are persistent, although they may be challenged in alternative ways.

Petrova's engagement with the energy access problems of the precariat highlights the significance of deprivation and how it becomes visible in an urban context. Here inequality is a landscape factor that shapes the extent to which an urban transition is possible. The perspective developed by Petrova, well known to urban studies scholars, is less influential in transition studies in the sense that their relevance to niche innovation and socio-technical transition is not immediately apparent. The existence of an urban precariat is agglutinated under an umbrella of landscape factors. Yet, this may be key. First, the precariat relates to a context of urban improvisation in which urban services are accessed in an uncommon manner. This requires a sort of everyday experimentation to make ends meet that may generate viable innovations. The issue is that while we understand the presence of this factor we do not really understand how innovations may emerge, mostly because, as Petrova illustrates, the presence of a precariat is largely ignored. Second, the lack of policy focus in relation to the complexity of energy access constitutes an area for potential innovation. There are possibilities for a rapid change in the policy landscape which may constitute an opportunity for sustainable innovation by coupling socio-technical innovations which address energy poverty simultaneously with emissions and pollution reduction.

Wiek et al. take a critical and analytical turn on urban experiments or as they define them 'urban sustainability transition labs' (USTL). They start with a working hypothesis that the general guidelines of experimentation need to be accounted for the different phases of the life-cycle of the experiment itself as well. In this way they bring forward the temporal dimension in experimentation that has been underexplored in current work of sustainability transitions. Their analysis framework provides a systematic lens to map the effort, guiding principles and impact of transition experiments. The case of Phoenix in the US shows how an urban sustainability transition experiment in a public urban space took place and unfolded, explicating the way interventions can bring up sustainability in practice. Despite the fact that experiments in the Phoenix lab were not completed, the case shows the effort and operational design needed to start a process of experimentation. Overall, this provides an insightful analysis of the 'soft part' of experimentation: setting up the process and create a new narrative explanation of the desired transformative intervention. With a very critical and reflective take on the case of Phoenix, the authors draw recommendations on how to proceed in setting up and researching urban experiments for sustainability transitions. From their overall recommendations we highlight here one: "Make sure not to get stuck in the early phases and move fast into the stage of strategically designed full transition experiments and scaling-up efforts (sustainability outcomes) – to demonstrate success and motivate collaborators and partners."

Haase et al. present a historical case on the confluence of social and ecological dynamics in the city of Leipzig in Germany. They provide an account of paradigms' changing over time that shape and have been shaped by social, political and ecological events (triggers of development). A strong conceptual contribution of the chapter is the issue of persistency as a dimension of urban sustainability transitions, as a combination of process and systemic dimensions. The case analysis shows that policy shifts and paradigm changes operate and are realised across spatio-temporal scales. The message from examining persistence as a dimension of urban sustainability transitions is that it provides a more pragmatic view of the challenges that need to be faced and navigated for governing urban sustainability transitions as long-term complex processes.

Part III – Politics of Urban Space and of Urban Sustainability Transitions

In this book we characterise urban sustainability transition as inherently political, moved forward by processes of (dis)agreement, contestation, competition, negotiation, compromise and conflict. As deliberate attempts to bring about a change, actions directed towards catalysing a transition confront first the generation of sustainability visions of the urban future that can help aligning the actors' objectives and resources which may initiate action; and to bridge the expectations created in such visions with the possibilities to act at the local level. Urban sustainability transitions are not smooth processes in which all actors find a common project and advance collectively through a well-marked, manageable path. Rather, transitions are unpredictable and unruly processes that different actors can influence in different ways. The opportunities opened in urban areas, to deliver services to newly constructed areas, to create spaces of intervention through planning and management and to give access to resources to multiple action may be central to energize the transition process.

Rohracher and Späth present two cases of urban transitions in Graz in Austria and in Freiburg in Germany that "create new zones of friction, pitch different actor worlds against each other and reframe visions of more sustainable cities". From both cases, it becomes evident that urban sustainability transitions unfold in a diverse way over different time-phases and involve multiple actors that create new meanings to spatial configuration and ideas of sustainability. The spatial projects create 'hotspots' where contestation and conflicts surface and "unexpected connections between initially separate issues are established". Amongst the theoretical contributions and highlights of this chapter, it is the conceptual proposition that for understanding the dynamics and politics of urban sustainability transitions, one has to move away from examining and explaining transitions as mere niche-regime interactions.

Pineda et al. examine the way two transition projects in Copenhagen play out with the politics of space in the city. The two lighthouse projects, the Carlsberg city district that is a redevelopment project and the Cycle Superhighway that is a low-carbon path-reinforcing project, both impact the city's spatial and social fabrics. In the Carlsberg spatial project, the actors involved in developing and shaping the way the project was envisioned and implemented created a new situation for the redeveloped area, even though in a more conforming way that enhanced unsustainable practices rather than disrupting them towards more sustainable ones. The Cycle Superhighway project case illustrates how actors, their perceptions and interests intermingle in transitions-in-the-making. As multi-actor processes where no single actor can navigate or mediate alone, urban sustainability transitions are ever evolving and changing processes.

Swilling et al. present an account of the current drivers of urban transitions in African cities, elaborating on systemic drivers as well as process conditions including the introduction of new narratives for urbanisation in African cities. The authors present a very good elaboration of the binding barriers of transitions and show the diversity of persistence that it is often missed in transition studies. They propose a proto-framework on connecting the transition thinking via the multilevel perspective with metabolic flows' model to explain urban sustainability transitions in African cities.

Kronenberg et al. present the social-ecological transitions of the city of Lodz, in Poland. The chapter presents how planning practices, policies and paradigms evolved over time and how they are imprinted in the urban spatial development of the city. Over the years, authors show how environmental modernization steered up more integrative and systemic thinking about sustainability of the city of Lodz. Prompted by researchers and NGOs, the authorities gave the environment the place that it had been missing in the documents prepared thus far. Kronenberg et al. show that this strategy opens the opportunity for Lodz to enter a delayed sustainability transition, and discuss the related drivers and challenges.

Cities as Transitionscapes: The New Pathway for Sustainability Transitions Studies

With this book we want to propose five avenues that we found relevant for future research to examine and understand sustainability transitions in cities. We hope that our reflections from the contributions of the authors in the book chapters will create a new terrain for expanding and enriching the research of urban sustainability transitions.

First, we propose that epistemological pluralism beyond the usual suspects in transition theory will benefit and enrich the academic dialogue about urban sustainability transitions. The book sets the scene for fruitful and constructive ways to engage with different theoretical frameworks to examine and understand dynamics of urban phenomena of transformations in cities. We found this epistemological plurality refreshing and opening up new debates about the multiple dimensions of urban transitions including the positioning of intermediaries, the way innovation influences ongoing transitions, the mapping of multiple actors for the transition and the way visions and conflicts confluence in the cities. We hope that in the future not only social sciences and engineering engage with the 'urban' in sustainability transitions but also that humanities and cultural studies can further the mosaic of explanations of the urban Anthropocene and its transitions (Catterall, 2014).

Second, we suggest that examining the politics of urban sustainability transitions will provide a fuller explanation of the ways solutions in cities are debated, adapted and hybridised. In this way, the meaning behind 'contested' concepts or solutions will become more evident and transparent, allowing for conflicts and contradictions to surface and provide meaning to urban choices (Fisher et al., 2012; Fratini and Jensen, this volume; Miller and Levanda, this volume) and transformations in urban social, ecological and economic fabrics. It will allow for a more in-depth examination of which solutions and which issues are contested and as such require more thorough exploration and research, steering away from universal assumptions on urban issues that may misdirect research efforts.

Third, we recommend shedding away mono-case explanations for urban sustainability transitions. As some of the contributions of the book already show, research and practice will benefit from multiple case or cross-case comparative examinations of similar phenomena also allowing (comparative or synthesis) research to unpack context. Methodological pluralism in the case study research can also enrich the explanations, and deepen our understanding of the impact contextual conditions play in the way sustainability transitions occur and unfold. Another way that is not explored in the present book, but it is at heart of sustainability transitions' studies is knowledge coproduction between practitioners and scientists for understanding complex phenomena and employing knowledge for transformative solutions and action. We hope that in the future we will also see transdisciplinary explanations of urban sustainability transitions that co-create new knowledge to demystify context and its influence in how transitions roll out (Han et al., 2012).

Fourth, we found it refreshing to understand change from an agency perspective, rather than a system perspective only. This provides a richer explanation on the role of visions, narratives, incentives and interests in transformative changes that relate to contemporary phenomena. Agency also brings historicity in a different way into the way transitions are formed and accelerated or stalled: history of interests, visions and incentives are embedded in the current actions and motives of agency as well as in the way agency's relations to events and structures are formed and reformed. It also allows for differentiation between providing explanations from a systems' perspective that is about the heuristic framework chosen to frame the explanations and in a systematic way that refers to the methodological conciseness of the research. An agency's perspective on urban sustainability transitions will allow us to also investigate how transformative solutions play out with resolving complex sustainability problems and how with problem displacement (processes that shift the space-location of environmental problems and as such shift between vulnerable and benefiting actor groups and redistributing responsibilities, see Romero-Lankao, 2012), resulting in changes in the socio-political urban fabric.

Fifth, we found that it is both relevant and challenging to look at cases from non-European contexts such as African cities (Simon and Leck, 2015; Swilling et al., this volume). With many European cities exemplifying stories of transitions that can be inspirational to other cities and their practitioners, there is a plethora of cities that face barriers to transitions and stalemates difficult to overcome. In these challenging contexts, it is where the knowledge of governance of and for sustainability transitions will make more benefit for global socio-ecological and socio-technical transformations.

Acknowledgements

First and foremost, we would like to thank Prof. John Grin who was the first to believe in our book project and was a supportive critical friend to our endeavour throughout the period it took from 'idea' to implementation. Second, we would like to thank all the contributing authors for committing their time, energy and inspiration through the chapters to our book. We want to thank you all for your perseverance through three rounds of reviews, for participating in our book workshop in August 2014 and for being the most responsive and time-responsible team we have worked with so far. The book was a truly collaborative effort and coproduced with a great team of authors. Third, we would like to thank three junior researchers of DRIFT for offering their assistance in the process of finalising this book: Felix Spira, Giorgia Silvestri, Matthew Bach and Michael Karner. Last but not least, as the editors of the book, we have been working in this book-project supported by a number of research funds that allowed us the time and the research focus to bring it forward. Specifically, Dr Niki Frantzeskaki worked on this book as part of the EU Funded ARTS research project (www.acceleratingtransitions. eu) and the NOW Biodiversa funded URBES project. Dr Derk Loorbach and Dr Lars Coenen worked on this book as part of the JPI Urban Europe funded GUST research project (www.urbanlivinglabs.eu). Dr Vanesa Castán Broto's participation in the project was supported by the Economic and Social Research Council, as part of the Future Research Leaders project Mapping Urban Energy Landscapes [grant number ES/K001361/1].

References

Bulkeley, H., Castan Broto, V., Hodson, M. and Marvin, S. (Eds.) (2010). *Cities and low carbon transitions*, London: Routledge.

Bulkeley, H., Castan Broto, V. and Maassen, A. (2014). Low-carbon transitions and the reconfiguration of urban infrastructure. *Urban Studies, 51*(7), 1471–1486.

Catterall, B., (2014), Towards the Great Transformation: (11) Where/what is culture in 'Planetary Urbanisation'? Towards a new paradigm, *City: analysis of urban trends, culture, theory, policy, action*, 18:3, 368–379, DOI: 10.1080/13604813.2014.892773

Coenen, L., Benneworth, P. and Truffer, B., (2012), Toward a spatial perspective on sustainability transitions, *Research policy*, 41:6, 968–979.

Fisher, D.R., Campbell, L.K., and Svendsen, E.S., (2012), The organisational structure of urban environmental stewardship, *Environmental Politics*, 21:1, 26–48, dx.doi. org/10.1080/09644016.2011.643367

Geels, F.W., Kemp, R., Dudley, G. and Lyons, G. (Eds.) (2012). *Automobility in transition? A socio-technical analysis of sustainable transport*, London, Routledge.

Glaeser, E.L. (2000). The New Economics of Urban and Regional Growth. In: G.L. Clark, M.P. Feldman and M.S. Gertler (Eds.) *The Oxford Handbook of Economic Geography* (pp. 83–98). Oxford, Oxford University Press.

Hall, P. (1998). *Cities in Civilization: Culture, Technology and Urban Order*, London: Weidenfeld and Nicolson.

Han, J., Fontanos, P., Fukushi, K., Herath, S., Heeren, N., Naso, V., Cecchi, C., Edwards, P. and Takeuchi, K., (2012), Innovation for sustainability: toward a sustainable urban future in industrialized cities, *Sustainability Science*, 7, 91–100, DOI 10.1007/s11625-011-0152-2

Hoffmann, M. (2013). Climate Change. In R. Wilkinson and T. Weiss (Eds.) *International Organization and Global Governance*. London, Routledge.

Loorbach, D. Wittmayer, J.M., Shiroyama, H., Fujino, J. and Mizuguchi, S. (Eds.) (2016). Governance of Urban Sustainability Transitions: European and Asian Experiences, Tokyo: Springer.

Markard, J., Raven, R. and Truffer, B. (2012). Sustainability transitions: An emerging field of research and its prospects, *Research Policy, 41*(6): 955–967.

McCormick, K., Anderberg, S., Coenen, L. and Neij, L. (2013). Advancing sustainable urban transformation, *Journal of Cleaner Production*, 50, 1–11.

Mieg, H. A. and Töpfer, K. (Eds.) (2013). *Institutional and social innovation for sustainable urban development*. London, Routledge.

Romero-Lankao, P. (2012): Governing carbon and climate in the cities: an overview of policy and planning challenges and options, *European Planning Studies*, 20:1, 7–26.

Rotmans, J., Kemp, R., and van Asselt, M. (2001). More evolution than revolution: transition management in public policy. *Foresight, 3*(1), 15–31.

Simon, D., and Leck, H., (2015), Understanding climate adaptation and transformation challenges in African cities, *Current Opinion in Environmental Sustainability*, 13, 109–116.

Spaargaren, G., Oosterveer, P. and Loeber, A. (Eds.) (2012). *Food practices in transition: changing food consumption, retail and production in the age of reflexive modernity*. London, Routledge.

Verbong, G. and Loorbach, D. (Eds.) (2012). *Governing the energy transition: reality, illusion or necessity?*, London, Routledge.

Tollefson, J., (2012), Megacities move to track emissions, *Nature*, 492, 20–21.

Part I
Characteristics and Distinctiveness of Urban Transitions

2 Anchoring Global Networks in Urban Niches

How On-site Water Recycling Emerged in Three Chinese Cities

Christian Binz and Bernhard Truffer

Introduction

Analyzing the spaces and places in which sustainability transitions evolve – and especially the crucial role of cities in this process – has moved center stage in academia and policy circles (Bulkeley et al., 2011; Hodson and Marvin, 2010). Evidence is growing that transition dynamics in urban contexts cannot be understood based solely on the specific actors and dynamics inside a city, but that they span actors and processes at multiple interrelated spatial scales (Betsill and Bulkeley, 2006; Hodson and Marvin, 2010). Yet, transition literature to date only provides a limited understanding on how multi-scalar spatial contexts influence transition pathways. It thus lacks explanations on why transitions emerge in specific places while they fail in others (Coenen and Truffer, 2012; Raven et al., 2012; Smith et al., 2010). As a consequence, it remains rather unclear by what strategies and under which conditions specific urban actors can make a difference in furthering sustainability transitions, for instance by acting as strategic niche managers for new technologies.

The present chapter aims at addressing this research gap by elaborating on the ability of urban actors to mediate local and global resource flows as a precondition for niche formation. Our analytical framework will draw on recent insights from economic geography and technological innovation system studies and argue that an important element in explaining early niche formation processes is urban actors' ability to combine territorially embedded innovation processes with mobilizing resources through networks reaching outside the city. We propose the concept of socio-spatial anchoring to analyze how local niche activities become connected to international technological innovation systems and analyze which key roles urban actors fulfill in these multi-scalar innovation systems.

Urban Actors as Intermediaries between Local Niches and Global Networks

Transition studies generally assume that sector-wide transformation is the outcome of interrelated processes at the niche, regime and landscape levels

(Geels, 2002). The emergence and development of socio-technical niches and the mechanisms through which they develop a constituency behind new technologies are especially crucial for transition theory (Kemp et al., 1998). Recent empirical evidence shows that actors in specific urban contexts can play an essential role in such niche upscaling dynamics (Bulkeley et al., 2011; Hodson and Marvin, 2010): for instance, urban governments can act as strategic niche managers by providing 'protected spaces' for experimentation (Hodson and Marvin, 2010), inducing targeted niche policies (Carvalho et al., 2012) and often even coordinating niche experiments in wider intercity networks (Betsill and Bulkeley, 2006). As Hodson and Marvin (2010, 477) point out, urban governments increasingly "have political aspirations to develop purposive and managed change in the socio-technical organization of infrastructure networks that can be characterized as 'systemic' transitions".

Yet, much of the work dealing with such urban transitions is still preoccupied with niche formation and governance processes at regional to national scales, and rather ignores international interdependencies (Coenen et al., 2012). Furthermore, the existing literature does not specify in much detail how preexisting urban, institutional and sectorial configurations influence niche formation processes. Recently, economic geographers have criticized this simplistic concept of geographic contexts in transition literature: in a globalizing knowledge economy, both regional (urban) contexts and global networks are key building blocks of a thorough understanding of innovation and niche formation processes (Bathelt et al., 2004; Coenen et al., 2012).

Insights from Economic Geography: Endogenous and Exogenous Transition Dynamics

Economic geography literature provides two helpful perspectives for analyzing cities' role in niche formation: on the one hand an 'endogenous' approach, which emphasizes innovation dynamics stemming from the preexisting social and institutional capital of territorial innovation systems; for example, specific capabilities, industrial structures and local institutional arrangements (Boschma and Frenken, 2011; Moulaert and Sekia, 2003). In this view, regions or cities with a diverse actor base and a historically grown culture which fosters reciprocal trust and mutual learning have a higher propensity for innovation and industrial renewal (Moulaert and Sekia, 2003). Urban niche actors would arguably profit from such dense localized institutional arrangements (Dewald and Truffer, 2012) and from historically grown positive externalities like specialized workforces, knowledge infrastructures and governance arrangements that support continuous innovation (Boschma and Frenken, 2011). To understand the determinants of successful niche upscaling, a close focus on the local socio-technological contexts is thus indispensable.

A second – 'exogenous' – perspective argues that innovation is increasingly shaped by international networks, mobile actors, and multi-locational knowledge dynamics (Crevoisier and Jeannerat, 2009). Today's globalizing knowledge economy has created a shift "from specialization within regional production systems to [...] knowledge and resources within multi-location networks of mobility and anchoring" (ibid.: 1225). Innovation is still conditioned by territorial agglomeration, but exchange processes between distant places are also becoming increasingly important. This especially applies to cities, whose actors often occupy central positions in networks of global knowledge, capital, or specialized labor (ibid.). Cities can accordingly be seen as unique spatial contexts in which radically new products and technologies can benefit from locally specific institutional structures as well as resources stemming from trans-local networks (Binz et al., 2016).

The early formation and later development of niche technologies in a given city thus depend on how well urban actors are able to mobilize extra-regional networks, resources and knowledge, and involve them in sustained local niche-formation processes. This involves a series of mediation activities between production and consumption, between different political priorities and between planning and implementation (see Hodson and Marvin, 2010: 482), which we here conceptualize as 'anchoring' (Crevoisier and Jeannerat, 2009). We understand anchoring as a *systemic* process through which actors in a city manage to actively embed external knowledge, actors and resources into local supply and demand structures and the wider institutional context.[1]

Analytical Framework: The Anchoring of Global Innovation System Resources

We conceptualize anchoring by drawing on recent insights from the technological innovation system (TIS) approach. TIS are generally defined as "a set of networks of actors and institutions that jointly interact in a specific technological field and contribute to the generation, diffusion and utilization of variants of a new technology and/or a new product" (Markard and Truffer, 2008: 611). Besides core structural elements (actors, networks and institutions), TIS research focuses on seven key formation processes (knowledge creation, entrepreneurial experimentation, market formation, guidance of the search, creation of legitimacy, resource mobilization and creation of positive externalities (for an overview see Bergek et al., 2008, and Hekkert et al., 2007)[2] to analyze early gestation processes in socio-technical niches (Bergek et al., 2008; Markard and Truffer, 2008). How well a niche is developing, diffusing and utilizing an innovation can be analyzed by assessing the performance of these processes (Bergek et al., 2008).

In this chapter, we thus assume a direct relationship between TIS formation and the evolution of urban niches: the better the TIS performs in a specific urban context – that is, the more system-building processes its actors activate and the more system structure they build in a cumulative causation process – the better the development potential of an emerging niche technology in a city. We furthermore posit that TIS performance cannot be assessed with a myopic focus on local system structure, but that international connections must be equally taken into account (Gosens et al., 2015). The development of the TIS thus depends on connections between actors and processes emerging both endogenously in the city and exogenously in wider networks of a 'global TIS' (for a more detailed discussion, see Binz et al., 2014; Binz et al., 2016).

Based on these foundations, we define anchoring as the buildup of a local innovation system, which embraces and supports local actors' capacity to access, interact with, and 'capture' knowledge, information, ideas or any form of tangible and intangible asset from other places in the global TIS. Through interactive learning and the continuous integration of local and extra-regional inputs, TIS formation may be anchored in a specific urban context, leading to spatially 'sticky' resources for (radical) innovation. Over time, relevant actors, networks, and institutions stabilize and the proto-TIS scales up, evolving into a proto-regime that increasingly challenges dominant regime structures within and beyond a given urban context.

On-site Water Recycling as an Empirical Case and Methodological Approach

We will illustrate this framework with the transition to on-site water recycling (OST) technology in China. OST is based on washing-machine-sized wastewater treatment plants which recycle water in the basements of buildings. It represents a disruptive innovation with transformational potential for the wastewater sector's dominant regime: instead of relying on extended sewer networks and centralized, utility-based organizational forms, OST allows for mass-produced modular treatment and decentralized operation and maintenance.

The technology has not yet left the niche stage. Except for Japan and the US, OST niches are mainly served by small- to medium-size enterprises, and no dominant design for OST plants has emerged yet (Truffer et al., 2012). Nevertheless, OST technologies' R&D networks are globalized, with associations and epistemic communities integrating experiences from different OST niches at an international level. A relevant 'global OST TIS' has formed, and OST applications are gradually expanding in many places around the world (Binz et al., 2014).

We focus on OST in China for two main reasons. First, Chinese cities are all latecomers in the OST field, so zooming in on China allows us to reconstruct the full development cycle of OST niches over a relatively condensed time span. Second, desk research showed that China's pressing urban water problems generated significant activity in the OST field, leading to easily comparable success and failure cases. So far, a considerable OST niche has emerged only in Beijing, where 2,000 to 3,000 OST systems have been installed over the last 20 years. Its success story was chosen for in-depth investigation, whereas Shanghai and Xi'an represent contrasting failure cases.

According to the existing literature elaborated in Section 2.2, we would expect strong OST niches to emerge in regions which provide either strong endogenous innovation potential (incumbent related industries, supportive institutional arrangements) and/or have strong access to international knowledge networks.

Of the three city regions studied, endogenous development potential was arguably strongest in Shanghai (see Table 2.1). When the first OST experiments started in the late '80s, the city could already provide basic know-how and a specialized workforce in related industries (e.g., pumping, process engineering). Xi'an and Beijing could not provide comparable industrial capabilities. In terms of exogenous development potential, both Xi'an and Shanghai had more promising preconditions than Beijing: Shanghai was China's most internationalized commercial center, while Xi'an hosted a very active returnee entrepreneur[3] who tried to push OST from the early '90s. Finally, in terms of landscape factors, both Beijing and Xi'an historically have very pressing water shortages that exert a strong push on local governments to explore new water-saving solutions. This pressure is less pronounced in Shanghai, which however struggles with heavy water pollution (Lee, 2006). As can be seen from this short discussion and Table 2.1, Beijing initially provided quite weak endogenous and exogenous development conditions, but still developed into the only Chinese city where substantial TIS development can be observed. In the remainder of this study, we will try to explain this seemingly contradictory observation based on our framework.

Methods

Applying functional TIS analysis (Bergek et al., 2008; Hekkert et al., 2007) with a focus on international linkages poses specific challenges to research design and methods (for an overview see, e.g., Binz et al., 2014; Gosens et al., 2015). In this study, we decided to use an expert interview-based, comparative case study design. Forty interviews were conducted between November 2010 and May 2011, covering experts from all relevant TIS actor groups (Table 2.2). Interview transcripts were codified and analyzed with qualitative content analysis and the results triangulated with secondary data sources and existing literature.

Table 2.1 Initial development potential and TIS performance in three Chinese cities

Location	Endogenous potential	Exogenous potential	Landscape pressure	Performance of OST TIS
Beijing	+	+	+++	+++
Shanghai	+++	+++	+	+
Xi'an	+	++	+++	+

+ weak, ++ medium, +++ strong

Table 2.2 Interviews in China

Actor group	Interviews Beijing	Interviews Shanghai	Interviews Xi'an	Sum
Academia	10	2	1	13
Companies	12	6	0	18
Policy experts	3	2	1	6
Associations	2	0	1	3
Total	27	10	3	40

Source: Adapted from Binz et al. (2016).

The Emergence of On-site Water Recycling in Beijing, Xi'an and Shanghai

We will first describe the emergence of Beijing's OST niche (for a more detailed discussion, see Binz et al., 2016) and then shortly compare it to the two unsuccessful cases of Shanghai and Xi'an.

OST in Beijing

1990–2000: OST is Established in an Internationalized Hotel Niche

The first OST activities in Beijing started in the late '80s, driven by strong water problems: in 1987, the city government formulated a regulation requiring large hotels to introduce on-site water recycling facilities and thereby created a protected niche market for OST (Mels et al., 2007). At the time, local know-how on wastewater treatment was still very limited, so hotels had to refer to foreign companies (mainly from Japan, Germany and France) to comply with that regulation.

The first OST systems in hotels performed quite well. As hotels could provide professional operation of their OST plants, basic *legitimacy* for the concept developed, and local engineers, policy makers and practitioners first realized OST's full potential. Several local universities and research institutes began experimenting with OST pilots. Yet, these *knowledge creation* activities were still explorative, aimed at scientific discoveries and not connected to local industrial partners. *Entrepreneurial experimentation* was almost exclusively imported from outside of China: many foreign firms competed in Beijing's small hotel market, but none of them could achieve a dominant market position. Domestic competition formed only in the late '90s when the first Chinese companies developed their own OST systems, though at a very basic technological level. As the hotel niche was strongly driven by extra-local actors and international hotel chains, *resource mobilization and guidance of the search* also did not emerge locally, but were mostly imported from outside Beijing.

Until the late '90s, few TIS structures and processes emerged locally. Beijing's hotel niche was mainly kept alive by connections to niche actors from other places in an otherwise globalized TIS. Only little anchoring could be observed.

2000–2007: Localized System-Building in a Residential Building Niche

In the early 2000s, Beijing's city government decided to extend the successful water recycling legislation from hotels to residential buildings. This small addition to existing city regulation essentially forced most new residential projects in Beijing to include on-site systems and opened a large new niche market, which induced a surge in local actors' system-building activities.

As the market potential of OST suddenly skyrocketed, new companies were established that tried to serve this market. Several firms were founded around the year 2000 by returnee entrepreneurs or as spin-offs from Beijing's universities (*entrepreneurial experimentation*). This emerging industry maintained strong international ties through migrating experts' personal networks and the city's internationally renowned universities. An early form of anchoring of international capability stocks can thus be observed in this development phase. According to our interviewees, in the first few years, new local actors were strongly involved in 'learning by doing': they installed preliminary designs of their making and then learned on the spot about the specific challenges in running and maintaining OST plants in residential buildings. Parallel to this practical learning, knowledge creation in local universities also intensified. As start-ups needed consulting expertise in configuring and operating OST plants, the local industry built up dense cooperation with local research institutes. *Knowledge creation* between local start-ups and research organizations took on an increasingly reciprocal character.

Yet, despite dynamic knowledge creation, the residential building niche ran into considerable problems after five years, mainly due to misalignments in residential OST projects' institutional contexts (weak regulation enforcement, dysfunctional operation and maintenance systems, low prices for recycled water, etc.). Our interviewees contend that a significant fraction of the residential OST systems are not fully operational anymore today. This fiasco strongly *delegitimized* OST in Beijing and made the technology increasingly appear as a very undesirable solution. Nevertheless, in the second phase other system-building processes began emerging locally: *resource mobilization* was provided by real estate developers who were essentially forced to integrate OST systems into new buildings and bear the capital costs. *Direction of the search* increasingly developed in regular meetings, trade fairs and policy symposia of the local industry associations and research groups.

In sum, despite clear problems in the residential OST market, a proto-TIS emerged in this second phase in Beijing, which increasingly anchored external knowledge and resources in a dynamic local entrepreneurial experimentation process. Nevertheless, connections to the global TIS remained crucial, mainly through returning experts and internationally well-connected academics.

2007–Today: Beijing's OST Niche Begins Scaling-up

In the last phase, the local industry increasingly consolidated and – through its growing lobbying power – convinced the city government to install several hundred OST systems in the rural suburbs of Beijing. These rural systems included a comprehensive operation and maintenance package, and operational costs were completely covered by the suburbs' local governments. Moreover, foreign OST companies reentered the Beijing market and induced further *entrepreneurial experimentation* in the rural niche. Concomitantly, OST *markets formed* in other Chinese regions, especially in rich Southern provinces or the urban fringes of large cities. Also *guidance of the search* was further pushed by academia, associations, and growing interpersonal ('guanxi-') networks. The Chinese Academy of Science founded a competence center for rural OST systems while international advocacy coalitions increased their influence in Beijing, mainly through highly devoted individuals and the organization of policy symposia and conferences. *Legitimacy* was still hampered by problems in the residential niche, but Beijing's TIS actors compensated by investing heavily in presentations and lobbying activities to re-establish political support for the concept. Finally, *knowledge creation* further intensified, mainly through tight university–industry linkages and an emerging specialized labor force.

In the last phase, a complex anchoring process that had lasted for about 30 years began bearing fruit: Beijing's OST niche scaled-up, and several local TIS actors started challenging the dominant centralized urban water management regime in Beijing, as well as in several other Chinese cities and more internationally. This success story will now briefly be compared to the two other case studies with seemingly better starting conditions.

OST in Shanghai

Actors in Shanghai – despite being in a very favorable initial position for developing OST activities – never created a viable OST niche and prioritized centralized wastewater technology. Our interviewees explained this outcome as follows: in the late '80s, the local government was confronted with very pressing water pollution problems, so together with international donor agencies, TNCs and consultants, city authorities implemented a massive infrastructure build-up project based on large-scale end of pipe solutions (see also Lee, 2006). As a consequence, international networks supported the importing of the centralized regime logic in Shanghai. In the process, OST became increasingly marginalized: resources were mobilized only for large-scale, centralized wastewater technologies, OST market formation was blocked, entrepreneurial experimentation was limited to mass-producing component suppliers and the local science system did not become involved in the international networks of OST technology. Incumbent companies and spin-offs took up OST activities only very recently and now mainly serve rural and industrial niche markets. Shanghai's actors thus missed the early formation phase and therefore still lag behind Beijing in anchoring external dynamics to build up a local TIS.

OST in Xi'an

Xi'an's experience with OST implementation again differs from the other two cases: its initial conditions in the early '90s were quite comparable to Beijing: the city was also confronted with pressing water scarcity and fast urbanization and could not provide much indigenous know-how on how to deal with the problem. Yet, in contrast to Beijing and Shanghai, OST in Xi'an was from the outset visible on the policy agenda. A very entrepreneurial professor tried to push OST with his research group at Xi'an University of Architecture and Technology. He had studied in Japan and learned about Japan's successful rural OST niches. Upon returning to Xi'an, he had a strong vision to introduce this idea into the city – and ultimately the rest of China. He was very active in building pilot plants and successfully implemented OST systems in several local residential districts (Wang et al., 2008). Yet, despite his enthusiasm and encouraging research results, Xi'an never developed a viable OST niche. Even though his research group was actively building-up local TIS structures and trying to leverage networks with local design institutes and authorities, they failed to induce broader system-building processes like in Beijing. The professor's activities significantly contributed to knowledge creation (which also became available for the other regions) and created legitimacy for the OST concept beyond the borders of Xi'an. Yet, other crucial processes such as market formation, entrepreneurial experimentation or resource mobilization did not develop in the city, leaving Xi'an as a lighthouse for OST, but without a niche with considerable upscaling potential.

Discussion

Table 2.3 condenses the insights from these three cases. In Beijing, TIS buildup evolved from a strongly internationalized structure to a more and more regionally anchored set-up: whereas in a first phase, most system-building processes were imported from the outside, they were gradually turned into sticky resources in later development stages. In a nutshell, Beijing actors' success lies in a three-step anchoring process: first, the city government attracted actors from other places by opening a small market to foreign companies.

Table 2.3 System-building processes in Beijing, Shanghai and Xi'an

Beijing		Knowledge creation	Market formation	Entrepreneurial experimentation	Creation of legitimacy	Guidance of the search	Resource mobilization	Pos. Ext.
Hotels 87-00	Exogenous	++		++	+++	+	++	+
	Endogenous	+	++					
Resi-dential 00-07	Exog.	+++		+	++	+		
	Endog.	++	+++	+++	--		++	+
Rural 07-12	Exog.	+		+		+	+	
	Endog.	++	+++	++	++	++	++	+

		Knowledge creation	Market formation	Entrepreneurial experimentation	Creation of legitimacy	Guidance of the search	Resource mobilization	Pos. Ext.
Shanghai	Exog.	+		+				
	Endog.	+		+				
Xi'an	Exog.	+						
	Endog.	+++		+	++	+		

+ weak; ++ medium; +++ strong; --- hindering
Source: Adapted from Binz et al. (2016).

This cutting-edge know-how was then transformed by local start-ups and universities through interactive learning-by-doing. Finally, a local TIS emerged that retained learning and capability buildup in a mix of local and global networks. In the process, local industry champions gradually upgraded their competencies and have now almost reached the international technological frontier. Beijing's OST niche thus developed thanks to co-evolving city regulation, market segments and the strategic agency of industry and academic experts that built and maintained network ties both locally and internationally. Interestingly, this process was not planned at the outset but emerged out of a favorable mix of regional policies and emergent local–global system-building processes.

Actors in Shanghai and Xi'an developed OST in a significantly less systemic way, which did not mobilize all key processes and provide constructive coupling to the global TIS level. Most significantly, a policy push and the succession of a set of differing market segments were crucial missing factors in both Xi'an and Shanghai. Furthermore, actors in Shanghai did not mobilize international connections for system-building in OST technology, but rather for developing conventional wastewater technologies. This shows how decisively urban niche upscaling depends on specific connections to external actors and the ways in which they are mobilized in a local system-building process. Interestingly, in all presented cases, the national level's influence on niche upscaling is less relevant than existing literature would expect. This further emphasizes urban actors' important role as direct intermediaries between local niche contexts and global networks.

Conclusions

This chapter aimed at complementing urban transition studies' focus on national to regional scales with a more international perspective on the early formation dynamics in urban niches. Our evidence suggests that a TIS-based anchoring framework can fruitfully account for the complex interplay of endogenous and exogenous innovation processes in early niche formation. Multi-scalar interdependencies in urban niches appeared to be just as complex as in regime structures. In fact, leveraging exogenous innovation resources was a key strategy for urban niche actors to improve their transformative capacity: in the Beijing case, connecting to resourceful actors in distant places allowed the local constituents of OST to develop the knowledge, resources, experimental spaces, markets and legitimacy needed to induce niche upscaling, and to begin challenging dominant regime structures. While such anchoring-based niche formation is certainly not an exclusively urban phenomenon, cities' high density of potential market niches, global knowledge networks, internationally mobile workforces and particularly pressing environmental problems are likely to increase the probability for successful anchoring in urban areas.

The anchoring process described in the Beijing case study could accordingly be used to inform policymakers and other actors involved in urban transition processes. Our case shows that not only local governments, but also companies and universities can play key roles in developing and maintaining connections between localized resources and international networks. When acting as strategic niche managers, they should accordingly focus not only on creating local coalitions and transition arenas, but also equally on connecting local stakeholders with the relevant TIS actors and resources in different places around the world. Policy interventions to support such anchored niche formation could include encouraging returnee entrepreneurship, supporting extra-regional knowledge networks (e.g., through conferences and symposia), providing global–local interaction platforms (associations, exchange programs, partnerships), as well as stimulating a variety of market segments for domestic and foreign actors.

In conclusion, this chapter illustrates a strong need to address urban transition dynamics from a more multi-scalar spatial perspective, and to improve our conceptual understanding of the geographic context in which the relevant niche formation processes take place (or not). The proposed TIS-based approach provides promising analytical guidance here, but also shows some limitations. In particular, it overemphasizes supply-side innovation dynamics and tends to downplay complex power struggles in niche–regime interactions. Future work should thus try to embrace a concept of niche–regime interaction (e.g., as proposed by Elzen et al. 2012) and better connect the multi-scalar view on niche formation with an equally multi-scalar view on regime dynamics. It should also further elaborate why and how TIS formation processes unfold in specific places.

Notes

1   Note that we understand anchoring in the geographic sense of Crevoisier et al. (2009), not related to regime–niche interaction (Elzen et al., 2012).
2   We refrain from analyzing positive externalities here, as urban studies usually see them as a cumulative outcome of the other system-building processes.
3   Prof. Wang Xiaochang at Xi'an University of Architecture and Technology (XAUAT).

References

Bathelt, H., Malmberg, A., Maskell, P., 2004. Clusters and knowledge: local buzz, global pipelines and the process of knowledge creation. *Progress in Human Geography* 28 (1), 31–56.

Bergek, A., Jacobsson, S., Carlsson, B., Lindmark, S., Rickne, A., 2008. Analyzing the functional dynamics of technological innovation systems: A scheme of analysis. *Research Policy* 37 (3), 407–429.

Betsill, M.M., Bulkeley, H., 2006. Cities and the multilevel governance of global climate change. *Global Governance* 12 (2), 141–159.

Binz, C., Truffer, B., Coenen, L., 2016. Path creation as a process of resource alignment and anchoring – Industry formation for on-site water recycling in Beijing. *Economic Geography* 92 (2), 172–200.

Binz, C., Truffer, B., Coenen, L., 2014. Why space matters in technological innovation systems – the global knowledge dynamics of membrane bioreactor technology. *Research Policy* 43 (1), 138–155.

Boschma, R., Frenken, K., 2011. Technological relatedness, related variety and economic geography. In: Cooke, P. (Ed.), *The Handbook of Regional Innovation and Growth*. Edward Elgar, Cheltenham, pp. 187–197.

Bulkeley H., Castán Broto V., Hodson M. and Marvin S. (Editors), 2011. *Cities and Low Carbon Transitions*. Routledge, New York.

Carvalho, L., Mingardo, G., van Haaren, J., 2012. Green urban transport policies and cleantech innovations: evidence from Curitiba, Göteborg and Hamburg. *European Planning Studies* 20 (3), 375–396.

Coenen, L., Benneworth, P., Truffer, B., 2012. Toward a spatial perspective on sustainability transitions. *Research Policy* 41 (6), 968–979.

Coenen, L., Truffer, B., 2012. Places and spaces of sustainability transitions: geographical contributions to an emerging research and policy field. *European Planning Studies* 20 (3), 367–374.

Crevoisier, O., Jeannerat, H., 2009. Territorial knowledge dynamics: from the proximity paradigm to multi-location milieus. *European Planning Studies* 17 (8), 1223–1241.

Dewald, U., Truffer, B., 2012. The local sources of market formation: explaining regional growth differentials in German photovoltaic markets. *European Planning Studies* (3), 397–420.

Elzen, B., van Mierlo, B., Leeuwis, C., 2012. Anchoring of innovations: assessing Dutch efforts to harvest energy from glasshouses. *Environmental Innovation and Societal Transitions* 5 (0), 1–18.

Geels, F.W., 2002. Technological transitions as evolutionary reconfiguration processes: a multi-level perspective and a case-study. *Research Policy* 31, 1257–1274.

Gosens, J., Lu, Y., Coenen, L., 2015. The role of transnational dimensions in emerging economy 'Technological Innovation Systems' for clean-tech. *Journal of Cleaner Production* 86 (1), 378–388.

Hekkert, M., Suurs, R., Negro, S., Kuhlmann, S., Smits, R., 2007. Functions of innovation systems: a new approach for analysing technological change. *Technological Forecasting and Social Change* 74 (4), 413–432.

Hodson, M., Marvin, S., 2010. Can cities shape socio-technical transitions and how would we know if they were? *Research Policy* 39 (4), 477–485.

Kemp, R., Schot, J., Hoogma, R., 1998. Regime shifts to sustainability through processes of niche formation: the Approach of strategic niche management. *Technology Analysis & Strategic Management* 10 (2), 175–195.

Lee, S., 2006. *Water and Development in China. The Political Economy of Shanghai Water Policy*. World Scientific Publishing, Singapore.

Markard, J., Truffer, B., 2008. Technological innovation systems and the multi-level perspective: towards an integrated framework. *Research Policy* 37, 596–615.

Mels, A., Guo, S., Zhang, C., Li, X., Wang, H., Liu, S., Braadbaart, O., 2007. Decentralised wastewater reclamation systems in Beijing – adoption and performance under field conditions. First SWITCH Scientific Meeting University of Birmingham, UK, 9–10 Jan 2006, 1–8. http://www.switchurbanwater.eu/outputs/pdfs/CBEI_PAP_Decentralised_wastewater_reclamation_systems.pdf, accessed on 10/08/2015.

Moulaert, F., Sekia, F., 2003. Territorial innovation models: a critical survey. *Regional Studies* 37 (3), 289–302.

Raven, R., Schot, J., Berkhout, F., 2012. Space and scale in socio-technical transitions. *Environmental Innovation and Societal Transitions* 4 (0), 63–78.

Smith, A., Voss, J., Grin, J., 2010. Innovation studies and sustainability transitions: the allure of the multi-level perspective, and its challenges. *Research Policy* 39 (4), 435–448.

Truffer, B., Binz, C., Gebauer, H., Störmer, E., 2012. Market success of on-site treatment: a systemic innovation problem. In: Larsen, T., Udert, K., Lienert, J. (Eds.), *Wastewater Treatment: Source Separation and Decentralisation*. IWA Publishing, London, pp. 209–223.

Wang, X., Chen, R., Zhang, Q.H., Li, K., 2008. Optimized plan of centralized and decentralized wastewater reuse systems for housing development in the urban area of Xi'an, China. *Water Science & Technology* 58 (5), 969–975.

3 Understanding the Policy Realities of Urban Transitions

Yvette Bettini, Tracey Arklay and Brian W. Head

Introduction

The global process of urbanization has left environmental, economic, and social consequences yet to be understood. One concern of scholars and urban administrators is the resilience of cities; how urban activities can 'bounce back' after a significant disturbance, and 'bounce forward' through learning and responding to these events (Seeliger and Turok 2013). This maintenance of urban function is salient in the context of cities, as their highly engineered landscapes can leave citizens vulnerable. With large socio-technical systems delivering essential services such as energy, water, transport, housing, and health care, there is an argument that urban populations in developed countries have moved from a modest level of self-reliance to high levels of technical reliance. Natural disasters provide the most frequent evidence of this vulnerability, exposing citizens when failure in large technocratic systems leaves them to provide for their own basic needs. In major cities in some developing countries, those without access to urban infrastructure services may be less reliant on central technologies, but their subsistence within the resources of the urban landscape is a daily struggle, made more difficult in times of crisis.

What does the engineered landscape of a city mean for its resilience in the face of climate change? More pertinently for this book, how do climatic variations and other forms of future uncertainty affect the way city administrators manage and modify the socio-technical systems on which cities depend? What influence do short-term shocks and long-term pressures have on the policy and administrative frameworks within which these technical systems are embedded? This chapter focuses on incidents of natural disaster to explore how cities can recover and learn from the experience by adjusting systems and services to anticipate the next hazard, and to explore the implications of shocks and incremental pressures on the policy context for ongoing socio-technical transitions.

The Policy Process and Transitions

Policy issues pertaining to urban sustainability and resilience are difficult to manage (Dovers 2005, Head 2008), not only due to the complex nature of the problems themselves, but the contested process of policymaking (Rhodes 1997).

Yet it is the policy process that provides a critical pathway to transitions, as technological solutions to society's sustainable development are legitimized and institutionalized through policy change (Huitema and Meijerink 2010). Flexibility and responsiveness in these governance processes are also needed, to ensure dependency on a single solution does not prevail in the face of changing circumstances and future uncertainty (Frantzeskaki, Loorbach and Meadowcroft 2012).

From its origins, the transition management (TM) approach recognized the importance of influencing policy (Rotmans, Kemp and van Asselt 2001); as a means of pursuing the structural change, both physical and institutional, needed to overcome persistent sustainable development problems (Grin, Rotmans and Schot 2010). Transition management emerged as a proposed alternative to the expert-informed, rationalist policymaking tradition dominant in western democracies. The TM approach rests within the framework of networked forms of governance; where deliberative, participatory coalitions are fostered to develop novel solutions, connected to shared long-term perspectives, outside the constraints of the bureaucracy (Loorbach 2010). The carefully selected membership of these coalitions, including 'champions,' 'frontrunners', 'policy entrepreneurs', and the like, in theory can provide the connections back into official policy processes to influence incremental change and provide a range of alternative policy options when the opportunity for radical change opens (Frantzeskaki, Loorbach, and Meadowcroft 2012).

Being designed as a 'shadow track' to official policy processes, TM offers advantages in providing space for innovation, collaborative learning, and fostering well-networked communities of practice. However, these coalitions remain only one voice among the many interest groups and agendas policy officials must manage and balance in the policy design, communication and implementation processes of decision-making. Policy processes are highly contested, even during periods of stability (Rhodes 1997). In times of crisis, tensions between embedded power structures, key interests, and political imperatives for quick solutions heighten the stakes (Pierre and Peters 2005). It is acknowledged that transition scholarship has not yet delved deep enough into the particulars and politics of governing transitions (Kern, 2012). This chapter aims to explore the policy realities of urban transitions, using a unique case of incremental pressure and rapid system shock. The research examines the governance interactions and activities behind policy responses to short-term shock (flood) and long-term pressure (drought) in Brisbane, Australia. This city experienced the 'creeping crisis' of a prolonged drought and a major urban flooding disaster in quick succession. These circumstances provide a unique opportunity, firstly, to examine the immediate management solutions and policy responses employed to deliver urban services following these two forms of system shock (bounce back resilience), and second, to explore the influence of these events on policy learning and development (bounce forward resilience).

Analytical Frame

So as to connect research findings of policy and governance activities observed in the case study to transition scholarship, we employed the multilevel governance framework (Loorbach, 2010) as the analytic lens for the study. This framework offers four dimensions of governance that are used as guideposts for the broad range of governance activities underlying management responses and policy change:

> **Strategic** activities set long term goals, develop policies and plans to realize these visions, and generate shared understandings, values, identity and culture.
> **Tactical** activities set agendas, design policy interventions, and strategize implementation plans and their steering mechanisms such as funding and resourcing systems, networks and partnerships.
> **Operational** activities encompass the range of 'on-ground' actions of policy implementation, infrastructure management, and service delivery.
> **Reflexive** activities monitor and evaluate the process through formal reviews and inquiries or individual practitioner reflection, to ensure learning outcomes.

The literature on the complex nature of many policy issues establishes that these governance activities often do not follow a logical or lineal pathway; activities may occur in parallel rather than sequentially (Rittel and Webber 1973, Head 2008). The four governance dimensions above provide a useful lens for examining policy aspects of the case study, particularly the role different governance activities play in steering through complex policy settings at different rates of change. This governance framework enables the analysis of case materials to be structured so as to capture the range of governance activities behind the two policy responses observed. Such examination offers initial insight for urban transition scholars into the policy challenges of long-term path dependency and short-term shocks, which are magnified in densely populated urban centers.

Context and Methods

Drought and flood occur frequently in Australia. As a consequence, water supply systems and disaster response and recovery are considered vital government services. The persistent natural resource management issue of drought versus the short-term management of disaster response and recovery after flooding offers two divergent policy problems. The recent Brisbane experience with both events in quick succession enables a comparison of the activities and interactions behind the policy responses used in both circumstances within the same case context. This study builds from earlier work, which examined the policy and political realities of these complex public-policy issues (Arklay 2012, Head 2014, Bettini and Frantzeskaki 2014). The circumstances relating to each case are described in brief below.

South East Queensland was subject to the 'creeping crisis' of water scarcity from 2001 to 2008, with the major city, Brisbane, facing a very real prospect of running out of water for its 2 million residents. Government authorities responded with major institutional reforms alongside large-scale, centralized infrastructure and demand management strategies. Our research collected and analyzed primary and secondary evidence throughout the latter stages of the drought to examine the policy activity and political pressures behind this infrastructure response. Primary data included six extensive interviews with urban water professionals from government, industry and NGOs at senior management to executive level, and workshops with a further ten professionals at the service delivery level from a range of government organizations. Secondary sources included policy documents, scientific and consultancy reports and media articles.

The flooding events of 2010–11 that followed the drought conditions were unprecedented, as torrential rain affected over 80 per cent of the state of Queensland's land mass, stretching emergency agencies to their limit. Over a period of six months in 2011, 24 semi-structured interviews were conducted with senior disaster managers across the relevant agencies, and conversations with 12 mayors and several councillors in the worst affected regions were also conducted. The information and experiences of these interviewees were then triangulated with the evidence and findings reported in the Queensland Flood Commission of Inquiry reports, press reports, and the scholarly literature.

Using data sources detailed above and the timeframe of the mid-stage of the drought in 2006 to the early aftermath of the flood in 2011, we identified the actions of organizations and individuals that enabled the city to respond to these events, and examined the impacts on policy and management directions for each domain (urban water and disaster management). We sought explanations pertaining to leadership, organizational culture, institutional conditions, policy networks and anything else that emerged within the strategic, tactical, operational and reflexive governance themes as important, to highlight how the policy governance of these two domains operated in periods of incremental pressure and crisis. While neither event provides the study of an urban transition, together they represent the two main velocities with which transitions are known to proceed: long-term incremental changes and short-term shocks. This is useful in developing an understanding of the types of policy interventions and governance activities that may help to progress transitions in the context of urban systems.

Results

The findings of the comparative study are now discussed, with supplementary representative quotes from those interviewed during the research.

Strategic Lens

Despite a statutory basis for long-term water planning, there was a noted lack of preparedness for the drought conditions. While water services (supply, sewerage and drainage) were delivered through a vertically integrated administrative structure within municipal councils, these arrangements and the geographic scope of statutory plans led to horizontally disconnected planning across water catchments. As one interviewee noted, *"at the time we had 13 local governments all managing their own water supply and trying to get some consistency within the region around water use, water restrictions, and [so] better management of water is very, very difficult"*. As water resources became scarce, and with catchments artificially connected through water supply infrastructure, it was apparent that collaborative planning was needed to secure supplies. A Regional Water Supply Strategy for South East Queensland was developed around 2004–05, but came too late to address water scarcity through better planning and allocations alone. As one interview reflected, *'Initially [demand management] was the only way that we could deal with it … we did not have the thinking and we did not have the planning done'*.

Queensland disaster management is underpinned by a complex network of intergovernmental bodies, operating under structures and procedures set out in the *Disaster Management Act 2003*. Legislation underpins local government responsibility in the first instance, but requires strong levels of coordination through statutory disaster plans based on the international tenets of 'Prevent, Prepare, Respond and Recover'. Federal constitutional arrangements also ensure primary responsibility for disaster management falls to State governments, with additional support provided when a certain threshold is reached. Thus, the strategic policy framework is focused on disaster coordination with collaboration across and between Australia's three tiers of government, as well as between non-government and volunteer organizations. This framework allows a response to be scaled up if the extent of the disaster requires. Still, all those interviewed agreed that 'it is the planning rather than the plans themselves that are important'. While training and preparedness within the emergency services and the broader community are a crucial element in these plans, it was noted that prior experiences in managing disasters increased the preparation and focus of plans. This translated to better prepared communities in those areas that were most at risk by recurring natural disasters (cyclones and floods). Thus, the planning process itself was generally seen to be a vital strategic governance success factor in generating preparedness.

Tactical Lens

As the drought deepened the state government abruptly entered the water management arena. The situation was framed as a 'crisis' to win political points and justify the state's intervention, which pursued an agenda of centralizing decision-making; infrastructure ownership and water services provision; corporatizing administration; and separating policy, regulatory and service delivery functions (Head 2014). At the time, many in the water policy community questioned the logic behind the reforms, as one interviewee noted: *"There was no integrated approach to water management … I think this kind of crisis event allowed those sorts of really major institutional and policy changes to happen"*.

Although crisis can provide the opportunity to pursue necessary reforms, once elevated to a major political issue, crisis-framed decision-making took over, and policy strategies were developed by inner policy networks with limited discussion with stakeholders and experts from the broader water policy community (Head 2010). Subjected to the legislative power of the state government, and with their influence and consultation avenues largely eroded, the water policy community got down to the task of implementing the changes. A new administrative landscape was created, and as organizational roles became established, actors began to look beyond the bounds of their own organizations to understand the positions of other key players. The use of political manoeuvring tactics were also employed – two examples identified were using a partnership program for industry capacity-building as a bargaining chip in negotiations between organizations, and communicating the costs of the state's decisions to the broader public.

Unlike the incremental problem of drought, where the predominant political tactic was to capitalize on the opportunity to separate the current administration from past decisions or to assign blame, the political behavior during a fast-moving crisis event such as a natural disaster is different. Disparate groupings of usually siloed government agencies, NGOs, charities and volunteers work in collaboration, recognizing the social, economic and political importance of a timely and effective response. During the 2010–11 events the State Disaster Management Group (SDMG), whose membership included the highest ranking government officials, provided a quick-response mechanism, coordinating and organizing resources and personnel with authoritative decision-making. Yet to work effectively, managing relationships between disparate groups was a vital task. In 2009 a senior police officer was given the role of State Disaster Coordinator. Initially, some local councils expressed concern about how police culture would fit with the more collaborative, bottom-up nature of emergency work. Post flood, one interviewee suggested the successful operation was *"testament to the leadership shown at the top of Queensland's disaster management agencies as well as within the police hierarchy.'* Yet, to achieve this, *'much shoe leather was worn out traversing the State with the Deputy Police Commissioner to get the local councils on side prior to the 2010–11 event"*. This statement highlights the importance of relationships in overcoming inter-organizational collaboration barriers and cultural differences, representing a significant tactical activity.

Operational Lens

During the drought the lack of preparedness, combined with the intervention by the State, resulted in less consultative decisions and quick-win solutions. Demand management, though laden with political risk, was utilized to buy time for infrastructure development. The choices of infrastructure focused on readily available off-the-shelf engineering solutions. Many in the water policy community saw the drought response as a missed opportunity for change, as the problem focus was narrowed to supply security and the solutions continued traditions of large, expensive and inflexible infrastructure. The lack of attention to planning for beyond the immediate drought conditions, in terms of investment in novel technologies and innovative system designs, was viewed as a significant backward step for the sector (Keath and Brown 2009, Head 2014). Many in the policy community expressed concern that the response – both the infrastructure and institutional reforms – geared the sector toward a single anticipated future (droughts), rather than developing greater resilience in the city. The corporatized business model of the service delivery organizations was also viewed as a potential barrier to achieving the best, multi-functional solutions for providing optimum benefits from water management (e.g., urban amenity, waterway health). As one interviewee noted, *"If there's not a return then they're not going to invest"*.

The relationships that had been established within the urban water policy community were recognized as a key instrument for making the sector operationally effective. A partnership catchment management program which included ecosystem monitoring, innovative research, industry capacity building, communication and education, and strategy coordination provided a locus for a policy community to form around water-quality/integrated-catchment management issues. This informal forum provided opportunities to share information and knowledge, discuss new thinking, consider new science and ecosystem monitoring results, trial new practices and consider emerging issues and policy implications. These activities built trust and shared cognitive frames around water management problems and solutions. Interviewees noted that this informal network was crucial to managing across the boundaries of the new administrative arrangements, navigating the disruption and instability to implement institutional and infrastructure reforms. As one interviewee noted, *"There are new boundaries that people are needing to manage across. So those informal networks in fact become pretty important"*.

While institutional arrangements and the SDMG established coordination mechanisms and responsibility, the disaster response also relied on the actions of responders and citizens on the ground to keep people safe, rescue those in trouble and help people return to some normalcy. In 2011 the police and emergency crews from the official agencies worked alongside trained volunteers, local councils and major charities. Along with the telecommunications and electricity companies, most of these groups were represented at the SDMG level, where they were part of a two way communication flow that enabled sharing of the most up-to-date information possible. Trust was a vital component. Interviewees indicated that understanding other agencies' cultures and the management of relationships was an ongoing issue and *"while we may not like each other, we respect each other's skills"*. Again, prior planning that had a purposefully consultative approach, not only set up the structures for response, but ensured they were operable during the crisis.

Reflexive Lens

Learning from the drought was evident in the stories of those interviewed. There was a general recognition that fundamental questions such as the purpose of water in society needed to be considered across the urban water sector, and the willingness to discuss this through informal forums existed. However, it is less clear whether this recognition extended to water management operations, planning activities and policy development. While long-term water planning and review processes were initiated during the drought, the broader water policy community members were unclear about the status of these activities post-drought. As such, policy processes remained disconnected to the professional expertise within the urban water sector, negating reflexive governance capacity. Further, the handling of the drought 'crisis' may have eroded some of the trust and collaborative relationships needed for this to occur, as one interviewee reflected: *"I think that the [water] utilities are hiding from it at the moment. I think ... they're just saying we'll stay out of the debate and we'll just let the politics and all that argue between each other"*. It remains to be seen whether the knowledge gained through Brisbane's experience translates into policy learning.

The disaster study highlights that learning from past experience matters. Front line perspectives, the importance of institutional memory and being prepared to review areas of weakness are all important aspects that Queensland had incorporated into its disaster policy framework. However, changes to disaster legislation often occur after findings from official inquiries. It is less certain whether longer-term learning for mitigation and resilience planning are included in the terms of reference of these exercises. Some have commented that the response post flood was a missed opportunity, in that substantial hardship payments to individuals increased unrealistic expectations of citizens and reduced their resilience, reflecting the choice of short-term political gain over long-term decisions to do with land planning and climate change strategies (see McGowan 2012, McClelland 2012).

Discussion

We now take the insights into policy activities and challenges in each study to canvas some of the implications for guiding urban transitions toward short- and long-term resilience.

The results suggest that city administrators and other levels of government are well versed in managing the operational activities required in both short-term events and incremental pressures to maintain public services like water supplies and disaster response and recovery. While this short-term resilience capacity is standard 'kit' for most developed cities and governments, these results show that the tactical activities of collaboration are also important. The results affirm the standard wisdom in the literature on managing system change, namely, that stakeholder buy-in and commitment to plans and processes are critical and are best ensured by genuine involvement in planning from the outset. The directly felt impacts of an immediate natural disaster like a flood create a sense of urgency and humanity to bring both authorities and communities together in response. Differences are set aside to pursue the immediate priority of ensuring the safety and well-being of city inhabitants. However this case study shows that this collegiality can be enhanced by taking a collaborative approach to planning for disaster response. It is difficult to garner this level of urgency in a more incremental change process like drought. Yet the study results demonstrate the risk of ignoring collaborative approaches prior to and during such a creeping crisis, including: impeded coordination, reduced trust and willingness to collaborate in the short term, and eroded collaborative capacity for activities with a longer-term outlook.

Within the diverse socio-cultural demography and concentration of interest groups characteristic of most modern cities, the need for collaborative foundations to public service design and delivery raises distinct challenges for city administrators and policy officials, and by proxy for transition managers. Questions of representation; appropriate communication and participatory process design; skills in negotiation, conflict, expectation and agenda management; and political engagement and risks come to the fore, along with the issue of resource availability for collaborative approaches. The drought case also suggests that a lack of planning can close opportunities for collaboration around a particular trigger event, because quick rather than consensual decisions are needed. One implication of these results for TM is the need to develop participatory and consensual processes that can shift to more decisive protocols to match the decision-making needs of administrators and policy officials during planning and crisis situations respectively. This may also have implications for managing the evolving membership of transition arenas, and perhaps the cohesiveness or collegiality of these coalitions.

Transition arenas may also have an active role to play in advocating for attention to issues in the absence of a perceived crisis; using their transition experiments not only to generate solution options but also to make the case for change by highlighting potential consequences of inaction, demonstrating costs of reactive decisions, and showing the political benefits of proactive responses in contrast to reactive or 'manufactured' crisis responses. The fundamental challenge is to find the resources, support and legitimacy for the network governance activities inherent in the TM approach, as both case examples have shown these networks to be largely undervalued. Attention to fostering these networks remained largely unrecognized in formal budget allocations and planning/policy procedures.

This study suggested that neither a short-term nor an incremental crisis provides an automatic mechanism for opening a system to new directions and opportunities. The drought presented a 'crisis' requiring fundamental structural change. While major change ensued, it reflected the continuation of past thinking and solutions. Likewise the catastrophic events of the flood provided the opportunity to reevaluate flood management once the water subsided. The resulting inquiry instead inadvertently encouraged a community focus on assigning blame and seeking compensation. The insights from both cases highlight that the opportunity for transformative change can be missed in the political nature of planning and service provision.

In democratic systems, activities with long-term outlooks are impacted by political factors like electoral cycles and budgetary processes. Individual actors and agencies may learn from operational mistakes and make efforts to improve them, if negative feedback is instant and easily attributable. However, the incentive to make long-term, often fundamental changes to controversial policy areas like land use planning and water allocation is weak when the negative consequences of inaction can be deferred, and hence blame shifted. Both studies highlight well the political opportunities provided by every crisis, whether real or manufactured. Sudden disasters attract significant media attention, providing the opportunity for political leadership to be displayed. Incremental problems can be blamed on past governments through framing as an underlying problem now needing to be solved, and provide an opportunity to show leadership and competency by averting a 'potential' crisis. Both cases showed how political motivations will frame the problem to suit the solution.

This political framing of problems and solutions suggests a need for close attention to careful political engagement in transitions processes, in order to grasp the windows of opportunity arising in these trigger events. Any attempt to promote alternative solutions for uptake into policy will need to be supported by a political rationale. Transition agendas would do well to include potential political ramifications as criteria within the case for change, along with the standard economic cost assessments and demonstration of non-monetary social and environmental benefits. Such a strategy will require a close appreciation of the policy and political context, and skills in anticipating what the gatekeepers to ministers and other officials are looking for in policy solutions.

These results also highlight the challenges of converting experience and learning from each type of trigger event into policy outcomes. Despite the different types of crisis, both studies showed disconnect between the lead-up and management of a crisis and the later reflexive activity. In the case of flooding, the response was borne out of immediate safety and survival needs – and the political imperative to restore normalcy and minimize anger in the electorate. However, the political choices made, such as the generous hand-outs, arguably wasted resources that could have been better spent on future mitigation measures. Furthermore, these actions contributed to shaping the communities' expectation about what governments should do, reinforcing apathy toward individual and local responsibility and potentially decreasing the city's resilience in future disaster events. In the drought case, it is arguable whether the response increased resilience of the city in the longer term. On the one hand, large capital investments in central reticulation systems are leaving a legacy of higher water prices and reduced opportunities for investment in innovation. On the other, 'climate independent' desalination has provided some flexibility in water-source provision, and demand management and household water-efficiency subsidies have empowered communities with some capacity for managing their own water supply. Yet it is clear this potential resilience is more fortuitous than planned. Policies and responses during the drought focused on water security. Once the crisis was averted, the focus shifted elsewhere, and a system optimized for dealing with water-scarce conditions remained.

In both studies, limited reflection on the longer term impacts of actions taken during the crisis hinder urban resilience by limiting policy learning and change. Neither good preparation in the flood case, nor near–system failure in the drought case, were enough to drive critical reflection of the public services provided and their system of delivery. How transition approaches deal with these legacy issues are critical to progressing a transition. The space for reflexive activities appears limited, difficult to recognize and hard to influence. Nevertheless, the iterative design and independence of TM 'shadow track' processes may set transition studies in good stead to fill this role – if the challenge of political legitimacy can be overcome.

Conclusion

This study has suggested that the respective governances of short-term and incremental change are not fundamentally dissimilar challenges. Both require good planning, clear but flexible policy frameworks and cohesive networks able to weather the relationship dynamics of political ebbs and flows. Delivering services and planning for complex policy issues are difficult in the context of modern cities that are highly engineered, culturally diverse and have unequal power distributions. Short-term shock and long-term pressure events may not act as the trigger for forward-looking, long-term policy outlooks needed to drive and support transitions to resilience cities. While this study has looked solely at cases in a developed city, there are implications for transitions in the context of developing cities in terms of access to resources, limitations of existing infrastructure and administrative systems and political instability. These issues are experienced even more intensely in the developing context, and the immediate priority of universal access to essential services will focus the transition agenda from future aspirations to current basic needs.

The problem of short electoral cycles and the difficulties of budgeting for future unknowns provide ongoing challenges. Particular networks may be motivated to be innovative and learn from past experience, but pressure to return to old modes is at times overwhelming. Nevertheless, this study has identified promising strategies for overcoming the policy-related pitfalls of urban transitions. Fostering urban policy networks from the diverse sociocultural and professional landscape of cities, and seeking to match collaborative processes to decision-making needs of authorities while maintaining a participatory design, will be critical to gaining legitimacy and a seat at the policy development table. Likewise, it may be possible to develop trusted sources of policy advice by using transition experiments to build an evidence base – political, economic and moral – for a change agenda. Finally, we can build on the strengths of TM to provide the network governance capability and reflexivity that are often missing in policy processes.

The organized, theoretically based approach of TM offers a governance structure capable of pursuing these strategies to enable policy change, while providing a support and learning mechanism for networks of professionals with a degree of independence from the hierarchy of government. With climate change predictions suggesting more frequent and unanticipated events, understanding how transitions can be progressed through periods of both stability and crisis in the 'crowded' urban context is vital if our cities, and the social and ecological systems which support them, are to develop resilience to future shocks and pressures.

References

Arklay, Tracey M. 2012. "Queensland's state disaster management group: an all agency response to an unprecedented natural disaster". *The Australian Journal of Emergency Management* 27 (3):9–19.

Bettini, Yvette, and Niki Frantzeskaki. 2014. "Linking practice to process: examining adaptive institutional capacity using the multi-level transition governance framework". Paper presented to the 5th International Sustainability Transitions Conference, Utrecht, the Netherlands, 27–29 August.

Dovers, Stephen. 2005. *Environment and Sustainability Policy: Creation, Implementation, Evaluation*. Sydney, Australia: Federation Press.

Frantzeskaki, Niki, Derk Loorbach and James Meadowcroft. 2012. "Governing societal transitions to sustainability". *International Journal of Sustainable Development* 15 (1–2):19–36.

Grin, John, Jan Rotmans and Johan Schot. 2010. "Conclusion: How to understand transitions? How to influence them?" In *Transitions to Sustainable Development: New Directions in the Study of Long Term Transformative Change*, edited by John Grin, Jan Rotmans, Johan Schot, Frank Geels and Derk Loorbach. New York: Routledge.

Head, Brian W. 2008. "Wicked problems in public policy". *Public Policy* 3 (2):101–118.

Head, Brian W. 2010. "Water policy – evidence, learning and the governance of uncertainty". *Policy and Society* 29 (2):171–180.

Head, Brian W. 2014. "Managing urban water crises: resilience challenges in Southeast Queensland". *Ecology and Society* 19 (2):33.

Huitema, Dave, and Sander Meijerink. 2010. "Realizing water transitions: the role of policy entrepreneurs in water policy change". *Ecology and Society* 15 (2):26.

Keath, Nina A., and Rebekah R. Brown. 2009. "Extreme events: being prepared for the pitfalls with progressing sustainable urban water management". *Water Science and Technology* 59 (7):1271–1280.

Kern, Florian. 2012. "Using the multi-level perspective on socio-technical transitions to assess innovation policy". *Technological Forecasting and Social Change* 79 (2):298–310.

Loorbach, Derk. 2010. "Transition management for sustainable development: A prescriptive, complexity-based governance framework". *Governance: An International Journal of Policy Administration and Institutions* 23 (1):161–183.

McClelland, Robert. 2012. "Federal MP questions disaster funding, Labor's future". *ABC Online*, 2 April. Accessed 1 April 2014. http://www.abc.net.au/worldtoday/content/2012/s3468713.htm.

McGowan, Jim. 2012. "A missed opportunity to promote community resilience – the Queensland Floods Commission of Inquiry". *Australian Journal of Public Administration* 71 (3):355–363.

Pierre, Jon, and Guy B. Peters. 2005. *Governing Complex Societies: Trajectories and Scenarios*. Basingstoke, UK: Palgrave MacMillan.

Rhodes, Roderick 1997. *Understanding Governance: Policy Networks, Governance, Reflexivity, and Accountability*. Maidenhead, UK: Open University Press.

Rittel, Horst W.J. and Melvin M. Webber. 1973. "Dilemmas in a general theory of planning". *Policy Sciences* 4 (2):155–169.

Rotmans, Jan, René Kemp and Marjolein van Asselt. 2001. "More evolution than revolution: transition management in public policy". *Foresight* 3 (1):15–31.

Seeliger, Leanne, and Ivan Turok. 2013. "Towards sustainable cities: extending resilience with insights from vulnerability and transition theory". *Sustainability* 5 (5):2108–2128.

4 The Governance of Transformative Change

Tracing the Pathway of the Sustainability Transition in Vancouver, Canada

Sarah Burch

Introduction

Sustainability transitions are fluid and multi-faceted phenomena, and may be characterized by multiple 'false starts', punctuated equilibria, and contradictory pressures (such as a shifting political landscape and economic stressors). Many of these transitions are taking place at very small, community-based scales and are driven by grassroots or bottom-up initiatives (Forrest and Wiek, 2014; Seyfang and Haxeltine, 2012). While the idiosyncrasies of a particular urban context may strain our capacity to garner lessons that apply to other cities, social learning is a crucial dimension of accelerated sustainability transitions. In particular, cases of established leadership and innovative responses to sustainability challenges provide important insights into the roots, enabling factors, and various pathways that sustainability transitions might follow. The City of Vancouver, in the province of British Columbia, Canada, is one such case, offering over two decades of clear action in response to climate change and the related issues of biodiversity, water quality, social cohesiveness and equity, waste management and energy use.

The City of Vancouver is consistently ranked one of the most livable cities in the world, and is also viewed as a Canadian leader in sustainability (Shaw et al., 2014). A wide-ranging suite of strategies has been implemented, including landfill gas recovery, neighborhood energy utilities, stringent green building standards and support for cycling and public transit. Targets and actions have become increasingly ambitious and comprehensive and are now fundamentally influencing sustainability indicators in the city (City of Vancouver, 2014). Although the municipality of Vancouver is granted unusually broad powers by the province of British Columbia under the Vancouver Charter, it faces some of the same constraints encountered by other municipalities in Canada's 'weak mayor[1]' system. As part of its sustainability transition, successive mayors have also taken significant political risks in order to implement sustainability measures (such as densification, organics collection, landfill gas recovery and others) – not all of which have paid off with reelection. This presents a puzzle of relevance to other urban actors: what particular mix of capacities, institutional structures, and networks of actors are giving rise to

Vancouver's ongoing transition? Furthermore, what is it about the urban or municipal context (geographically, jurisdictionally and socio-politically) that has enabled or inhibited this transition?

To uncover the roots and chart the pathway of Vancouver's transition, this chapter employs an approach that integrates theoretical tools from core strands of transition scholarship. The goal of this chapter is to reveal the transferable lessons demonstrated by Vancouver's leadership, with a particular focus on innovative modes of governance and networks of actors. Ultimately, this chapter contributes to longitudinal analysis that begins to demonstrate whether sustainability strategies put in place over the last two decades have actually borne fruit.

Sustainability Governance: Engagement, Fluidity, and the Potential for Accelerated Transitions

Transformative change in socio-technical systems has given rise to an everexpanding, and increasingly influential, body of theory. The roots and primary thrusts of this theory (and related domains such as sustainability science) have been coherently captured by a handful of recent reviews (Markard et al., 2012; Spangenberg, 2011). These reviews highlight the fundamentally trans- and interdisciplinary and action-oriented nature of this work, while suggesting that gaps remain in our capacity to understand the politics that characterize transitions (Markard et al., 2012), the broader socio-cultural context that gives rise to them, and the multi-system or non-static nature (Jacobsson and Johnson, 2000) of transformative change towards sustainability (Burch et al., 2014).

While this chapter will not offer a detailed review of transition theory, distinctions between the four central strands of this work help to elucidate the dimensions of transformative change in an urban context that may prove to be instructive to other cities currently considering sustainability experiments. In particular, two branches of sustainability transition theory, namely strategic niche management and transition management, offer particularly useful insights into the case of Vancouver.

Strategic niche management focuses on the cultivation of 'niche' spaces in which novel patterns of actor/network/technology relations can develop (Geels and Schot, 2008; Hoogma et al., 2002; Raven and Geels, 2010). Examples include public–private partnerships, fiscal policies such as subsidies or tax shifting and the use of public funds to support the uptake of new technologies as they become increasingly competitive. Strategic niche management suggests that cities may be viewed as niche spaces in which novel modes of governance can emerge, and suggests the importance of tracing the policies that can give rise to these niches.

Transition management (Kern and Smith, 2008; Loorbach, 2010), in contrast, employs a long-term, systems-level perspective to explore ways to guide a socio-technical system from one path to another, paying attention to actor–technology–institution interactions and governance mechanisms

(Smith et al., 2005). The challenge, in part, becomes linking radical short-term innovations with a longer-term sustainability vision (Loorbach, 2010) and creating opportunities for collaborative course-correction in light of new information or unexpected outcomes.

The challenge of governing sustainability transitions is made manifest in the urban context (Nevens et al., 2013), in which a variety of decisions are made that fundamentally shape energy consumption, greenhouse gas (GHG) emissions, waste production and water quality. Governance at this scale, however, is also deeply constrained by activities at higher (state/provincial and national) levels of government, creating the potential for policy incoherence and contradictory aims. The field of multilevel governance (Hooghe and Marks, 2003), which has its roots in analyses of European integration and federalism (Deutsch, 1954; Riker, 1964), has been brought to bear with increasing frequency on the question of climate change action and sustainability experience in cities (Betsill and Bulkeley, 2006; Bulkeley and Betsill, 2005).

It is the transition management approach that mostly actively informs the chapter that follows: tools from both transition theory and multilevel governance theory are employed to explore the overlapping spheres of influence that may characterize the governance of sustainability in urban spaces. Blending multilevel governance theory with a systems lens entails a consideration of human and natural systems as fundamentally intertwined, with change in one cascading in complex and often unpredictable ways through the other. It regards non-state actors to be of equal importance to nation states in policy development and implementation, engaging with often poorly understood actors such as small businesses and networks. Finally, it draws attention to the complex 'development path' (Burch et al., 2014) that shapes the capacities, drivers of GHG emissions and vulnerability and also the response options available. One might call this constellation of insights 'sustainability governance', representing a move forward from 'environmental governance', which may have a distinctly biophysical flavor (i.e., focusing on preservation of natural resources and ecosystems without exploring the ways that human world views construct the value of these systems), lack an explicitly normative lens and view change as linear or systems as static.

A sustainability governance approach suggests several elements of analysis that may elucidate the nature of Vancouver's transition. These elements include the innovative actions and policies that set Vancouver apart as a niche space; the range of actors, the networks in which they participate and the influence of these networks on Vancouver's pathway; and the evolution and distribution of fluid, issue-oriented governance arrangements.

Vancouver: Leadership, Evolution, and Potential for Development Path Transformation

The urban core of the third-largest metropolitan region in Canada, Vancouver has a long history of leadership on environmental issues, including climate change. The majority of its 578,000 residents typically vote for provincial and federal parties that are left of center on the political spectrum. While the city has a history of addressing both corporate (municipally controlled) and community emissions, many strategies designed by the city have focused on voluntary efforts and individual behavior change – such as active transportation and home energy retrofits (Burch et al., 2013). More transformative steps, discussed in greater detail below, have gained momentum as the provincial political context shifted and a constituency for more ambitious climate-change policy grew.

Faltering national leadership on climate change in Canada left room for the province of British Columbia to emerge as a major legislative driver of municipal climate change action.[2] Recent provincial policies, for instance, include the requirement that municipalities be carbon neutral in their own operations by 2012, and legislating a revenue-neutral carbon tax that applies to the purchase and use of fossil fuels. This tax began at only $10 per tonne of CO_2 but increased by $5/tonne each year until the tax held steady at $30/ton in 2014. This translated into around 7 cents per liter of gasoline: a modest fee that has nonetheless contributed to a 16% reduction in fuel consumption in the province (Beaty et al., 2014). Furthermore, municipalities are required to deliver GHG inventories of community emissions, as well as action plans for addressing these emissions (with the ultimate provincial goal of reducing GHG emissions by 33% from 2006 levels by 2020) (Province of British Columbia, 2008). The Climate Action Secretariat (CAS), a provincial unit in the Ministry of Environment designed to implement provincial climate policy and provide stakeholder support, was formed in 2008 alongside the controversial Pacific Carbon Trust (a Crown corporation created to invest public dollars in carbon offset projects to facilitate the achievement of 'carbon neutral' status, now replaced by the Climate Investment Branch located in the CAS). These provincial policies have stimulated a vast mobilization of efforts to mitigate GHG emissions on the part of municipalities, regional districts and public-sector organizations (Burch et al., 2014; Shaw et al., 2014). Recent reports show that the province met its interim GHG reduction target of 6% below 2007 levels by 2012, in part due to carbon offset projects, including forest management (Province of British Columbia, 2014).

Long before the provincial government began employing legislative tools to trigger action on climate change, however, the City of Vancouver had developed and implemented a wide array of sustainability measures, public engagement strategies and long-range planning processes. Taken together, these efforts represent significant steps along the pathway to an urban sustainability transition. The sections that follow will summarize how these activities have unfolded over time and space, with the ultimate goal of revealing both the crucial ingredients of this transition and its ultimate transformative potential.

Methods

This analysis is based on longitudinal interview data gathered from key informants involved in Vancouver's sustainability activities in 2007, 2009, and 2012[3], sustainability policy document analysis since 1993, and a meta-analysis of climate change and sustainability research since 2005. A series of semi-structured key informant interviews were carried out in Vancouver as part of three separate, yet related, projects. Participants in the interviews included municipal employees, local incumbent politicians, representatives from non-governmental organizations involved in climate change and small businesses taking steps to mitigate GHG emissions. Approximately 95% of the individuals who were contacted for interviews participated in the study.

While the basic script that was followed during each series of interviews varied according to the goals of the project, some questions were common to all series. These questions pertained to the key ingredients of success, organizational culture, role of nongovernmental actors, sources of leadership and the broader interjurisdictional context. Notes were taken during and following each interview, and interviews were recorded with the permission of the participant. Interviews were coded and analyzed using qualitative analysis software.

The sections that follow present the central findings gathered through these three series of interviews, enhanced by analyses of sustainability and climate-change policy documents. The purpose of these sections is to trace how Vancouver's sustainability transition has unfolded over space and time, but also to highlight the key policies and actors that comprise this transition. Ultimately, the goal is to consider the extent to which the actions taken in Vancouver are transformative, highlight the drivers of this shift and draw out lessons for other urban contexts.

Policies and Politics: Sustainability Innovations in the City of Vancouver

While a large number of municipalities in the province of British Columbia have implemented climate change and sustainability policies (Burch et al., 2014), data collected over a period of 8 years (and covering a period of nearly 30 years) show that the City of Vancouver was one of the first Canadian municipalities to devote significant resources to these issues. Long before the development of the Kyoto Protocol, for instance, the City of Vancouver Task Force on Atmospheric Change produced the 1990 Clouds of Change report that set out targets for the reduction of both carbon dioxide and ozone-depleting substances (City of Vancouver, 1990). This report committed the city to reducing total community emissions by 20% below 1988 levels by 2005, a target that far exceeded the level of ambition embodied in Canada's future Kyoto commitments of 6% below 1990 levels by 2012 (and also exceeded any future targets that the city set for itself). A multilevel governance approach was proposed, in which the provincial and federal governments align their plans to address climate change, and municipal tools such as rezoning and urban reforestation were highlighted. A period of relative quiet followed the release of this report, however, with no further council reports or policy documents emerging from the City of Vancouver in the subsequent 12 years.

Climate change remerged on the municipal radar in 2003 and 2005, when the Vancouver City Council approved both a corporate (emissions under the control of the municipality) and community climate-change action plan (City of Vancouver, 2003, 2005). Based on the model provided by the Task Force on Atmospheric Change, and fundamentally shaping the multi-actor engagement that was to come, both plans drew upon expertise provided by the Cool Vancouver Task Force, an assemblage of corporate leaders, politicians, environmentalists and scientists, designed to provide the city with recommendations regarding GHG reduction (Kear, M., 2007). These plans committed the City of Vancouver to achieving a 20% reduction in civic (or corporate) GHG emissions from 1990 levels by 2010, and a 6% reduction in community emissions from 1990 levels by 2012 (Kear, M., 2007). While no interviewees spoke directly to this issue of diminished ambition, potential explanations may include a changing political landscape both municipally and provincially, a nationwide economic recession in the early 1990s (immediately following the Clouds of Change report) and a greater understanding of the challenges posed by dramatic GHG reductions.

In July of 2007, the City of Vancouver began to consider long-range GHG planning and the issue of carbon neutrality, and city council adopted targets to reduce community GHG emissions by 33% below 2006 levels by 2030 and 80% below 1990 levels by 2050 (Kear, M., 2007). This represents steps towards a more transformative approach to climate change responses, and opened the door to strategies that might be considered to fall within the broader domain of sustainability. For example, the City of Vancouver has designated the area of Southeast False Creek, approximately 80 acres of former industrial land near downtown Vancouver and future site of the 2010 Winter Olympic Village, as a model sustainable community. This includes the design of a Neighbourhood Energy Utility and a minimum building standard of LEED[4] Silver (Kear, M., 2007). In 2005, the City of Vancouver approved the Green Building Strategy, the purpose of which was to develop new zoning guidelines and bylaws to enhance the environmental performance of new buildings in Vancouver (City of Vancouver, 2008). In 2008, the city Council unanimously approved the Green Homes Program, which broadened the scope of the Green Building Strategy and applies significant energy efficiency bylaws to one- and two-family dwellings. These changes are accompanied by increased spending on public transit throughout the region; retrofits of existing commercial, residential, and institutional buildings for energy efficiency; and enhanced provision of biodiesel fuel blends throughout the city.

Despite frequent engagement with large corporate partners, crown corporations (such as BC Hydro) and nongovernmental organizations, Vancouver has less-frequently drawn small businesses into the climate change mitigation process. Since 2010, however, the City of Vancouver has partnered with the region of Metro Vancouver, Vancouver Economic Commission (an offshoot of the City of Vancouver that focuses on local business development) and a local social enterprise (Climate Smart Businesses Inc.) to train small businesses in GHG measurement and management. An initial pilot program has now grown to include over 150 local businesses in this training, and forms the foundation of the broader Corporate Climate Leaders program.

Rather than focusing solely on the impacts of this partnership on the community GHG inventory, municipal interviewees in 2010 suggested that their goal was to build a repertoire of tangible examples of results that local, relatable businesses have achieved through managing GHGs; build awareness of the city's sustainability efforts; and highlight the responsibility that businesses have for managing their own operations in a sustainable manner.

More recently, the focus in the City of Vancouver has shifted towards a more integrated approach to sustainability rather than the narrower priority of climate change mitigation. This has taken the form of the Greenest City Action Plan (City of Vancouver, 2012), a comprehensive policy document that addresses issues such as transportation, green business, waste and access to nature, water, air and local food. If somewhat hyperbolic, the goal of this plan is to develop a roadmap that will make Vancouver the 'greenest city in the world' by 2020. Ongoing assessments show that significant progress is being made on many of the sustainability indicators (See Table 4.1).

Also of note is the *process* that was followed in the development (and now implementation) of the Greenest City Action Plan. Relatively unusual methods were employed to engage with Vancouverites, such as Pecha Kucha[5]–style idea presentation, and ongoing collaboration with local university researchers and students. The Greenest City Action Team and the "Talk Green to Us" processes, which fundamentally informed the actions that were to come did not emerge spontaneously, but were based on a tradition that had been cemented through the COOL Vancouver Task Force in the 1990s and decades of participatory planning.

Actors and Spheres of Influence

The branch of sustainability transitions that pertains to transition management, along with multilevel governance theory, suggest that new, more flexible, multi-actor network-based governance is required to address the constellation of sustainability challenges in the urban context. This is in stark contrast to more traditional, top-down, centralized government that may exclude the meaningful participation of the private sector, civil society, scholars and other groups. Over the course of its two-decade sustainability journey, the City of Vancouver has increasingly engaged with a wide variety of actors, each of which brings a particular piece of the sustainability puzzle.

While a range of actors has played central roles, political leadership is a key trigger of Vancouver's sustainability transition. A political directive from high-level politicians has the power to rearrange the priorities set before municipal employees, and ultimately translates into the day-to-day directions managers give to junior staff. Interviewees indicated that clear municipal priorities are critical to shaping the job description and standard operating procedures of municipal employees, and shape the uses to which various resources are put (Burch, 2010b).

The importance of political leadership was raised, for instance, by a junior employee of Vancouver's Sustainability Group (the branch of the municipal organization in which climate change is housed), who said that "political leadership is fundamentally the most important thing. We have a climate change action plan because people in Council ... directed staff to do something about it".

Woven throughout more recent efforts is a strong theme of connecting with the private sector to transform the local economy and enable environmentally sustainable innovation. This is a marked departure from the more traditional municipal climate change or sustainability rhetoric, which has often focused on the small actions that municipalities can take in relation to the services they provide and the infrastructure they own. While the proportion of emissions that municipalities directly control varies quite widely from city to city (Bulkeley et al., 2011), it is clear that municipalities must engage with the private sector if ambitious targets are to be reached.

Both formal and informal networks are evident in Vancouver, of the type that is required to produce new, more effective solutions to a deeply complex set of problems (Loorbach, 2010). These networks include formal associations like the International Council for Local Environmental Initiatives (ICLEI) but also informal networks among employees at the City of Vancouver, the region of Metro Vancouver, the provincial Climate Action Secretariat, surrounding municipalities, and local civil society groups.

Figure 4.1[6] below presents a timeline of sustainability activities in Vancouver, including key policies and organizational units involved in this transition. These are shaped in part by provincial policy, such as the carbon tax and Green Communities legislation, but also build upon nearly three decades of explicit action on climate change and sustainability issues. As explored in the sections that follow, the linkages between the actors and initiatives shown below, as well as the political, social and technical inertia built over time that shed some light on Vancouver's success in the realm of urban sustainability governance.

Potential for Transformative Sustainability Governance

It is clear that Vancouver is carving out a more sustainable development path. Table 4.1 shows progress on a number of environmental indicators between 2007 and 2013. These data demonstrate a steady decline in GHG emissions, reduced water consumption, creation of new local food and green jobs, and increased use of public transit, cycling and walking over single-occupancy vehicle use. As skills grow and learning occurs, Vancouver may be more likely to successfully act in the future because it has acted in the past.

It is often the case that policies at the regional, provincial and federal level are inconsistent, however, with the ongoing climate-change efforts in the city.

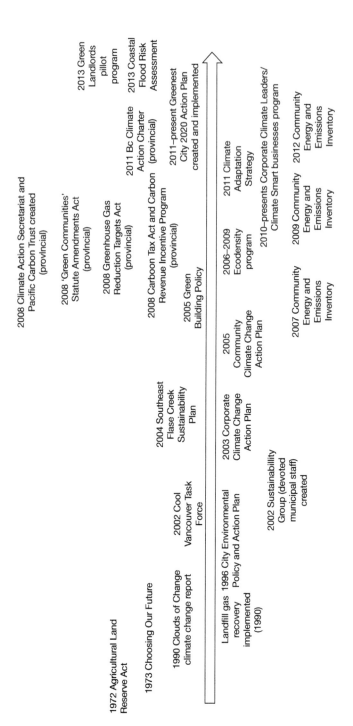

Figure 4.1 Timeline of selected City of Vancouver (unless otherwise noted) climate change and sustainability policies.

Table 4.1 Selected City of Vancouver Greenest City targets, indicators, and progress in 2013. Adapted from City of Vancouver, 2014.

Target	Indicator	Baseline	2013	% change
Reduce community-based GHGs by 33% from 2007 levels by 2020	Total tonnes of CO_2e emissions	2,755,000 tCO_2e (2007)	2,585,000 tCO_2e	-6%
Double the number of green jobs over 2010 levels by 2020	Total number of local food and green jobs	16,700 jobs (2010)	19,900 green jobs	19%
Reduce solid waste going to landfill or incinerator by 50% from 2007 levels	Annual solid waste disposed to landfill or incin-erator from Vancouver	480,000 tonnes (2008)	424,000 tonnes (2012)	-12%
Plant 150,000 additional trees in the city between 2010 and 2020	Total number of additional trees planted	---(2010)	23,400 trees	---
Increase citywide and neighborhood food assets by a minimum of 50% over 2010 levels	Total number of neighbor-hood food assets[1] in Vancouver	3,340 food assets (2010)	4,332 food assets	30%
Reduce per capita water consumption by 33% from 2006 levels	Total water consumption per capita	585 L/person/day (2006)	480 L/person/day	-18%
Make the majority of trips (over 50%) by foot, bicycle and public transit	Percent mode share by walk, bike and transit	40% of trips (2008)	44% of trips (2012)	10%

Source: European Commission, 2013

---

1 Food assets include: number of community garden plots, farmers markets, community orchards, community composting facilities, community kitchens, community produce stands and urban farms.

Interviewees indicated that this inconsistency can have two effects: any progress in GHG reductions may be offset by increases resulting from policies imposed by higher levels of government, and staff may feel disempowered by forces beyond their control leading to diminished motivation and creativity. Other such intervening factors must be explored if action on climate change is to be effectively enabled.

The City of Vancouver's sustainability framing highlights the potential power of exploring and exploiting co-benefits between strategies. For instance, during a 2008 interview a senior transportation planner said:

> There is a huge focus on moving people away from auto [single occupancy vehicle] modes as a priority. And that was done primarily ... to ease the burden on infrastructure, so we wouldn't have to build any new roads. If we could get people on bikes and get them using public transit and walking we wouldn't have to build a bridge ... and we would save ourselves hundreds of millions of dollars.

These synergies can most revealed most effectively if the city is operating under a high-level, integrated sustainability strategy like the Greenest City Action Plan. Prior to its creation, in fact, one member of the City of Vancouver sustainability group said:

> The decentralized model whereby we would have a small core group of professionals that provide leadership and support and training and fill in the gaps and execute on a citywide sustainability strategy and plan it seems like a good model to me. I think the absence of a strategic sustainability strategy for the organization has really hampered ... a decentralized model from being as effective as it could be. We exist without necessarily a mandate from Council that we can cite and ... something to compel departments to act.

It is just this function that GCAP has provided, simulating citywide action on a host of indicators.

Although it is impossible to predict the future, the City of Vancouver has accumulated significant momentum behind its identity as a livable, sustainable city, with a focus on green growth. The surrounding municipalities, however, are deeply interdependent on one another and with Vancouver, however, creating challenges for sustainable transit and land-use planning at the regional level. Vancouver itself may reach its greenhouse gas reduction targets, spurring further densification and more sustainable resource use, but it is important to look beyond the municipal boundaries to the region and province as a whole. Smaller, rural, resource-dependent or largely suburban municipalities face distinctly different sustainability challenges than does Vancouver, highlighting the need for ongoing provincial support and policy coherence.

Conclusions

This chapter has shown that sustainability is a constantly shifting proposition that is deeply rooted in values, political context and complex governance arrangements. Scale-related conflicts can emerge in which policies at a higher (i.e., provincial) level of government directly contravene actions taken at the urban scale, such as regional transportation plans that lead to increasing emissions or land-use planning that encourages commuting. Cities are often faced with a particular scarcity of both financial resources and legislative tools (Burch, 2010a), but this case illustrates that a shift in political culture and meaningful civil society involvement can support the radical redefinition of the way an urban system should function.

The ongoing sustainability transition in the City of Vancouver appears to hinge on three central factors: (1) governance models that engage new actors in creative ways; (2) exploring and exploiting synergies between climate change, sustainability and other urban priorities; and (3) the growing inertia behind a political calculus that favors environmental risk-taking and leadership.

Vancouver has not completed its sustainability journey, nor is continued success a foregone conclusion. In order to reach transformative levels of greenhouse gas reductions (such as an 80% reduction by 2050), for instance, the city must not simply create more 'green' businesses and buildings, but work to fundamentally alter the emissions profiles of its existing businesses and building stock. This requires exponentially increasing engagement of the private sector, along with large-scale retrofit programs. Furthermore, while modes of production are targeted through a number of initiatives, material consumption is a domain that remained largely untouched. Support and leadership on sustainability issues at the federal level also remain a missing piece of the puzzle, but one that could serve to accelerate Vancouver's sustainability transition.

The lessons learned in Vancouver have resonance with other developed and developing cities around the world, and challenge the notion that economic development is fundamentally at odds with environmental and social sustainability. The path followed by Vancouver demonstrates that sustainability governance requires innovative and iterative participatory processes, policies that encourage a profound rethinking of modes of production and consumption, and synergies between multiple scales of government.

Notes

1 A municipality is considered to have a 'weak mayor' if it has a chief administrative officer, the mayor does not have veto power over decisions made by council, and the mayor shares responsibility for appointing department heads and preparing the budget (DeSantis and Renner, 2002).
2 The increasingly central role of sub-national levels of government in the multilevel governance of climate change has been extensively analyzed in the context of provincial and state action in Canada and the United States. (Rabe, 2007; 2008), as well as emerging action in cities (Betsill, 2001; Bulkeley and Betsill, 2005).

3   A portion of the data used in this paper is employed with grateful acknowledgement
    to Meg Holden. The research for this article is drawn from cross-analysis and
    comparison of interview data from a series of four separate qualitative research
    interventions by three independent researchers into the sustainability and climate
    change policies and actions in the City of Vancouver. The first set of 11 interviews,
    conducted in 2007–08, with City of Vancouver staff and political leaders, was a
    case study of Vancouver's climate change and sustainability initiatives and organi-
    zational structure (Burch, 2010a and 2010b). The second set of nine interviews,
    conducted in 2010, included City of Vancouver staff as well as businesspeople and
    regional government staff engaged in a climate change initiative designed to sup-
    port local businesses (Burch et al., 2013). The third and final set of nine interviews
    was conducted in 2012 with city employees as well as other professionals engaged
    in climate change and sustainability initiatives (Holden, 2013). As a result of the
    common themes in each of these four sets of independent interviews, their longitu-
    dinal spread over four years and the fact that they were completed by two research-
    ers independently, this data set has strengthened validity.
4   LEED, or Leadership in Energy and Environmental Design, is a green building
    certification that addresses such issues as energy efficiency, building materials,
    building siting and water performance.
5   Pecha Kucha is a method of idea exchange and presentation that allows presenters
    only 20 slides, shown for 20 seconds each. The goal is the swift engagement of the
    audience, delivery of innovative concepts and potentially wider appeal than tradi-
    tional public presentations.
6   Brief summaries of many of the key Provincial climate change and energy policies
    can be found on this website: http://www2.gov.bc.ca/gov/topic.page?id=60E1E781
    0BC145C6B6FC00EE31F41EC5

References

Beaty, R., Lipsey, R., Elgie, S. (2014) The shocking truth about B.C.'s carbon tax: It
    works. *Globe and Mail*, Toronto, Canada.
Betsill, M. (2001) Mitigating climate change in US cities: Opportunities and obstacles.
    Local Environment 6, 393–406.
Betsill, M., Bulkeley, H. (2006) Cities and the multilevel governance of global climate
    change. *Global Governance* 12, 141–159.
Bulkeley, H., Betsill, M. (2005) Rethinking sustainable cities: Multi-level governance
    and the 'urban' politics of climate change. Environmental Politics 14, 42–63.
Bulkeley, H., Schroeder, H., Janda, K., Zhao, J., Armstrong, A., Chu, S., Ghosh, S.
    (2011) The role of institutions, governance and planning for mitigation and adap-
    tation by cities, in: Hoornweg, D., Frire, M., Lee, M., Bhada, P., Yuen, B. (Eds.),
    Cities and Climate Change: Responding to an Urgent Agenda. The World Bank,
    Washington, DC, pp. 68–88.
Burch, S. (2010a) In pursuit of resilient, low-carbon communities: An examination of
    barriers to action in three Canadian cities. *Energy Policy* 38, 7575–7585.
Burch, S. (2010b) Transforming barriers into enablers of action on climate change:
    Insights from three case studies in British Columbia, Canada. *Global Environmental
    Change* 20, 287–297.
Burch, S., Schroeder, H., Rayner, S., Wilson, J. (2013) Novel multi-sector networks and
    entrepreneurship in Metro Vancouver: A study of small business as an emerging non-
    state actor on climate change mitigation. *Environment and Planning C* 31, 822–840.
Burch, S., Shaw, A., Dale, A., Robinson, J. (2014) Triggering transformative change:
    A development path approach to climate change response in communities. *Climate
    Policy* 14, 467–487.

City of Vancouver (1990) Clouds of change: Final report of the city of Vancouver task force on atmospheric change. City of Vancouver Department of Planning, Vancouver.

City of Vancouver (2003) A corporate climate change action plan for the city of Vancouver. City of Vancouver, Vancouver.

City of Vancouver (2005) Community climate change action plan: Creating opportunities. City of Vancouver, Vancouver.

City of Vancouver, (2008) Vancouver Ecodensity Charter: How density, design and land use will contribute to environmental sustainability, affordability and livability. City of Vancouver, Vancouver.

City of Vancouver (2012) Greenest City 2020 Action Plan. City of Vancouver, Vancouver.

City of Vancouver (2014) Greenest City 2020 Action Plan: 2012–2013 Implementation Update. City of Vancouver, Vancouver.

DeSantis, V., Renner, T. (2002) City government structures: An attempt at clarification. *State & Local Government Review* 34, 95–104.

Deutsch, K. (1954) *Political Community at the International Level: Problems of Definition and Measurement*. Doubleday and Company, New York.

Forrest, N., Wiek, A. (2014) Learning from success – toward evidence-informed sustainability transitions in communities. *Environmental Innovation and Societal Transitions* 12, 66–88.

Geels, F.W., Schot, J. (2008) Strategic niche management and sustainable innovation journeys: theory, findings, research agenda, and policy. *Technology Analysis and Strategic Management* 20, 537–554.

Holden, M. (2013) City of Vancouver Case Study. Meeting the Climate Change Challenge Case Study Reports. Published on-line at: http://www.mc-3.ca/

Hooghe, L., Marks, G. (2003) Unraveling the Central State, but how? Types of multi-level governance. *American Political Science Review* 97, 233–243.

Hoogma, R., Kemp, R., Schot, J., Truffer, B. (2002) *Experimenting for Sustainable Transport: The Approach of Strategic Niche Management*. Spon Press, London.

Jacobsson, S., Johnson, A. (2000) The diffusion of renewable energy technology: an analytical framework and key issues for research. *Energy Policy* 28, 625–640.

Kear, M. (2007) Spaces of transition spaces of tomorrow: Making a sustainable future in Southeast False Creek, vancouver. Cities 24, 324–334.

Kern, F., Smith, A. (2008) Restructuring energy systems for sustainability? Energy transition policy in the Netherlands. *Energy Policy* 36, 4093–4103.

Loorbach, D. (2010) Transition management for sustainable development: A prescriptive, complexity-based governance framework. *Governance: An International Journal of Policy, Administration, and Institutions* 23, 161–183.

Markard, J., Raven, R., Truffer, B. (2012) Sustainability transitions: An emerging field of research and its prospects. *Research Policy* 41, 955–967.

Nevens, F., Frantzeskaki, N., Gorissen, L., Loorbach, D. (2013) Urban transition labs: co-creating transformative action for sustainable cities. *Journal of Cleaner Production* 50, 111–122.

Province of British Columbia (2008) Climate Action for the 21st Century. Province of British Columbia, Victoria, B.C.

Province of British Columbia (2014) Climate Action in British Columbia: 2014 Progress Report. Province of British Colubmia, Victoria, BC.

Rabe, B. (2007) Beyond Kyoto: Climate change policy in multilevel governance systems. *Governance* 20, 423–444.

Rabe, B. (2008) States on steroids: The intergovernmental odyssey of American climate policy. *Review of Policy Research* 25, 105–128.

Raven, R., Geels, F.W. (2010) Socio-cognitive evolution in niche development: comparative analyssi of biogas development in Denmark and the Netherlands (1973–2004). *Technovation* 30, 87–99.

Riker, W.H. (1964) *Federalism: Origin, Operation, Significance*. Little, Brown, and Co., Boston.

Seyfang, G., Haxeltine, A. (2012) Growing grassroots innovations: Exploring the role of community-based initiatives in governing sustainable energy transitions. *Environment and Planning C* 30, 381.

Shaw, A., Burch, S., Kristensen, F., Robinson, J., Dale, A. (2014) Accelerating the sustainability transition: Exploring synergies between adaptation and mitigation in British Columbian communities. *Global Environmental Change* 25, 41–51.

Smith, A., Sterling, S., Berkhout, F. (2005) The governance of sustainable socio-technical transitions. *Research Policy* 34, 1491–1510.

Spangenberg, J. (2011) Sustainability science: a review, and analysis and some empirical lessons. *Environmental Conservation* 38, 275–287.

5 Transitioning Complex Urban Systems

The Importance of Urban Ecology for Sustainability in New York City

Timon McPhearson and Katinka Wijsman

Introduction

New York City, like other cities, is rarely considered as a hotspot for nature. Rather, it is primarily considered in popular discourse as a mix of man-made structures and artifacts, diverse assemblages of social institutions and cultural landmarks, and concentrations of urban development, all supported by complex infrastructure systems for transportation, sanitation, housing, and utilities. In such imaginaries, nature is rarely considered as one of the most fundamental components of urban systems. The view that nature is distinct from the life of cities is not a new one. Despite renewed focus in New York City and other cities advancing sustainability agendas, the remark of leading urban sociologist Louis Wirth, from 1938, that "nowhere has mankind been farther removed from organic nature than under the conditions of life characteristic of great cities", remains a typical modern lament (Wirth, 1938). This still widely pervasive human exemptionalist paradigm which views humans and nature as fundamentally separate (McPhearson and Tidball, 2013) is at the forefront of a deep misunderstanding that nature actually exists in cities, and that there is an extremely close relationship that exist between humans and nature in cities (Gomez-Baggethun et al., 2013).

Cities, including NYC, are literally teaming with nature (Aronson et al., 2014). Though NYC comprises a small proportion of the land area of New York State, it contains nearly 85% of the state's bird, mammal, reptile and amphibian species (McPhearson et al., 2013b). Additionally, 40% of the state's rare and endangered plant species are resident in the city. Increasingly scientists are showing that the city is in fact rich in nature and NYC is starting to be seen as an important ecological hotspot, with more species diversity than the surrounding suburbs and rural areas (Stille, 2002). Within the city limits, New York City harbors lakes, marshes, freshwater wetlands, centuries-old woods and rare flora and fauna. A 2010 survey in Jamaica Bay Wildlife Refuge (located next to JFK airport) counted more bird species than in Yosemite and Yellowstone National Park combined (Sullivan, 2010). Similar observations are being made for other cities with cities and urban areas increasingly studied as places where rich biodiversity can and does exist (CBD, 2013; Aronson et al., 2014). With nature often thriving in cities, and increasingly understood as critical to planning and governing for human health, well-being and livability (Elmqvist et al., 2013), the need to put the nail in the coffin of the human exemptionalism paradigm is now more important than ever (McPhearson and Tidball, 2013).

The city is increasingly recognized as an appropriate level for analysis and intervention in tackling persistent problems associated with urban development and goals for sustainability (Bulkeley et al., 2011; Betsill, 2001; Hammer et al., 2011). It is therefore crucial to understand the ways in which urban life and nature intersect and support (or challenge) each other. Thinking about the role of nature for the livability and sustainability of cities is not new. In New York the use of urban ecosystems is exemplified in Olmsted and Vaux's design for Central Park in 1858 that considered the role nature could play for public health (Gandy, 2002). However, scholars and practitioners have only recently had the benefit of fundamental research on the relationships between social and ecological dynamics in urban areas, benefitting from the emergence in the early 1990s of the modern field of urban ecology (McPhearson et al., 2016a) Devoting empirical attention to social and ecological transformation in highly populated areas, urban ecologists have contributed to understanding interactions and feedbacks between components of the biophysical and the social foundations of urban systems. For example, lifestyle behavior, housing age, family size, marriage rates and other demographic characteristics of neighborhood residents have been linked to vegetation cover, biodiversity and ecosystem services in urban areas (Grove et al., 2006; McPhearson et al., 2013a).

In this chapter, we elaborate on the urban ecology approach and its relevance for urban sustainability transitions. We argue that understanding urban areas as complex social-ecological-technical systems (SETS) (McPhearson et al., 2016a,b), in which people, ecological processes and built environments are inextricably linked, is pivotal in addressing urban problems precipitated by climate change, inequity, environmental pollution and many other causes. Explicitly including ecological knowledge in the theory and practice of sustainability transitions is crucial to understanding and transitioning complex urban systems, as ecological processes provide the fundamental basis for urban sustainability and livability. Transitions thinking in turn pushes urban ecological thinking in that it explicates processes of human governance and human valuation of urban nature and ecology, which – despite recognition of social aspects to urban ecology – are not addressed thoroughly in the field. In emphasizing historical and social processes in the emergence and perpetuation of specific kinds of SETS, the transitions approach can help deal with some of the critiques on urban ecology expressed by (among others) political ecologists. We explicate the urban ecology approach, its value for urban sustainability transitions and the ways in which the approach is pushed by transitions thinking, using a case study of urban vacant lots in NYC. Vacant lots in urban areas can provide important social and ecological benefits to both human and nonhuman inhabitants of the city through the ecosystem services they provide and therefore open up opportunity for sustainability transitions. This case study illustrates the benefits associated with taking an urban ecology approach in making sense of the city.

Sustainability Transitions, Resilience, and the Nature of Cities: An Urban Ecology Approach

As truly complex SETS, cities consist of dynamically interacting infrastructures of multiple kinds – social, ecological, economic and technological – that feed back on one another, producing more or less resilient, but not necessarily sustainable or equitable, patterns and dynamics (Batty, 2008; Pickett et al., 2013; McPhearson et al., 2015). Transitioning cities towards more sustainable trajectories not only requires knowledge on each of these infrastructures; it also means dealing with the inherent complexity of urban systems and emergent properties of the system, thus recognizing and working with the interactions between multiple components which are constantly undergoing change (McPhearson, 2013). This can be daunting, but the necessity of understanding urban SETS, and characterizing its components in terms of vulnerability to perturbations and other impacts of global environmental change, is a precondition for building sustainable and resilient communities. Superstorm Sandy, which struck NYC on October 29, 2012, illustrates the necessity of a systems-level understanding of urban SETS dynamics.

In New York City, Sandy destroyed 72,000 homes, displaced thousands of residents, caused the death of 43 people, caused tens of billions of dollars in infrastructural damage (knocking out power regionally for millions of residents and flooding major transit routes) and completely disrupted the second largest regional economy in the world. Sandy exposed the sensitivity and vulnerability of the complex SETS of NYC, where a single storm decimated components and connections between components of the city system, creating extreme difficulty in supplying energy, communication, food and other basic life support to affected residents (McPhearson, 2013). Moreover, the nature of the problems caused by the storm evolved over time, as problems posed by high winds and flooding evolved into a myriad of new problems, such as providing residents with fuel to warm their homes. The dynamic and complex nature of the problems posed by Sandy made appropriate responses difficult. As Sandy demonstrated, and with increased frequency and severity of heat waves, drought and flooding becoming harbingers of a "new normal" (Grimm et al., 2013), understanding how city systems and their SETS components will respond to shock and disturbance is crucial for cities to plan and govern for resilience and sustainability (McPhearson et al., 2016). Further, understanding the relations and dynamics in cities not only informs dealing with emergencies, but may also initiate alterations in the cities' social-ecological fabric under less stressful circumstances that can provide an opportunity to address critical issues of social justice.

Urban ecology proves a useful approach to tackling the challenge of examining the connections, relationships and feedbacks within urban systems through recent theoretical and empirical advances within the field (McHale et al., 2015). The urban ecology perspective firmly grounds sustainability transitions in biophysical and social dynamics that affect the course of such transitions, both in terms of issues to be dealt with (e.g., changing urban climate) and feasible alterations (e.g., multi-functionality and ecosystem services of urban green infrastructure). In order to make sense of urban system dynamics, urban ecologists examine the city as a complex, dynamic SETS (Grimm et al., 2000; Pickett et al., 2001; McPhearson et al., 2016) and argue that processes within natural ecosystems can be a model for urban planning and development (Gomez-Baggethun et al., 2013). Such an approach is well positioned to cut across sectors and social domains to study how social-ecological and social-technical patterns affect urban sustainability and resilience on the one hand, and how their relationships and interactions are affected as a result of other processes (e.g., climate change) on the other.

Cities as SETS are seen as made up of intersecting social and ecological flows in a context of built, technological and economical infrastructures. The focus on interactions between humans and the environment has helped to move contemporary urban ecology beyond classical approaches focusing on, for example, species distribution patterns to instead address process questions in which dynamics and temporal and spatial changes are emphasized (McDonnell and Hahs, 2008; Pickett et al., 2008). Grimm et al. (2000) and Pickett et al. (2001) therefore distinguish between two approaches in urban ecology: the 'ecology *in* cities' and the 'ecology *of* cities' approach.

The ecology *in* cities approach provides the fundamental ecological science for urban planning, management and design (McDonnell, 2011). Shifting focus from 'pristine' natural areas to urban settings, ecologists since early studies in post-WWII in Berlin in the 1950s (Sukopp et al., 2001) have asked how urban climates and city form influence ecological patterns and processes in cities. Focusing on the physical environment, soils, plants and vegetation, and animals and wildlife, this approach forms the foundation of urban ecology (McDonnell, 2011). Examples of the ecological research in urban areas include work on the urban heat island effect (the phenomenon that a metropolitan area is significantly warmer than the surrounding suburbs or rural areas) (Rozensweig et al., 2009); on heavy metal distribution in urban soils (Yesilonis et al., 2008); and on structural and compositional changes patterns in urban species richness (Aronson et al., 2014; Groffman et al., 2014). Studies have shown for example that urbanization affects biophysical aspects of the city (e.g., soil chemistry, climate, ecosystem functions) (Pickett et al., 2008; Groffman et al., 2014); that cities are hotspots of accumulation of certain chemicals and metals (Pickett et al., 2001; Grimm et al., 2008); and that predictions based on trends in pollution, stress or exotic species alone are inadequate to understand the complex feedback mechanisms that exist between them and other social dynamics (Pickett et al., 2008). These studies have also provide insights relevant for urban planning, including that plants and animals evolve in response to local conditions, and spatial heterogeneity in cities is important (Pickett et al., 2001; McDonnell and Hahs 2008; Alberti, 2015). Findings from the ecology *in* cities approach are important in sustainability transition processes, as they provide essential insights into ecological dynamics and processes of urban SETS that are needed for managing, governing and planning ecosystems in ways that can support healthy urban environments (Gomez-Baggethun et al., 2013; Andersson et al., 2015a; McPhearson et al., 2016).

The ecology *of* cities approach goes further by incorporating insights from social sciences, urban planning and design in integrative even long-term studies of urban areas as SETS with humans and nature as fundamental components of urban systems (McDonnell, 2011; Pickett et al., 2014). The assessment of feedbacks and dynamics of ecological linkages and interactions between numerous subsystems of an urban region is centralized in this approach. Ecology *of* cities allows for the scrutiny of the interaction between human and nonhuman elements of the urban system (Grimm et al., 2000), or, as Newman (1999:221) puts it, this approach makes it possible to "specify the physical and biological basis of the city, as well as its human basis". In a similar way that inherently links humans and ecosystems, the ecosystem services framework assesses the human benefits resulting from functioning ecosystems and gained broad currency in assessing and comparing the productive aspects of nature for supporting urban life (Elmqvist et al., 2013). Another integrative framework, urban metabolism, examines longitudinal trends in consumption and waste generation of cities, using the analogy of the city as an organism. This approach quantitatively takes into account energy, food, water and other required resources together with waste production, allowing examination of flows into and out of the urban system (Grimm et al., 2008). Using these integrative approaches and advancing them in ways that more

Table 5.1 Categories of urban ecosystem services

Provisioning services	Regulating services	Habitat/supporting services	Cultural services
Food Fresh water Medicinal resources Raw materials	Local climate and air quality Carbon sequestration and storage Moderation of extreme events Wastewater treatment Erosion prevention and maintenance of soil fertility	Habitat for species Maintenance of genetic diversity	Recreation Mental and physical health Tourism Aesthetic appreciation and inspiration for culture, art and design Spiritual experience and sense of place

Source: Adapted from McPhearson et al., 2014.

explicitly include humans as components of urban systems, urban ecologists have elucidated important relationship in cities. Findings include that social and ecological change occurs at different rates (manifested in the observation that the ecological structure of certain neighborhoods does not reflect the social structures existent); that lawns have beneficial functions in urban systems (as biogeochemical sinks and as catalyst for revitalization of certain neighborhoods); and that the feedbacks between environmental change and human change contributes to transformations in social geography (Pickett et al., 2008). These and other insights from urban ecology are critical to incorporate as part of urban sustainability transitions precisely because urban ecology explicitly links biophysical and social sciences to urban planning, management and policymaking for sustainability (Grimm et al., 2008; 2013; Alberti, 2015).

The Ecology of New York City: The Case of Vacant Lots

As ecological processes provide the fundamental basis for healthy living environments in urban settings (Gomez-Baggethun et al., 2013), understanding the how to plan, manage and govern the green infrastructure of cities is critical in transitioning cities towards sustainability (Schewenius et al., 2014). The ecosystem services provide a useful approach for assessing human derived benefits of ecological functioning and planning for its improvement. Assessing, mapping and valuing urban ecosystem services for human health and well-being can be useful for setting goals, identifying benchmarks and prioritizing approaches for transitioning urban green space (Daily et al., 2009; Niemela et al., 2010; Sukhdev et al., 2010; McPhearson et al., 2013a; Haase et al., 2014). As the levels of access to ecosystem services differ among urban dwellers, identifying which ecosystem services are provided to which groups of urban residents and finding potential gaps between social needs for these services and the actual level and location of service provisioning are crucial steps in creating more just, equitable and sustainable environments (McPhearson et al., 2014; Andersson et al., 2015b).

Urban ecologists have long recognized that the ecosystems in cities is not found merely in parks and protected areas, but exists everywhere: on rooftops, sidewalk cracks, in backyards, soils, rivers and streams (McPhearson and Marshall, 2015). Providing ecosystem services to urban residents sufficient to support livability and public health in densely populated cities requires identifying alternative areas that can provide opportunities for development of novel ecosystems, including various types of green infrastructure. One of the important identified sources of ecosystem services in urban areas are vacant lots: underutilized land such as bare soil, uncultivated land, derelict land, brown fields, green fields and land with abandoned buildings and structures (Kremer et al., 2013). Although vacant lots are often associated with negative phenomena, such as crime, abandonment, trash, depressed real estate values, overgrown weeds, pests and failure (Accordino and Johnson,

2000; Goldstein et al., 2001), they can also be considered an opportunity for building sustainable communities, in part through the provision of ecosystem services (Burkholder, 2012; Little, 2008; Kremer et al., 2013). In New York City, there are 29,782 parcels designated by city tax codes as vacant lots that together make up about 3,000 ha (or 7,300 acres). These lots represent a sizable opportunity for urban development (Figure 5.1). Historically, management of urban vacant land has been meager, as lots were often overlooked or neglected (McPhearson, 2013), but over the last seven years the NYC council has addressed the role of vacant lots in revitalization projects, affordable housing and community gardens (Kremer et al., 2013). This development mirrors the recognition that vacant lots could serve beneficial uses as community gardens, wildlife gardens, recreational areas and sites for urban agriculture (Bonham et al., 2002).

As vacant lands are the result of historical development patterns, including human migration, deindustrialization, environmental disaster, contamination and demographic shifts (Burkholder, 2012; McPhearson, 2013), their locations and ecological quality are highly diverse. The existence and development of ecosystem services on specific vacant lots depend on the environmental conditions of the land, the surrounding natural habitats and the current and historic uses of the lot (Burkholder, 2012). In order to assess the specific social and ecological value of lots and their potential to contribute to policy and planning goals of increasing biodiversity, ecosystem provisioning and social justice, vacant lots have to be made legible to decision-makers. This legibility is key in overcoming some of the barriers in adopting policy strategies for sustainable land-use transformation, as a lack of data on urban vacant land has been a complicating factor for management and governance practices (Alexander, 2005; Bonham et al. 2002).

For New York City, Kremer et al. (2013) and McPhearson et al. (2013a) brought together data from various sources to map the social-ecological value of vacant lots using an ecosystem services assessment and valuation approach. In this approach, the benefits urban residents accrue from ecosystems in particular lots are evaluated using a combination of land cover data, land use data, published empirical measures of ecosystem functions and estimates of the actual use of the lots. The measurement of ecosystem services in turn is linked to the direct ecological environment (e.g., concentration of green space) and social-economic environment of the plots (e.g., population density, indicating the need for ecosystem services in these urban communities), thereby making social-ecological relations between humans and ecosystems where humans live legible in a spatially explicit way (McPhearson et al., 2013). By our assessing the vacant lot uses and the ecological and social characteristics of their environment, clusters of vacant lots in areas with low ecological value and high social need can be identified, providing policymakers a map of priority locations for vacant land transformation in support of urban sustainability and resilience (Figure 5.5).

N

Figure 5.1 Vacant land in New York City. Light grey areas are privately owned
vacant lots and dark grey areas are publically owned vacant lots. There are
29,782 parcels designated by city tax codes as vacant lots that together
make up about 3,000 ha (or 7,300 acres), a sizable percent of total land in
the city. (Adapted from McPhearson, 2013.)

Using ArcGIS and Google Earth, Kremer et al. (2013) conducted a visual
survey of 5% of New York City's vacant lots through a stratified random sample
(N=1502) of vacant lots in each of its five boroughs. Through this method, land

cover data as provided through MapPLUTO (the city's land use and geographical data) could be complimented by actual land use data, which correspond to the actual social and ecological processes taking place in vacant lots (Table 5.2, Figure 5.2). Linking the actual use of the vacant lots with social characteristics (in terms of income and population density) and "greenness" (green density) of neighborhoods, a number of correlations were established: population density

Table 5.2 NYC vacant lot characteristics for the entire population (N=29,782)

Size	Range m2	Average m2	< 100m2	100–300m2	300–500m2	>500m2
	≈ 0–900,000	996	16%	46%	17%	21%
Ownership	Public lot	Private lot (owner known)	Private lot (owner unknown)	Public land size	Public land size	
	23%	38.5%	38.5%	44%	56%	
Location	Low-density residential area, private owners	High-density residential area, private owner	Low-density residential area, public owner	Commercial zone	Manufacturing zone	Mixed use districts
	± 50%	14.6%	10.8%	4%	9.5%	≈ 0 %

Source: Adapted from Kremer et al., 2013.

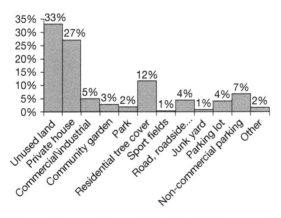

Figure 5.2 Actual uses of surveyed vacant lots (N = 1502) across all five of NYC's boroughs as determined by a visual survey. (Adapted from Kremer et al., 2013.)

was negatively correlated with distance to green space, income and neighborhood density (the first being a weak correlation); distance to green space was negatively correlated with population density and neighborhood green density, and weakly positively correlated with income; and in general, greener vacant lots were located in relatively greener neighborhoods with higher income levels (Kremer et al., 2013:228). In addition, actual land-use categories associate significantly with income. Community gardens, for example, had the strongest association with neighborhood income (−), in addition to strong associations with population density (+) and distance to green space (−). These correlations point out the importance of considering the interactions between various land use practices and land covers in vacant lots in order to prioritize management for maintaining or increasing ecosystem service provisioning.

As many vacant lots in New York City (62%) have vegetated land cover (Figure 5.3), these lots are already providing many ecosystem services to urban residents (Kremer et al., 2013). However, there are major differences in kind and differences in degree with respect to the ecosystem services that are provided and needed in specific urban areas. Bringing together data estimating the productivity of ecosystems from different literatures and connecting those to the specific ecological characteristics of the vacant lots, the approach provides insight into the specific productivity of vacant lots (Table 5.3). This productivity can be linked with the social need for ecosystem services (based on the indicators median household income, median real estate value, population density and density of green and open space, as depicted in Table 5.4) by splitting both ecological value and social need into high and low designation categories and mapping these together (Figure 5.4). The mapping of the emerging social-ecological interaction across the city

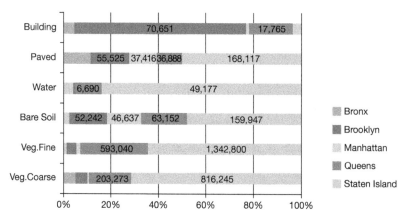

Figure 5.3 Survey results of landcover in sampled vacant lots (N=1502) in NYC. Results present the distribution of different landcover types (coarse vegetation, fine vegetation, bare soil, water, building and paved) for the five boroughs of NYC. (Adapted from Kremer et al., 2013.)

Table 5.3 Ecosystem services provision in vacant lot sample (N=1502)

		Indicator	New York City estimate average	Vacant lots sample
				Averages for regulating services
Regulating services	Carbon sequestration	Coarse vegetation area × average sequestration rate (kg/m²)	0.12 kgC/ m²/yr	66–91
	Carbon storage	Coarse vegetation area × average storage rate (kgC/m²) Fine vegetation area × average storage rate (kgC/m²) Soil area × carbon density/m² (kgC/m²)	7.3 kgC/m²/yr 0.18 kgC/ m²/yr 8.2 kgC/m²/yr	20,061– 25,134
Air pollution removal	SO$_2$	Coarse vegetation area × pollution removal rate (g/yr) Fine vegetation area × pollution removal rate (g/yr)	1.32 g/m²/yr 0.65 g/m²/yr	1541–1905
	NO$_2$	Coarse vegetation area × pollution removal rate (g/yr) Fine vegetation area × pollution removal rate (g/yr)	2.54 g/m²/yr 2.33 g/m²/yr	4315–5163
	PM$_{10}$	Coarse vegetation area × pollution removal rate (g/yr) Fine vegetation area × pollution removal rate (g/yr)	2.73 g/m²/yr 1.12 g/m²/yr	2907–3629

(*continued*)

Table 5.3 Ecosystem services provision in vacant lot sample (N=1502) (*continued*)

			Indicator	New York City estimate average	Vacant lots sample
					Averages for regulating services
		O_3	Coarse vegetation area × pollution removal rate (g/yr)	3.06 g/m²/yr	1689–2327
		CO	Coarse vegetation area × pollution removal rate (g/yr)	0.58 g/m²/yr	320–441
	Local temperature regulation		Cooling by vegetation (degree Celcius)	− 0.05°C per +1% tree cover	1.3–1.6
	Runoff mitigation		Runoff coefficient (% precipitation absorbed per 5 inch/24 hr rain event)		37% (38m³)
Provisioning services	Food production		Community garden (yes/no)		2%
Supporting services	Provision of habitat for biodiversity	Availability	% total coarse and fine vegetation (green, blue and brown)		70–96
		Sensitivity	Situated in ecological high-priority area according to the nature conservancy (yes/no)		197
		Connectivity	Proximity to green areas in meters		454
		Shape	Compactness (approximation of circle) on scale 0–1; 1= most compact)		0.65

	Indicator			New York City estimate average	Vacant lots sample
					Averages for regulating services
Cultural services	Recreation	Public access	Publically owned		23%
		Actual use	Use for at least one of multiple uses, including recreation		67%

Note: Estimations are conservative.
Source: Adapted from McPhearson et al., 2013 and Kremer et al., 2013.

Table 5.4 Indicator values for social need for ecosystem services (within a 500 meter buffer of each vacant lot) for the sample (N=1502)

	Median household income in US$	Average population density per km²	Median property value in US$	Green density (%)
Mean	42,581	12,984	52,254	11
Median	40,900	12,033	34,583	5

Source: Adapted from McPhearson et al., 2013.

was possible because calculations of ecological value and social need were attributed to specific lots.

The approach taken by McPhearson et al. (2013a) considers the social-ecological conditions and relationships among multiple ecosystem services, while giving insight into spatial patterns of distribution. Using a social-ecological matrix approach, the analysis provided a method for prioritizing locations for focusing investment for sustainability transitions. This is especially important, given the prediction that pressure will increase on local urban ecosystems to provide critical ecosystem services under scenarios of changing urban climate (Rosenzweig et al., 2009). Making the production of and need for ecosystem services legible to decision-makers and stakeholders at all levels can provide the means for identifying priority areas for social-ecological transformation to increase resilience to predicted near-term effects of climate change and other priorities for improving urban livability and sustainability transitions (McPhearson et al., 2013a).

Despite challenges associated with the stacking of multiple ecosystem services (due to trade-offs and synergies between ecosystem services) (Table 5.4),

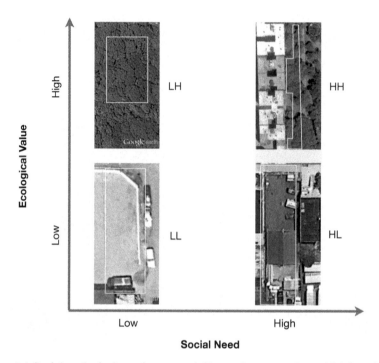

Figure 5.4 Social-ecological matrix approach illustrating vacant lots which have high
or low social need for ecosystem services combined with an assessment
of the low or high value of ecosystem services currently being supplied
by vacant lots in NYC (N=1502). Vacant lots pictured illustrate a typical
situation in the four quadrants of the matrix. High social need combined
with low ecological value spaces are examples of places of high priority
for social-ecological transformation.

varying spatial distributions of specific social needs, assigning weights and
ranking to services and needs, and the obfuscation of details of specific indicators in aggregated maps, the ecosystem services approach is an important
tool for policymakers concerned with urban livability and transitions. The
spatially explicit method provides the opportunity to identify clusters of
high need: clusters of conditions of low ecological value combined with high
social need should be priority areas for urban planning and social-ecological
transformation (McPhearson et al., 2013a; Larondelle et al., 2014; Hamstead
et al., 2015) (Figure 5.4). Using the indicators for ecological value and social
need, giving these a weighting and mapping them in classes thus helps identifying spatial hotspots: vacant lots that share social-ecological configuration
and proximity to one another (Figure 5.5). In New York, major clusters with
low ecological value and high need for ecosystem services are primarily concentrated in East Harlem, South Bronx and Central and South Brooklyn.
Focusing on these areas gives policymakers the opportunity to enhance just
and sustainable environments and resilient communities.

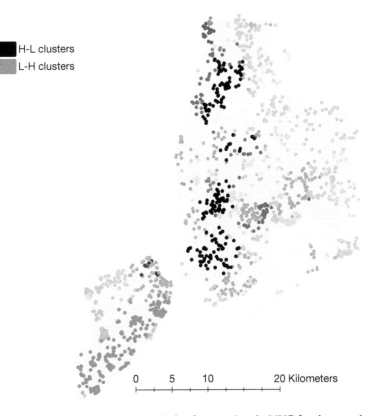

Figure 5.5 Social-ecological cluster analysis of vacant lots in NYC for the sample
(N=1502). Black H-L clusters represent areas where social need is high
and ecological value is low, representing priority areas for transformation.
Dark grey L-H clusters where social need is low and ecological value
is high represent areas that are performing well and of low priority for
transformation. (Adapted from McPhearson et al., 2013.)

Sustainable Urban SETS: Transitioning Cities Through Urban Ecology

The vacant lot case demonstrates the utility of incorporating SETS components
in an urban ecological approach to understanding complex urban phenomena in
ways that can improve decision-making for urban sustainability transitions. To
transition cities to more sustainable pathways, it is critical to consider the role of
the green infrastructure and other ecological spaces as well as their connections
with other urban infrastructures. By bringing together and linking different kinds
of data from different sources, as exhibited in the case study, the urban ecology
approach provides insights into the workings of SETS necessary for urban sustainability transitions. Applying these and other urban ecology approaches can
help establish planning and management priorities for governance actors aiming
to advance ecologically resilient and socially just environments.

Despite the potential contribution for governance for sustainability, the urban ecology community has only recently begun to intersect with governance practices and processes. In many ways, the role of knowledge in governance issues is still considered along the lines of a relatively outdated paradigm that presumes a clear division of roles of researchers (producers of objective knowledge) and governance actors (weighting and using knowledge in planning). However, knowledge production is not an objective endeavor but involves choices and decision-making and can therefore be seen as an activity that involves politics and power, which long has been recognized by many social scholars, even since Foucault. Similarly, diverse literatures have recognized that change through governance interventions is more likely to occur when those involved have been through a process of mutual learning (e.g., Grin and Loeber, 2007). If urban ecologists want to make profound contributions to advance sustainability, the discipline will need to advance studies that better intersect with power dynamics and politics well understood in other disciplines.

Recent efforts to advance, planning, management and governance for sustainability is precisely where the urban ecology approach can learn from the transitions approach, especially the work on governance and transitions management. Focusing on processes of group learning and knowledge sharing among actors from different backgrounds, the transitions approach can explicate the politics involved in the urban ecology approach. Discussing definitions and operationalization of concepts and social categories and using different data sources and methodologies make for a less technical and richer analysis. If we consider the vacant lots case, this may mean, for example, a reassessment of the leading principle for distribution for social justice (as it can be based on need, entitlement or other) as well as more ethnographically focused approaches which involve communities in priority setting and determining appropriate transformations, as needs and wants are not universally given. Social justice and environmental sustainability are not always compatible objectives (Dobson, 2003a, 2003b); therefore, attention should be given to the inherent trade-offs among multiple objectives and the differences in ways various communities are affected by (non)intervention. The transitions approach offers possibilities for deeper and broader commitment for the social aspects being explored in the ecology *of* cities approach.

Explicating human governance and valuation, voicing difference and inequality, and historicizing SETS, a combined approach of urban ecology and sustainability transitions can provide insights into the functionalist components of the city (the material and biophysical world that needs to be sustained for environmental sustainability; for example, critical natural capital, biodiversity, value of natural objects), while addressing the social and political construction and meaning of this material and biophysical world (addressing the unevenness in access to utilizing these) and making sure that social-ecological relationships are not uncritically reproduced. As young and still maturing academic disciplines, urban ecology and sustainability transitions require rethinking modes of analysis based in both natural science traditions and interpretative approaches for both urban ecology and transition studies.

Conclusion

The quality of life in cities changes over time, depending on the biophysical systems in place and their use and alteration through social and technical processes. In rethinking, reimaging, retrofitting and even creating new cities along more sustainable pathways, it is imperative to address the complex interplay among different types of infrastructure, including green infrastructure and other ecological spaces. Transitioning cities towards sustainability requires explicit inclusion of the biophysical and material world as provided by ecosystems, areas of inquiry where urban ecology has made substantial theoretical and empirical contributions. Bringing urban ecology more directly into urban sustainability transitions could provide new modes of inquiry and practices for transitioning urban systems towards more sustainable development trajectories. We argue that linking transitions studies and urban ecology approaches could improve our ability to deal with urban complexity and address persistent problems affecting cities around the world. Still, we recognize that urban ecology needs to continue to develop from an originally biophysical basis to one that engages critically with the social sciences to better understand the political basis of urban system dynamics, so that systems transform towards social equity as a fundamental goal within urban sustainability and resilience agendas. Truly dealing with complexity and emergence, important concepts in both transitions studies and urban ecology, means acknowledging that knowledge is partial. Our understanding of the urban system is always contextual and temporal, and recognition of not only the dynamics of the system but also of the dynamics in understanding the system is essential. We find urban ecology to be important to understanding and effecting transitions, and the case study described illustrates the utility of SETS analysis for developing priorities for decision-making towards more livable, sustainable and resilient urban futures.

References

Accordino, J. and G.T. Johnson. (2000). "Addressing the vacant and abandoned property problem". *Journal of Urban Affairs*, 22 (3): 301–315.

Alberti, M. (2015). "Eco-evolutionary dynamics in an urbanizing planet". *TREE*, http://dx.doi.org/10.1016/j.tree.2014.11.007

Alexander, F.S. (2005). *Land bank authorities: a guide for the creation and operation of local land banks*. Fannie Mae Foundation, available at http://www.nhc.org/media/files/Land_Bank_Authorities-Alexander.pdf

Andersson, E., T. McPhearson, P. Kremer, E. Gomez-Baggethun, D. Haase, M. Tuvendal and D. Wurster. (2015a). "Scale and context dependence of ecosystem service providing units". *Ecosystem Services* (Special Issue), http://dx.doi.org/10.1016/j.ecoser.2014.08.001

Andersson, E. T., M. Tengö, T. McPhearson and P. Kremer. (2015b). "Cultural ecosystem services as a platform for working towards urban sustainability". *Ecosystem Services* (Special Issue), http://dx.doi.org/10.1016/j.ecoser.2014.08.002

Myla F. J. Aronson, Frank A. La Sorte, Charles H. Nilon, Madhusudan Katti, Mark A. Goddard, Christopher A. Lepczyk, Paige S. Warren, Nicholas S. G. Williams, Sarel Cilliers, Bruce Clarkson, Cynnamon Dobbs, Rebecca Dolan, Marcus Hedblom, Stefan Klotz, Jip Louwe Kooijmans, Ingolf Kühn, Ian MacGregor-Fors, Mark McDonnell, Ulla Mörtberg, Petr Pyšek, Stefan Siebert, Jessica Sushinsky, Peter Werner and Marten Winter. 2014. "A global analysis of the impacts of urbanization on bird and plant diversity reveals key anthropogenic drivers". *Proc. R. Soc. B*, 281: 20133330. http://dx.doi.org/10.1098/rspb.2013.3330

Batty, M. (2008). "The size, scale, and shape of cities". *Science*, 319 (5864): 769–771.

Betsill, M.M. (2001). "Mitigating climate change in US cities: opportunities and obstacles". *Local Environment*, 6 (4): 393–406.

Bonham, J.B., G. Spilka and D. Rastorfer. (2002). "Old cities/green cities. Communities transform unmanaged land". APA Planning advisory service report number 506/507. Chicago, IL.

Bulkeley, H., V. Castan Broto and A. Maassen. (2011). "Governing low carbon transitions" in H. Bulkeley and V. Castan Broto. *Cities and Low Carbon Transitions*. New York: Routledge, pp. 29–41.

Burkholder, S. (2012). "The new ecology of vacancy: Rethinking land use in shrinking cities". *Sustainability*, 4 (12): 1154–1172.

CBD (Secretariat of the Convention on Biological Diversity). (2012) *Cities and Biodiversity Outlook*. (ISBN 92-9225-432-2) is an open access publication, subject to the terms of the Creative Commons Attribution License (http://creativecommons.org/licenses/by-nc/3.0/).

Gretchen C Daily, Harold A Mooney, Liba Pejchar, Joshua Goldstein, Stephen Polasky, Peter M Kareiva, Taylor H Ricketts, James Salzman, and Robert Shallenberger (2009). "Ecosystem services in decision making: time to deliver". *Frontiers in Ecology and the Environment*, 7 (1): 21–28.

Dobson, A. (2003a). *Justice and the Environment: Conceptions of Environmental Sustainability and dimensions of Social Justice*. Oxford: Oxford University Press.

Dobson, A. (2003b). "Social justice and environmental sustainability: Ne'er the twain shall meet?" in J. Agyeman, R. Bullard, B. Evans, Bullard and Evans (eds.) *Just Sustainabilities: Development in an Unequal World*. Cambridge: MIT Press, pp. 83–95.

Elmqvist, T. et al. (eds.) 2013a. *Urbanization, Biodiversity and Ecosystem Services: Challenges and Opportunities: A Global Assessment*. Springer Open. DOI: 10.1007/978-94-007-7088-1_33

Gandy, M. (2002). *Concrete and Clay: Reworking Nature in New York City*. Cambridge, MA: MIT Press.

Goldstein, J., M. Jensen and E. Reiskin. (2001). *Urban Vacant Land Redevelopment: Challenges and Cambridge, MA*. Lincoln Institute of Land Policy.

Gómez-Baggethun, E., Å. Gren, D.N. Barton, J. Langemeyer, T. McPhearson, P. O'Farrell, E. Andersson, Z. Hamstead and P. Kremer. (2013). "Urban ecosystem services". In: Thomas Elmqvist, Michail Fragkias, Julie Goodness, Burak Güneralp, Peter J. Marcotullio, Robert I. McDonald, Susan Parnell, Maria Schewenius, Marte Sendstad, Karen C. Seto, Cathy Wilkinson), (Eds.) *Cities and Biodiversity Outlook: Urbanization, Biodiversity and Ecosystem Services: Challenges and Opportunities*, Springer Netherlands, pp. 175–251, DOI:10.1007/978-94-007-7088-1_11

Grimm, N.B., J.M. Grove, S.T.A. Pickett and C.A. Redman. (2000). "Integrated approaches to long-term studies of urban ecological systems". *BioScience*, 50 (7): 571. doi:10.1641/0006-3568(2000)050[0571:IATLTO]2.0.CO;2

Grimm, N.B., S.H. Faeth, N.E. Golubiewski, C.L. Redman, J. Wu, X. Bai and J.M. Briggs. (2008). "Global change and the ecology of cities". *Science* 319: 756–760.

Grimm, N.B., F.S. Chapin, B. Bierwagen, P. Gonzalez, P.M. Groffman, Y. Luo, F. Melton, K. Nadelhoffer, A. Pairis, P.A. Raymond, J. Schimel and C.E. Williamson. (2013). "The impacts of climate change on ecosystem structure and function". *Frontiers in Ecology and the Environment* 11: 474–482.

Grin, J. and A. Loeber (2007). "Theories of policy learning: agency, structure and change". In: F. Fischer, G. Miller and M. Sidney (eds.) *Handbook of Public Policy Analysis: Theory, Politics, and Methods.* London: Taylor and Francis.

Groffman, P.M., J. Cavender-Bares, N.D Bettez, J.M. Grove, S.J. Hall, J.B. Heffernan, S.E. Hobbie, K.L. Larson, J.L. Morse, C. Neill, K. Nelson, J. O'Neil-Dunne, L. Ogden, D.E. Pataki, C. Polsky, R.R. Chowdhury, and M.K. Steele. (2014). "Ecological homogenization of urban USA". *Frontiers in Ecology and the Environment* 12: 74–81. http://dx.doi.org/10.1890/120374

Grove, J.M., A.R. Troy, J.P.M. O'Neill-Dunne, W.R. Burch Jr, M.L. Cadenasso and S.T.A. Pickett. (2006). "Characterization of households and its implications for the vegetation of urban ecosystems". *Ecosystems* 9: 578–597.

Haase, D., N. Larondelle, E. Andersson, M. Artmann, S. Borgström, J. Breuste, E. Gomez-Baggethun, Å. Gren, Z. Hamstead, R. Hansen, N. Kabisch, P. Kremer, J. Langemeyer, E.L. Rall, T. McPhearson, S. Pauleit, S. Qureshi, N. Schwarz, A. Voigt, D. Wurster and T. Elmqvist. (2014). "A quantitative review of urban ecosystem services assessments: concepts, models, and implementation". *AMBIO* (Special Issue), 43: 413–433, DOI 10.1007/s13280-014-0504-0

Hammer, S., L. Kamal-Chaoui, A. Robert and M. Plouin. (2011). "Cities and green growth: a conceptual framework". OECD Regional Development Working Papers. Available at http://www.oecd.org/gov/regional-policy/49330120.pdf

Hamstead, Z.A., P. Kremer, N. Larondelle, T. McPhearson and D. Haase. (2015). "Classification of the heterogenous structure of urban landscapes (STURLA) as an indicator of landscape function applied to surface temperature in New York City". *Ecological Indicators*, http://dx.doi.org/10.1016/j.ecolind.2015.10.014

Kremer, P., Z. Hamstead and T. McPhearson. (2013). "A social-ecological assessment of vacant lots in New York City". *Landscape and Urban Planning*, 120: 218–233.

Larondelle, N., Z.A. Hamstead, P. Kremer, D. Haase and T. McPhearson. (2014). "Applying a novel urban structure classification to compare the relationships of urban structure and surface temperature in Berlin and New York City". *Applied Geography*, 53: 427–437. http://dx.doi.org/10.1016/j.apgeog.2014.07.004

Little, G.M. (2008). *692 Main Street – A revisioning of an urban void: An exploration into challenging cultural perceptions of an urban vacant lot.* University of Manitoba. Available at http://mspace.lib.umanitoba.ca/jspui/handle/1993/23124

McDonnell, M.J. and A.K. Hahs. (2008). "The use of gradient analysis studies in advancing our understanding of the ecology of urbanizing landscapes: Current status and future directions". *Landscape Ecology*, 23:1143–1155.

McDonnell, M.J. (2011). "The history of urban ecology". In: J. Niemelä, J.H. Breuste, G. Guntenspergen, N.E. McIntyre, T. Elmqvist and P. James P (eds.) *Urban Ecology: Patterns, Processes, and Applications.* Oxford University Press, Oxford.

McHale, M.R., T.A. Steward, Pickett, O.Barbosa, D.N. Bunn, M.L. Cadenasso, D.L. Childers, M. Gartin, G. Hess, D. M. Iwaniec, T. McPhearson, M.N. Peterson, A.K. Poole, L. Rivers III, S.T. Shutters and W. Zhou. (2015). "The new global urban realm: complex, connected, diffuse, and diverse social-ecological systems". *Sustainability* (Special Issue), 7: 5211–5240, doi:10.3390/su7055211

McPhearson, T. (2012). "Vacant land in cities could provide important social and eco-logical benefits". *The Nature of Cities*, http://www.thenatureofcities.com/?p=656

McPhearson, T. (2013). "Wicked problems, social-ecological systems, and the utility of systems thinking". *The Nature of Cities*, http://www.thenatureofcities. com/?p=2180

McPhearson, T. and K. G. Tidball. 2013. "Disturbances in urban social-ecological systems: niche opportunities for environmental education". In: M. Krasny and J. Dillon (eds.) *Trading Zones in Environmental Education: Creating Transdisciplinary Dialogue*. Peter Lang, New York.

McPhearson, T., P. Kremer, and Z. Hamstead. (2013a). "Mapping Ecosystem Services in New York City: Applying a Social-Ecological Approach in Urban Vacant Land." *Ecosystem Services* 11–26, http://dx.doi.org/10.1016/j.ecoser.2013.06.005

McPhearson, T., D. Maddox, B. Gunther and D. Bragdon. (2013b.) "New York City biodiversity, green space, and ecosystem services". In: T. Elmqvist et al. (eds.) *Cities and Biodiversity Outlook: Urbanization, Biodiversity and Ecosystem Services: Challenges and Opportunities*, Springer Netherlands, pp. 355–383, DOI:10.1007/978-94-007-7088-1_19

McPhearson, T., Zoé Hamstead, and Peleg Kremer. (2014). "Urban ecosystem services for resilience planning and management in New York City". *AMBIO: Journal of the Human Environment, Special Issue* (2014) 43: 502–515. DOI: 10.1007/ s13280-014-0509-8

McPhearson, T., E. Andersson, T. Elmqvist and N. Frantzeskaki. (2015). "Resilience of and through urban ecosystem services". *Ecosystem Services* (Special Issue), DOI: 10.1016/j.ecoser.2014.07.012

McPhearson, T. and V. Marshall. (2015). "Micro_Urban: the ecological and social potential of small-scale urban spaces". *The Nature of Cities*, http://www. thenatureofcities.com/2015/01/03/micro_urban-the-ecological-and-social-potential-of-small-scale-urban-spaces/

McPhearson, Timon, S.T.A. Pickett, N. Grimm, J. Niemelä, M. Alberti, T. Elmqvist, C. Weber, D. Haase, J. Breuste, and S. Qureshi. 2016. "Advancing Urban Ecology Toward a Science of Cities." *BioScience* 66(3):198–212, doi: 10.1093/biosci/biw002.

McPhearson, Timon, Dagmar Haase, Nadja Kabisch, Åsa Gren. 2016b. "Advancing understanding of the complex nature of urban systems." *Ecological Indicators* 70: 566–573, http://dx.doi.org/10.1016/j.ecolind.2016.03.054

Newman, P.W.G. 1999. "Sustainability and cities: extending the metabolism model". *Landscape and Urban Planning* 44: 219–226.

Niemela, J., S.-R. Saarela, T. Soderman, L. Kopperoinen, V. Yli-Pelkonen, S. Vare and D.J. Kotze. (2010). "Using the ecosystem services approach for better planning and conservation of urban green spaces: a Finland case study". *Biodiversity & Conservation*, 19 (11): 3225–3243.

Pickett, S.T.A., J.M. Grove, C.H. Nilon, R.V. Pouyat, W.C. Zipperer and R. Costanza. (2001). "Urban ecological systems: linking terrestrial ecological, physical, and socialeconomic components of metropolitan areas". *Annual Review of Ecology and Systematics*, p. 32.

Steward T. A. Pickett, Mary L. Cadenasso, J. Morgan Grove, Peter M. Groffman, Lawrence E. Band, Christopher G. Boone, William R. Burch Jr., C. Susan B. Grimmond, John Hom, Jennifer C. Jenkins, Neely L. Law, Charles H. Nilon, Richard V. Pouyat, Katalin Szlavecz, Paige S. Warren, And Matthew A. Wilson. (2008). "Beyond urban legends: an emerging framework of urban ecology, as illustrated by the Baltimore Ecosystem study". *BioScience*, 58 (2): 139–150.

Pickett, S.T.A., M.L. Cadenasso and B. McGrath. (2013). *Resilience in Ecology and Urban Design: Linking Theory and Practice for Sustainable Cities*. New York, ISBN 978-9400753433

Pickett, S.T.A., B. McGrath, M.L. Cadenasso and A.J. Felson. (2014). "Ecological resilience and resilient cities". *Building Research and Information*, 42(2): 143–157. DOI:10.1080/09613218.2014.873593

Rosenzweig, C., W.D. Solecki, J. Cox, S. Hodges, L. Parshall, B. Lynn, Cynthia Rosenzweig, William D. Solecki, Lily Parshall, Barry lynn, Jennifer Cox, Richard Goldberg, Sara Hodges, Stuart Gaffin, Ronald B. Slosberg, Peter Savio, Frank Dunstan, and Mark Watson and F. Dunstan. (2009). "Mitigating New York City's heat island: integrating stakeholder perspectives and scientific evaluation". *Bulletin of the American Meteorological Society*, 90 (9): 1297–1312. DOI:10.1175/2009BAMS2308.1

Schewenius, M., T. McPhearson and T. Elmqvist. (2014). "Opportunities for increasing resilience and sustainability of urban social–ecological systems: insights from the URBES and the Cities Biodiversity Outlook Projects". *AMBIO* (Special Issue), 43: 434–444, DOI: 10.1007/s13280-014-0505-z

Stille, A. (2002). "Wild cities: it's a jungle out there". *New York Times*, November 23, 2002. Accessed on 1-21-15 at http://www.nytimes.com/2002/11/23/arts/wild-cities-it-s-a-jungle-out-there.html

Sukhdev, P., H. Wittmer, C. Schröter-Schlaack, C. Nesshöver, J. Bishop, P. Ten, H.G. Brink, Pavan Sukhdev, Heidi Wittmer, Christoph Schröter-Schlaack, Carsten Nesshöver, Joshua Bishop, Patrick ten Brink, Haripriya Gundimeda, Pushpam Kumar and Ben Simmons. (2010). *The Economics of Ecosystems and Biodiversity: Mainstreaming the Economics of Nature. A Synthesis of the Approach, Conclusions and Recommendations of TEEB*, available at http://www.unep.org/pdf/LinkClick.pdf

Sukopp, H., M. Numata and A. Huber. (2001). Urban ecology as the basis of urban planning. Biologia Plantarum 44 (1):110. DOI: 10.1023/A:1017940320214

Sullivan, R. (2010). "The concrete jungle". *New York Magazine*, available at http://nymag.com/news/features/68087/

Wirth, L. (1938). "Urbanism as a way of life". *American Journal of Sociology*, 44 (1): 1–24.

Yesilonis, I. D., R. V. Pouyat and N. K. Neerchal. (2008). "Spatial distribution of metals in soils in Baltimore, Maryland: role of native parent material, proximity to major roads, housing age and screening guidelines". *Environmental Pollution*, 156: 723–731.

6 The Role of Place-specific Dynamics in the Destabilization of the Danish Water Regime

An Actor–Network View on Urban Sustainability Transitions

C. F. Fratini and J. S. Jensen

Introduction

In a time of environmental and economic predicaments and of a growing world population increasingly concentrated in urban settlements, the role of cities as arenas where impacts are most visible, and thus most debated and acted upon, has been largely acknowledged (UN-HABITAT, 2012; Hodson and Marvin, 2010). At the same time, the role of large technological systems, like those concerned with water, energy and food provision, has been identified as an empirical theme of central relevance for the development of sustainable urban futures (Bulkeley et al., 2011; Späth and Rohracher, 2015). On one hand, expectations on utility services are changing as networked infrastructure is turning out to be critical in improving urban living while simultaneously protecting the natural environment (Kaika and Swyngedouw, 2000; Monstadt, 2009). On the other hand, utility organizations are experiencing important transformations in governance models (Hodson et al., in print). Influenced by the neoliberal paradigm dominating European policies, market-oriented management approaches are drastically changing the socio-technical priorities of urban services (Graham and Marvin, 2001; Jensen et al., 2015b). Kaika and Swyngedouw (2012) suggest that the emergence of a diversity of urban imaginaries and discursive formations requires recasting sustainability transitions as a decidedly political project "to ask questions about what visions of nature and what urban socio-environmental relations we wish to inhabit".

Networked infrastructures are deeply embedded in daily practices within and between urban fabrics, and their character is highly contingent to specific "places" and their different socio-political constructs (Pierce et al., 2011; Murphy, 2015). In this study, the term "place" is used in a thick descriptive sense as employed in disciplines such as human and environmental geography and anthropology, in order to refer not only to the physical features of a place but also to characteristics such as culture, communities, history, human relations and socio-political settings, which define a specific place with respect to others (Healey, 2006; Hodson and Marvin, 2010; Pierce et al., 2011; Murphy, 2015). Despite the fact that scholars increasingly emphasize the role of geographies in transition dynamics (Coenen et al., 2012; Raven et al., 2012; Truffer and Coenen, 2012), the relational qualities of places remain largely unexplored by transition scholars (Jensen et al., 2015a; 2015b; Hodson et al., in print; Longhurst, 2015). In particular, Murphy (2015) argues that "transition studies could benefit from analyses of the competing place-frames associated with sustainability initiatives and the networks and actor- or institution-specific positional ties that stabilize, obstruct, and/or promote development visions". In doing so, it becomes fundamental to develop 'thick' descriptions of the double interrelations of the ongoing restructuring of both infrastructures' networks and cities (Blok, 2013).

In Jensen et al. (2015b) we explored "why the boundaries, functions and challenges of large scale systems typically are framed differently at the urban level of governance rather than at more aggregated levels of governance [national level]". By examining the conflicting framings of the Danish water system and their enactment at the urban and national levels of governance, we concluded that their juxtaposition produced transition dynamics which are currently destabilizing the Danish water regime. In particular, we suggested that place-specific framings enacted at the urban level have more transformative potential than those enforced at the national level because "they can associate systems with new objectives and thereby challenge the traditional boundaries and interrelations between systems and their contexts". In this chapter, our aim is to explore in more depth how such place-specific transformative dynamics emerged, and which role they are having in the current transition of the water regime in Denmark. Inspired by Geels (2014), our ambition is to contribute to ongoing debates on regime destabilization through an in-depth description of regime dynamics by studying the role of regime actors, power and politics in transition processes. We seek to explore how socio-technical transitions are mobilized through "situated city-making practices" (Blok, 2013), thus positioning this study at the intersection of cross-cutting debates on urban sustainability transitions and the geographies of transition governance.

Inspired by Murphy (2015), in this chapter we present "thick" descriptions of places and place-making processes to "reveal novel insights into the power relations and political processes underlying transition processes, and thus enable transition researchers to better account for the rationalities and context-specific forces determining the pace, scale, and direction of socio-technical change". Drawing from recent studies attempting to bring actor-network theory (ANT) epistemologies closer to studies of sustainability transitions with the use of the Arena of Development approach (AoD) as an analytical framework (Jørgensen, 2012; Jensen et al., 2015a; 2015b; Späth and Rohracher, 2015), we argue that ANT can offer an alternative analytical lens enabling "the study of those concrete and plural sites at which urban sustainability is known, practiced, scaled, negotiated, and contested, in heterogeneous and dynamic assemblages of humans and non-humans" (Blok, 2013).

An ANT View on Urban Sustainability Transitions

Geels (2014) has recently argued that "an important topic for future research is to better understand not just regime resistance but also the destabilization and decline of existing regimes". Consequently, he argues for the need of developing conceptual frameworks able to integrate the role of agency, power and politics in a process of regime transformation.

A similar argument has been promoted by the Arena of Development approach (AoD). According to Jørgensen (2012), the "AoD approach downplays the consistency of rules and mechanism of the regimes level, as the introduction of regime level tensions and inconsistencies allows for studying situated actors' political engagement in conflicts and sense-making dynamics through their performed interventions". Following the same line of reasoning, Jensen et al. (2015b) highlight how "drawing on actor-network theory, (…) the arena approach thus calls for sensitivity to how representations of large-scale systems are typically related to inter-ests", and how "the relevance of such systems is defined by specific actor constellations". On the base of such considerations, we suggest that the AoD approach might be a productive framework to analyze processes of resistance, destabilization and decline of existing regimes. Inspired by the ANT vocabulary, in this section we would like to contribute to this line of inquire by introducing a set of concepts which offer insights on the role of situated urban dynamics on the destabilization and decline of socio-technical regimes.

According to the ANT epistemology, urban contexts should not be studied as single orchestrated orders that can be analytically decomposed into a set of well-defined functions and socio-material flows. To take into account the intrinsic multiplicity and tension that characterize the generation of urban orders in the "urban fabric", ANT scholars employ the concept of *"urban assemblages"*. The concept of assemblage urbanism suggests that there is no city as a whole, but a multiplicity of situated processes assembling the city in different ways (Farías, 2011; McFarlane, 2011). This analytical approach has three important consequences for conceptualizing cities (Blok, 2013): (1) cities should be addressed as the precarious outcome of a multiplicity of interdependent yet relatively autonomous socio-material assemblages that are performed by a variety of situated actors and actor constellations, informed by different myopic and distributed understandings of the situ-ation at hand; (2) the city is described as the product of "a multiplicity of sites, the connections among which are changing and contingent", thus spa-tiality is a variable end-product of actor-networks' activities and scale-mak-ing practices; 3) there are no overarching power structures governing cities: thus actors' capacities, resources and power end up being unequally distrib-uted within specific urban relations. An urban assemblage is hence defined as an ensemble of "heterogeneous actors, human and non-human, which orient themselves to the gradual redesign of urban eco-socio-technical relations". Therefore, assemblages emerge as a consequence of "the way actors forge urban ecological connections between otherwise non-related sites and practices, (…) enrolling technologies, inscriptions, standards and natures in the process" (Blok, 2013).

Therefore, urban governance is conceptualized as a distributed and myopic enterprise that is performed from within a variety of assemblages, which due to their different socio-material compositions promote different and sometimes incompatible conceptions of what an urban socio-technical system is, and what it should be. This entails that at the urban scale, socio-technical systems are typically subjected to multiple and sometimes competing framings that associate the system with a diversity of (sometimes competing) urban functions. Key dynamics of urban transitions are therefore the controversies and negotiations over those boundaries that define the relation between socio-technical systems and the wider urban context, among a variety of assemblages that operate from different socio-material positions. Therefore, urban configurations are products of the place-specific patterns by which these assemblages intersect one another, based on spatial proximity and overlaps.

Such a dynamic approach to urban governance does not rule out that an urban socio-technical system may appear as coherent governance objects that can be planned and developed in relation to fixed and well-defined urban functions for a longer period of time. Nevertheless, such hegemonic conceptions of urban socio-technical system need to be seen as the product of a particular governance configuration which is capable of marginalizing or suppressing alternative system framings at a certain point in time, and of monopolizing knowledge production in support of the hegemonic framing. In Jensen et al. (2015a) we introduced the notion of *"junction"* to describe those sites "where conventional boundaries and interdependencies among material systems and social practices are transgressed, where the established order and identity of the urban fabric has become unstable". Junctions are important locations in which to study processes of urban transitions and their effect on socio-technical regimes because in such places "different visions and perspectives of urban change are confronted with each other and are negotiated and may eventually lead to the emergence of new socio-technical configurations" (Späth and Rohracher, 2015).

Because contradiction becomes tangible at these specific sites, actors engage in repair-work activities to reconfigure boundaries and relationships among those systems and spaces that have been compromised. Jensen et al. (2015a) employ the notion of "navigation" to describe "how change often is moulded by loosely coordinated micro-political manoeuvres of actors and actor constellations operating in the absence of a predefined strategic vision". In order to describe the concept of navigational agency more accurately, we will use the notion of *"boundary work"* in this chapter (Gieryn, 1983; Owens et al., 2006) to account for the existence of fixed and potentially precarious system frames within urban governance that, over specific time periods, have succeeded in monopolizing knowledge production and in marginalizing alternative system framings.

On these premises, the notions of assemblage urbanism, junctions and boundary-work allow the analyst to account for all those asymmetries and conflicts that emerge in specific urban places. Such asymmetries and power struggles emerge as the result of the ways elements of the world, the city and their mutual connections unfold and become tangible as "matters of concern" (Latour, 2005; Jensen et al., 2015b). A deeper understanding of such place-specific asymmetries, power relations and their potential for influencing transformation processes might open up new spaces for democratic experimentation to drive socio-technical transitions in sustainable directions (Jørgensen, 2012; Kaika and Swyngedouw, 2012; Blok, 2013).

Research Design

In the following section, we present an empirical exploration of how place-specific junctions have contributed to transformations within the Danish water regime. The core empirical material consists of 66 face-to-face narrative interviews (Kvale, 2007). The interviewees were selected to encompass most of the professional disciplines and organizational roles involved in water governance and urban development in Denmark, as well as various levels of seniority and association at differing scales of governance. A summary of the interviewees sample is presented in Table 6.1. The interviews were conducted between 2008 and 2014 as part of a long-term study of water governance in Denmark (Fratini, 2009;2014; Jensen et al., 2015a). Interview data was selectively transcribed, coded and analyzed. This material has been complemented by a study of grey literature conducted to gain an understanding of historical developments in water governance in Denmark. This drew upon a variety of documents, including policy reports, municipal and regional plans and national legislation and research.

Table 6.1 Categorization of interviewees

Interviewee category	Number of interviewees
Water and wastewater utility managers	19
Local government administrators	17
National regulators	4
Consultants	13
Researchers	13

The Case: The Urban Transition of the Danish Water Regime

The analysis begins with a short introduction of the competing urban and national boundary-work activities which have contributed to the destabilization of the Danish water regime from the beginning of the 21st century onwards. Our analysis then explores how those dynamics played out in place-specific urban junctions where the socio-technical boundaries of the water system were contested or entered into conflict with situated urban orders. Finally, we examine how tensions among different urban assemblages and their mediating role in sustainable urban transitions are presently shaping the transition of the water regime in Denmark.

The Context: A Destabilized Water Regime in Between Innovation of Functions and Innovation of Place

In Denmark, the development and operation of water infrastructures took off in the 18th century as cities gained an increasingly central position within societal development, due to rapid urbanization catalyzed by the industrialization of production. These processes generated pressures for more active involvement in the development and operation of collective infrastructures by national as well as urban public administrations (Lindegaard, 2001). The main authority overseeing water infrastructure development resided in the local municipal administrations. Most waterworks were owned and operated by municipalities, and the planning, construction and maintenance of sewage systems was conducted by sewage offices located within public municipal administrations.

In Denmark, the period from 1970 to 1989 was characterized by economic growth and increasing public environmental concerns. New environmental policies were developed which pushed the implementation of wastewater treatment plants and the implementation of new environmental regulations to prevent the pollution of water recipients (Andersen, 2001). At the same time, further developments of the water infrastructure had rendered water increasingly invisible to the average citizen. Water had become a basic need/resource that was taken care of by means of a discrete and invisible infrastructure with the aim of providing clean water and safe urban environments.

The Emergence of the 'Place-making Water' Framing

From the end of the 20th century, new important socio-technical pressures pushed for a new framing of urban water. On one hand, expanding urban development significantly increased water runoff into sewage facilities. This caused uncomfortable overloads of the wastewater system, which represented a critical problem because discharges from treatment plants were highly regulated and monitored by the strict environmental regulations set in the

1980s. New water solutions were needed to respond to such predicaments. On the other hand, a new paradigm started to emerge in urban planning practices. Local politicians' ambitions to improve municipal finances created an interest for relocating parts of the wealthy suburban population back to city centers. New principles for urban renewal planning were adopted by the municipal administration. This broader reorientation in urban planning in Copenhagen was largely influenced and represented in the concept of 'life between buildings' promoted in particular by the urban architect Jan Gehl. As a consequence of such urban imaginaries, the boundaries of the sociotechnical configuration of water that rendered water invisible through the development of a discrete underground piped water network was questioned. Water integrated the notion of urban livability and was framed as a value-adding asset that should actively be integrated into above-ground constructions and infrastructure.

In 2007, an early expression of this idea was a nationally funded research project named 2BG (Black blue green – integrated infrastructure planning as key to sustainable urban water systems). Rather than narrowly focusing on the development and optimization of the piped water network, this project argued for the need to actively include green urban infrastructures in the management of urban water (Fryd et al., 2013). It was argued that a water-oriented redesigning of the green city could simultaneously relieve pressure on traditional piped water networks in case of storms, and generate urban value in the guise of new green areas, wetlands and watercourses in the city. The vision to actively integrate green infrastructure in the urban management of water was further explored and developed in two subsequent nationally funded projects (called '19K' and 'vand-i-byer') that aimed at engaging more actively with municipal water professionals and the water industry. These projects generated a network of incumbent actors involved in administrative positions all over the country who engaged in experimentations with integrated and multifunctional above-ground water infrastructures.

The Emergence of the 'Sectorial Water' Framing

From 2001 onwards, the traditional sociotechnical configuration of water was also questioned by a quite different set of reform processes trigged by a new policy discourse that emerged within the Ministry of Environment, in which the national regulation of the water infrastructures resided. Until 2001, the ministry had not taken a very active interest in the detailed ways in which the water infrastructure was operated and developed by the municipalities. Rather, the ministry had been focusing on ensuring clean hygienic water and reducing the impact of wastewater on the aquatic environment. In 2001, this human health regulatory focus was replaced by a new efficiency focus (Regeringen, 2003).

A benchmark study succeeded in framing the municipally operated water infrastructures as a target of the ministry's efficiency-oriented policy approach. The study estimated yearly 'inefficiencies' deriving from water infrastructure operation as a whole at 1.3 billion DKK (174 million Euro) (Konkurrencestyrelsen, 2003). These estimated inefficiencies were addressed by a governmental advisory board that consisted of recognized professionals within economics. The board explained the identified inefficiencies as a consequence of public administration:

> Public production can entail poorer efficiency than private production. This can be due to secondary objectives (e.g. to prioritize the requests of staff groups) poorer incentives for cost reductions due to softer budget constraints, or that the political priorities are not realized because the administration enforces its own agenda. (Det økonomiske råd 2004:276)

In expressing the rationale for the reform, the Ministry of Finances framed water governance as follows: (1) the area is not politically involved with other political areas which are within the public administration; (2) there are market opportunities in the utility assets which are now corporatized.[2] The new efficiency-oriented framing suggested that while local political administration should retain some authority to develop local infrastructure performance goals (in the guise of so-called service goals and environmental goals), the means by which to meet these performance goals should be left to professional organizations operating as independently as possible of the politically driven public administration.

In 2009, the Water Sector Reform thus enforced corporatization by establishing water utilities that operated independently of municipal administration. This entailed that the municipal ownership of the water infrastructure and the responsibility over the activities associated with the development and operation of water infrastructures had to be separated from the leadership of local politicians and transformed into municipally owned corporatized utilities. Thus, these corporatized utilities were not placed under the authority of local politicians, but rather under the management of a professional and independent board. The central objective of these boards was to meet the politically set performance goals with maximum economic efficiency. Local political authorities were thus no longer in command of water infrastructure planning, but rather translated into a client in charge of defining performance goals.

In order to promote sectorial competition, the water sector reform furthermore shifted the authority over water tariffs from the municipalities to a newly established national 'Utility Secretariat', located in the national competition authority. Based on a national benchmarking system that assessed the efficiency of each utility, this secretariat was authorized to regulate the tariffs for each individual water utility on an annual basis. Each year, these tariffs were reduced by an individually calculated 'efficiency factor', derived from a comparison with the calculated efficiency of other utilities. At the same time, a series of new boundaries was set in regard to what should be defined water infrastructure and the activities associated with the development and operation of that same infrastructure. The reforms defined the new utilities as strictly 'infrastructural' companies. Their activities were thus restricted to the operation and development of 'infrastructure related to water provisions'. They were thereby allowed to invest only in those infrastructures owned, operated and financed exclusively by themselves. The utilities were thus cut off from engaging in the development of cross-sectorial and multifunctional above-ground integration of water into urban development projects.

The reform established the piped water infrastructure as a discrete sectorial object of economic optimization. This was done by weakening the power of local political authority over system development, and by defining water utilities as strictly infrastructural companies, the activities of which were delimited to the development and operation of the piped water infrastructure.

To conclude, the two boundary-work activities described above, summarized and compared in Table 6.2, have pushed the Danish urban water regime into two different and competing transition pathways, which framed urban water as mediator of two distinctive goals: urban renewal and economic efficiency. These two distinctive frames have pushed incumbent actors into exploring two different innovation trajectories for the transformation of urban water infrastructures: that of 'functions' and that of 'places'. As a consequence of these two boundary-work activities initiated by different groups of incumbent actors, the Danish water regime has been largely destabilized and is today in a process of transformation.

Table 6.2 Place-making versus sectorial framings of water

	Place-making water	*Sectorial water*
Matter of concern/ Imaginary	Urban renewal and livability	Economic efficiency in service provision
Framing of water infrastructure	Cross-sectorial integration of above- and below-ground components	Discrete and below-ground pipe system
Planning unit	Municipal administration	Corporatized water utility
Management approach	Experimental	Deterministic
Innovation trajectory	Innovation of place	Innovation of functions

Contested Boundaries at Fundamental Urban Junctions

In the previous section, we introduced the two sociotechnical framings that are currently guiding the Danish water regime's transition. In this section, we analyze how these two framings emerged and juxtaposed within place-specific urban junctions, and how the dynamics at these junctions supported regime resistance, destabilization and transformation.

The Copenhagen Harbor Junction: The Emergence of the Urban Livability Assemblage

An early example of the place-making framing of water was the transformation of the Copenhagen's inner harbor from an industrial site into a swimming facility, which took place between 1980 and 2002 as traditional industrial production activities were relocated to areas outside the inner harbor. This transition was not the outcome of a deliberate and far-sighted master plan or a political vision, but the fruit of the gradual alignment of a number of independent, myopic, boundary-work activities in response to several assemblages that began emerging and overlapped in 1987 when the first Action Plan for the Aquatic Environment (APAE-I) was published by the Ministry of Environment. Initially, the sewage office was divided between water engineers who believed this was an opportunity for action, and those who did not see the APAE-I as a strong political priority. This provoked one of the water engineers from the sewage department to write a letter to the Director of Planning and Development describing the situation of inertia within the sewage department. With the support of some of his colleagues, he was placed in charge of a new planning entity responsible for infrastructural investments in the municipality. Two retention basins were planned to increase the retention capacity of the infrastructure and thus prevent sewage overflows to the harbor. According to a senior engineer from the utility company managing the water infrastructure in Copenhagen, the boundary-work activity of the municipal water engineer in charge of dimensioning the basins was a key prerequisite for the harbor's transformation:

> [W]hat he saw in the future was that when you build those tanks you will not be able to go back to expand them if somebody makes a decision for stronger regulations (…). Then he asked: "What could the strongest regulation that anybody could demand be?" His answer was: "Bacteria and bathing. If we achieve this then a lot of other pollutants will be reduced" (…). They [the group of municipal engineers planning water infrastructure development] decided to go as far as they could justify with strong environmental criteria.[1]

The retention basins' implementation resulted in the biggest wastewater infrastructure investment in decades. Nevertheless, the decision was taken outside the public radar and without a political mandate. At that time, large breweries were major water users in Copenhagen, and it was feared that they would have opposed the use of water tariffs as a means to ensure the harbor's water quality (Jensen et al., 2015a). Consequently, "within the water planning department the endorsement of the larger design was perceived as an affirmation that infrastructure investments did not need to be constrained by political targets" (Jensen et al., 2015a). Furthermore, the decision was taken in a context of internal municipal tensions provoking a number of different visions for the harbor's future: those who still viewed it as an industrial area and an integrated component of the wastewater treatment system, and those who viewed it as a potential biological habitat instead.

New opportunities for transformation emerged as a consequence of the formation of a new assemblage, linking metropolitan cities and their political and administrative community in a competition through a number of ranking systems measuring sustainability and livability based on a variety of indicators. The assemblage was developed and supported by media and international political and research institutions. The municipality of Copenhagen dedicated important resources and political attention to enter both the international rankings for livable cities and the European Commission's Green Capital competition. In particular, Copenhagen has long been vying with Stockholm for obtaining the title of green capital of Europe. Because swimming was possible in Stockholm's harbor, the Environmental Mayor of Copenhagen, elected in 1997, made this goal one of his political agenda's major highlights.

Despite all these developments, Copenhagen's inner harbor remained an unstructured and ill-defined junction for a number of years. Despite the fact that the bathing quality of the harbor's water was coming under increased scrutiny, the framing of the harbor as a bathing facility had not yet stabilized. Two imaginaries were competing with each other: (1) the "harbor aquarium", to provide an experience of "wild" nature as an alternative to city life or (2) the harbor as a space for recreational activities (canoeing, fishing, bathing etc.) within the city.

Nevertheless, the opportunity for a more tangible transformation was actually provided by a local diving association that applied for permissions to use the inner harbor for a series of diving shows. Considering the improved water quality in the harbor, the municipality granted permission. Nevertheless, during the festival a municipal employee made regular visits to assess that no sewage overflows would compromise human safety. The event had such a large public success that the president of the association organized a petition campaign to claim permanent diving and swimming permission for the harbor. As a consequence of the support and the occurrence of a municipal budget negotiation in his favor, the Environmental Mayor finally succeeded in promoting the establishment of the first bathing facility in the harbor.

The harbor junction was finally disentangled as a consequence of the sudden alignment of the boundary-work activities described above. Harbor bathing was established as an urban practice in 2002 when the new Environmental Mayor first dived in the harbor at the newly implemented bathing facility. The implementation

Figure 6.1 The first bathing facility in the Inner Copenhagen Harbor.

also included computer-based monitoring systems simulating how water quality is affected by wastewater infrastructure overflow in the event of rain.

To conclude, the establishment of swimming in the inner harbor of Copenhagen was the outcome of the alignment of various boundary-work activities, but not a specific predefined goal in a long-term master plan. Today, harbor bathing is promoted as the symbol of urban livability and green innovation in municipal discourses supporting urban renewal projects. Furthermore, as a consequence of this development, hygienic water quality has been extended beyond sewage infrastructure requirements. New plans to establish another bathing facility in the southern part of Copenhagen include the large-scale retrofitting of a local creek and the disconnection of 60% of urban water run-off from sewage (Fryd et al., 2013). In Copenhagen's Northern Harbor (*Nordhavn*), an ongoing urban redevelopment aimed at achieving hygienic water quality standards suitable for bathing has become a source of inspiration for architects and urban planners in charge of urban redesign (Blok, 2013). Similar developments have been and are happening in other major cities in Denmark and abroad – for example, Aarhus, Aalborg and New York. As reflected by a senior water engineer from Copenhagen:

> Harbor bathing … everybody wants that now! Even New York has put that in the design plans for city development.[1,3]

Inspired by the introduction of harbor bathing, water was no longer perceived as a phenomenon that should be hidden underground. Instead, water has been translated into a highly visible and highly valued quality among the public, as reflected by a senior engineer from the water utility in Copenhagen:

> We made an analysis of costumers' preferences (…) in 2007, asking them about their estimation of the value of having bathing water in the inner harbor. They provided a fantastic high figure! Actually, just having the knowledge that the water was clean enough for bathing was judged a lot worth. It doubled when they also used it. If you had made that questionnaire two, three years before opening the first harbor bath, they would have preferred us not to build it.[1]

The new role of water is also reflected in new identities among some water engineers, as noted by the former chief of R&D in the utility of Copenhagen:

> [T]the major innovation [produced by harbor bathing] has been that we [water professionals] have realized that we are really key players in urban development, which we never thought before! We just thought, OK somebody else will design the city and then they will ask us to supply the utility. But now we know that we are very indispensable players in designing cities.[1]

As a consequence, a new and more visible role in urban development was ascribed to water. It was attributed a new function: to generate 'place making' urban values. Such political interest has been translated by the water engineers, with a shift in focus from the improvement of technologies for wastewater treatment plants to the reduction of the number of overflows from combined sewer systems. As a consequence, the reduction of the number of discharges from combined sewers overflows per year has become the central priority in a number of municipal strategies for sewer infrastructure planning across Denmark.

The Climate-Neighborhood Junction: Aligning Climate Adaptation and Livability Assemblages

Despite the strong influence of water recipient quality requirements supported by the harbor transformations which strongly contributed to the emergence of the place-making framing of water, this framing did not manage to drastically influence regime transformations because incumbent actors' resistance was supported by sectorial water framing, which promoted water efficiency as opposed to the role of water infrastructure in urban renewal projects. After the Water Sector Reform, most Danish utilities kept prioritizing system optimization rather than fostering opportunities for collaboration with the municipal planning department. This was especially the case in municipalities that did not have enough financial and organizational capacity to build or maintain collaborative routines with their water utilities.

However, a series of storm-water events fundamentally challenged the sectorial conception of the urban water infrastructure as a discrete physical network that could be clearly demarcated from the surrounding urban fabric. Due to these storm-water events, roads, parks and entire neighborhoods were flooded (Fryd, 2011). The traditional water infrastructure was thus deemed inefficient in dealing with storm-water events, and so were the corporatized utilities which had been established to optimize this infrastructure. The limitations of the sectorial configuration of water in dealing with storm-water were thus increasingly articulated, and the focus on cross-sectorial, above-ground integrations of water that had been promoted by the place-making water agenda was slowly reintroduced.

©Morten Mejlhede Rolsted

Figure 6.2 The flooding of Lyngbyvej after the storm of 2 July 2011.

The prioritization of above-ground solutions was most prominently pursued in the Skt. Kjelds neighborhood. During a storm-water event in 2011, the entire neighborhood was largely flooded (Figure 6.2). The neighborhood was thereby translated into a critical urban junction, where societal infrastructure and social practices needed to be reorganized.

The municipal response to this junction was an ambitions climate adaptation strategy. Its objective was to provide a showcase for how to disconnect 30% of rainwater from traditional piped sewage infrastructure by increasing retention capacity and infiltration in the area, and by developing green waterways on the surface. In order to achieve these objectives, plans were devised to transform private yards and parts of public road infrastructure into green areas that allowed for infiltration and could function as green waterways. Furthermore, this strategy was tightly coupled to the idea of promoting urban livability, as illustrated in the quotation below:

> The climate-neighborhood project choses to see the cloud burst challenge from a positive angle and to see rainwater as a recreational potential. If we succeed in managing rainwater better, we avoid the large costs related to flooding of basements and infrastructures. We also gain the opportunities for some new and unique urban experiences with rainwater as our primary tool. Rainwater should be seen as a resource rather than a problem. (Københavns Kommune, 2013:8)

The climate adaptation strategy was furthermore linked to a boarder urban regeneration program aiming to engage with citizens in new ways and thereby reinforce social cohesion in the SKt. Kjelds neighborhood, characterized by diverse and stratified social groups. Figure 6.3 shows one of the designs for the

Figure 6.3 A vision for the future of Skt. Kjelds Square at the heart of the climate neighborhood by Tredje Natur (Københavns Kommune 2012:4)

redevelopment of the area. Cross-sectorial concerns such as greening, recreation and social cohesion by far transcended the legally defined objectives and responsibilities of the corporatized utility, whose role in developing the climate-neighborhood strategy remained limited. This provoked a tenacious endeavor by the Copenhagen water utility and municipality to influence new political processes towards easing collaborations among them for the implementation of the climate adaptation strategy.

In parallel, the national interest organizations of Danish Water Utilities (DANVA), informed by similar situated experiences, began to actively criticize the systems boundaries enforced by the sector reform by arguing that

> water knows no boundaries, and in case of a storm-water event, urban spaces, viaducts, roads and gardens are flooded from water-courses, the sea, waste-water, rainwater and groundwater. (DANVA: 2012:5)

DANVA thus suggested that the corporatized water utilities should be assigned greater responsibility and authority over the governance of the entire water resource cycle – including natural waterways – and not just over the piped water infrastructure.

Moreover, the national interest organization of the Danish municipalities (KL) argued for integrated policies between climate adaptation planning and urban renewal as illustrated in a report on climate adaptation strategies:

> In case of storm water events, even the largest sewers cannot protect us from flooding. Instead, we need to conceive of water in an entirely new way. We are used to thinking of water as something that should be channelled away. But water is also a resource that we cannot do without, and there is much to gain by using water to make cities a better place to live i (KL, 2012)

In 2013, these boundary-work activities provoked an easing of the sectorial legislation by the national authorities. A revision of the water sector law allowed corporatized utilities to co-finance privately and municipally owned projects designed to cope with surface water in roads, water courses and recreational areas by applying water tariffs.

To conclude, the clear-cut boundaries between water infrastructure and the urban fabric designed by the water sector reforms were difficult to maintain in the light of urban junctions such as the flooding of Skt. Kjelds neighborhood. Both municipalities and utilities demanded less rigid system boundaries in the legislation. This also elevated the place-making configuration of water through the emergent livability agenda spreading across Danish municipalities. Nevertheless, national authorities still strive to maintain a strict separation between investments related to the responsibilities of the corporatized utilities and the political priorities of cities.

Conclusions

Our study indicates that a particular transformative potential pertaining to urban contexts resides in the inherent ambivalence between system boundaries and system functions that characterize urban governance, due to its place-sensitive nature. Urban governance thus plays out in the contexts of micro-political negotiations and controversies among system framings promoted by actor constellations with different spatial orientations. This indicates that a governance challenge is to cope with organizational and institutional tensions between place-specific development activities within the urban context, and system-specific governance arrangements promoted at various other scales.

Our study offers a perspective on the urban governance of socio-technical transitions which highlights the fluidity of relations among systems boundaries and place-specific dynamics. Such fluidity allows urban contexts to maintain emergent properties of path creation rather than path-dependent lock-ins. In such contexts, the shaping of large socio-technical systems occurs as a consequence of specific tensions and the resulting distributed boundary-work activities, with the ability to frame emerging configurations that are sensitive to the place-specific functions, boundaries and relations that characterize urban contexts in which system transformation is bound to occur.

This suggests that sustainable transformation journeys are destined to remain incomplete, especially those developing in urban contexts, as also advocated by Jørgensen (2012) and Garud and Gehman (2012). Therefore, system transformation is more likely to be supported by actors able to sustain and co-create such journeys on an 'ongoing basis'. This dialectic characteristic of sustainable transitions makes urban contexts particularly productive arenas for supporting and driving socio-technical transitions in sustainable directions. On the base of these reflections, we recommend policymakers to engage more closely with contingent urban dynamics. Rather than trying to contain the creative potentials of place-specific dynamics in discrete and sectorial framings, it is necessary to design policies which are able to empower distributed and path-creating agency capable of developing a variety of sometimes competing and sometimes aligning place-specific framings. Discrete and sectorial framings might appear sustainable in the short term, because they facilitate centralized management practices, but in the long run may prevent urban actors from engaging in long-sighted, and thus sustainable or, in other words, 'durable' journeys.

Acknowledgements

This work draws on data collected with the involvement of a Danish partnership called 'Vand i Byer' [Water in Urban Areas] aimed at developing new water management practices in Denmark with the purpose of helping the water sector to contribute to climate change adaptation, green innovation and liveability of Danish cities. Particular thanks go to all the interviewees for sharing with us their knowledge and data on water governance in Denmark.

Notes

1   Interview with water and wastewater utility manager, carried out in 2013; conf. Table 6.1.
2   Interview with local government administrator, carried out in 2012, conf. Table 6.1
3   We would like to underline that according to this interviewee, the development of strategies for harbor bathing in New York has been influenced by the installations made in Copenhagen. In fact, the municipality of New York has asked the municipality of Copenhagen for advice in improving their urban water infrastructure, especially in response to disaster storms (i.e., Hurricane Sandy). This information was provided by the same interviewee a few minutes before in the same interview.

References

Andersen, M.S. (2001). Economic instruments and clean water: why institutions and policy design matter. OECD: Paris. Available online at: https://www1.oecd.org/governance/regulatory-policy/1910825.pdf (Accessed 13-07-2013).

Blok, A. (2013). Urban green assemblages: an ANT view on sustainable city building projects. *Science and Technology Studies*, 26(1), 5–24.

Bulkeley, H., Broto, V.C., Hodson, M. and Marvin, S. (2011). *Cities and Low Carbon Transitions*. Routledge, London.

Coenen, L., Benneworth, P. and Truffer, B. (2012). Toward a spatial perspective on sustainability transitions. *Research Policy* 41, 968–979.

DANVA (2012). Danskvand – Fra kildevand til spildevand, Årgang 80, nr. 3.

Det økonomiske råd (2004). Dansk økonomi efteråret 2004, Det økonomiske rød.

Farías, I. (2011). The politics of urban assemblages. *City: analysis of urban trends, culture, theory, policy, action*, 15(3–4), 365–374.

Fratini, C.F. (2009). Urban flood risk management: implementation of the Three Points approach. M.Sc. Thesis. Department of Environmental Engineering. Technical University of Denmark, Lyngby, Denmark.

Fratini, C.F. (2014). Integrated urban water management for sustainable transition: innovation of functions or innovation of place? An explorative study on the evolution and innovation of urban water management practices in Denmark. PhD thesis. Aalborg University, Denmark.

Fryd, O. (2011). Planning for sustainable urban drainage systems. PhD Thesis. Danish Center for Forest, Landscape and Planning. University of Copenhagen. Denmark.

Fryd, O., Backhaus, A., Birch, H., Fratini, C.F., Ingvertsen, S.T., Jeppesen, J., Panduro, T.E., Roldin, M. and Jensen, M.B. (2013). Water sensitive urban design retrofits in Copenhagen: 40% to the sewer, 60% to the city. *Water Science and Technology*, 67, 1945–1952.

Garud, R. and Gehman, J. (2012). Metatheoretical perspectives on sustainability journeys: evolutionary, relational and durational. *Research Policy*, 41, 980–995.

Geels, F.W. (2014). Regime resistance against low-carbon transitions: introducing politics and power into the multi-level perspective. *Theory, Culture & Society*, 31(5), 21–40.

Geiryn, T.F. (1983). Boundary-Work and the demarcation of science from non-science: strains and interests in professional ideologies of scientists. *American Sociological Review*, 48(6), 781–795.

Graham, S. and Marvin, S. (2001). *Splintering Urbanism: Networked Infrastructures, Technological Motilities and the Urban Condition*. Routledge, London.

Healey, P. (2006). Relational complexity and the imaginative power of strategic spatial planning. *European Planning Studies*, 14(4), 525–546.

Hodson, M. and Marvin S. (2010). Can cities shape socio-technical transitions and how would we know if they were?. *Research Policy* 39, 477–485.

Hodson, M., Marvin, S. and Späth, P. (2016). Subnational, inter-scalar dynamics: the differentiated geographies of governing low carbon transitions – with examples from the UK. In H.G. Brauch, Ú.O. Spring, .J. Grin and J. Scheffran (eds), *Handbook on Sustainability Transition and Sustainable Peace Springer International Publishing: Switzerland.*

Jensen, J.S., Lauridsen E.H., Fratini, C.F. and Hoffmann, B. (2015a) Harbor bathing and the urban transition of water in Copenhagen: Junctions, mediators and urban navigations. *Environment and Planning A,* 47(3), 554–570.

Jensen, J.S., Fratini, C.F. and Cashmore, M.A. (2015b). Socio-technical systems as place-specific matters of concern: the role of urban governance in the transition of the wastewater system in Denmark. *Journal of Environmental Policy and Planning.* Published online 17 Aug. 2015.

Jørgensen, U. (2012). Mapping and navigating transitions – the multilevel perspective compared with arenas of development. *Research Policy*, 41, 996–1010.

Kaika, M. and Swyngedouw, E. (2013). The Urbanization of Nature: Great Promises, Impasse, and New Beginnings. In G. Bridge and S. Watson (eds), *The New Blackwell Companion to the City.* Chapter 9, pp 96-108. John Wiley & Sons Ltd, West Sussex, UK.

Kaika, M. and Swyngedouw, E. (2000). Fetishizing the modern city: the phantasmagoria of urban technological networks. *International Journal of Urban and Regional Research*, 24(1), 120–138.

KL (2012). Et robust Danmark – Hvordan vi sikrer Danmark mod oversvømmelser. Local government Denmark (KL).

Københavns Kommune (2012)Velkommen til Københavns første klimakvarter, Københavns Kommune. Available at: http://www.klimakvarter.dk/wp-content/2012/07/klimakvarter_samlet_publ_netversion.pdf [Accesses March 15th, 2017

Københavns Kommune (2013). Velkommen til Københavns første klimakvarter, Københavns Kommune.

Konkurrencestyreslen (2003). konkurrenceredegørelse 2003. Konkurrencestyrelsen.

Kvale, S. (2007). Doing interviews. In *The Sage Qualitative Research Kit.* Sage Publications, London.

Latour, B. (2005). *Reassembling the Social – An Introduction to Actor-Network-Theory.* Oxford University Press, Oxford.

Lindegaard, H. (2001). The debate on the sewerage system in Copenhagen from the 1840s to the 1930s. *Ambio* 30(4/5), 323–326.

Longhurst, N. (2015). Towards an 'alternative' geography of innovation: Alternative milieu, socio-cognitive protection and sustainability experimentation. *Environmental Innovation and Societal Transitions.* Available online: doi:10.1016/j.eist.2014.12.001

McFarlane, C. (2011) Assemblages and critical urbanism. *City* analysis of urban trends, culture, theory, policy, action. 15(2), 204–224.

Monstadt, J. (2009). Conceptualizing the political ecology of urban infrastructure: insights from technology and urban studies. *Environmental and Planning* A 41, 1924–1942.

Murphy, J.T. (2015). Human geography and socio-technical transition studies: promising intersections. *Environmental Innovation and Societal Transitions*17, pp 73–91.

Owen, S., Petts, J. and Bulkeley, H. (2006). Boundary work: knowledge, policy and the urban environment. *Environment and Planning C*, 24, 633–643.

Pierce, J., Martin, D.G., Murphy, J.T., 2011. Relational place-making: the networked politics of place. *Transactions of the Institute of British Geographers* 36(1), 54–70.

Raven, R., Schot, J. and Berkhout, F. (2012) Space and scale in socio-technical transitions. *Environmental Innovation and Societal Transitions*, 4, 63–78.

Regeringen (2003) Grøn markedsøkonomi – mere miljø for pengene. Regeringen.

Späth, P. and Rohracher, H. (2015). Conflicting strategies towards sustainable heating at an urban junction of heat infrastructure and building standards. *Energy Policy*, 78, 273–280.

Team Bede (2014). Picture of the Copenhagen Inner Harbour Bath Facility. Available at: https://www.flickr.com/photos/52754570@N04/with/14800829155/ [Accessed on March 15th 2017]

Truffer, B. and Coenen, L., (2012). Environmental innovation and sustainability transitions in regional studies. *Regional Studies*. 46(1), 1–21.

UN-HABITAT (United Nations Human Settlements Programme) (2012). State of the world's cities 2012/2013. *Prosperity of Cities. World Urban Forum Edition*. Nairobi, Kenya.

7 Village Communities and Social Innovation Policies in Seoul

Exploring the Urban Dimension of Grassroots Niches

Marc Wolfram

Introduction

Research on cities and socio-technical transitions has developed a strong focus on urban infrastructure systems, examining how they shape and are shaped by cities under conditions of global environmental change and economic destabilization (Guy et al. 2001; Guy et al. 2011; Monstadt 2009; Hodson and Marvin 2010; Bulkeley et al. 2011). This has shed light on why and how actors at various scales engage in new forms of governance arrangements and local experimentation in order to reconfigure urban energy, water, waste or transport systems (Berkhout et al. 2010; Bai et al. 2010; Coutard and Rutherford 2010; Hodson and Marvin 2012; Späth and Rohracher 2012; Hamann and April 2012; Castán Broto and Bulkeley 2013; Hodson et al. 2013; Moloney and Horne 2015). Nevertheless, other urban dimensions of socio-technical change and related experiments have so far remained largely unexplored.

In particular, studies of everyday practices as basic constituents of socio-technical systems (Shove and Walker 2010; Shove et al. 2012), as well as of grassroots innovations and niche formation (Seyfang and Smith 2007; Seyfang and Longhurst 2013) have implications for cities deriving from the ways in which citizens and local civil society actors become involved in the spatially-embedded reproduction of socio-technical regimes and/or creation of sustainability innovations (Bulkeley et al. 2014a; Baker and Mehmood 2015). Urban contexts enable and require the social and physical interconnection or 'bundling' (Shove et al. 2012) of diverse social practices that (de-) stabilize not only single systems, but 'multi-regime' configurations (Smith et al. 2010; Papachristos et al. 2013; Næss and Vogel 2012; Mizuguchi et al. 2015). At the same time, cities also provide 'protected spaces' that allow people to articulate and enact diverse 'alternative ontologies' and 'spatial imaginaries' of socio-technical change (Longhurst 2015), since they fundamentally enable the manifestation of diversity (Castells 1983; Fincher and Iveson 2008). Most importantly, cities draw on substantive policy capacities that directly affect their citizens across all life domains, including housing, green space, employment, consumption, education or culture, among others.

This range of local policies also implies approaches for enabling citizen participation in planning and decision-making, as well as for community support linked to a variety of purposes. Urban policies and related interaction forms thus have an immediate bearing on the constitution of social practices and related (multi-)regime configurations, as well as on association- and coalition-building processes for place-based socio-technical change, and may also be used strategically in this regard (Aylett 2013, 870; Cohen and Ilieva 2015; cf. de Wildt-Liesveld et al. 2015).

Complementary to recognizing cities as contested sites of multi-level 'low-carbon politics' (Bulkeley et al. 2014b; Moloney and Horne 2015), there is thus a need to account for the role cities (can) play locally in shaping civil society-driven sustainability innovations. Especially regarding place-making activities that mutually engage citizens, local authorities and businesses in the transformation of the diverse socio-technical systems embedded in the urban fabric, this role appears to be more influential than discussed so far. Therefore, this chapter takes up this perspective and explores how cities enable or constrain the emergence and formation of grassroots niches. In particular, it examines the implications for urban policy and governance and perspectives for a purposeful orientation of sustainability transitions. To start with, basic conditions for grassroots niche formation and their relation to urban contexts are deducted from research dealing with grassroots movements and their socio-technical transformation potential, and with spatially embedded social innovations. Second, these conditions are then explored empirically through the study of a highly pertinent urban case – the evolving approach for 'village community' governance in Seoul – accounting for their articulation, identifying critical issues that arise from implementation, and deriving new insights for theory and practice. Finally, the conceptual and empirical results obtained are discussed to provide responses to the above questions, and to conclude about implications for future research and policy.

Grassroots Niches in the Urban Context

The two research fields invoked here respectively deal with grassroots socio-technical niches, and with urban social innovations. They offer distinctive insights about enabling conditions for civil-society driven innovations and niche formation, as well as about the roles of urban place and urban policy in this process. To engage with these two fields, the concepts of 'niche' and 'strategic niche management' first need to be briefly expanded.

Strategic niche management (SNM) has been suggested as a crucial form of policy intervention to enable the creation of robust and influential niches (Kemp et al. 1998; Schot and Geels 2008). From an SNM perspective, niches are seen as 'protected spaces' for experimenting with alternative socio-technical configurations, liberated from the selection pressures of the regime (Smith and Raven 2012). Yet, niches are not spatial configurations but conceived as 'cosmopolitan' networks constituted of 'local initiatives' and 'trans-local' intermediaries that may span across scales (Geels and Deuten 2006). Niche formation is described as a process in which intermediaries distill lessons from initiatives and offer transferrable knowledge to new initiatives, who then reinterpret and apply it in their local contexts. This supports the consolidation of learnings and replication of successful practices, thereby increasing the influence of the niche on regime actors to adopt new solutions (Raven et al. 2008). The formation process is therefore sequenced into phases, beginning with isolated initiatives ('local phase'), to the first exchanges of experiences among initiatives ('inter-local phase'), and the increased aggregation of knowledge across initiatives ('trans-local phase'), towards the consolidation of a robust niche that coordinates local projects and exerts strong influence on the regime ('global phase') (Geels and Deuten 2006).

Grassroots Innovations and Grassroots Niches

Based on SNM, most analyses of niches dynamics have so far focused on market-oriented technological innovations featuring industry and state actors. However, a growing body of literature addresses sustainability innovations that are driven and implemented by civil society actors instead, dealing with issues such as energy, mobility, housing, food or complementary currencies. This perspective acknowledges the potentials and accomplishments of diverse types of community initiatives and grassroots movements regarding transformative change for sustainability articulated around alternative values and social practices (Smith 2006a; Smith 2006b; Seyfang and Smith 2007; Seyfang and Haxeltine 2012; Ornetzeder and Rohracher 2013; Seyfang and Longhurst 2013). It also identifies the particularities of these innovations in terms of their motives, constitution and development, and the policy requirements that derive from them.

In line with the assumptions of SNM, three basic conditions have been confirmed empirically that appear to shape the development path and diffusion prospects of grassroots niches: (1) the *expectations* of what an innovation will achieve need to be widely shared among niche members and stakeholders, as well as being specific and realistic (concrete and feasible targets); (2) *networking* is needed beyond members, not only to mediate expectations, but also to diversify the interests involved and thus broaden support for the innovation's objectives, and to obtain access to resource types required for implementation (knowledge, skills, human, organizational, institutional, technological and/ or financial); (3) *learning* should be experiential and occur in the wider social context of communities, organizations and institutions, thereby also changing actor preferences and practices (second-order learning). This highlights the particular importance of the intermediaries involved in enabling and facilitating the required communication, interactions and transfers (Bai et al. 2010; Seyfang and Haxeltine 2012; Davies 2012; Seyfang et al. 2014).

However, there are several particularities of grassroots niches, which demand specific attention. First of all, they are essentially *value-driven* and focused on *social needs*. Therefore, intrinsic benefits for the community in terms of needs fulfilment, identity, self-expression, recognition, belonging and/or aspirations of its members form the primary motive, rather than wider diffusion benefits (Smith and Seyfang 2013). Correspondingly, the risks and potentials of innovation are also assessed differently here, which points to specific needs in terms of 'protection': while radical experiments may become feasible more easily and rapidly (Aylett 2013), they also 'cannot afford to fail' with a view to the motivational damage caused (Heiskanen et al. 2015). Moreover, while working on similar topics, different grassroots initiatives may use different narratives underpinned by distinct ethical orientations that frame the structure and form of their actions and interactions, and affect their ability to form wider coalitions (Feola 2014).

Particular sensitivity is thus required to effectively support grassroots niches while avoiding stifling their motivation through attempts of management and control. Especially developing social competences and soft skills (e.g., conflict management, confidence building) of both members and intermediaries appears to be crucial for building trusted relations and helping narratives to converge. Furthermore, since the resource needs and assets of individual initiatives vary considerably (knowledge, skills, networks, human, financial, technology, etc.), more tailored backing that adjusts as initiatives mature is also needed (e.g., from social competence to project management skills). Likewise, instead of standardized guidance, grassroots require personal interaction to help the application of new knowledge in specific local contexts, and to enable the use of tacit knowledge (Seyfang and Haxeltine 2012; Seyfang et al. 2014). Furthermore, given their orientation at social needs instead of particular technologies or markets, grassroots tend to create innovations that address several socio-technical systems simultaneously (e.g., combining community gardens, rainwater harvesting and consumer cooperatives). This particular quality opens up multiple new pathways as it challenges various regimes and their interrelations (cf. Rydin et al. 2013), but it also questions a straightforward management approach focused on moving innovations from protected spaces into markets (Ornetzeder and Rohracher 2013, 866; Seyfang et al. 2014, 42). It rather points to the need for a deliberation process linked to grassroots innovations in order to define transformation strategies based on collective goals.

Despite these useful orientations for studying the specific dynamics and requirements of grassroots niches formation, two aspects are usually sidelined in analyses informed by SNM. On the one hand, while being sensitive to the implications of scale, there is very limited consideration of the potentially distinctive role of *place* (cf. Coenen and Truffer 2012; Maassen 2012) and in particular *urban* place. Based on the 'cosmopolitan' conception of niches, the initiatives examined usually include issue-driven *and* place-based innovations in urban or rural contexts, but do not discuss their differences (cf. Seyfang and Smith 2007; Seyfang and Haxeltine 2012; Seyfang et al. 2014).

Yet, various research perspectives on the UK Transition Towns movement and its diffusion have highlighted this issue, critically questioning the future wider impacts of these initiatives regarding their rural embedding (Brown et al. 2012; Mason and Whitehead 2012; Neal 2013; Atkinson and Viloria 2013): 'Cities, having a diversity of actors able to do the work of transition, provide the institutional thickness (Amin and Thrift, 1995; Amin et al., 2002) for this to happen, and might therefore be, long term, more fertile ground for a deeper transition involving systemic change than the smaller towns where [the Transition Town movement] currently flourishes' (North and Longhurst 2013, 1435). Hence, the formation of grassroots niches and the up-scaling and translation of their innovations could potentially benefit from the dense web of local institutions, personal relations and discourses available in cities (Taylor 2012; North and Longhurst 2013; cf. Boyer 2015, 32). Moreover, differences between places in terms of cultural frames, identity and consumption habits have been highlighted as critical to socio-technical transitions (Cooke and Rehfeld 2011; Mulugetta, Jackson, and van der Horst 2010). This equally points to distinctive transition dynamics *in cities* linked to the articulation of urban lifestyles, as well as to the concentration of artistic activity – regarding its potential to expose, question and modify place-related narratives (Stuiver et al. 2013). Last but not least, further spatial differentiation is also required *within* cities regarding the particular qualities of 'creative' milieus or 'alternative' neighborhood communities, as well as the conditions of periphery versus the urban center (Boyer 2015, 335).

On the other hand, and related to the question of place, subjects of analysis have so far been *existing and relatively successful* grassroots initiatives, regardeless of the preconditions of their emergence and endurance (Ornetzeder and Rohracher 2013, 866). The very definition of grassroots initiatives as "networks of activists and organizations generating novel bottom–up solutions for sustainable development" (Seyfang and Smith, 2007, 585) presupposes activist subjects, organizational structures and resource availabilities that are reflective of certain levels of civil society engagement and capacity. However, depending on the issue and the context, this may not be a given and should therefore in itself represents a basic concern for the formation of grassroots niches. As widely discussed in development studies, weaker civil society structures require to first enable the articulation of value orientations and social needs that may drive grassroots activity, and to simultaneously facilitate the association and organization of initiatives that could then become autonomous governance subjects (Eade 1997; OECD 2006; Ubels et al. 2010; UNDP 2011; Greijn et al. 2015). This draws attention to the shaping of grassroots niche formation pathways well before take-off or acceleration dynamics can occur, but also to the place-specific conditions of this.

Social Innovation and Empowerment in Cities

The second important research strand referred to here is more broadly concerned with the emergence and diffusion of social innovations while emphasizing the particular role of urban place in this. Social innovations may include a wide range of incremental or disruptive changes in social practices, including 'new (combinations of) ideas, models, rules, social relations and/ or products' (Avelino et al. 2014, 9). However, the core motive remains to solve problems of unmet social needs and to improve living conditions where state and market actors do not provide satisfactory solutions (Nicholls et al. 2012; Mulgan 2012; Moulaert et al. 2013). Regarding the potential for disruptive systemic change, increasing attention has been paid to social innovations *for sustainability* (Westley et al. 2011; Mieg and Töpfer 2013; Mehmood and Parra 2013). In this sense, the grassroots innovations discussed above represent a specific form of social innovation with a strong orientation at environmental and sustainability values.

Three conditions have been highlighted to nurture social innovation dynamics, all of which complement the findings regarding grassroots niches. First of all, social innovations are understood as *institutionally and spatially embedded social struggles*, thus also recognizing their correlation with urban agglomeration processes (Castells 1983; Moulaert et al. 2005). Their trajectories are seen to lead from the local emergence of alternative development discourses and practices (e.g., in households, neighborhoods and/or community initiatives), to the selective adoption of these alternatives by dominant regime actors, towards a reconfiguration of institutions, territories and urban governance arrangements. Urban place and place-based experimentation are therefore attributed a genuine potential for reshaping values, identities and governance relations (Friedmann 1992, 31; Moulaert et al. 2007, 200). Understanding place as a *social and physical construct* (Agnew 1987; Lefebvre 1992; Soja 1996) frames both the immediate experience of social needs and the means through which these can be addressed. Therefore, it is concrete urban settings such as streets, blocks, neighborhoods or districts that are identified here as the 'protected spaces' for experimenting with alternative forms of living and working that mediate between local livelihoods, global sustainability issues and prevailing institutions (Moulaert et al. 2010, 233; Baker and Mehmood 2015).

Second, active involvement and *empowerment* are underlined as a necessary condition. To obtain access to resources and acquire the capabilities needed for meeting their needs, civil society actors require deliberate and targeted forms of support. This may include material assistance (funding, space, tools), but even more importantly deals with knowledge, skills, social networks and organization, as well as surplus time, shared through direct interaction in various formats (e.g., participation in formal policy-making, training, mentoring) (Friedmann 1992, 57; Moulaert et al. 2005, 1976; 2013; MacCallum et al. 2009; Oliveira and Breda-Vázquez 2012). Individuals, organizations and communities thus need to be actively helped to engage, articulate needs, self-organize, improve their ability for co-creating solutions and acquire autonomy as a stakeholder. Whether such empowerment effectively enables stakeholders to develop a 'sense of meaning, competence and impact' remains decisive (Avelino 2009, 386).

Third, there is a corresponding requirement for a *redefinition of social roles* both within communities and governance structures, to enable the targeted satisfaction of social needs. At the community level, this revolves around modifying established roles, identities and practices that alter what people do and how they relate to each other in their everyday lives, considering, for example, new forms of collective action in initiatives, cooperatives or associations for diverse purposes (e.g., culture, education, health, energy). Within governance structures, this recognizes the need for more inclusive formal and informal networks, involving state, civil society and private actors, and the (re-)positioning of (new) intermediaries and/or hybrid agencies (Mulgan 2006; Mulugetta et al. 2010; Aylett 2013; Baker and Mehmood 2015). Given the dependence on trusted relations and in order to overcome the perceived or factual antagonism between civil society initiatives and corporate coalitions (state and private sector), intermediation provided by independent organizations and especially offered in proximity (Oliveira and Breda-Vázquez 2012), as well as individual mediation and leadership, for example, in the form of 'institutional entrepreneurs' (Westley et al. 2013), 'civic entrepreneurs' (Etzkowitz 2015), or 'transformative leaders' (Ardoin et al. 2015) have a key role to play.

Enabling Conditions for Urban Grassroots Niches

As the above discussion reflects, both fields offer complementary insights to understand and explore the role of cities in grassroots niche formation, and to discern options for intervention through policy and governance approaches. While the basic model of niche formation and its conditions suggested by SNM remains valid (formation phases, importance of shared expectations, networking and learning processes), significant extensions and specifications appear to be required when focusing on urban grassroots.

Most importantly, the preconditions for the very emergence of local initiatives have to be addressed. This shifts attention to actions for *empowerment*, and thus attributes a key role and responsibility for urban policy. To meet the specific requirements of value-driven grassroots initiatives, effective empowerment also has to develop sensitive methods based on proximity and personal interaction. Moreover, the 'protected spaces' required for experimentation are not only abstract entities here, but *concrete places embedded within urban contexts* that enable people to deeply engage with various manifestations of socio-technical change, while forming part of a dense web of social and physical relations. Urban social innovation thus equally deepens the concern for change in social relations: not only networking and relations with key stakeholders matter (in order to improve resource access and develop social and political capital), but also reconfiguring *roles and interactions at the community level* in support of alternative values and identities of place becomes important. Last but not least, the focus on urban place has implications in terms of the type and scope of expectations formulated (i.e., 'alternative urban futures', rather than alternative systems of provision), and consequently also regarding the range of regimes addressed and the possible delimitation(s) of niches. It equally involves a wider range of government agencies, policies, businesses and intermediaries, thus diversifying the sites and arenas where socio-technical change is negotiated.

In synthesis, the specific conditions for urban grassroots niche formation identified so far have been categorized by their principal targeted purpose (Table 1): civil society empowerment, reconfigured urban governance, reconfigured

Table 7.1 Conditions for urban grassroots niche formation and innovation diffusion

Purpose	*Conditions*
Civil society empowerment	• Protected spaces and places for free expression of alternative values are (made) available • Civil society actors are enabled to articulate social needs, and to associate and organize grassroots initiatives for meeting these needs • Development of social competences and soft skills within grassroots initiatives and intermediary organizations is aided • The specific resource needs of grassroots initiatives are supported, especially through direct interaction, and support is adjusted as initiatives mature
Reconfigured urban governance	• Direct involvement of grassroots initiatives in formal and informal governance structures is actively supported • Changes in governance modes contribute to developing social and political capital • Effective intermediaries (organizations, individuals) are positioned between grassroots initiatives, and between initiatives, authorities and businesses, especially articulated around proximity
Reconfigured urban place	• Grassroots initiatives reconfigure social roles and relations at the community level (identities, interaction, practices) • Grassroots initiatives experiment with innovations in concrete urban settings • Urban places are reframed discursively, reused culturally, and reshaped physically through grassroots experiments • Authorities and businesses become involved in place-based experimentation beyond empowerment (especially implementation, monitoring)
Multiple pathways	• Grassroots initiatives develop diverse integrated solutions, connecting multiple socio-technical systems • The diversity of grassroots innovation is recognized and supported as a value • Alternative options for grassroots niche formation of a different scope and scale are identified and deliberated among stakeholders

(*continued*)

Table 7.1 Conditions for urban grassroots niche formation and innovation diffusion (*continued*)

Purpose	Conditions
Shared expectations	• Support for grassroots initiatives is sensitive to their particular values, discourses and intrinsic benefits: value-driven development is safeguarded, control avoided • Collaborative actions are taken to develop shared expectations, both among grassroots initiatives and in the wider stakeholder arena • Integrated narratives of alternative urban futures become articulated • Expectations are translated into concrete tasks and feasible targets
Social learning	• Learning is experiential and supported through diverse formats and methods involving all key stakeholders, as well as intermediaries • Learnings from grassroots initiatives are aggregated and disseminated • Personal interaction is used to help initiatives adopt generic lessons

urban place, multiple pathways, shared expectations and social learning. These purposes and their supporting conditions are closely interrelated and provide an operational framework for analyzing grassroots niches formation in urban contexts, and the role of urban policy and governance in this.

Village Communities and Social Innovation Policies in Seoul: Case Study Approach and Methods

In order to obtain further insights about the role of cities in grassroots niche formation, and in particular their policy and governance implications, an exploratory case study has been carried out. Based on the set of categories deducted above, it analyzes the approach to urban community development and social innovation adopted in the city of Seoul since 2012. The case was selected because it represents an outstanding example of an attempt by a 'global' city to enable and foster urban grassroots innovations. As such, it forms a large-scale urban policy and governance experiment that offers valuable insights in terms of grassroots niche formation dynamics and emerging challenges related to the six purposes identified above. This 'critical case' approach serves primarily to generate new theory and practical knowledge for its application (Flyvbjerg 2006, 230; Donmoyer 2000), but also to validate existing theory (Patton 2002, 180; Yin 2009, 38). The patterns and processes observed are thus interpreted in terms of their implications for research and policy addressing cities and their influence on grassroots niche formation.

For data collection and analysis, a mix of quantitative and qualitative methods were employed. This included document analysis (websites, policy documents, research reports, grassroots publications), site visits and participant observation, mapping, as well as exploratory and semi-structured personal interviews with 23 selected individuals (I1–I23) that together provide for a balanced representation of all relevant stakeholders (Table 2). Basic data on those grassroots initiatives supported by the novel policy approach since 2012 were obtainable from a local agency (date of initiation, location, category, title, budget by category). For the calibration and validation of the final interpretations made, and in order to initiate a transdisciplinary dialogue on future requirements, results were also discussed in a focus group (FG) involving five key stakeholder representatives. These tasks were realized between October 2013 and April 2015.

Table 7.2 Representation of stakeholder groups in the interview sample (I) and focus group (FG)

Ref.	Affiliation	Stakeholder group	I	FG
I1	Seoul Green Trust	NGO (local)	X	
I2	Climate Change Center	NGO (local)	X	
I3	Urban Association	NGO (local)	X	
I4	Local Sustainability Alliance of Korea	NGO (national)	X	
I5	Greenfunds	NGO (national)	X	
I6	ICLEI Local Gov. for Sustainability, Korea	NGO (inter-/national)	X	
I7	Korea Climate Change & Environment Network	NGO (national)	X	
I8	Seoul Metropolitan Govmt., Climate Change Department	Local government	X	
I9	Seoul Metropolitan Govmt., Innovation Bureau, Social Innovation Division	Local government	X	
I10	Seoul Metropolitan Govmt., Innovation Bureau, Village Community Division	Local government	X	X
I11	Seoul Metropolitan Govmt., Innovation Bureau	Local government	X	
I12	Village community district network, Seodaemun-gu (Seoul)	Civil society		X

(continued)

Table 7.2 Representation of stakeholder groups in the interview sample (I) and focus group (FG) (*continued*)

Ref.	Affiliation	Stakeholder group	I	FG
I13	Sungmisan village community, Mapo-gu (Seoul)	Civil society	X	
I14	Consumer and housing cooperative, Yeongdeungpo-gu (Seoul)	Civil society	X	
I15	Multi-unit housing community, Songpa-gu (Seoul)	Civil society	X	
I16	Energy self-reliant village community, Dongjak-gu (Seoul)	Civil society	X	X
I17	Seoul Village Community Support Center	Intermediary	X	X
I18	Seoul Village Community Support Center, Training and Education Division	Intermediary	X	
I19	Village Community District Support Center, Dobong-gu (Seoul)	Intermediary	X	X
I20	Social Economy Support Center	Intermediary	X	
I21	Seoul Institute	Research	X	
I22	Korea Research Institute for Human Settlements (KRIHS)	Research	X	
I23	University of Seoul	Research	X	

Background: Village Communities in Seoul

Since 2011, a novel approach to urban community governance and social innovation has been developed and implemented in Seoul. Its stated primary objective is to 'grow and diversify village communities for achieving autonomy and improving democracy' (SMG 2012, 5262:1), and to achieve a status of maturity and self-organization of such communities by 2017 (Seoul Institute 2012). This new emphasis on active community development has its antecedents in local grassroots initiatives as well as in policy. Both draw on the spatial concept of 'village', which here refers to place-based, self-organizing citizen networks that are only loosely delimited by their socio-spatial identity, and pursue the fulfilment of local social needs (Yu 2010; Wi 2013; Jung and Nam 2014).

After South Korea became a democracy in 1987, local activists turned to community building in the early 1990s as a response to pressing social and ecological problems, thus filling gaps in policy and institutions. Citizen-driven initiatives that were emerging in different Seoul districts adopted the notion of 'village making', and a first practical guide for establishing 'ecological villages' within cities was produced in 1998 (KISS 1998; Green Korea United 1998). A particularly influential community has been 'Sungmisan village' – a Seoul neighborhood of 5,000 households today. Initiated in 1994, this community has since implemented a range of social innovations dealing with diverse social needs (e.g., cooperatives for child care, eco-consumption and housing, an alternative school, a community center, various restaurants and stores), but also fought fierce battles over the destruction of urban green spaces with local government in 2004 and 2010 (I13; I17; Yu 2010; Wi 2013).

Since the 1990s, grassroots community activities in Seoul thus offered important lessons regarding the potential of place-based collective action and problem solving. Yet, from 2007 policy also began embracing the concept of urban 'villages' – although with diverse objectives. Several national ministries subsidized 'villages', for example, for supporting economic growth (local enterprises), social welfare (housing quality) or environmental quality (green infrastructures) – without creating a coherent approach (Seoul Institute, 2012). At the local level, 'villages' were also supported in Seoul from 2009, focusing on management transparency and maintenance in the large apartment complexes that dominate the housing market (I19; I21; Park 2013).

By 2010, a certain shared understanding had therefore developed both in public discourse and policy regarding the *practices* involved in 'village community' development. Yet, the *objectives* pursued by both sides, continued to vary. At that point, it was essentially the political leadership provided by a new mayor (Park Won Soon) elected in October 2011 that triggered a redesign of the local policy approach to 'villages', linked to a political agenda emphasizing empowerment and social justice (I11; I17; SMG 2012; VCSC 2015).

Civil Society Empowerment

The novel approach actively aids citizens to form village communities that address self-defined needs. Proposals for community initiatives are collected twice a year and receive support if they are evaluated as showing high potential in terms of "necessity, public benefit, feasibility, durability, creativity, participation, resources, partnership, expected results" (Seoul Institute 2012). In 2014, the budget allocated to finance various forms of assistance for 487 initiatives was $7.6 million, that is, 0.4% of the city's total budget, which corresponds to an average of $16,000 per initiative.

A conceptual stage model has been adopted for specifying what type of support is needed and when, specifically targeting individual activists that provide the necessary leadership, motivation and endurance. The model assumes an initial 'seed stage' in which citizen collaboration for defining and prioritizing needs is aided through on-site trainings and joint seminars, for example. for collective decision-making, conflict management or option assessment. At the 'sprout stage', integration between various earlier activities into wider solutions is helped by trainings on management, organization or business planning skills. Finally, at the 'hope stage' communities' self-organizing capability for maintaining solutions and creating new ones is strengthened; for example, through evaluation skills and networking (Seoul Institute 2012; SMG 2013).

On this basis, a total of 1,709 new village communities have been formed in Seoul between 2012 and 2014, largely adding to the existing fabric of grassroots initiatives, and demand has been growing (from 757 proposals in 2012 to 1,810 in 2014). The support offered and its openness for bottom-up proposals have effectively enhanced urban 'protected spaces' for articulating social needs and expressing alternative values, including through art and cultural activity (Figure 7.1). In this sense, direct interaction has been decisive for building trust and enabling communities to adopt new knowledge, but also for the continuous adjustment of support structures (VCSC 2014; VCSC 2015).

Nevertheless, the empowerment approach has also met major contextual barriers. Most importantly, access to community support in Seoul has been constrained in practice due to factors that limit civil society engagement more generally: excessive working hours, minimum wages, extremely high real estate prices and resulting household fluctuations, but also the lack of open spaces for people to meet imply that especially younger generations and full-time employed men (can) hardly get involved, while the majority of activists are women who are more than 40 years old. In a context of rapid socio-demographic change and strong gender inequalities, this 'empowerment bias' has therefore led to criticism regarding the legitimacy, effectiveness and future reach of the new initiatives (I13–16; FG).

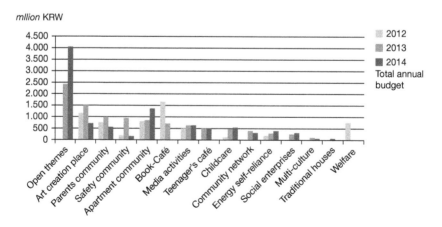

Figure 7.1 Budget evolution for new village community initiatives in Seoul Metropolitan Area 2012–2014 (Data: VCSC 2014)

Reconfigured Urban Governance

These community-level shifts have been accompanied by major changes in local institutions, articulating new relations between civil society and authorities, but also between positions within Seoul Metropolitan Government (SMG – the local authority responsible for the Seoul metropolitan area and its 25 autonomous districts). These changes have been driven and coordinated by the 'Seoul Innovation Bureau' (SIB), newly created in 2011 and directly adjoined to the Mayor's office. Its staff has been recruited mainly from civil society and private organizations, while senior government officials occupy half of the lead positions. This set-up has been highly instrumental in mediating between new ideas and established routines within SMG and building ownership of the new policies in the sectoral departments (I11; I17).

The main terms and principles of village community development, however, have been elaborated by a task force of grassroots activists, convoked by the SIB between 2011 and 2012. On this basis, a regulation for village community development was adopted in 2013 that lays down a basic governance system. A newly created intermediary, the 'Village Community Support Center' (VCSC), is responsible for managing the development process, including proposal selection, support organization and coordination with SMG departments. While being funded by SMG, the VCSC is fully independent in its operations and has been staffed with non-officials only. It is therefore crucial to bridging the gaps between civil society and local government in terms of trust, skills and language (FG: Seoul Institute 2012; SMG 2012).

The system for village community governance co-created in Seoul is still in evolution. Especially the intermediation capacity has been steadily expanded, diversified and brought into proximity. In 2013, 25 district-level (Gu) support entities have been established, and further ones are currently being built up for the 423 administrative 'neighborhoods' (Dong). While differing considerably in size and set-up (authority- vs. civil-society-led, formal organizations vs. loose networks, Gu- vs. Dong-scale), these new entities gradually take over direct community interaction tasks from the central VCSC, which in turn focuses more on managing relations with SMG departments (I9; I10; I17; FG) (Figure 7.2). These shifts thus respond both to the need to facilitate knowledge transfers through trusted personal relations, and to deal with the heritage of an authoritarian administrative culture.

Reconfigured Urban Place

Since the 1960s, rapid urban growth and top-down policy making and planning in Seoul have shaped an urban environment characterized by socio-spatial segregation and poor ecological performance. While 70% of Seoul's inhabitants live in densely packed high-rise apartment blocks, clearly differentiated by their socio-economic status, 30% occupy older low-rise areas that mostly remain in a state of constant precariousness, between development

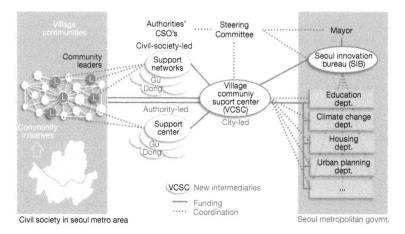

Figure 7.2 Governance structure for village community development in
Seoul 2015. (Source: Author.)

pressures and neglect. Both area types massively lack green and open spaces,
as well as compliance with basic green building standards. Household fluctuation is thus very high (17.4% p.a.), weakening social ties and cohesion within
and between neighborhoods, and undermining citizens' sense of ownership
and responsibility for the built environment and green spaces (Gelézeau 2003;
Park 2013; SMG 2013).

The village initiatives directly respond to these conditions, trying to shape
the qualities of place according to community needs and priorities. An important starting point is often the creation of open spaces located within the neighborhood to enable interaction and proximity association (e.g., community
center, book café, youth club). Communities then experiment with alternative
solutions that link substantive concerns (e.g., education, care, healthy food,
green space, clean energy) with physical change (public space, buildings, technologies, etc.), institutional change (social enterprises, networks, cooperatives,
etc.), cultural activities (festivals, sports, cooking, etc.), and manifestations of
difference in discourse, design and aesthetics (FG; VCSC 2014; VCSC 2015).

Social roles, identities and relations within communities have also gradually become modified. Value orientations concerning existing systems of
provision have been made more transparent, leading to both new coalitions
but also to new conflicts within neighborhoods about shaping everyday life
practices and environments. Differences have surfaced between 'progressive'
and 'conservative' residents, and between new 'professional' and pre-existing
'laymen' initiatives, leading to struggles over representation. Therefore, the
communication, conflict management and leadership skills of activists and
intermediaries are continuously challenged to enable a constructive dialogue
and realize shared projects (I13–16; FG).

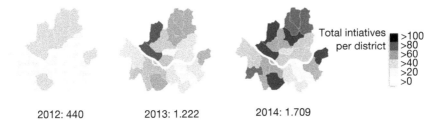

Figure 7.3 Spatial distribution of new village community initiatives in Seoul
Metropolitan Area 2012–2014 (Data: VCSC 2014)

Although many of the initiatives have remained confined at the neighborhood scale so far, the collective discourses they create are opening up new
perspectives for reframing place-making activities in individual districts,
as well as in the wider metropolitan context. Existing differences and similarities between districts have shaped a particular spatial pattern of village
activity that reflects their socio-economic and cultural profile (income, education, immigrants), urban environments (density, typology, green space),
institutional thickness (presence of NGOs and intermediaries), and political
leadership (Figure 7.3). As common concerns emerge among villages within
districts or in the wider metropolitan area, they are likely to create strong
political leverage for the translation of social innovations into policy at the
corresponding scale (I17; I19; FG; VCSC 2014; VCSC 2015).

Multiple Pathways

Seoul has seen the emergence of a plethora of neighborhood initiatives since
2012. This diversity has been an explicit objective from the start, but became
further prioritized in the course of implementation. Initially, proposals were
required to respond to a set of issues defined by the VCSC, mainly revolving
around education, culture, cohesion and community spaces. From 2013, however, new open categories were introduced ("open themes") and budget allocations for these have grown considerably (cf. Figure 7.1), thus allowing for a
much wider range of initiatives. In addition, 'open' initiatives mostly address
a wider spectrum of innovations that integrate existing and new activities,
rather than single issues (e.g., community center, child care, community garden, co-housing). Moreover, villages increasingly articulate economic (social
enterprises) and environmental sustainability concerns (e.g., renewables, sustainable products and services, sharing, green education) in conjunction with
social ones. This place-based accumulation and integration of social innovations also occurs in those initiatives that had been initiated with a clear sectoral focus. for example, on education or energy (FG; VCSC 2014; VCSC 2015).

The emerging diversity of social innovations poses a major challenge
for intermediaries and policy that is increasingly recognized. To synergize

and enhance impacts beyond individual villages, initiatives may become framed and connected in many ways and for diverse objectives, targeting established policy fields (e.g., housing, welfare, parks) and/or rather new and integrated action domains operating at different scales (e.g., 'green roofs', 'energy cooperatives'). More differentiated monitoring is needed to obtain deeper insights into the reality on the ground and identify options for niche formation. Yet, the categories used by the VCSC so far do not provide for this (I17; I19). A first clustering attempt has been based on the funding category of 'energy self-reliant' villages, now reassigned directly to the department of climate change for coordination. However, communities demand further 'trans-local' networks for mutual learning and to obtain leverage on policy change; for example, related to green education, social enterprises and various urban regeneration issues (FG; I16). Moreover, a more diffuse translation effect of the diverse community activities on sectoral policies transpires in the fact that an increasing share of the total village community budget is actually covered by *other* SMG departments (2012: 1/4; 2014: 2/3) (SMG 2014).

Shared Expectations

Based on the early interactions between authorities (SIB) and grassroots activists for the formulation of village community policies, the main goal of creating autonomous communities for meeting social needs and the instruments used for achieving this have gained wide support by stakeholders. However, expectations have generally remained far from concrete, with the 'self-organizing ecosystem' targeted for 2017 and 'happiness' as its outcome being the most explicit formulations used (FG; Seoul Institute 2012). In turn, individual communities must set and agree on specific targets for their villages, both locally and with the VCSC, as part of the support procedure (cf. evaluation criteria in section 7.8 above). In the absence of concrete (sectoral) policy objectives that would impose stronger management directions, this approach has provided latitude to define community targets, thus allowing for diversity in terms of values, activities and maturity, while also preserving their particular motivations (I12-16; FG; VCSC 2015).

However, the gap between an overarching vision and concrete project targets has not been clearly addressed yet. Communication and exchange across communities are insufficient to elucidate and juxtapose narratives, expectations and visions developing independently in the villages. Targeted analysis is missing to identify commonalities and differences regarding both the village scale and wider urban change. Nevertheless, the SIB recently highlighted new priorities focusing on 'urban regeneration' and the 'social economy', thus partly addressing motives and solutions emerging from the villages (cf. Ah 2015). The urban planning department has also started to amend ongoing regeneration initiatives (mainly focused on the built environment) with a view to community development. But pressures are growing both from communities and from within the administration (SIB, climate change) to modify a wider array of planning and development practices, for example, regarding housing, energy, as well as green infrastructure (FG; I16).

Social Learning

The approach adopted in Seoul embraces experiential learning for community building and social innovation. Drawing on the stage model, it addresses changing community requirements, and largely through personal interaction. Learning-by-doing has equally guided the establishment and evolution of the governance framework, which reflects various instances of policy learning resulting from interactions between villages, SIB and VCSC regarding. for example, support forms, organizational structures or intermediary organization (I9–11; I18).

Nevertheless, the noted lack of concrete expectations beyond individual villages appears to constrain wider social learning and therefore inter- and trans-local niche formation dynamics. Initiatives are evaluated individually and ex-post as part of the reporting process, mainly using quantitative criteria defined by the SIB and VCSC. Since this rather bureaucratic approach has not enabled the reflexivity that communities desired, they have demanded more autonomy for evaluation, including the use of interactive methods and qualitative criteria. But evaluation efforts remained focused on defining and promoting 'good practice' cases to facilitate peer-to-peer knowledge transfers – and to demonstrate policy effectiveness. Only recently, the concern for understanding has finally outweighed the (political) pressures on the SIB and VCSC for justifying expenditures, resulting in a proposal for a 'self-evaluation' approach (I12–16; I19).

Discussion and Conclusions

The results obtained through the exploratory case study allow us to connect and expand the available research findings discussed above. Four overarching and interdependent aspects appear to be crucial here for further conceptualizing the role of cities in grassroots niche formation, and to specify key implications for urban policy and governance: (1) holistic socio-technical innovation, (2) dis-/empowerment through urban policy, (3) community governance experiments, and (4) urban niche/regime interactions.

First of all, cities shape the *holistic character* of the practices and visions developed by 'local initiatives'. Unlike issue-driven social innovations, urban grassroots initiatives respond to conditions of place and the diverse frictions these cause with subjective life-worlds, needs and values. In doing so, they necessarily create and accumulate *integrated solutions* that offer various types of benefits and synergies (social, economic, environmental). This is clearly illustrated by the villages in Seoul, driven by the deficits accumulated over the past decades, and creating diverse embedded solutions that combine aspects of, for example, education, care, welfare, cohesion, housing, green space, energy and consumption.

It is through this integration that urban grassroots innovations stand out and may be able to provide key contributions for sustainability transitions. By connecting the search for a better quality of life to the 'multidimensional design problem' of sustainable urban development (cf. McCormick et al. 2013, 5), they produce holistic visions of sustainable places – rather than reproducing dominant discourses of socio-technical change and the biases they imply (e.g., "low-carbon transitions", "decoupling", "resource security" – cf. Hodson and Marvin 2014). Moreover, change itself becomes framed as actively shaped by engaged communities experimenting with alternative values and lifestyles, and less as driven by critical landscape pressures (e.g., 'climate change'). These features provide a crucial motivational advantage that offers opportunities for broader involvement and coalitions in cities, as observed in the Seoul case.

However, holistic innovations also imply a dilemma in terms of niche formation because of their *socio-technical polyvalence*. Urban grassroots initiatives may in principle exert pressures on multiple systems of provision (e.g., 'roof gardens': energy, water, construction, green infrastructure, food), but their integrated approach is at odds with the differentiated institutional logic of the regimes concerned. This requires distinct forms of intermediation that are able to connect individual initiatives with various niche formation processes, and to link between actors of different regimes for translating integrated niche innovations.

Thus, cities also turn out to be in a crucial position for purposefully exploiting potentials for integrated multi-regime transformations that arise from urban grassroots. This demands new forms of collective action to develop differentiated insights regarding the narratives and practices of local initiatives. Not only 'aggregating learnings', but also identifying and assessing different incipient options for niche formation and translation become important. Here the case points to the vital need for social innovation monitoring and intermediation at city scale. This would allow making emerging visions for urban development explicit, and transparently deliberating what kind of support is needed, for what phase, and at which scale in order to strengthen collectively desired socio-technical niches. It would equally inform any actions taken to transcend the socio-spatial (auto-) delimitation of initiatives ('inter-local' phase), and to facilitate the involvement of external actors and resources ('trans-local' to 'global' phases).

Second, due to their *policy capacity and institutional thickness*, empowerment is enabled and implemented differently in cities, thus meeting a crucial prerequisite for generating social innovation. Cities and their local stakeholders draw on substantial experiences with a variety of policies and instruments for community empowerment and participation. These provide a rich collective repertoire of resources, knowledge and social capital, deployed for different policy objectives – partly including social innovation. This repertoire also allows them to selectively reinforce the basic 'protection' offered by urban areas for articulating difference and diversity by granting additional freedoms (e.g., spaces, subsidies, rights, nonintervention).

In Seoul, the available experiences with various types of urban 'village' policies formed a critical precondition for designing and implementing the novel approach. Yet, given the burden of the prevailing authoritarian administrative culture, it was also important to build up new empowerment capacity. Urban proximity and institutional thickness thereby strongly bene-fitted the approach considering, for example, the close ties between the VCSC and Sungmisan, the proliferation and spatial differentiation of support enti-ties, or the 'stage model'. These conditions have had clear implications for enabling trusted relations, tacit knowledge transfer, and sensitivity for deal-ing with individual community requirements. In addition, discourses of place ('village making') have already provided initiatives with a sense of meaning and impact at the neighborhood scale, but this may become further reinforced to the degree that they also induce changes at the district and/or metropolitan scale.

Nevertheless, the Seoul case equally reflects that this urban amplification of empowerment simultaneously applies to its genuinely inseparable effect of *disempowerment* (Avelino 2009; Avelino and Rotmans 2011). Because empow-erment always implies selectivity, social conflicts between diverse groups have become (re-)accentuated in the villages along divides of value orientations, age, gender and/or socio-economic status. Such conflicts require not only distinct forms of mediation, but also an in-depth assessment of who 'wins' and who 'loses'. Thus, gearing urban empowerment capacity towards grass-roots innovation also calls for the development of strategies and methods that enable effective socio-political feedback and learning, thereby ensuring the transparency and legitimacy of the choices made.

Third, cities give rise to *experimentation with community governance* that incorporates the above particularities in terms of holistic socio-technical inno-vation and place-based interaction. Such experimentation does not necessar-ily follow the same pattern as 'governance experiments' for socio-technical change that have been recognized as a response to growing pressures on the political economy and ecology of cities (Bai et al. 2010; Castán Broto and Bulkeley 2013; Bulkeley et al. 2014b; Moloney and Horne 2015). Rather than global environmental change, in Seoul it is the *social problems* related to wel-fare, inclusion, education and care issues that are heavily concentrated in the city that motivate the creation of novel community governance arrangements. Correspondingly, the key actors also diverge, involving organizations and individuals from the local public and civil society sector that are engaged with place-based social change, and therefore tend to share a basic set of concerns and expectations.

As demonstrated in the Seoul context, this opens up special possibilities for institutional hybridization, institutional entrepreneurship, intermediation and participation that reconfigure relations between all stakeholders, as well as within local government (levels, domains), gradually reframing what is gov-erned, how and by whom (e.g., "community-led, municipality supported" – Aylett 2013, 867; cf. Etzkowitz 2015). Therefore, community governance experimentation may also prepare and enable more fundamental shifts in governmentality that modify the way in which social practices, urban policies and business interests clash or converge in reshaping socio-technical system configurations (cf. Appadurai 2001; Bulkeley et al. 2014b). It thus provides a distinct and potentially powerful leverage for sustainability transitions, firmly rooted in urban contexts.

The characteristics of such experimentation are revealing of the political project that governs a city's approach to 'social innovation', 'community empowerment' or 'devolution' – especially considering the widespread use of an 'empowerment' rhetoric to legitimize neoliberal urban development agendas (Lawless and Pearson 2012; Bacqué and Biewener 2013; Lawson and Kearns 2014; Rich and Stoker 2014; Fabian and Samson 2015). In Seoul, it has been the increasing openness of the approach for bottom-up initiatives in any domain that has so far disabled such criticisms. Yet, the same openness also implied high political risk and created strong justification pressures, thereby constraining the required social and political learning process. This points to a critical policy dilemma for community-oriented governance experiments in that they (necessarily) tend to question the institutions that have enabled them.

Fourth, taken together these urban characteristics have clear implications for (conceptualizing) processes of grassroots niche formation and the forging of transition pathways. As discussed above, cities strongly condition the emergence and practices of place-based grassroots innovations, as well as the interaction and learning processes that may contribute to niche formation. However, within contexts of high institutional thickness, these processes co-evolve with the regimes they confront *from the outset*. This spatial and temporal conflation of niche formation and regime structuration in cities enables a continuous translation of innovations into various regimes simultaneously. It thus allows grassroots innovators and regime actors to build mutual trust and achieve legitimization for modifications in practices, regulations and technology through collective experience (urban place), cognitive changes (e.g., neighborhoods reframed as 'villages') and knowledge transfer (e.g., understanding community needs) (cf. Murphy 2015).

As described for Seoul, the novel discourse of social justice in neighborhoods jointly developed by SIB and grassroots activists has paved the way for direct translations into sectoral policies (welfare, education, care and energy) but is also affecting incumbent agendas in urban planning and infrastructure development regarding, for example, community development, building retrofitting and green spaces. Therefore, while creating pressures for simultaneous change in various sectoral regimes, urban conditions appear to favor incremental 'transformation' or 'reconfiguration' pathways rather than radical 'substitution' (cf. Geels and Schot 2007). This provides for a distinctive influence of cities on the formation, selection and translation of grassroots niche innovations in terms of the regime(s) addressed and the transition dynamics created.

In sum, the four aspects highlighted above underline the relevance of a focus on cities and their role in shaping grassroots niches, while offering new directions for future research and policy. Key issues are thus the potential for and management of holistic socio-technical innovations, the use and development of urban empowerment capacities, the design of novel community-oriented urban governance modes, and the dynamics of urban niche/regime interactions.

References

Agnew, J. A. 1987. *Place and politics the geographical mediation of state and society.* London: Routledge.

Ah, S. J. 2015. Village is innovation. Conference presentation at the ADeKo Forum 2015 "Shaping urban transitions towards sustainability," May 28, Seoul.

Amin, A., Thrift, N., 1995. Institutional issues for the European regions: from markets and plans to socioeconomics and powers of association. Econ. Soc. 24, 41–66. doi:10.1080/03085149500000002.

Amin, A., Thrift, N., 2002. Cities: reimagining the urban. Polity Press, Cambridge.

Appadurai, A. 2001. Deep democracy: urban governmentality and the horizon of politics. *Environment and Urbanization* 13: 23–43. doi:10.1177/095624780101300203.

Ardoin, N. M., R. K. Gould, E. Kelsey, and P. Fielding-Singh. 2015. Collaborative and transformational leadership in the environmental realm. *Journal of Environmental Policy & Planning* 17: 360–380. doi:10.1080/1523908X.2014.954075.

Atkinson, A., and J. Viloria. 2013. Readjusting to reality 2: Transition? *City* 17: 1–26. doi:10.1080/13604813.2013.827843.

Avelino, F. 2009. Empowerment and the challenge of applying transition management to ongoing projects. *Policy Science* 42: 369–390.

Avelino, F., and J. Rotmans. 2011. A dynamic conceptualization of power for sustainability research. *Journal of Cleaner Production* 19: 796–804. doi:10.1016/j.jclepro.2010.11.012.

Avelino, F., J. M. Wittmayer, A. Haxeltine, R. Kemp, T. O'Riordan, P. M. Weaver, D. Loorbach, and J. Rotmans. 2014. Game Changers and Transformative Social Innovation. The Case of the Economic Crisis and the New Economy. TRANSIT working paper. EU SSH.2013.3.2-1 Grant agreement no: 613169. TRANSIT.

Aylett, A. 2013. Networked urban climate governance: neighborhood-scale residential solar energy systems and the example of Solarize Portland. *Environment and Planning C: Government and Policy* 31: 858–875. doi:10.1068/c11304.

Bacqué, M.-H., and C. Biewener. 2013. Different manifestations of the concept of empowerment: the politics of urban renewal in the United States and the United Kingdom. *International Journal of Urban and Regional Research* 37: 2198–2213. doi:10.1111/j.1468-2427.2012.01169.x.

Bai, X., B. Roberts, and J. Chen. 2010. Urban sustainability experiments in Asia: patterns and pathways. *Environmental Science & Policy* 13: 312–325. doi:10.1016/j.envsci.2010.03.011.

Baker, S., and A. Mehmood. 2015. Social innovation and the governance of sustainable places. *Local Environment* 20: 321–334. doi:10.1080/13549839.2013.842964.

Berkhout, F., G. Verbong, A. J. Wieczorek, R. Raven, L. Lebel, and X. Bai. 2010. Sustainability experiments in Asia: innovations shaping alternative development pathways? *Environmental Science & Policy* 13: 261–271. doi:10.1016/j.envsci.2010.03.010.

Boyer, R. H. W. 2015. Grassroots innovation for urban sustainability: comparing the diffusion pathways of three ecovillage projects. *Environment and Planning A* 47: 320–337. doi:10.1068/a140250p.

Brown, G., P. Kraftl, J. Pickerill, and C. Upton. 2012. Holding the future together: towards a theorisation of the spaces and times of transition. *Environment and Planning A* 44: 1607–1623. doi:10.1068/a44608.

Bulkeley, H., V. Castán Broto, M. Hodson, and S. Marvin, ed. 2011. *Cities and Low Carbon Transitions*. New York: Routledge.

Bulkeley, H., V. Castán Broto, and A. Maassen. 2014a. Low-carbon transitions and the reconfiguration of urban infrastructure. *Urban Studies* 51: 1471–1486. doi:10.1177/0042098013500089.

Bulkeley, H., V. Castán Broto, and G. Edwards. 2014b. *An Urban Politics of Climate Change: Experimentation and the Governing of Socio-Technical Transitions*. London; New York: Routledge.

Castán Broto, V., and H. Bulkeley. 2013. A survey of urban climate change experiments in 100 cities. *Global Environmental Change* 23: 92–102. doi:10.1016/j. gloenvcha.2012.07.005.

Castells, M. 1983. *The City and the Grassroots: A Cross-Cultural Theory of Urban Social Movements*. California Series in Urban Development. Berkeley, CA: University of California Press.

Coenen, L., and B. Truffer. 2012. Places and spaces of sustainability transitions: geographical contributions to an emerging research and policy field. *European Planning Studies* 20: 367–374. doi:10.1080/09654313.2012.651802.

Cohen, N., and R. T. Ilieva. 2015. Transitioning the food system: a strategic practice management approach for cities. *Environmental Innovation and Societal Transitions* 17: 199–217. doi:10.1016/j.eist.2015.01.003.

Cooke, P., Rehfeld, D. 2011. Path Dependence and New Paths in Regional Evolution: In Search of the Role of Culture. *Eur. Plan. Stud.* 19, 1909–1929. doi:10.1080/096 54313.2011.618685.

Coutard, O., and J. Rutherford. 2010. Energy transition and city–region planning: understanding the spatial politics of systemic change. *Technology Analysis & Strategic Management* 22: 711–727. doi:10.1080/09537325.2010.496284.

Davies, A. 2012. *Enterprising Communities: Grassroots Sustainability Innovations*. Advances in Ecopolitics 9. Bingley, UK: Emerald.

Donmoyer, R. 2000. Generalizability and the single case study. In *Case Study Method: Key Issues, Key Texts*, ed. R. Gomm, M. Hammersley, and P. Foster, 45–68. London: Sage.

Eade, D. 1997. *Capacity-Building: An Approach to People-Centred Development*. Development Guidelines. Oxford: Humanities Press International.

Etzkowitz, H. 2015. Making a humanities town: knowledge-infused clusters, civic entrepreneurship and civil society in local innovation systems. *Triple Helix* 2: 1. doi:10.1186/s40604-014-0012-z.

Fabian, L., and K. Samson. 2015. Claiming participation – a comparative analysis of DIY urbanism in Denmark. *Journal of Urbanism: International Research on Placemaking and Urban Sustainability*: 1–19. doi:10.1080/17549175.2015.1056207.

Feola, G., 2014. Narratives of grassroots innovations: a comparison of voluntary simplicity and the transition movement in Italy. *Int. J. Innov. Sustain. Dev.* 8, 250–269. doi:10.1504/IJISD.2014.066612.

Fincher, R., and K. Iveson. 2008. *Planning and Diversity in the City: Redistribution, Recognition and Encounter*. Houndmills/New York: Palgrave Macmillan.

Flyvbjerg, B. 2006. Five misunderstandings about case-study research. *Qualitative Inquiry* 12: 219–245. doi:10.1177/1077800405284363.

Friedmann, J. 1992. *Empowerment: The Politics of Alternative Development*. Cambridge, MA: Blackwell.

Geels, F., and J. J. Deuten. 2006. Local and global dynamics in technological development: a socio-cognitive perspective on knowledge flows and lessons from reinforced concrete. *Science and Public Policy* 33: 265–275. doi:10.3152/147154306781778984.

Geels, F., and J. Schot. 2007. Typology of sociotechnical transition pathways. *Research Policy* 36: 399–417. doi:10.1016/j.respol.2007.01.003.

Gelézeau, V. 2003. *Séoul, ville géante, cités radieuses*. Collection Asie Orientale. Paris: CNRS éditions.

Green Korea United. 1998. 생태마을 지침서 *(Eco village guidance)*. Seoul: Green Korea United.

Greijn, H., V. Hauck, A. Land, and J. Ubels, ed. 2015. *Capacity Development Beyond Aid*. The Hague: SNV Netherlands Development Organisation; European Centre for Development Policy Management (ECDPM).

Guy, S., S. Marvin, and T. Moss, ed. 2001. *Urban Infrastructure in Transition: Networks, Buildings, Plans*. London; Sterling, VA: Earthscan Publication.

Guy, S., S. Marvin, W. Medd, and T. Moss, ed. 2011. *Shaping Urban Infrastructures: Intermediaries and the Governance of Socio-Technical Networks*. London; Washington, DC: Earthscan.

Hamann, R., and K. April. 2012. On the role and capabilities of collaborative intermediary organisations in urban sustainability transitions. *Journal of Cleaner Production* 50: 12–21. doi:10.1016/j.jclepro.2012.11.017.

Heiskanen, E., M. Jalas, J. Rinkinen, and P. Tainio. 2015. The local community as a "low-carbon lab": Promises and perils. *Environmental Innovation and Societal Transitions* 14: 149–164. doi:10.1016/j.eist.2014.08.001.

Hodson, M., and S. Marvin. 2010. Can cities shape socio-technical transitions and how would we know if they were? *Research Policy* 39: 477–485. doi:10.1016/j.respol.2010.01.020.

Hodson, M., and S. Marvin. 2012. Mediating low-carbon urban transitions? Forms of organization, knowledge and action. *European Planning Studies* 20: 421–439. doi:10.1080/09654313.2012.651804.

Hodson, M., and S. Marvin. 2014. *After Sustainable Cities?* New York: Routledge.

Hodson, M., S. Marvin, and H. Bulkeley. 2013. The intermediary organisation of low carbon cities: a comparative analysis of transitions in greater London and greater Manchester. *Urban Studies* 50: 1403–1422. doi:10.1177/0042098013480967.

Jung, W. Y., and H. B. Nam. 2014. 한국새마을운동의 전개과정과 방향 (A study on the development process of the Saemaeul Movement). *AKPAH* 34: 272–302.

Kemp, R., J. Schot, and R. Hoogma. 1998. Regime shifts to sustainability through processes of niche formation: The approach of strategic niche management. *Technology Analysis & Strategic Management* 10: 175–198. doi:10.1080/09537329808524310.

KISS. 1998. 무주군 진도리 생태마을 기본계획 *(Muju-Gun Jindo-ri eco village basic plan)*. Seoul: Korea Institute for Sustainable Society.

Lawless, P., and S. Pearson. 2012. Outcomes from community engagement in urban regeneration: evidence from England's New Deal for Communities programme. *Planning Theory & Practice* 13: 509–527. doi:10.1080/14649357.2012.728003.

Lawson, L., and A. Kearns. 2014. Rethinking the purpose of community empowerment in neighbourhood regeneration: The need for policy clarity. *Local Economy* 29: 65–81. doi:10.1177/0269094213519307.

Lefebvre, H. 1992. *The Production of Space*. Malden, MA: Blackwell.

Longhurst, N. 2015. Towards an "alternative" geography of innovation: Alternative milieu, socio-cognitive protection and sustainability experimentation. *Environmental Innovation and Societal Transitions*. doi:10.1016/j.eist.2014.12.001.

Maassen, A. 2012. Heterogeneity of lock-in and the role of strategic technological interventions in urban infrastructural transformations. *European Planning Studies* 20: 441–460. doi:10.1080/09654313.2012.651807.

MacCallum, D., F. Moulaert, J. Hillier, and S. Vicari Haddock, ed. 2009. *Social Innovation and Territorial Development*. Farnham; Burlington: Ashgate.

Mason, K., and M. Whitehead. 2012. Transition urbanism and the contested politics of ethical place making. *Antipode* 44: 493–516. doi:10.1111/j.1467-8330.2010.00868.x.

McCormick, K., S. Anderberg, L. Coenen, and L. Neij. 2013. Advancing sustainable urban transformation. *Journal of Cleaner Production* 50: 1–11. doi:10.1016/j.jclepro.2013.01.003.

Mehmood, A., and C. Parra. 2013. Social innovation in an unsustainable world. In *The International Handbook on Social Innovation Collective Action, Social Learning and Transdisciplinary Research*, ed. F. Moulaert, D. MacCallum, A. Mehmood, and A. Hamdouch. Cheltenham: Edward Elgar.

Mieg, H. A., and K. Töpfer, ed. 2013. *Institutional and Social Innovation for Sustainable Urban Development*. London; New York: Routledge.

Mizuguchi, S., K. Ohta, P. J. Beers, M. Yamaguchi, T. Nishimura, D. A. Loorbach, J. Shiroyama, J. Wittmayer, et al. 2015. Interactions among multiple niche-innovations and multi-regimes: the case of the "Welfare Mall" in Higashiomi. In *Theory and Practice of Urban Sustainability Transitions*. New York: Springer.

Moloney, S., and R. Horne. 2015. Low carbon urban transitioning: from local experimentation to urban transformation? *Sustainability* 7: 2437–2453. doi:10.3390/su7032437.

Monstadt, J. 2009. Conceptualizing the political ecology of urban infrastructures: insights from technology and urban studies. *Environment and Planning A* 41: 1924–1942. doi:10.1068/a4145.

Moulaert, F., F. Martinelli, E. Swyngedouw, and S. González. 2005. Towards alternative model(s) of local innovation. *Urban Studies* 42: 1969–1990. doi:10.1080/00420980500279893.

Moulaert, F., F. Martinelli, S. Gonzalez, and E. Swyngedouw. 2007. Introduction: social innovation and governance in European cities: urban development between path dependency and radical innovation. *European Urban and Regional Studies* 14: 195–209. doi:10.1177/0969776407077737.

Moulaert, F., E. Swyngedouw, F. Martinelli, and S. González, ed. 2010. *Can Neighbourhoods Save the City?: Community Development and Social Innovation*. London: Routledge.

Moulaert, F., D. MacCallum, and J. Hillier. 2013. Social innovation: intuition, precept, concept, theory and practice. In *The International Handbook on Social Innovation Collective Action, Social Learning and Transdisciplinary Research*, ed. F. Moulaert, D. MacCallum, A. Mehmood, and A. Hamdouch, 13–24. Cheltenham: Edward Elgar.

Mulgan, G. 2006. The process of social innovation. *Innovations: Technology, Governance, Globalization* 1: 145–162. doi:10.1162/itgg.2006.1.2.145.

Mulgan, G. 2012. The theoretical foundations of social innovation. In *Social Innovation: Blurring Boundaries to Reconfigure Markets*, ed. A. Nicholls and A. Murdock, 33–65. Basingstoke: Palgrave Macmillan.

Mulugetta, Y., T. Jackson, and D. van der Horst. 2010. Carbon reduction at community scale. *Energy Policy* 38: 7541–7545. doi:10.1016/j.enpol.2010.05.050.

Murphy, J. T. 2015. Human geography and socio-technical transition studies: Promising intersections. *Environmental Innovation and Societal Transitions* 17: 73–91. doi:10.1016/j.eist.2015.03.002.

Næss, P., and N. Vogel. 2012. Sustainable urban development and the multi-level transition perspective. *Environmental Innovation and Societal Transitions* 4: 36–50. doi:10.1016/j.eist.2012.07.001.

Neal, S. 2013. Transition culture: Politics, localities and ruralities. *Journal of Rural Studies* 32: 60–69. doi:10.1016/j.jrurstud.2013.04.001.

Nicholls, A., A. Murdock, A. Nicholls, and A. Murdock, ed. 2012. The nature of social innovation. In *Social Innovation: Blurring Boundaries to Reconfigure Markets*, 1–30. Basingstoke: Palgrave Macmillan.

North, P., and N. Longhurst. 2013. Grassroots Localisation? The scalar potential of and limits of the "transition" approach to climate change and resource constraint. *Urban Studies* 50: 1423–1438. doi:10.1177/0042098013480966.

OECD. 2006. *The Challenge of Capacity Development. Working towards Good Practice*. DAC Guidelines and Reference Series. Paris: Organization of Economic Co-operation and Development.

Oliveira, C., and I. Breda-Vázquez. 2012. Creativity and social innovation: What can urban policies learn from sectoral experiences? *International Journal of Urban and Regional Research* 36: 522–538. doi:10.1111/j.1468-2427.2011.01024.x.

Ornetzeder, M., and H. Rohracher. 2013. Of solar collectors, wind power, and car sharing: Comparing and understanding successful cases of grassroots innovations. *Global Environmental Change* 23: 856–867. doi:10.1016/j.gloenvcha.2012.12.007.

Papachristos, G., A. Sofianos, and E. Adamides. 2013. System interactions in socio-technical transitions: Extending the multi-level perspective. *Environmental Innovation and Societal Transitions* 7: 53–69. doi:10.1016/j.eist.2013.03.002.

Park, C. 2013. 아파트 _ 공적 냉소와 사적 정b이 지배하는 사회 *(Apartment - A society dominated by public cynicism and private passion)*. Seoul: Mati.

Patton, M. Q. 2002. *Qualitative Research and Evaluation Methods*. 3d ed. Thousand Oaks, CA: Sage Publications.

Raven, R. P. J. M., E. Heiskanen, R. Lovio, M. Hodson, and B. Brohmann. 2008. The contribution of local experiments and negotiation processes to field-level learning in emerging (niche) technologies: meta-analysis of 27 new energy projects in Europe. *Bulletin of Science, Technology & Society* 28: 464–477. doi:10.1177/0270467608317523.

Rich, M. J., and R. P. Stoker. 2014. *Collaborative Governance for Urban Revitalization: Lessons from Empowerment Zones*. New York: Cornell University Press.

Rydin, Y., C. Turcu, S. Guy, and P. Austin. 2013. Mapping the coevolution of urban energy systems: pathways of change. *Environment and Planning A* 45: 634–649. doi:10.1068/a45199.

Schot, J., and F. W. Geels. 2008. Strategic niche management and sustainable innovation journeys: theory, findings, research agenda, and policy. *Technology Analysis & Strategic Management* 20: 537–554. doi:10.1080/09537320802292651.

Seoul Institute. 2012. 서울특별시 마을공동체 기본 계획 *(Seoul village community basic plan)*. Seoul: Seoul Institute.

Seyfang, G., and A. Haxeltine. 2012. Growing grassroots innovations: exploring the role of community-based initiatives in governing sustainable energy transitions. *Environment and Planning C: Government and Policy* 30: 381–400. doi:10.1068/c10222.

Seyfang, G., and N. Longhurst. 2013. Desperately seeking niches: Grassroots innovations and niche development in the community currency field. *Global Environmental Change* 23: 881–891. doi:10.1016/j.gloenvcha.2013.02.007.

Seyfang, G., and A. Smith. 2007. Grassroots innovations for sustainable development: Towards a new research and policy agenda. *Environmental Politics* 16: 584–603. doi:10.1080/09644010701419121.

Seyfang, G., S. Hielscher, T. Hargreaves, M. Martiskainen, and A. Smith. 2014. A grassroots sustainable energy niche? Reflections on community energy in the UK. *Environmental Innovation and Societal Transitions* 13: 21–44. doi:10.1016/j.eist.2014.04.004.

Shove, E., and G. Walker. 2010. Governing transitions in the sustainability of everyday life. *Research Policy* 39: 471–476. doi:10.1016/j.respol.2010.01.019.

Shove, E., M. Pantzar, and M. Watson. 2012. *The Dynamics of Social Practice: Everyday Life and How It Changes*. Los Angeles: Sage.

SMG. 2012. 서울특별시 마을공동체 만들기 지원 등에 관한 조례 *(Building a village community in Seoul)*. Vol. 5262. Seoul: Seoul Metropolitan Government.

SMG. 2013. 2013 희망서울 시정운영계획 (2013 Hee-mang Seoul plan). Seoul: Seoul Metropolitan Government.

SMG. 2014. 서울마을이야기 *(Seoul Maeul story)*. Seoul: Seoul Metropolitan Government.

Smith, A. 2006a. Green niches in sustainable development: the case of organic food in the United Kingdom. *Environment and Planning C: Government and Policy* 24: 439–458. doi:10.1068/c0514j.

Smith, A. 2006b. Niche-based approaches to sustainable development: radical activists versus strategic managers. In *Reflexive Governance for Sustainable Development*, ed. J.-P. Voß, D. Bauknecht, and R. Kemp, 313–336. Cheltenham: Edward Elgar.

Smith, A., and R. Raven. 2012. What is protective space? Reconsidering niches in transitions to sustainability. *Research Policy* 41: 1025–1036. doi:10.1016/j.respol.2011.12.012.

Smith, A., and G. Seyfang. 2013. Constructing grassroots innovations for sustainability. *Global Environmental Change* 23: 827–829. doi:10.1016/j.gloenvcha.2013.07.003.

Smith, A., J.-P. Voß, and J. Grin. 2010. Innovation studies and sustainability transitions: The allure of the multi-level perspective and its challenges. *Research Policy* 39: 435–448. doi:10.1016/j.respol.2010.01.023.

Soja, E. W. 1996. *Thirdspace: Journeys to Los Angeles and Other Real-and-Imagined Places*. Cambridge, MA: Blackwell.

Späth, P., and H. Rohracher. 2012. Local demonstrations for global transitions – dynamics across governance levels fostering socio-technical regime change towards sustainability. *European Planning Studies* 20: 461–479. doi:10.1080/09654313.2012.651800.

Stuiver, M., Jagt, P. van der, Erven, E. van, Hoving, I. 2013. The potentials of art to involve citizens in regional transitions: exploring a site-specific performance in Haarzuilens, the Netherlands. Community Dev. J. 48, 298–312. doi:10.1093/cdj/bss022.

Taylor, P. J. 2012. Transition towns and world cities: towards green networks of cities. *Local Environment* 17: 495–508. doi:10.1080/13549839.2012.678310.

Ubels, J., N.-A. Acquaye-Baddoo, and A. Fowler, ed. 2010. *Capacity Development in Practice*. London; Washington, DC: Earthscan.

UNDP. 2011. *Practitioner's Guide: Capacity Development for Environmental Sustainability*. New York: United Nations Development Program.

VCSC. 2014. 마을은 형성되고 있는가 *(Is Maeul forming?)*. Seoul: Village Community Support Center.

VCSC. 2015. 서울시 마을공동체 지원사업 성과연구보고서 *(Seoul Village Community Outcome Report)*. 2014-03-002. Seoul: Village Community Support Center.

Westley, F., P. Olsson, C. Folke, T. Homer-Dixon, H. Vredenburg, D. Loorbach, J. Thompson, M. Nilsson, Lambin E, Sendzimir J, Banerjee B, Galaz V, van der Leeuw S. 2011. Tipping Toward Sustainability: Emerging Pathways of Transformation. *AMBIO* 40: 762–780. doi:10.1007/s13280-011-0186-9.

Westley, F. R., O. Tjornbo, L. Schultz, P. Olsson, C. Folke, B. Crona, and Ö. Bodin. 2013. A theory of transformative agency in linked social-ecological systems. *Ecology and Society* 18. doi:10.5751/ES-05072-180327.

de Wildt-Liesveld, R., J. F. G. Bunders, and B. J. Regeer. 2015. Governance strategies to enhance the adaptive capacity of niche experiments. *Environmental Innovation and Societal Transitions*. doi:10.1016/j.eist.2015.04.001.

Wi, S. N. 2013. 마을하기, 성미산마을의 역사와 생각 *(The history and thinking of Seongmisan village)*. Seoul: Korea Research Institute for Human Settlements (KRIHS).

Yin, R. K. 2009. *Case Study Research: Design and Methods*. Los Angeles: Sage Publications.

Yu, C. B. 2010. 우린 마을에서 논다 *(We have fun in the village)*. Seoul: Another Culture.

8   Spatialising Urban Sustainability Transitions

Eco-cities, Multilevel Perspectives and the Political Ecology of Scale in the Bohai Rim, China

Federico Caprotti and Nichola Harmer

Introduction

In this chapter, we critically engage with a range of literatures on urban sustainability transitions by focusing on the ways in which transitional strategies focused on eco-city projects become fluid across different geographical scales of enquiry. To do this, we explore a multilevel case study, focused on the Sino-Singapore Tianjin Eco-City (hereafter 'Tianjin eco-city'), an eco-city mega-project which has been under construction since 2007, and which is presented by the Chinese government as the flagship project within a wider context of central government support for approximately 200 transitional eco-city projects planned in China at the time of writing. In this context, Tianjin eco-city can be seen an experimental niche which may, if successful, effect change across other eco-city projects and across the country (Caprotti, 2015). The eco-city itself can be seen as a bounded socio-technical experiment that, nonetheless, displays close links to the wider region. In this light, we situate Tianjin eco-city within its regional context in terms of China's Bohai Rim: an area of rapid urban growth and significant environmental despoliation. This region contains key urban centres such as Beijing and Tianjin and houses nearly a fifth of the country's population, being one of the major targets of rural-urban migratory flows. Indeed, the Bohai Rim is increasingly being called the 'Bohai Megalopolis'. It is also one of the most environmentally affected regions in China. Overlaid on this is a wider, national and international landscape of urban experimentation with eco-cities and associated transition strategies as a way of informing national, regional and urban sustainability policies.

This chapter's theoretical contribution is in establishing a dialogue between literatures on low-carbon sustainability transitions, urban socio-technical experiments, and the political ecology of scale. Specifically, we argue for the need to spatialise studies of transition, by focusing on cities as sites *and* places within interlinked spatial scales. This implies a refocusing of studies of urban governance for sustainability transitions on the city as a geographically specific entity, which nonetheless emerges from a complex set of multilevel and multi-scalar interactions. In the chapter's final section, we draw some conclusions both in terms of the implications of spatialising studies of transition, and for conceptualising urban governance for sustainability.

Eco-Cities and Transition

In recent years, eco-cities have received increasing attention as sites with the potential for innovative responses to global environmental change (Hodson and Marvin, 2010b; Bulkeley and Castán Broto 2012). Definitions of what an eco-city is are generally vague, but initiatives range from interventions in specific sectors, to retrofitting existing urban areas, to the creation of eco-suburbs or entire cities (Joss, 2010; Bulkeley and Castán Broto, 2012). The latter are predominantly being built in Asia and the Gulf, with a 2011 census showing 14 out of 24 new builds being constructed in Asia (Joss, Cowley and Tomozeiu, 2013). The scale and number of these entities arguably represent an "eco-revolution" (Wu, 2012: 169), and an attempt to envision and shape new cities as a way of building solutions to the challenges of climate change (and other issues) by building new, ecologically sensitive urban areas. Some of the largest new-build eco-cities being built to date include Masdar eco-city, in Abu Dhabi (Caprotti and Romanowicz, 2013; Cugurullo, 2013a, 2013b); the Sino-Singapore Tianjin Eco-City, China (Baeumler et al., 2009); and Songdo City in South Korea (Shwayri, 2013).

A central feature of many of these eco-city initiatives is a focus on advances in green technology (Joss, Cowley and Tomozeiu, 2013; Joss and Molella, 2013; Shwayri, 2013), with cities seen as models with potential for replication elsewhere (Cheng and Hu, 2010). Eco-cities play an important role in knowledge transfer and exchange both domestically and internationally (Wu, 2012; Joss, Cowley and Tomozeiu, 2013), and in terms of enabling a transitional, greener economy to emerge in and around these experimental urban sites (Bailey and Caprotti, 2014; Caprotti & Cowley 2016). Eco-city developments are often characterised by the involvement of a wide range of public and private actors (Joss, Cowley and Tomozeiu, 2013), and based on transnational links and partnerships (Baeumler et al., 2009; de Jong, Wang and Yu, 2013; Hult, 2013; Joss and Molella, 2013). The close involvement of state and corporate actors, and the existence of international networks of knowledge and policymaking in the delivery of eco-city visions and plans can be seen as an example of (a) the complex process of imagining and delivering emergent urban and economic futures (Caprotti, 2012a); and (b) the workings of a wider landscape of state-led neoliberal environmental and economic management, with the state focusing on the market as a source of solutions to environmental and societal problems (Caprotti, 2012b). Consequently, eco-cities can be seen as bounded experimental sites which, crucially, also need to be viewed through a multifaceted lens which considers these sites' characteristics in terms of enabling technological innovations, and wider (economic, political, governance-related) transitional contexts.

In recent years, and in parallel with the emergence of an ever-wider number of experimental eco-city projects worldwide, there has been a significant critique of eco-cities specifically, and eco-urbanism more generally. Recent scholarship has questioned the extent to which eco-cities may in actuality be expected to fully address the wider social and environmental aspects of sustainability. The potential environmental impacts of developments on local ecology (Chang and Sheppard, 2013), such as sensitive wetlands (Cheng and Hu, 2010), or in respect of CO_2 emissions created through the construction of these cities, has been queried (Joss and Molella, 2013). The provision made for existing local land users, for whom the cost of proposed affordable housing may be prohibitive, has also been problematised (Cheng and Hu, 2010). Writing of the now stalled Dongtan development, Chang and Sheppard (2013) argue that the emphasis was on housing for elites rather than wider social provision. The World Bank echoed similar concerns in a report on preliminary plans for the Sino-Singapore Tianjin Eco-City (Baeumler et al., 2009). By 2014, several authors had highlighted the fact that many eco-cities seemed to be targeted squarely at a market of wealthy potential residents (Rapoport, 2014), thus raising fears of the construction of "eco-enclaves" (Hodson and Marvin, 2010b). Similar critiques have been raised with regard to specific, high-profile and "flagship" eco-cities such as Tianjin eco-city (Caprotti, 2014a, 2014b; Caprotti, Springer and Harmer, 2015), Masdar eco-city (Caprotti and Romanowicz, 2013; Cugurullo, 2013a, 2013b) and Songdo (Yigitcanlar and Lee, 2013).

Another key criticism levelled at eco-cities has been the challenge of encouraging participation, both in the planning process and in the continued governance of eco-cities after construction (Cheng and Hu, 2010; de Jong, Wang and Yu, 2013; Joss, Cowley and Tomozeiu, 2013; Joss and Molella, 2013). Furthermore, the literature has critiqued the extent to which sustainable solutions developed within an eco-city may be able to diffuse regionally to help address environmental problems associated with industrialisation (Joss and Molella, 2013), problematising the relationship between new-build eco-cities and their contribution towards social justice on a wider spatial scale (Hodson and Marvin, 2010a). This is apparent even although eco-cities have also been seen as part of concerted wider efforts to tackle environmental problems on a regional scale, as is the case in China (Cooke, 2011).

Notwithstanding the multiple critiques that can (and should) be made of current eco-urban projects, there are nonetheless some key aspects of current eco-city developments which make them interesting from both an empirical and a theoretical perspective. Empirically, eco-cities are increasingly seen as envelopes for new and innovative policy and market mechanisms (from incentive systems to new and experimental policies to sustainability indicator and evaluation frameworks) that are aimed at *transition*, broadly understood. This means that eco-cities can be analysed in light of their experimental nature, as built environments engineered as innovative spaces where specific transitional pathways and target points can potentially be achieved. In this sense, they can be understood as bounded socio-technical experiments (Brown and Vergragt, 2008). In the case of Masdar eco-city, for example, the city's function is part of a wider initiative to foster economic diversification away from Abu Dhabi's largely hydrocarbon-based economy and towards a high-tech, renewables-based knowledge economy for the future.

Therefore, in theoretical terms eco-cities are of interest because they represent a *spatial* intervention aimed at influencing wider, national and (in some cases) international contexts. Thus, eco-cities (and especially the large, new-build examples mentioned above) can be investigated in light of the state's spatial and territorial strategies aimed at harnessing and controlling processes of economic-environmental and technological change. It is at this juncture (between the materiality of eco-city projects and the spatial transitions strategies that they represent) that eco-cities can be analysed through the lens of a multilevel standpoint that adequately accounts for the spatial element in transition strategies.

Spatialising the Multilevel Perspective on Socio-Technical Transitions

In order to investigate the link between eco-cities and transition strategies, it is fitting to use the multilevel perspective (MLP) on socio-technical transitions (Geels and Schot, 2010). The MLP can be used to explore relations between urban sustainability transitions in the Tianjin area, China, which in itself is set within the wider region of the Bohai Rim. The MLP is an appropriate theoretical and interpretive lens because it provides a framework for analysing sustainability transitions (such as eco-city developments) as technical innovations, which develop in relation to their wider social context (Geels and Schot, 2010). This allows us to explore Tianjin eco-city as more than the delivery of a technical accomplishment in eco-engineering and also to examine its genesis and manifestation within the context of wider social, political and economic processes taking place at varying spatial scales in China.

Geels and Schot (2010) define transitions as "shifts from one socio-technical system to another", leading to the adoption within a society of new technologies and practices (Geels and Schot, 2010: 11). These are large-scale changes, usually occurring over several decades (Geels and Schot, 2010), which are brought about by the "multi-dimensional *interactions* between industry, technology, markets, policy, culture and civil society" (Geels, 2012: 472). The MLP posits three levels: the niche, regime and landscape (Geels and Schot, 2010). Niches are usually small and unstable social networks attempting to innovate; regimes are larger and more established networks, which include markets and infrastructures, legislation, practices and norms; landscapes are wider social structures that cannot be influenced in the short term. As Geels and Schot explain, "niches provide the locus for the generation of radical novelties (variation) but the selection and broader diffusion of these novelties depends on alignments with regime and landscape levels" (2010: 19). Because regimes are fairly stable, the types of socio-technical systems they support are hard to change unless disruptions within a regime or pressure from the external landscape open up "windows of opportunity" (ibid.: 21). This may allow "niches", or "experimental projects" to develop in protective spaces and to diffuse into the mainstream in the form of transition (ibid.: 22). This is not a linear process but involves interactions within and among the three levels and an acceptance of both structure and agency in the creation of sustainable transitions (ibid.). It is important to note that whereas MLP-based approaches deploy the analytical levels of "niche", "regime" and "landscape", these are not generally understood in the MLP literature as strictly *scalar* or *spatial* levels. Rather, they are defined in more abstract and non-spatial terms.

One of the key aims of this chapter is to show how, through our analysis of the Tianjin eco-city case, the MLP can be effectively spatialised by adequately considering the spatial-geographical context in which transition strategies take place. This has been the concern of recent critical research on the so-called political ecology of scale, which seeks to understand and explain uneven urban development in its geographical specificity (Swyngedouw and Heynen, 2003). As we detail below, Tianjin may be understood as a niche innovation, brought about through landscape level pressures in the form of global and regional environmental challenges, particularly climate change, as well as regime-level disruptions caused by China's recent rapid economic development and urbanisation. This emphasis responds to recent critiques of the MLP that have focused on a lack of consideration of space and geographical scale in analyses of transition. It is widely acknowledged, for example, that there are spatial dimensions to processes of socio-technical change, and that leaving space out of the MLP means that important spatial perspectives, such as transitions in the Global South, are effectively ignored (Hodson and Marvin, 2010a; Lawhon and Murphy, 2012). It is clear that, as will be shown in the case of Tianjin eco-city, the regime and niche levels can be seen as spatially nested. The eco-city itself becomes, then, a spatially specific, bounded and yet porous (in policy, economic and other terms) "container" of socio-technical niches. Niches which develop and are successful within the spatial context of the eco-city can then be seen to potentially influence the wider regime level, identified in the case discussed below with the wider Bohai Rim, and eventually the wider Chinese national urban landscape.

In addition to the utility of spatialising the various levels within the MLP, a spatial dimension to the MLP can be useful in that, as some scholars have pointed out, this would enable studies of transition to pay closer attention to the role of politics and power in transitions strategies (Lawhon and Murphy, 2012; Truffer and Coenen, 2012) – a point which is clearly of importance in the context of those eco-city mega-projects, such as Masdar and Tianjin eco-cities, which exist in non-democratic contexts. This will enable scholars using the MLP to provide a fuller account of (a) unequal power relations, (b) how power influences discourse and knowledge creation on sustainability, and (c) exclusions of the public from participation and input into the planning and development of sustainability transitions strategies (Lawhon and Murphy, 2012). A more spatially nuanced, regional focus can thus help to provide a more spatially engaged exploration of how and where transitions occur, and particularly "the role of cities and regions as strategic sites and actors to promote or even manage sustainability transitions" (Truffer and Coenen, 2012: 13). This, in turn, enables an understanding of how niches and innovations at the urban level can influence wider spatial contexts on a national scale, allowing for analysis of how "the wider network configurations within which territorial transitions dynamics are embedded, and the institutional environments and arrangements particular to those territories, come to shape transition processes" (Coenen, Benneworth and Truffer, 2012: 969).

There are a wide variety of critiques of the MLP and associated approaches in the current literature (Smith, Voß and Grin, 2010; Coenen, Benneworth and Truffer, 2012; Lawhon and Murphy, 2012; Truffer and Coenen, 2012). Most of these critiques are sympathetic to the broader project of studying and understanding the processes of change and transition. Several critiques have focused not on the spatial aspects of transition, but on other aspects, such as the fact that many studies of innovation rooted in the MLP overemphasise the role of technology at the expense of social and political contexts, and in many cases exhibit a bias towards elite actors whilst ignoring the agency and perspectives of more grassroots actors and networks (Lawhon and Murphy, 2012). All these additional critiques are clearly relevant to the case of transitions-focused eco-city projects, rooted as they are in elite policy, urban planning and engineering networks, marketed to wealthy potential "consumers" of new and "green" urban environments, and massively focused on technological innovations as the central motifs on which the eco-city label is based. While cognisant of these critical aspects of transitional eco-city projects, the rest of this chapter focuses more closely on the need to consider transitional eco-cities through a spatialised MLP. Focusing on the case of Tianjin eco-city provides an example of transition in an emerging economy; pays attention to the involvement of elite actors (state and corporate, international, national and regional); and attends to how discourses and material elements of change may work at different spatial scales to inscribe a particular technology-focused definition of transition.

There are several further challenges to the application of the MLP framework in the case of Tianjin eco-city. First, as raised by Karanikolas et al. (forthcoming) in relation to transitions in agriculture, is the definition of a regime where the focus of the analysis is a broad sector and, in the case of an eco-city, one which potentially embraces multiple regimes. Second, the MLP suggests that niche innovations are usually bottom-up processes: Geels describes "radical alternatives" being put forward by "pioneers, entrepreneurs, social movements and relative outsiders (to the existing regime)" (2012: 472). However, the Tianjin project is to a large extent state-supported, although it also involves significant corporate stakeholders (especially in real estate, engineering and urban planning consultancy roles) in delivering innovations in the city. However, this concern perhaps emphasises actor affiliation over the scale and experimental nature of the endeavour. In this context, Geels (2012) gives the example of the military (a state-affiliated actor) as a protected niche where innovation may occur, and Hodson and Marvin (2010b) have noted how eco-city projects have tended to be led by corporations and governments.

The MLP has been used to look at socio-technical transitions within cities, although this has often been within established major world cities (Hodson and Marvin, 2010a) rather than new-build creations such as Tianjin. This difference is significant, as the lack of an existing polity within a new-build complicates the question posed by Hodson and Marvin of "who is doing this and who is claiming to speak on behalf of these cities?" (2010a: 481). Finally, some authors have raised the issue of whether it is possible and useful to study transitions as they happen. Most of the literature on socio-technical transitions has, indeed, focused on historical case studies as ways of ascertaining and assessing processes and determinants of change over specific timescales. Geels and Schot (2010), for example, emphasise the importance of relying on historical examples. They argue that "studies of future transitions cannot be tested as of yet" and "studies of present or on-going transitions are also limited, because they cannot cover entire transitions from beginning to end" (Geels and Schot, 2010: 15). However a recent study of "emerging transitions" in European agriculture (Sutherland et al., 2015) suggests the utility of examining ongoing transitions such as we explore in the case of Tianjin. Furthermore, we would argue that "endpoints" to transition are useful analytical points, but that studying specific processes as they happen (as in the case of Tianjin eco-city) is fruitful in identifying and bringing to light processes of transition *as they happen*. This may be a messier and more complex story than normally desired, but transitions are rarely simple or linear (Bailey and Wilson, 2009).

Space and Socio-Technical Transitions: Tianjin Eco-City as an Urban Niche

The Sino-Singapore Tianjin Eco-City is a new city being built on a former salt marsh near Tianjin's cargo and cruise port. At the time of writing, the eco-city is an enormous construction project, with an initial Start-Up Area (SUA) largely completed: this comprises blocks of (partly occupied) residential accommodation, some shops, and wide multi-lane avenues and pedestrian and cycle paths. The eco-city is a government-backed project, and it is also an international joint venture between the governments of China and Singapore. As such, it is truly a city which is "too big to fail", as it is a key showcase for China-Singapore collaboration and cooperation. It involves significant levels of investment not only in terms of capital, but also with regard to political goodwill and the sharing of planning and technical knowledge between the planning and policy elites in both countries. The city is an experimental urban zone, in the sense that it represents an attempt to build a cleaner, greener city focused on a viable and sustainable green economic basis (Caprotti, 2015). As such, Tianjin eco-city is also an area of experimental policy interventions focused on the development of green industry and service sectors in and around the city, and also on attracting white-collar, knowledge-economy professionals to the city.

In transitional terms, the city is in itself an experimental site for technologies, innovations and ways of performing urban life (from the use of micro renewables such as solar-powered lighting to vacuum-based, centralised waste collection systems to the citywide water recycling and purification system imported from Singapore). These innovations can be tested within the experimental envelope of the eco-city, and eventually spread to other urban areas in China (and perhaps abroad) (Yu, 2014). This points to the spatial and scalar components of the transitional strategies focused on the eco-city. The following focuses on the ways in which the eco-city is being envisioned and constructed in transitional terms, by placing the project within a scalar and spatial framework that is sensitive to analytical approaches based in the MLP *and* to the need to territorialise and spatialise transitions.

Tianjin Eco-City: The International Scale

Tianjin eco-city's status as an international joint venture means that the broadest geographical scale at which the eco-city project can be considered is the international one (Pow and Neo, 2014). The eco-city was international from its beginnings: the city's master plan was chosen following a call, in 2007, by the central government for the development of a flagship eco-city to be planned and built in China. Tianjin municipality's proposed eco-city was a clear winner of the call due to its ability to leverage high-level international partners. Tianjin eco-city was announced as the government's favoured project for eco-city development in late 2007. The involvement of Singapore as a key state partner was crucial to this development. Singapore was a highly favoured partner in part because of the history of China–Singapore collaboration on industrial and urban projects in China from the 1990s: these projects helped develop industrial and business parks in key Chinese urban areas, and enabled the Chinese government to see Singapore as a capable partner in ensuring efficient and high-tech project development and completion in the case of Tianjin eco-city.

Tianjin eco-city's international nature is also evident in its organizational structure. The institution responsible for developing the eco-city project is the Sino-Singapore Tianjin Eco-City Investment and Development Corporation (SSTECIDC). The SSTECIDC is a corporation which therefore functions not just as a managing entity, but is also the interface between the Chinese and Singaporean governments. The corporation is jointly owned and operated by a Chinese consortium led by the Tianjin TEDA Investment Holding Company, and a Singaporean consortium headed by the Keppel Corporation, a real estate development business. The organizational and planning system through which the city is being developed is highly hierarchical, reflecting the tiers of stakeholders active in the project. At the highest level, one meeting takes place between the premiers of the two countries every year. Other meetings, involving government ministers working on national construction projects, occur once or twice per annum. At the level of the municipality itself, meetings take place several times a year between local city officials from Tianjin municipality and executives from private corporations such as development firms. At this level, the specific outputs of these organizational meetings include reports and plans for specific buildings within the eco-city. It can be argued that these organizational levels are the mechanisms through which attempts to enable niches in the eco-city project are promoted.

Another aspect of the international scale which was important in the selection of Tianjin eco-city by the Chinese government was its location within the Tianjin Binhai New Area (TBNA) Special Economic Zone (SEZ). The TBNA is managed by the Tianjin Economic-Technological Development Area (TEDA), which was the first state-sponsored techno-logical development zone in northern China (TEDA, 2010). The TEDA is a successful transitional economic zone, as is the TBNA. The latter was formed in 2006 as part of the Chinese government's strategy to promote economic development in transitional, experimental zones where industrial reforms could be tested (Ministry of Finance and the State Administration of Taxation, 2006). A series of economic incentives, including corporate income tax incentives for high-tech firms, were deployed to stimulate indus-trial and commercial development in the TBNA. The SEZ's economy devel-oped rapidly, reaching a growth rate of 24% per annum in 2009, more than double China's overall GDP growth rate. This growth rate is reflected in the economic performance of Tianjin's metropolitan area, where the economy grew at an average of 16% in 1999–2009 (SSTECIDC, 2010). Thus, whereas Tianjin eco-city can be placed within an international scale which features bilateral China-Singapore relations, it can also be spatially situated within the wider industrial transitional zones of TEDA and the TBNA, special zones effectively constructed as interfaces between domestic manufactur-ing and the international market, and envisioned as sites where techno-logical transition and knowledge transfer could occur. Tianjin eco-city is therefore an experimental site and a socio-technical niche, but it is also a site which is placed within a wider cascade of spatial and regional elements focused on the international scale.

The Bohai Rim and the Regional Scale

The focus of Tianjin eco-city is transitional not only at the scale of the state and national and international economic policy, but also within the wider context of the region around Tianjin. Indeed, at a regional scale the eco-city can be considered within the broad context of the Bohai Rim, a broadly coastal area in north-east China. The Bohai Sea coast fea-tures some of China's largest cities, such as Tianjin, Tangshan, Shenyang and Qingdao and the provinces of Hebei, Shandong and Liaoning con-tain around 18% of China's total population – leading to the area being dubbed the "Bohai Megalopolis" (Zhou, Dai and Bu, 2013). Thus, this is an area which is a predominant target for rural–urban migratory flows and for hyper-urbanization. It is also an area which suffers from the exter-nalities produced as a result of the development of heavy industries and rapidly growing cities in the Bohai Rim: externalities which are not just environmental, but socio-economic and demographic as well.

Economically, the Bohai Rim is the third most important region in China after the delta areas around the Pearl and Yangtze rivers. As a result of policies promoting heavy industries in the area during the pre-reform era, coupled with reform policies after 1978, the Bohai Rim is highly industrialised. The environmental impacts have been significant, as 'natural resource shortages and environmental pollution have been caused by the incompatibility of heavy and chemical industry aggregation with a sustainable environment' (Lin et al., 2011). This has led to challenges in terms of creating or maintaining a sustainable and healthy living environment in the region's rapidly expanding cities. Indeed, by 2007 the Bohai Rim was estimated to have exceeded its estimated environmental carrying capacity by around 36% (Lin et al., 2011). This has had repercussions in urban areas: Beijing and Tianjin, two of China's top ten most polluted cities in 2013, are part of the Bohai Megalopolis (Na, 2013).

The Bohai Megalopolis region is thus of central importance to the Chinese government's focus on establishing socio-technical, environmental-economic transitions. The regional scale is important because the socio-technical niches enabled within the Sino-Singapore Tianjin Eco-City are in part meant to be both replicable and scalable (Baeumler et al., 2009). This points to the Chinese government's ambition for using the eco-city as an experimental trial within which successful niches may develop and emerge, influencing the wider socio-technical regime and landscape levels. These effects will eventually be seen – if the eco-city functions as expected – at a wider national scale.

The City Scale: Tianjin Municipality

Having considered the importance of the international, national and regional geographical scales in situating the planned transitions within Tianjin eco-city, the remainder of this section focuses on the scale of the eco-city itself. Indeed, the city can be seen as a key space within which socio-technical transition strategies can be enacted, monitored and analysed.

Situated within the wider urban remit of Tianjin municipality Tianjin eco-city is China's third-largest urban area, and of high political importance. Indeed, it is one of the country's five "National Central Cities", and thus holds a similar status to a whole province. Further underlining the key political importance of Tianjin municipality is the fact that the city is one of just four urban areas under the direct control of the central government of the People's Republic of China.

Tianjin faces similar challenges to those of the wider Bohai Megalopolis. The city's population of 13 million has grown at a rapid pace since 2000, and overall, its population has almost doubled since 1980. In response to the pressures of rapid urbanization fuelled by migration-driven demographic growth, the city's planners are expected to provide housing for over 3 million extra inhabitants by 2020. The city's socio-economic mix is also changing, with a significant proportion of its population composed of migrants who have little or no access to public services such as health care. It is revealing that by the end of the 2000–2010 period, one in six inhabitants of Tianjin (between one-and-a-half and two million people) did not hold a Tianjin household registration (*hukou*) (Li, 2008). This means that the city currently incorporates a large number of socio-economically and politically disadvantaged migrants, which may affect the city's social sustainability. In addition to population and socio-economic pressures, the municipality suffers from the same environmental externalities affecting the Bohai Rim.

It is in this context of demographic pressure and environmental decline that the Tianjin eco-city project makes sense for Tianjin municipality: not so much as a solution to rising levels of population, but as a way of enabling a set of urban niches focused on engineering and technical "solutions" which promise a new way of organising the urban. Thus, in light of the MLP, the eco-city itself can be seen as a planned, experimental set of niches, whereas the wider urban context of Tianjin municipality provides the background in which these niche developments start *making sense*.

Conclusion: Space, Scale and the Multilevel Perspective

This chapter has used the example of a single experimental transitional eco-city project to argue for the necessity to consider the spatial, scalar and territorial context within which socio-technical transitions take place. The case of Tianjin eco-city clearly represents a transition strategy in progress, and therefore endpoints cannot yet be assessed. Nonetheless, what is important about analysing an urban case such as Tianjin is the light that it sheds on the key role of different geographical scales in making sense of transition. This is because the agency and transitional visions of networks of different actors (from high-level policymakers to local municipal governments to real estate development corporations) can be adequately considered only when they are spatialised and territorialised. By placing significant emphasis on the link between scale, space and transition, this viewpoint enables a much-needed spatialisation of the MLP. In the case of Tianjin eco-city, for example, the city can be seen as a bounded experimental site in which niches are allowed to emerge, but it is also very clearly a geographical *place* which makes sense not in abstract terms but precisely because of the cascade of, and interactions between, geographical scales. The case of a single eco-urban project such as Tianjin eco-city thus highlights the relevance of the MLP for studying the development of socio-technical transitions across space.

Building on this, our spatialisation of the MLP through the case study of Tianjin eco-city underlines the utility of considering bounded cases which are predominantly *urban* in focus and character. In part, this is a question of relevance: cities are the loci where transitions strategies are most likely to be focused. They are also the sites of concentration of environmental externalities and of potential for wider socio-technical change. Furthermore, cities lend themselves well to approaches which seek to *manage* transition pathways and strategies. Urban experiments thus enable both the backcasting and forecasting of transition pathways, strategies and interventions (Nevens et al., 2013). An experimental transitions management focus, which is centred on the city as a site of transformation, necessarily incorporates the *spatial* character of transitions to sustainability in the city.

A further point, which emerges from the above discussion, is the need for transition approaches to move past a focus on sites of transition as simply sites of *technological* change and innovation. As has been recently argued (Berkhout, Marcotullio and Hanaoka, 2012), a techno-centric view of transition strategies is inherently limited. Considering geographically bounded urban sustainability transition projects such as Tianjin eco-city highlights the need to consider transitions to sustainability not only in spatial terms, but also in more complex ways that encompass elements of governance, culture, politics and international relations in conceptualising transition strategies.

There are, however, some critical points to be considered when analysing cities as places and spaces of transition. The first of these is that the city scale cannot, in and by itself, be treated as a single site where transition strategies and pathways can be studied in the absence of other spatial and multilevel scales. This is because to do so would be to reify the city as a self-sufficient site of experimentation, separate from other contexts, be they regional, national or global. As seen through our case study of Tianjin, cities are more appropriately spatialised as sites, or moments, *within* wider spatial spheres of emergence of sustainability transitions. This has implications both for a reassessment of studies of sustainability transitions, and for the governance of sustainability transitions in the urban context. With regard to the former, it is clear that spatialising the study of sustainability transitions needs to take into account multiple spatial scales, and the processes and mechanisms through which these are co-constituted. With regard to urban governance, it is becoming increasingly clear that the governance of urban sustainability necessitates a broader spatial perspective, to include not only a range of spatial scales and places, but a city's wider biological, geophysical, economic, political and cultural region (Doughty and Hammond, 2004): a region that may or may not be easily bounded in geographical terms, but within which the life of the city pulses and emerges, and thus a region which does not lend itself well to static governance interventions rooted in notions of the city as bounded cartographic locations. This implies a need for integrated governance, and for sensitivity to the different governance, policy and political contexts within which specific cities exist and function. A consideration of the complexity and diversity of emergent urban sustainabilities thus enables a more dynamic, if also more intricate, multilevel understanding of transition.

References

Baeumler, A., Chen, M., Dastur, A., Zhang, Y., Filewood, R., Al-Jamal, K., Peterson, C., Randale, M. and Pinnoi, N. (2009) *Sino-Singapore Tianjin Eco-City: A Case Study of an Emerging Eco-City in China*. World Bank, Washington, DC.

Bailey, I. and Caprotti, F. (2014) 'The green economy: functional domains and theoretical directions of enquiry'. *Environment and Planning A*, 46(8), 1797–1813.

Bailey, I. and Wilson, G. (2009) 'Theorising transitional pathways in response to climate change: technocentrism, ecocentrism, and the carbon economy'. *Environment and Planning A*, 41(10), 2324–41.

Berkhout, F., Marcotullio, P. and Hanaoka, T. (2012) 'Understanding energy transitions'. *Sustainability Science*, 7(2), 109–11.

Brown, H. S. and Vergragt, P. J. (2008) 'Bounded socio-technical experiments as agents of systemic change: the case of a zero-energy residential building'. *Technological Forecasting and Social Change*, 75(1), 107–30.

Bulkeley, H. and Castán Broto, V. (2012) 'Government by experiment? Global cities and the governing of climate change'. *Transactions of the Institute of British Geographers*, 38(3), 361–75.

Caprotti, F. (2012a) 'The cultural economy of cleantech: environmental discourse and the emergence of a new technology sector'. *Transactions of the Institute of British Geographers*, 37(3), 370–85.

Caprotti, F. (2012b) 'Environment, business and the firm'. *Geography Compass*, 6(3), 163–74.

Caprotti, F. (2014a) 'Critical research on eco-cities? A walk through the Sino-Singapore Tianjin Eco-City'. *Cities: The International Journal of Urban Policy and Planning*, 36(1), 10–17.

Caprotti, F. (2014b) 'Eco-urbanism and the eco-city, or denying the right to the city?' *Antipode*, 46(5), 1285–1303.

Caprotti, F. (2015) *Eco-Cities and the Transition to Low Carbon Economies*. Palgrave, London, UK.

Caprotti, F. & Cowley, R. (2016) 'Interrogating urban experiments'. Urban Geography, DOI: 10.1080/02723638.2016.1265870

Caprotti, F. and Romanowicz, J. (2013) 'Thermal eco-cities: green building and urban thermal metabolism'. *International Journal of Urban and Regional Research*, 37(6), 1949–67.

Caprotti, F., Springer, C. and Harmer, N. (2015) '"Eco" for whom? Envisioning eco-urbanism in the Sino-Singapore Tianjin Eco-City, China'. *International Journal of Urban and Regional Research*, 39(3), 495–517.

Chang I-C.C. and Sheppard, E. (2013) 'China's eco-cities as variegated urban sustainability: Dongtan Eco-City and Chongming Eco-Island'. *Journal of Urban Technology*, 20(1), 57–75.

Cheng, H. and Hu, Y. (2010) 'Planning for sustainability in China's urban development: Status and challenges for Dongtan eco-city project'. *Journal of Environmental Monitoring*, 12(1), 119–26.

Coenen, L., Benneworth, P. and Truffer, B. (2012) 'Toward a spatial perspective on sustainability transitions'. *Research Policy*, 41, 968–79.

Cooke, P. (2011) 'Transition regions: Regional–national eco-innovation systems and strategies'. *Progress in Planning*, 76(3), 105–46.

Cugurullo, F. (2013a) 'How to build a sandcastle: an analysis of the genesis and development of Masdar city'. *Journal of Urban Technology*, 20(1), 23–37.

Cugurullo, F. (2013b) 'The business of utopia: Estidama and the road to the sustainable city'. *Utopian Studies*, 24(1), 66–88.

de Jong, M., Wang, D. and Yu, C. (2013) 'Exploring the relevance of the eco-city concept in China: the case of Shenzhen Sino-Dutch Low Carbon City'. *Journal of Urban Technology*, 20(1), 95–113.

Doughty, M. R. C. and Hammond, G. P. (2004) 'Sustainability and the built environment at and beyond the city scale'. *Building and Environment*, 39(10), 1223–33.

Geels, F. (2012) 'A socio-technical analysis of low-carbon transitions: introducing the multi-level perspective into transport studies'. *Journal of Transport Geography*, 24, 471–82.

Geels, F. and Schot, J. (2010) 'Introduction and exploration of the research topic' in Grin, J., Rotmans, J. and Schot, J. (ed), *Transitions to Sustainable Development: New Directions in the Study of Long Term Transformative Change*. Routledge, London.

Hodson, M. and Marvin, S. (2010a) 'Can cities shape socio-technical transitions and how would we know if they were?' *Research Policy*, 39, 477–85.

Hodson, M. and Marvin, S. (2010b) 'Urbanism in the anthropocene: ecological urbanism or premium ecological enclaves?' *City*, 14(3), 298–313.

Hult, A. (2013) 'Swedish production of sustainable urban imaginaries in China'. *Journal of Urban Technology*, 20(1), 77–94.

Joss, S. (2010) 'Eco-cities: a global survey 2009' in Brebbia, C., Hernandez, S. and Tiezzi, A. (eds) *The Sustainable City VI: Urban Regeneration and Sustainability*. WIT Press, Southampton, 239–50.

Joss, S., Cowley, R. and Tomozeiu, D. (2013) 'Towards the "ubiquitous eco-city": an analysis of the internationalisation of eco-city policy and practice'. *Urban Research and Practice*, 6(1), 54–74.

Joss, S. and Molella, A. (2013) 'The eco-city as urban technology: perspectives on Caofeidan International Eco-City (China)'. *Journal of Urban Technology*, 20(1), 115–37.

Karanikolas, P., Vlahos, G. and Sutherland, L.-A. (forthcoming) 'Utilising the Multi-Level Perspective in empirical field research: methodological considerations' in Sutherland, L.-A., Darnhofer, I., Zagata, L. and Wilson, G.A. (ed) *Transition Pathways Towards Sustainability in European Agriculture*. CABI, Wallingford, UK.

Lawhon, M. and Murphy, J.T. (2012) 'Socio-technical regimes and sustainability transitions: insights from political ecology'. *Progress in Human Geography*, 36, 354–78.

Li, B. (2008) 'Why do migrant workers not participate in urban social security schemes? The case of the construction and service sectors in Tianjin' in Nielsen, I. & Russell, Smyth (eds) Migration and Social Protection in China. World Scientific Publishing, Singapore, 92-117.

Lin, L., Liu, Y., Chen, J., Zhang, T. and Zeng, S. (2011) Comparative analysis of environmental carrying capacity of the Bohai Sea Rim area in China. *Journal of Environmental Monitoring*, 13(11), 3178–84.

Ministry of Finance and the State Administration of Taxation (2006) 'Incentives of the corporate income tax to support the development of the TBNA'. 130(2006), 15 November 2006. Available at: http://en.investteda.org/download/revised20070115. doc Accessed 1 March 2014.

Na, L. (2013) 'Top 10 most polluted Chinese cities in 2012'. *China.org.cn*, 15 April 2013. Available at: http://www.china.org.cn/top10/2013-04/15/content_28541619. htm Accessed 1 March 2014.

Nevens, F., Frantzeskaki, N., Gorissen, L. and Loorbach, D. (2013) 'Urban transition labs: co-creating transformative action for sustainable cities'. *Journal of Cleaner Production*, 50(1), 111–22.

Pow, H. and Neo, H. (2014) 'Modelling green urbanism in China.' *Area*, DOI: 10.1111/area.12128

Rapoport, E. (2014) 'Utopian visions and real estate dreams: the eco-city past, present and future'. *Geography Compass*, 8(2), 137–49.

Shwayri, S. (2013) 'A model Korean ubiquitous eco-city? The politics of making Songdo'. *Journal of Urban Technology*, 20(1), 39–55.

Smith, A., Voß, J.-P. and Grin, J. (2010) 'Innovation studies and sustainability transitions: The allure of the multi-level perspective and its challenges.' *Research Policy*, 39(4), 435–48.

SSTECIDC. 2010. Celebrating eco. Available at: http://events.cleantech.com/tianjin/sites/default/files/SSTECBrochureFinal.pdf Accessed 1 March 2014.

Sutherland, L.A., Darnhofer, I., Wilson, G. and Zagata, L. (eds) (2015) *Transition Pathways Towards Sustainability in Agriculture: Case Studies from Europe*. CABI, Wallingford, UK.

Swyngedouw, E. and Heynen, N. (2003) 'Urban political ecology, justice and the politics of scale'. *Antipode*, 35(5), 898–918.

TEDA (2010) 'Tianjin Binhai New Area'. Available at: http://en.investteda.org/ BinhaiNewArea/default.htm Last accessed 1 March 2014.

Truffer, B. and Coenen, L. (2012) 'Environmental innovation and sustainability transitions in regional studies'. *Regional Studies* 46(1), 1–21.

Yigitcanlar, T. and Lee, S. H. (2013) 'Korean ubiquitous eco-city: a smart sustainable urban form or a branding hoax?' *Technological Forecasting and Social Change*, 89, 100–14.

Yu, L. (2014) 'Low carbon eco-city: new approach for Chinese urbanization.' *Habitat International* 44, 102–10.

Wu, F. (2012) 'China's eco-cities'. *Geoforum*, 43(2), 169–71.

Zhou, S., Dai, J. and Bu, J. (2013) City size distributions in China 1949 to 2010 and the impacts of government policies'. *Cities*, 32(1), S51–7.

INTERLUDE

9 Urban Sustainability Transitions

Opportunities and Challenges for Institutional Change

Lea Fuenfschilling

Introduction

Part I of this book presented eight case studies that shed light on various processes and characteristics that are specific to urban transitions. This chapter summarizes and reflects upon some of the most pertinent particularities of urban transitions, and evaluates them with regard to their potential for institutional change. It is increasingly acknowledged that many of the 'grand societal challenges', for example, climate change, environmental degradation or resource depletion, are related to unsustainable consumption and production processes (Grin et al., 2010; OECD, 2011; UNEP, 2011; van den Bergh et al., 2011). Especially utility sectors like energy, food, transport or water are substantially pressured to transition to a more sustainable mode of operation. However, the transformation of established, highly institutionalized social structures and technologies has proven challenging. Infrastructures are comprised of extremely interrelated technical and social elements that have co-evolved and aligned over long periods of time. This causes a significant amount of path-dependency and inertia, which is generally viewed as an obstacle to radical change. The question of how a transition from the current dominant socio-technical configuration to a potentially more sustainable one could be achieved has thus taken center stage in research on sustainability transitions (Markard et al., 2012).

Scholarly literature has characterized sustainability transitions as long-term, socio-technical transformations (Bergek et al., 2008; Grin et al., 2010; Smith et al., 2005). The co-evolution of institutions and technologies is thereby emphasized (Nelson and Winter, 1982; Rip and Kemp, 1998). Change and innovation are thus conceived of as systemic processes, in which material and non-material aspects develop together; for example, as a simultaneous re-organization of business models, laws, technologies, user practices and cultural expectations. This reorganization can also be conceptualized as institutional change, since it involves the dismantling or de-institutionalization of existing structures (i.e., of the socio-technical regime) as well as the buildup or institutionalization of a new socio-technical configuration (i.e., of a niche), which at some point might be able to replace the old system. Sustainability transitions have therefore been characterized as processes of institutional change with specific focus on technologies and materiality (Fuenfschilling and Truffer, 2014). Associated research questions focus on how such processes of (de-)institutionalization unfold (Barley and Tolbert, 1997; Berger and Luckmann, 1966; Zucker, 1977), which roles actors and agency play (Battilana et al., 2009; Lawrence et al., 2009), how technologies exert their influence (Garud et al., 2010; Perez, 1983) or how discourses matter (Penna and Geels, 2012; Philips et al., 2004).

A somewhat understudied aspect of institutional change in the context of sustainability transitions refers to the question of where such changes take place, that is, to their spatial dimensions (Coenen et al., 2012). Are there places with specific characteristics – for example, institutional conditions or technological capabilities – which foster transition processes, or do they take place anywhere? In this respect, urban spaces, that is, cities, have been identified as particularly relevant loci for sustainable development (Bulkeley et al., 2011; Mieg and Töpfer, 2013; Pickett et al., 2013). On the one hand, this is due to their ever-increasing dominance regarding energy consumption (ca. two-thirds of global energy demand), CO_2 emissions (ca. 70%) and population growth (estimates suggest that by 2050, 70% of people will live in cities). On the other hand, the question arises whether cities play a particular role in contributing to a transition as spaces that provide specific opportunities for institutional change. For instance, research suggests that many new initiatives and interventions to counteract unsustainable behavior and practices have originated in cities (IEA, 2011; UN (DESA), 2012). Do urban spaces have the potential to act as institutional entrepreneurs (i.e., agents of change), for example, by coining progressive policies or by providing opportunities for technological experimentation? However, the specific features of urban spaces and their consequences for sustainability transitions have so far been rather neglected. The following section will thus reflect on some of the most important characteristics of cities, many of which have been described in detail in the previous empirical case studies, and discuss their relevance for processes of institutional change.

Characteristics of Urban Spaces and Implications for Institutional Change

A central assumption about cities is that they are often able to provide the intellectual, financial and political resources necessary to develop initiatives and blueprints for sustainable change. As *"engines of socioeconomic development"* and *"centers of cultural transformation and technological innovation"*, cities offer the critical mass of expertise, money and political power to initiate change (Wu, 2014, p. 201). Institutional theory places special emphasis on the importance of resources in order to create, disrupt or maintain institutions (Lawrence and Suddaby, 2006), that is, to initiate or prevent transitions. Resources may refer to the mobilization of financial support or political and regulatory interventions through lobbying, the creation of networks or monitoring processes. But they also include less tangible aspects aiming at the (de) construction of rationales: for example, through theorizing (elaboration of abstract categories and chains of cause and effect), demonizing a certain practice or technology or educating people via the skills and know-how transfer necessary to support a new institution (Hardy and Maguire, 2008; Lawrence and Suddaby, 2006). The application of resources in such a manner is called institutional work (Lawrence et al., 2009). It is especially relevant for transitions with regard to the establishment of new mindsets and novel practices that comply with the values of sustainability.

However, the array of actors and potential resources found in urban spaces might also be a source of conflict and contestation. Actors are generally highly diverse, have different vested interests and come from a variety of socio-economic backgrounds. As some of the case studies in this book have shown, creating shared narratives and visions for the future has proven a challenging task, and the success of an initiative often depends on actors' ability to generate such common ground. For instance, Bettini et al. (Chapter 3 in this volume), describe how the tensions between established power structures, vested interests from key stakeholders and political imperatives for finding timely solutions have led to suboptimal policy decisions in Brisbane's water sector. In a similar vein, Fratini and Jensen (Chapter 6 in this volume) identify the existence of two very distinct framings of the use and virtue of water in Denmark, leading to a highly contested and often contradictory innovation agenda for the urban water sector in the city of Copenhagen. However, research also suggests that it is precisely those areas of contestation that are able to bring about innovations (Greenwood et al., 2011; Kraatz and Block, 2008; Thornton et al., 2012). A structural overlap of originally separate spheres with distinct rationalities, such as the market and the public sector, carries the potential to bring about new practices or business models that have implications for the innovativeness of an industry. An example is the corporatization of public utilities or the outsourcing of activities to private firms that has happened in various infrastructure sectors (Lieberherr and Truffer, in press). In this sense, innovations might be the result of finding a compromise between actors and aligning different interests and belief and value systems.

A similar argument can be made with regard to the high complexity of urban systems. McPhearson and Wijsman (Chapter 5 in this volume) show that cities involve a dynamic interaction of ecological, social and technological infrastructures that are highly interdependent and create various feedback loops. For instance, energy systems are related to water infrastructure – for example, via hydropower – and waste disposal is closely linked to issues of recycling and energy production, as shown by the case of biogas. On the one hand, such extraordinary complexity increases the challenges for successful management of sustainable change, and has brought about the call for a holistic and systemic governance approach that takes these interdependencies into account (Loorbach, 2007). On the other hand, the proximity and interrelatedness of systems in urban spaces have also been identified as an opportunity to carve out synergies between the various elements that have the potential to increase the overall sustainability of a city (Ravetz, 2011). Establishing an integrated conceptualization of diverse systems can be interpreted as one of the major consequences of applying a sustainability perspective to urban governance. For example, this is visible in the emergence of a 'water-energy-nexus', which tries to integrate two previously separate domains of cities that are usually placed in different government departments and that have their own specific legislation (Kenway, 2013). Looking at the interrelatedness of these two industries might provide economic, ecological, socio-cultural and governance synergies, since an integrated view enables thinking about new finance models and value exchanges, different approaches to spatial planning or building design, novel practices for more networked resource management and ecosystem services, or sustainable community development and stakeholder integration.

From an institutional perspective, such a reconceptualization of once highly separate but nevertheless interrelated societal spheres is a challenging endeavor. One of the main reasons is that the complexity and interdependence of urban systems are not only a functional matter, but also to a great extent a historical and institutional one. Cities can be interpreted as historically grown, highly path-dependent socio-technical configurations. As transitions research has shown, this does not apply only to cities in general but especially to their relevant subsystems, such as energy, water or transport. Hence, the complexity of a city may reinforce the rigidity and inertia found in socio-technical systems, which poses great challenges for transition management. The currently highly institutionalized 'rules of the game' in cities, such as standards, practices or governance modes, have historically been developed with regard to values such as functionality, technical efficiency, resource depletion, national sovereignty or economic growth. Sustainability, on the other hand, is a rather new overarching societal value that emerged in the 1970s (Fuenfschilling and Truffer, 2014). Hence, the current dominant social and material structures of many urban spaces often present a strong mismatch with sustainable practices. It could thus be argued that urban spaces may be too rigid and complex to initiate change, while places with more flexibility, that is, lesser degrees of structuration, might be more likely to innovate. An indication thereof is found in the city of Seoul. Wolfram (Chapter 7 in this volume) describes in detail how change in the city was initiated at a neighborhood scale, and not at the city level. The complexity of a large-scale city is thereby reduced through a focus on more rural, village-like dimensions. It could thus make sense to think of a city as entailing heterogeneous, multi-scalar configurations, where transitions take place in a decentralized yet interconnected manner. Another example is the development of the photovoltaic market in Germany, which can, among other things, be traced back to various private initiatives in predominantly rural or community-based areas (Dewald and Truffer, 2012).

This has important implications regarding the question of how institutional work leads to institutional change, that is, transforms the mindsets and practices towards sustainability: Is it a bottom-up, decentralized process or a top-down guided transformation? As is often the case, research suggests that both aspects are necessary and should preferably be combined (Loorbach and

Rotmans, 2010; Rotmans and Loorbach, 2009). Whereas the interrelatedness of socio-technical configurations as well as possible synergies may require a holistic and top-down approach that takes various aspects into considerations (e.g., Fratini and Jensen, Chapter 6 in this volume), the identification and interpretation of local sustainability issues as well as the emergence of innovative solutions to them might better unfold in a decentralized manner through bottom-up activities initiated by a diverse range of actors (e.g., Wolfram, Chapter 7 in this volume).

Despite the high path-dependency and rigidity of cities, there is also evidence that urban spaces could serve as exemplary niches of how to address and govern sustainable change, because they possess favorable socio-technical structures that enable the creation of new sustainable practices. Using the case of on-site water recycling in various Chinese cities, Binz and Truffer (Chapter 2 in this volume) argue that some cities are able to act as strategic niche managers for new technologies because they are in a favorable position to access resources provided locally as well as through international networks. Seeing cities as favorable niche spaces is especially fruitful if (technological) innovation is viewed as a global process. Research has shown that cities are not isolated spaces, but instead depend on and are connected to resources provided via global networks (Hodson and Marvin, 2010). To understand the transition dynamics of urban spaces, it is thus sensible to account for their multi-scalar networks and contexts (Coenen and Truffer, 2012; Raven et al., 2012). Once such potentially more sustainable niche technologies are established in a city, that is, have developed a corresponding institutional setting, the whole package might be transferrable as best-practice models to other places. Thus, cities could serve as places for experimentation and learning and become role models in the transition towards sustainability. This point is also made by Burch (Chapter 4 in this volume), who shows that the city of Vancouver in Canada began applying sustainability measures long before the provincial government, making it a role model for other municipalities in the area who copy successful initiatives and learn from the city's experience.

Looking at cities as intermediaries in global innovation and transformation processes obviously has consequences for the development and governance of institutional change. For one, it implies that transition arenas need to be thought of as international. This contradicts the long-standing tradition and dominance of national policy making, which is most visible in many efforts to achieve supranational, binding agreements through the EU or the UN (e.g., climate conferences). However, there are plenty of other, less formal international interactions that aim at (de)institutionalizing old and new practices: for example, within the scientific realm (conferences, journal articles, professional associations), the globalized economy (multinational corporations, trade unions, lobby groups) or civil society (international non-governmental organizations). All of these actors are heavily influential in the build-up and diffusion of new socio-technical structures, such as the creation of markets in public sectors through economists, the manufacturing of technological innovations at university spin-offs or the development of standards for industries through labelling (e.g., ISO norms, fair trade, corporate social responsibility). All these processes shape institutional change in a bottom-up, non-governmental but nevertheless highly binding and powerful way (Boli and Thomas, 1997). To account for such processes of institutional change, a combined local and global – that is, a glocal – perspective on sustainability transition seems crucial. The role of cities in this context is vital; for example, as hosts and facilitators of transnational actors and global transformation processes, or as places where new global practices are implemented and refined.

Concluding Remarks

Based on the insights of the empirical case studies presented in this part of the book, this chapter has analyzed central characteristics of urban spaces and their potential for institutional change. It can be argued that the particularities of urban spaces simultaneously provide opportunities and challenges for sustainability transitions. The concentration of resources and actors in cities can be viewed either as providing the necessary capacities for institutional work that aims at contributing to a transition, or as a source for conflict and contestation that undermines the creation of a shared vision. Conflict, however, often results from the different rationalities applied by actors (e.g., economic vs. technological vs. sustainable), and it is the combination or resolution of this kind of institutional plurality that can enable innovation. Similarly, the ecological, technical and social complexity of cities can either be interpreted as uncontrollable and irresolvable interdependence, or as a potential for yet unused synergies. The highly institutionalized socio-technical configurations of cities and the related path-dependency can on the one hand be seen as a challenge for change, implying that urban spaces are too rigid and structured to allow for innovation or grass-root movements. On the other hand, certain configurations might be highly beneficial as cities become strategic niches, develop best-practices and act as global role models. Furthermore, cities are multi-scalar – they are themselves heterogeneous configurations that comprise smaller scales such as neighborhoods or districts. At the same time, they are connected to the global level. Whereas sometimes it makes sense to break them down into smaller units of analysis and look for specific neighborhood structures, at other times it is necessary to conceptualize them as knots in an international arena, highly influenced by transnational actors of all sorts.

The characteristics of cities described in this chapter point towards the distinctiveness of urban sustainability transitions. Urban spaces can thus be viewed as having a particular relevance for achieving radical socio-technical change. Placing an analytical focus on processes of institutional change furthermore provides for novel insights into the origin of cities' path-dependency, the maintenance or disruption of dominant structures, or the institutionalization of new socio-technical configurations. More detailed research investigating the particularities of urban spaces for institutional change is thus expected to lead to relevant findings for sustainability transitions as a whole.

References

Barley, S.R., Tolbert, P.S., 1997. Institutionalization and structuration: Studying the link between action and institution. *Organization Studies* 18 (1), 93–117.

Battilana, J., Leca, B., Boxenbaum, E., 2009. How actors change institutions: Towards a theory of institutional entrepreneurship. *Academy of Management Annuals* 3, 65–107.

Bergek, A., Hekkert, M., Jacobsson, S., 2008. Functions in innovation systems: A framework for analysing energy system dynamics and identifying goals for system-building activities by entrepreneurs and policy makers. In: Foxon, T., Köhler, J., Oughton, C. (Eds.), *Innovation for a Low Carbon Economy: Economic, Institutional and Management Approaches*. Edward Elgar, Cheltenham, pp. 79–111.

Berger, P.L., Luckmann, T., 1966. *The Social Construction of Reality*. Doubleday, New York.

Boli, J., Thomas, G.M., 1997. World culture in the world polity: A century of international non-governmental organization. *American Sociological Review* 62 (2), 171–190.

Bulkeley H., Castán Broto V., Hodson, M., Marvin, S. (Eds), 2011. *Cities and Low Carbon Transitions*. Routledge, New York.

Coenen, L., Benneworth, P., Truffer, B., 2012. Toward a spatial perspective on sustainability transitions. *Research Policy* 41 (6), 968–979.

Coenen, L., Truffer, B., 2012. Places and spaces of sustainability transitions: Geographical contributions to an emerging research and policy field. *European Planning Studies* 20 (3), 367–374.

Dewald, U., Truffer, B., 2012. The local sources of market formation: Explaining regional growth differentials in German photovoltaic markets. *European Planning Studies* (3), 397–420.

Fuenfschilling, L., Truffer, B., 2014. The structuration of socio-technical regimes – Conceptual foundations from institutional theory. *Research Policy* 43 (4), 772–791.

Garud, R., Gehman, J., Karnoe, P., 2010. Categorization by association: Nuclear technology and emission-free electricity. In: Sine, W., David, R., Keister, L. (Eds.), *Institutions and Entrepreneurship*. Emerald Group Publishing Limited. Bingley, United Kingdom, pp. 51–93.

Greenwood, R., Raynard, M., Kodeih, F., Micelotta, E.R., Lounsbury, M., 2011. Institutional complexity and organizational responses. *The Academy of Management Annals* 5 (1), 317–371.

Grin, J., Rotmans, J., Schot, J. (Eds), 2010. *Transitions to Sustainable Development: New Directions in the Study of Long Term Transformative Change*. Routledge, New York.

Hardy, C., Maguire, S., 2008. Institutional entrepreuneurship. In: Greenwood, R., Oliver, C., Sahlin, K., Suddaby, R. (Eds.), *Organizational Institutionalism*. Sage Publications, London, pp. 198–217.

Hodson, M., Marvin, S., 2010. Can cities shape socio-technical transitions and how would we know if they were? *Research Policy* 39 (4), 477–485.

IEA, 2011. *World Energy Outook 2011*. International Energy Agency, Paris.

Kenway, S., 2013. The water-energy nexus and urban metabolism – Connections in cities. Urban Water Security Research Alliance Technical Report No. 100.

Kraatz, M., Block, E., 2008. Organizational implications of institutional pluralism. In: Greenwood, R., Oliver, C., Sahlin, K., Suddaby, R. (Eds.), *Organizational Institutionalism*. Sage, London, pp. 243–275.

Lawrence, T.B., Suddaby, R., Leca, B., 2009. *Institutional Work: Actors and Agency in Institutional Studies or Organizations*. Cambridge University Press, Cambridge.

Lawrence, T.B., Suddaby, R., 2006. Institutions and institutional work. In: Clegg, S., Hardy, C.,Lawrence, T.B., Nord, W. (Eds.), *The Sage Handbook of Organizational Studies*. Sage Publications, London, pp. 215–254.

Lieberherr, E., Truffer, B., in press. The impact of privatization on sustainability transitions: A comparative analysis of dynamic capabilities in three water utilities. *Environmental Innovation and Societal Transitions* (0).

Loorbach, D., Rotmans, J., 2010. The practice of transition management: Examples and lessons from four distinct cases. *Futures* 42 (3), 237–246.

Loorbach, D., 2007. *Tranistion Management: New Mode of Governance for Sustainable Development*. International Books, Utrecht.

Markard, J., Raven, R., Truffer, B., 2012. Sustainability transitions: An emerging field of research and its prospects. *Research Policy* 41 (6), 955–967.

Mieg H.A., Töpfer K. (Eds), 2013. *Institutional and Social Innovation for Sustainable Urban Development*. Routledge, New York.

Nelson, R.R., Winter, S.G., 1982. *An Evolutionary Theory of Economic Change*. Belknap Press of Harvard University Press, Cambridge, MA.

OECD, 2011. *Towards Green Growth – A Summary for Policy Makers*. Organization for Economic Co-operation and Development, Paris.

Penna, C.C.R., Geels, F.W., 2012. Multi-dimensional struggles in the greening of industry: A dialectic issue lifecycle model and case study. *Technological Forecasting and Social Change* 79 (6), 999–1020.

Perez, C., 1983. Structural change and assimilation of new technologies in the economic and social systems. *Futures* 15 (5), 357–375.

Philips, N., Lawrence, T.B., Hardy, C., 2004. Discourse and institutions. *Academy of Management Review* 29 (4), 635–652.

Pickett, S.T.A., Boone, C.G., McGrath, B.P., Cadenasso, M.L., Childers, D.L., Ogden, L.A., McHale, M., Grove, J.M., 2013. Ecological science and transformation to the sustainable city. *Cities 32*, Supplement 1 (0), S10–S20.

Raven, R., Schot, J., Berkhout, F., 2012. Space and scale in socio-technical transitions. *Environmental Innovation and Societal Transitions* 4 (0), 63–78.

Ravetz, J., 2011. Urban synergy foresight. In: *Urban Governance in the EU: Current Challenges and Forward Prospects*. EU Committee of the Regions, Brussels, pp. 31–44.

Rip, A., Kemp, R., 1998. Technological change. In: Rayner, S., Malone, E.L. (Eds.), *Human Choice and Climate Change - Resources and Technology*. Battelle Press, Columbus, pp. 327–399.

Rotmans, J., Loorbach, D., 2009. Complexity and transition management. *Journal of Industrial Ecology* 13 (2), 184–196.

Smith, A., Stirling, A., Berkhout, F., 2005. The governance of sustainable socio-technical transitions. *Research Policy* 34 (10), 1491–1510.

Thornton, P.H., Ocasio, W., Lounsbury, M., 2012. *The Institutional Logics Perspective: A New Approach to Culture, Structure, and Process*. Oxford University Press, Oxford.

UN (DESA), 2012. *World Urbanization Prospects, the 2011 Revisions*. United Nations, Department of Economic and Social Affairs, New York.

UNEP, 2011. Towards a green economy: Pathways to sustainable development and poverty eradication. United Nations Environment Programme, www.unep.org.

van den Bergh, J., Truffer, B., Kallis, G., 2011. Environmental innovation and societal transitions: Introduction and overview. *Environmental Innovation and Societal Transitions* 1 (1), 1–23.

Wu, C.-Y., 2014. Comparisons of technological innovation capabilities in the solar photovoltaic industries of Taiwan, China, and Korea. *Scientometrics* 98 (1), 429–446.

Zucker, L.G., 1977. The role of institutionalization in cultural persistence. *American Sociological Review* 42 (5), 726–743.

Part II

Experimentation and Urban Sustainability Transitions

10 The Rise, Fall and Resurrection of Waste-to-energy Technologies in Berlin's Infrastructure History

Timothy Moss

Introduction

In February 2012, a ceremony was held in Berlin to launch the building of a state-of-the-art biogas plant by the city's own waste utility BSR (*Berliner Stadtreinigung*). The fermentation plant, now in production, has a capacity for processing 60,000 tons of biodegradable waste into biogas, comprising 98% methane. Each year, 3.4 million m^3 of purified gas from this plant is fed into the city's natural gas network (BSR 2010). In conjunction with the new plant, BSR will increase the number of its gas-powered waste collection vehicles to 150, thereby saving 2.5 million litres of diesel per year. This represents an annual CO_2 emissions reduction of 4.000–5.000 tons (t). Announcing the planned plant in a press statement, BSR claimed: "This project is setting new standards for Germany as a whole and will make a significant contribution to climate protection in the capital"[1]. The impression given is that we are witnessing the application of a novel, experimental technology never seen before. Within the living memory of most Berliners, this is certainly the case.

However, if we look back 80 years, the picture is rather different. In many German cities in the 1930s, the production and use of biogas derived from waste or wastewater was prevalent on a surprising scale (Deublein and Steinhauser 2011: 32). At the time, it was claimed that methane gas produced from wastewater alone amounted to some 15.5 million m^3 per year (Heilmann 1937: 353). This was used to run heating systems at sewage treatment plants, to drive machinery and vehicles, for heating and lighting, as well as to feed into city gas networks. Methane gas stations for vehicles were in operation in Stuttgart, Halle, Pforzheim, Essen, Erfurt, Pößneck and Munich, and proved very cost-effective.

If waste-to-energy technologies were widely applied in German cities in the 1930s, as we will demonstrate, how can their disappearance since then be explained? What can the reasons behind their original emergence, subsequent disappearance and current re-emergence tell us about how urban socio-technical transitions unfold over time? This chapter takes an historical perspective on current attempts to 'open up' established, centralized urban infrastructure systems to alternative technologies intended to reduce the use of natural resources, minimise environmental pollution and save costs. Its point of departure is the assertion that the process of introducing experimental, small-scale technologies into, or alongside, established, centralized urban infrastructures is not a novel phenomenon, as is widely assumed. In view of the difficulties experienced today in reconfiguring urban infrastructures, it is worth exploring historical examples of (attempted) adaptations of large technical systems (LTS) involving unconventional socio-technical solutions. This historical perspective is used not to illustrate the path dependency of current urban configurations, but rather to draw lessons from past processes of infrastructure reconfiguration and how they were bound up in broader issues of urban (and national) change.

As a case study, the chapter investigates a number of alternative technologies from the field of waste-to-energy applied in Berlin, focusing on the interwar period (1920–1939)[2]. Berlin is chosen by virtue of its role in pioneering several of these technologies at this time, but also in acknowledgement of its showcase effect for technological innovation today, having regained its status as Germany's capital city. The empirical analysis is based primarily on a systematic survey of relevant professional journals on energy and wastewater management published in Germany from 1920 to the present. In the following sections, I firstly frame the study in terms of three strands of scholarly debate: on socio-technical transitions, path dependency and creation and urban infrastructures in transition. I then describe the rise, fall and resurrection of selected waste-to-energy technologies, setting the Berlin case in the broader context of national technology policy. The chequered trajectories of these technologies and their relevance for urban sustainability transitions are subsequently interpreted with the help of the three research strands above. The chapter concludes with a summary of the main arguments and their relevance for today's attempts at reconfiguring urban socio-technical networks.

Conceptualising Time and Space in Socio-technical Research

The historical and urban perspectives of this chapter call for conceptual guidance on how socio-technical transitions unfold over time and space. To this end, I draw on two strands of recent research addressing temporality – transitions theory and path creation – and one body of literature addressing spatiality; specifically, urban infrastructures in transition.

Time

The multilevel perspective (MLP) on socio-technical transitions has attracted considerable attention as a conceptual framework for explaining processes of change (Geels 2002; Geels and Kemp 2007). According to the MLP, transitions are the result of interaction between three levels: technological niches (or protected spaces) at the micro level, socio-technical regimes at the meso level and landscapes (or exogenous factors) at the macro level. Incremental processes of reconfiguration are characteristic of established socio-technical regimes, as elements of a system become realigned to accommodate new developments. Radical innovations, by contrast, are generated in technological niches or by shifts in exogenous factors. The MLP framework has been applied in a number of historical case studies to analyse transitions from one stable socio-technical configuration to another. This chapter uses the history of waste-to-energy technologies in Berlin to question some of the assumptions underpinning this notion of regime shift by exploring processes of emergence, disappearance and re-emergence.

It also sheds fresh light on a second established body of scholarship related to the path dependency of socio-technical systems (Hughes 1983; Melosi 2005). This chapter shares a common interest in the history of technology and how it frames today's practices and decisions. It does not, however, set out to retrospectively reconstruct how we got to where we are today, in terms of the path dependency of a dominant socio-technical regime and how it constrains current options. It seeks, rather, to uncover and explain the existence and use of alternative technologies in the shadow of LTS. This resonates with Dirk van Laak's description of the history of infrastructure as being characterised by catastrophes, misplanning, dead ends and reuse (2005: 87) and Bernhard Joerge's critique of the linear model of LTS development from invention to stabilisation (1999). Recent work by James Simmie (2012) is helpful in conceptualising the role of "reflexive agents" in socio-technical transitions. His understanding of path creation is not as a shift from one path to another, but as an iterative, dynamic process characterised by three types of technology diffusion: displacement, layering and conversion. 'Displacement' refers to a dominant technology being superseded by a subordinate one, but continuing to exist for some time afterwards. 'Layering' refers to the addition of a new technology while previous technologies remain in use. 'Conversion' refers to how old technologies are modified, but not displaced. These categories will be applied and developed further in this chapter.

Space

One of the most prominent critiques of the MLP literature is that it is largely blind to the spatiality of socio-technical transitions, viewing cities either as homogenous actors of transition or merely as locations of innovation (Hodson and Marvin 2010; Bulkeley et al. 2011). In recent years, scholarship in the fields of urban and regional studies and human geography has made important inroads into explaining the relationship between urban and socio-technical transitions. They highlight the benefits that can be derived from connecting research on infrastructural, ecological and urban transitions (Monstadt 2009; Coutard and Rutherford 2011), on low-carbon and urban futures (Bulkeley et al. 2011), on sustainability transitions and regional studies (Truffer and Coenen 2012) and on urban and socio-technical transitions

(Hodson and Marvin 2009; 2010). Collectively, this literature challenges simplistic notions of cities as being bounded objects, jurisdictional territories or levels of action. Instead, it promotes, firstly, a co-evolutionary perspective in which cities and their socio-technical networks shape each other. Secondly, the city is treated in relational terms as a multiple entity. Rather than being a clearly defined territory 'out there', the city can be a policy actor, a niche for experimentation or a network of socio-technical relationships reaching within and beyond the confines of a municipal entity. Thirdly, the relationship between the city and its infrastructure is thoroughly political (McFarlane and Rutherford 2008), meaning that socio-technical change is never benign but benefits some more than others. These three dimensions will later be used to interpret the 'urban' aspect of the case study, which is presented in the following section.

Waste-to-energy Technologies in Berlin

From the 1920s onwards, and increasingly in the 1930s, a number of waste-to-energy technologies were developed and applied in cities across Germany. The production and use of biogas derived from waste or wastewater as referred to in the introduction was one such innovation. In this field, Berlin was a pioneer, producing gas from its wastewater pre-treatment plant at Waßmannsdorf as early as 1927 (Langbein 1927; Langbein and Kroll 1931). This plant alone produced 1.85 million m^3 of biogas in 1929, which was used to serve the wastewater utility's own energy requirements[3]. The director of the utility, *Berliner Stadtentwässerung*, calculated at the time that if all of Berlin's six planned sewage treatment plants could produce biogas to the same degree, this would cover the gas consumption of 275,000 people (Langbein and Kroll 1931: 476). Writing after the Nazi seizure of power, having left his post, Langbein remained an ardent supporter of the technology, demonstrating how biogas derived from Germany's sewers and treatment plants could provide 130 million m^3 of methane per year – that is, over 5% of the country's total gas production (Langbein 1936). Used as a substitute for petrol or diesel, this gas could be used to fuel 10,000 cars and save 14 million *Reichsmark*. During the war, under conditions of severe fuel shortages, gas derived from wastewater became a significant vehicle fuel – although, as another leading engineer, Imhoff, wryly noted, the poor nutrition of the population had a negative impact on the gas production potential of wastewater (Imhoff 1947: 67). After the war, there was no further reference to the technology in any of the professional journals or utility reports studied. It disappeared from view in Berlin and in Germany as a whole for many decades. Its re-emergence today in the form of biogas plants supplied by the city's waste and wastewater utilities is being widely advertised (see Figure 10.1). Besides the BSR, the Berlin Water Company BWB concluded a contractual agreement with the Berlin city-state government in July 2008, under which it commits itself to converting five of its sewage treatment plants to produce biogas to drive

Figure 10.1 Poster of BSR advertising campaign for its waste-to-energy strategy.
(Published with kind permission of BSR Berliner Stadtreinigung
© Berliner Stadtreinigung, 2014.)

on-site combined heat-and-power plants as a major contribution to climate protection. With this technology, BWB generates electricity and heating amounting to 115,000 MWh/a, representing an annual CO_2 saving of 21,900t[4].

Deriving biogas from waste products was not the only form of waste-to-energy practised in the 1930s. Considerable effort was also made to extract and recycle fats and oils from wastewater for reuse as soap, lubrication or fuel. A survey conducted by the national association of municipal authorities (*Deutscher Gemeindetag*) of all German towns over 10,000 inhabitants in 1936 revealed a wide range of practices of fat and oil extraction from wastewater (Heilmann 1937). With the help of fat or grease separators installed in establishments with high used-fat levels, such as canteens, hotels, meat processing plants and hospitals, around 10,000 t of fat was extracted and collected across Germany each year. The cities of Cologne, Duisburg-Hamborn, Aachen, Krefeld, Mühlheim/Ruhr, Mönchengladbach and Bonn were cited as being particularly active in this field (Heilmann 1937). In Berlin, one company alone collected and processed fat and grease from some 500 restaurants and 2,000 butchers, as well as 50 canteens, 20 barracks and 35 hospitals (Heilmann 1937: 323; Pallasch 1937: 336). Once purified, the fat was used primarily for soap and industrial lubricants, but also as a fuel substitute. It was estimated, however, that the costs of collecting and treating the used fat were twice as high as the income generated by its reuse. For this reason, wastewater utilities managers pressed for the mandatory installation of fat separators in all major waste fat producers, arguing that the investment would reduce the considerable costs to the utility of removing solidified fat from blocked sewers (Heilmann 1937).

Used motor oils were also extracted from wastewater, refined and subsequently reused as a fuel or lubricant. Berlin's wastewater utility operated a local collection system for used oils (petrol, diesel, turpentine, lubricating oil) in 8,500 garages across the city (Pallasch 1937). The purified oils were then used by the utility itself, for instance as fuels for its own vehicle fleet. In contrast to solid fat collection, the financial savings made here covered most of the costs incurred, including all costs for collection vehicles and local separation appliances, as well as those for running the purification plant. Only the running costs of the collection itself required utility subsidies.

As with the extraction of biogas, these technologies for recycling fats and oils were not pursued after the war. They re-emerged on the public agenda in 2008 in the climate protection agreement between the Berlin water/wastewater utility and the city-state government referred to above. Here, amongst the list of future measures by the utility, are two proposals for recycling waste fats as energy sources. The first is to substitute heating oil for fire sludge incineration plants with used fats extracted from wastewater, primarily via fat separators in restaurants. The second is to ferment used fat with wastewater sludge to produce a gas substitute for natural gas. It is estimated that, once introduced, these technologies will reduce CO_2 emissions each year by ca. 6,000 t and 1,000 t respectively. In both cases, experiments and tests are currently being conducted by the utility.

Explaining the Rise, Fall and Resurrection of Waste-to-energy Technologies

Popular histories of Berlin's infrastructure, written primarily by engineers, have cultivated our ignorance of these waste-to-energy technologies (e.g., Bärthel 2006; Tepasse 2006; Mohajeri 2005). At pains to emphasise the continuity and resilience of the city's infrastructure systems in the face of political turbulence throughout the 20th century, they disregard technologies which do not contribute to the linear, modernist narrative of centralized systems. This is particularly the case with technologies promoted under the National Socialist regime, such as waste-to-energy. In the general course of technological progress the Nazi period and the war are regarded in this literature as an "interruption" (Seeger 1999: 55). If mentioned at all, the alternative technologies of the 1930s are dismissed as aberrations and their disappearance after the war is explained solely in terms of technical shortcomings and inefficiencies (Mohajeri 2005: 258–259). This literature fails to address the multiple ways in which such technologies have been inextricably bound up in the city's political and socio-economic fabric, being both a product and medium of Berlin's highly diverse political regimes. As a result, waste-to-energy technologies have effectively been written out of Berlin's history.

Reasons for Emergence

Given these qualms about proximity to Nazi ideology, the first important point to make is that all the technologies addressed in this chapter originated before the Nazi seizure of power in 1933. Biogas, for instance, was being produced at the city's wastewater treatment plant in Waßmannsdorf in 1927. They were, therefore, not originally 'Nazi technologies' at all, but the product of the Weimar Republic and multiple drivers, ranging from a culture of innovation and technological prowess in the technical-scientific community to the pressures exercised by socio-economic hardship, with a prominent role played by strong municipal leadership of the utilities.

The major push for these technologies came, however, from the second 4-year plan of the Nazi regime, introduced in October 1936 (Ludwig 1974; Maier 1996). This plan was presented to the public as an ambitious programme to achieve economic independence (autarky) for Germany within 4 years, comprising a series of policies and measures to reduce foreign imports of raw materials. We now know that it was based on a memo written by Hitler himself setting out its hidden military agenda: to put the German economy in a position to attack the Soviet Union (Ludwig 1974: 161). The 4-year plan was widely publicised in engineering journals with powerful, emotive appeals to German engineers to rise to the call and contribute through their creativity and expertise to meeting the targets. These appeals were backed up with considerable funding and political support for technologies which could substitute imported raw materials, encourage resource use or recycle waste products. This also applied to the waste-to-energy technologies described above (Mohajeri 2005: 258–259). At the time, the 4-year plan was announced as "the beginning of a new technical era" (Heilmann 1937: 366), creating hitherto unknown freedom for compliant engineers (Maier 1996: 260ff). The underlying military purpose of Nazi policy on new technologies promoting self-sufficiency was certainly not concealed, being openly discussed in the Nazi journal *Deutsche Technik*.

Reasons for Disappearance

The disappearance of technologies to derive biogas, fats and fuels from waste products after the war can be explained in a number of different ways, all of which are valid to some degree. The most straightforward of explanations is that the technologies were not advanced enough to survive. Many engineers today take this line, arguing that such technologies were neither technically nor economically viable (Bärthel 2006; Tepasse 2006; Mohajeri 2005). When the funding programmes were axed towards the end of the war and political support collapsed with the Nazi regime in 1945, the flaws of these technologies were revealed and they were consequently discarded. This view attributes major significance to the inherent quality of a technology as the driving factor behind its diffusion.

A second explanation is that the path dependency of existing centralized socio-technical regimes reasserted itself after 1945. The line of argument here is that the dominant technological systems for the centralized collection and disposal of wastewater were never seriously challenged by the alternative technologies in terms of their relative significance. These enjoyed temporary prominence in debates amongst experts, but only insofar as they did not threaten the operational effectiveness and institutional arrangements of the LTS. This perspective is much broader in scope than the first, considering not only the technology itself, but also the whole socio-technical configuration.

There is, however, a third explanation, which is peculiar to the post-war period in Germany. This has to do with the strong association seen at the time between the technologies discussed here and the Nazi regime. The recycling technologies heralded under the 4-year plan became a political liability after the war. Those who had made careers in promoting them in the 1930s were keen to disassociate themselves from them in post-war Germany. Their future careers depended on demonstrating that they, individually and as a profession, were returning to the fold of mainstream sanitary and energy engineering. This is evident in the professional journals published after 1945, which addressed solely conventional infrastructure technologies without any reference to past alternatives or, indeed, to the need for recycling and saving natural resources (e.g., Imhoff 1947). From this perspective, the alternative technologies disappeared because they were tarnished with the brown brush of Nazism. This resonates with David Blackbourn's criticism of the "Nazi taint" preventing a differentiated analysis of German environmental history (Blackbourn 2006: 18). For this reason, we ascertain that Germany's early waste recycling technologies did not just disappear; they were – and still are – deliberately ignored.

Reasons for Re-emergence Today

The re-emergence of waste-to-energy technologies can also be attributed to multiple drivers. Firstly, the policy environment is creating new opportunities for using renewables, recycling materials and saving energy in the interests of environmental and climate protection. Subsidies and feed-in tariffs for power generated from renewable sources have provided a crucial boost to biogas production (Deublein and Steinhauser 2011). Secondly, technological developments in Germany are increasingly influenced by global discourses on renewables and recycling and their applications worldwide, creating new markets for Berlin's utilities. Thirdly, intense debates over the privatisation and re-municipalisation of Berlin's power and water/wastewater utilities since the 1990s have sensitised local politics and the city's utilities to the need to address popular concerns over environmental sustainability and public accountability. The agreements made by all the city's utilities with the Berlin city government to save natural resources and protect the climate underline the importance given to their 'green' public image. All these factors have enabled the application of waste-to-energy technologies as complements to the city's established socio-technical systems.

Reflections

In what ways can the findings and explanations of this chapter contribute to ongoing debates on urban infrastructure systems in transition? How can the empirical case of Berlin help substantiate or challenge the various approaches to conceptualising how urban sustainability transitions unfold in time and space? To answer these questions we refer back to the literatures introduced in Section 10.2.

Understanding the Transitional

The historical thrust of this chapter was not directed at reconstructing the transition from one socio-technical system to another, but at tracing the chequered trajectories of Berlin's waste-to-energy technologies over a long period. The findings challenge the assumption in some MLP studies that technological innovations are generated primarily at the micro scale, in technological niches, and rely on a supportive socio-technical regime or favourable exogenous factors to flourish. The massive interventions by the Nazi elites for national autarky, backed by the regime, were *the* driving force behind the diffusion of alternative technologies at the time, and cannot simply be subsumed as a favourable exogenous factor. Our study would suggest that 'landscape' factors influencing transitions are not something 'above' socio-technical niches and regimes, but very much part of them. This can be illustrated by the insidious ways in which Nazi ideology became internalised by individual engineers to advance their own careers during the 1930s and to reconfigure the established wastewater regime. The same can be said for the desire of these engineers to adapt to the post-war order. It follows that the distinction between the three levels of niche, regime and landscape may be a useful analytical heuristic, but runs the risk of downplaying processes of permeation across these levels.

In terms of path dependency and creation the story told is, again, not about one path replacing another but about the non-linear careers of waste-to-energy technologies, marked by unexpected fillips, sudden reversals and adaptive continuity. Path dependency is powerfully evident over the whole period. Following Simmie's terminology (Simmie 2012), there was no 'displacement' of the dominant socio-technical systems for wastewater treatment or energy generation, despite radical shifts in Berlin's political regimes. However, certain political regimes did create the conditions for alternative technologies to flourish alongside the established systems, which can be interpreted as a form of 'layering'. To this typology we would add, based on our findings, the categories of 'submersion' and 're-emersion' to describe processes by which technologies disappeared from the policy agenda and re-emerged in a modernised form to address new challenges. A powerful argument emerging from this chapter is that acts of 'submersion' can involve the wilful discarding of technologies deemed politically undesirable by key actors. This highlights the huge significance of agency and power working both for and against socio-technical transitions.

Understanding the Urban

This chapter adds to the literature on urban infrastructures in several ways. Firstly, it illustrates the multiple geographies at play in socio-technical transitions. The careers of Berlin's waste-to-energy technologies described here were shaped by a combination of physical geographies (e.g., the spatial range of its sewers or the non-availability of natural resources during wartime), environmental geographies (e.g., the use of on-site biogas by sewage treatment plants), political geographies (e.g., the role of Berlin as national capital) and institutional geographies (e.g., municipal responsibility for service provision). These different geographies are not simply a given, but socially constructed to serve specific purposes. Thus, Berlin's waste-to-energy technologies were enrolled by the Nazis in a narrative of self-dependence for the urban region as its contribution to national autarky. Secondly, the chapter draws particular attention to the importance of political conflict and power at different spatial levels, from the city and city-region to national and international arenas (cf. McFarlane and Rutherford 2008; Moss 2014). At several stages in their trajectories, the technologies we studied acted either as symbols of Berlin's technological prowess, a medium for implementing national autarky or expressions of municipal self-government. Thirdly, we have emphasised the importance of a city's (hidden) history of technological trajectories for understanding ongoing processes of socio-technical reconfiguration, building on a long tradition of work on the connections between urbanisation processes, urban governance and the emergence of modern urban infrastructures (e.g., Tarr and Dupuy 1988; Melosi 2000). By revealing the roots of today's alternative technologies, we have attempted to demonstrate the importance of acknowledging not only the existence of forerunners, but also how these can be ignored or even deliberately discarded by commentators past and present.

Conclusion

This chapter has set out to challenge a common assumption in policy and research circles that today's alternative urban technologies are something radically new. Using examples from the field of waste-to-energy developed and applied in and around Berlin during the interwar period, I have traced their chequered trajectories through to the present to show that the history of these technologies is not linear and gradual, but one marked by phases of emergence, disappearance and re-emergence. More importantly, this chapter has revealed how these processes of emergence, disappearance and re-emergence were not predetermined by some inherent qualities or deficiencies of the technologies themselves, but by human agency. We should not therefore speak of 'lost' alternatives, but rather of ones that were intentionally discarded and subsequently ignored, or even repressed from collective memory. Similarly, this practice of deliberate exclusion cannot be explained primarily in terms of dissatisfaction with the functionality or performance of these technologies. More significant was how they were perceived and judged by those responsible for their (non-)implementation, as well as by later generations of engineers. The factors influencing these perceptions were multiple and dynamic, and sometimes involved radical shifts in the appeal of individual technologies in professional circles. They ranged from concerns over environmental degradation to the desire to promote national autarky, and from the career aspirations of sanitary engineers to the racist-nationalist ideology of the Nazi regime.

The lessons that can be drawn for today's attempts at sustainable urban transitions are fourfold. Firstly, the Berlin case instructs us that the role of agency is crucial not only in promoting certain technologies, but also in hindering or overlooking them. Exploring the roots of current technological innovations will illustrate processes of contestation, collaboration, adaptation, realignment and suppression, which can be helpful in understanding ongoing transitions. Secondly, the case highlights the importance of politics to socio-technical systems and their transition. It suggests that in the future, we need to pay greater attention to how interests and power become bound up in the material form, the institutional arrangements and the symbolic value of urban infrastructure systems, and to how political shifts reverberate across these systems in diverse ways. Thirdly, we have indicated the multiple geographies at play in socio-technical transitions – whether physical, environmental, political or institutional – and how they combine to frame socio-technical pathways. Finally, we have argued for more awareness of the history of urban technologies in order to gain a better appreciation of the non-linearity, context-dependency and contingency so characteristic of socio-technical transitions.

Notes

1 www.bsr.de/9495.html accessed 08.06.2012
2 The chapter is based on a longer article on alternative technologies in Berlin published in Moss (2016).
3 This figure represents over half of the amount produced at the new BSR plant referred to above.
4 http://www.stadtentwicklung.berlin.de/umwelt/klimaschutz/aktiv/vereinbarung/download/bwb-ks_senguv.pdf accessed on 08.06.2012.

References

Bärthel, H. (2006): Anlagen und Bauten der Stadtentwässerung. In: Architekten- und Ingenieur-Verein zu Berlin (ed.): *Berlin und seine Bauten. Part X, Vol. A (2) Stadttechnik*. Michael Imhof Verlag, Petersberg, pp.111–186.

Blackbourn, D. (2006): *The Conquest of Nature. Water, Landscape, and the Making of Modern Germany*. Norton, New York/London.

BSR (Berliner Stadtreinigungsbetriebe A.ö.R.) (2010): Genehmigungsantrag nach § 4 BImSchG für eine Trockenvergärungsanlage. Kurzbeschreibung. Online: http://www.bsr.de/assets/downloads/2010-06-28_Kurzbeschreibung_BSR-Genehm-2010.pdf. Accessed on 29.06.2012.

Bulkeley, H.; Castán Broto, V.; Maassen, A. (2011): Governing urban local carbon transitions. In: H. Bulkeley, V. Castán Broto, M. Hodson, S. Marvin (eds.): *Cities and Low Carbon Transitions*. Routledge, London, pp.29–41.

Coutard, O.; Rutherford, J. (2011): The rise of post-networked cities in Europe? Recombining infrastructural, ecological and urban transformations in low carbon transitions. In: H. Bulkeley, V. Castán Broto, M. Hodson, S. Marvin (eds.): *Cities and Low Carbon Transitions*. Routledge, London, pp.107–125.

Deublein, D.; Steinhauser, A. (2011): *Biogas from Waste and Renewable Resources. An Introduction*. Wiley, Weinheim.

Geels, F.W. (2002): Technological transitions as evolutionary reconfiguration processes: A multi-level perspective and a case-study. In: *Research Policy*, 31, pp. 1257–1274.

Geels, F.W.; Kemp, R. (2007) Dynamics in socio-technical systems: Typology of change processes and contrasting case studies. In: *Technology in Society*, 29(4), pp. 441–455.

Heilmann, A. (1937): Städtereinigung und Vierjahresplan. In: *Gesundheits-Ingenieur*, 60(21), pp.321–327 & 60(22), pp.351–366.

Hodson, M.; Marvin, S. (2009): Cities mediating technological transitions: understanding visions, intermediation and consequences. In: *Technology Analysis & Strategic Management*, 21(4), pp.515–534.

Hodson, M.; Marvin, S. (2010): Can cities shape socio-technical transitions and how would we know if they were? In: *Research Policy*, 39, pp.477–485.

Hughes, T.P. (1983): *Networks of Power: Electrification in Western Society, 1880–1930*. John Hopkins University Press, Baltimore and London.

Imhoff, K. (1947): Die deutsche Abwasser-Wissenschaft in der Kriegszeit. In: *Gesundheits-Ingenieur*, 68 (3), pp.65–70.

Joerges, B. (1999): High variability discourse in the history and sociology of large technical systems. In: O. Coutard (ed.): *The Governance of Large Technical Systems*. Routledge, London/New York, pp.258–290.

Laak, D. van (2005): Infrastrukturen. Anthropologische und alltagsgeschichtliche Perspektiven. In: G.M. König (ed.): *Alltagsdinge. Erkundungen der materiellen Kultur*. Tübinger Vereinigung für Völkskunde e.V., Tübingen, pp.81–91.

Langbein, F. (1927): Die Abwasservorkläranlage auf dem Bölkensberge des Berliner Rieselfeldes Waßmannsdorf als Gaslieferer. In: *Das Gas- und Wasserfach*, 70 (46), pp.1109–1118.

Langbein, F. (1936): Die volkswirtschaftliche Bedeutung des Abwassers. In: *Gesundheits-Ingenieur*, 59 (19), pp.268–272.

Langbein, F.; Kroll, F. (1931): Die Gewinnung und Verwertung des Faulgases auf der Berliner Abwasservorkläranlage in Waßmannsdorf. In: *Das Gas- und Wasserfach*, 74 (21), pp.469–476.

Ludwig, K.-H. (1974): *Technik und Ingenieure im Dritten Reich*. Droste Verlag, Düsseldorf.

Maier, H. (1996): Nationalsozialistische Technikideologie und die Politisierung des "Technikerstandes": Fritz Todt und die Zeitschrift "Deutsche Technik". In: B. Dietz, M. Fessner, H. Maier (eds.): *Technische Intelligenz und „Kulturfaktor Technik". Kulturvorstellung von Technikern und Ingenieuren zwischen Kaiserreich und früher Bundesrepublik Deutschland*. Waxmann, Münster/New York/München/Berlin, pp.253–268.

McFarlane, C.; Rutherford, J. (2008): Political infrastructures: Governing and experiencing the fabric of the city. In: *International Journal of Urban and Regional Research*, 32, pp.415–435.

Melosi, M. (2005): Path dependence and urban history: Is a marriage possible? In: D. Schott, B. Luckin, G. Massard-Guilbaud (eds.): *Resources of the City: Contributions to an Environmental History of Modern Europe*. Aldershot: Ashgate, pp. 262–275.

Melosi, M. (2000): *The Sanitary City. Urban Infrastructure in America from Colonial Times to the Present*. John Hopkins University Press, Baltimore and London.

Mohajeri, S. (2005): *100 Jahre Berliner Wasserversorgung und Abwasserentsorgung 1840–1940* (Schriftenreihe des Zentrums Technik und Gesellschaft der TU Berlin, Band 2). Franz Steiner Verlag, Stuttgart.

Monstadt, J. (2009): Conceptualizing the political ecology of urban infrastructures: insights from technology and urban studies. In: *Environment and Planning A*, 41, pp.1924–1942.

Moss, T. (2014): Socio-technical change and the politics of urban infrastructure: Managing energy in Berlin between dictatorship and democracy, *Urban Studies*, 51(7), pp.1432–1448.

Moss, T. (2016): Discarded surrogates, modified traditions, welcome complements: The chequered careers of alternative technologies in Berlin's infrastructure systems, Social Studies of Science, online under DOI: 10.1177/0306312716657205.

Pallasch, O. (1937): Reinigung und Verwertung gewerblicher Abwässer in Berlin. In: *Gesundheits-Ingenieur*, 60 (21), pp.334–337.

Seeger, H. (1999): The history of German waste water treatment. In: *European Water Management*, 2(5), pp.51–56.

Simmie, J. (2012): Path dependence and new technological path creation in the Danish wind power endustry. In: *European Planning Studies*, 20(5), pp.753–772.

Tarr, J.; Dupuy, G. (eds.) (1988): *Technology and the Rise of the Networked City in Europe and America*. Philadelphia: Temple University Press.

Tepasse, H. (2006): *Stadttechnik im Städtebau Berlins. 20. Jahrhundert*. Gebr. Mann Verlag, Berlin.

Truffer, B.; Coenen, L. (2012): Environmental innovation and sustainability transitions in regional studies. In: *Regional Studies*, 46(1), pp.1–21.

11 The Spatial Complexity of Sustainability Transitions in the 'Cities of the East'

Anne Maassen

Introduction

The 'Cities of the East' – a phrase used expansively in this chapter to encompass urban settlements in Eastern Europe, the Russian Federation and Central Asia – are in transition. Multiple and parallel processes are currently unfolding: in particular, political reforms towards market economies and socio-economic transformations in public and private life, including commercialization, regeneration and suburbanisation (e.g., Collier 2011; Lane 2006; Shirokanova 2010; Sýkora and Bouzarovski 2011). The present chapter is concerned with one particular aspect of contemporary transformations – namely, those that endeavour to decrease the negative environmental externalities of urban systems of provision. This is a topic of great importance, given that the region's economies are amongst the most energy-, carbon- and water-intensive on earth: carbon intensity is almost twice the EU-15 average in Eastern Europe, and more than four times as high as the EU-15 average in Central Asia (EBRD 2011). Expected climate change impacts include high to extremely high water risk (WRI 2014), which is expected to further intensify existing subnational and trans-boundary conflicts over water for electricity generation and irrigation (UNECE 2011). From Belarus in Eastern Europe to Uzbekistan in Central Asia, climate change exacerbate existing resource management issues, and threaten to further deepen poverty, corruption and alienation from the state (International Crisis Group 2011).

Therefore, understanding, catalysing and achieving sustainability transitions is critical for avoiding the high environmental, economic and often human costs of the intensifying unsustainabilities in the post-Socialist East. Yet, applying transitions theory to this hitherto understudied geographical area reveals the limitations of existing conceptualisations of how place-specific and other spatial relations shape transition processes. Although this field is constantly growing in analytical sophistication (Smith et al. 2010), current approaches are relatively ill-equipped to capture a situation characterized by a pronounced local need for transformation, but where endogenous capacity is largely lacking. Contrary to Western contexts that have tended to be the focus of existing scholarship, in the Cities of the East state capability for leading transformation is weak, technical capacity extremely low and finance scarce. This situation – which represents in many ways an accentuated case of transition challenges elsewhere – is useful for interrogating existing approaches' ability to account for how place-specificity shapes the emergence of the need for transformation, as well the capacity to respond to it. Questioning the origins of transition potential opens up a long-overdue conceptual discussion about how contextual factors impact the prospects and trajectories of innovation processes – and is therefore of general interest to transition scholarship.

To develop an approach that captures the intricacies of transition dynamics in the Cities of the East, this chapter begins by exploring existing entry points for understanding the place-specificity of transition processes. Building on existing insights within transition studies and relational approaches to space, it introduces the notion of *spatial complexity* to understand multilevel transition processes. This brief conceptual discussion is followed by an account of the spatial complexity of unfolding transition processes in the Cities of the East. First, the chapter discusses the scalar legacies of the Soviet-era urban planning regime, which strongly shapes the nature and origins of sustainability challenges in the Cities of the East. The chapter then explores emerging responses to the significant urban unsustainabilities affecting post-socialist cities. In the absence of technical and financial resources, responses are strongly driven by extra-local networks of actors, which channel resources through a range of relatively codified interactions and processes. By exploring various spatialities – urban territories, scales and networks – involved in the transition process at hand, this chapter posits that transition studies have much to benefit from understanding transitions as emerging and unfolding phenomena at the intersection of multiple spatial forms.

Spatial Complexity and Transitions

Sustainability transitions have gained ground in policy and civil society circles (e.g. EC, 2008; DECC, 2009) and received increasing scholarly attention over the recent years. In parallel, there is a growing consensus that geography and space matter for sustainability transition processes. This relatively recent, more overt concern with the spatial dimensions of transitions can be seen as emerging from a reaction to approaches such as the multi-level perspective and strategic niche management, in which the spatial dimensions of transitions are largely implicit (e.g., Schot and Geels 2008; Van Driel and Schot 2005; Verbong and Geels 2007; Rotmans et al. 2001). In response, a number of recent contributions have begun to grapple with the importance of geography and place-specificity for shaping the conditions under which sustainability transitions take place. An explicitly geographical entry point has led scholars to use the 'regional' (Späth and Rohracher 2010), the 'urban' (Hodson and Marvin 2010; Bulkeley et al. (2014) and the local 'community' or 'grassroots' level (Smith 2010; Seyfang et al. 2014) as foci and loci of analysis, and the multi-scalar innovation systems for specific technologies (e.g., Binz and

Truffer 2011). In such approaches, transitions are increasingly understood as "a geographical process, involving the reconfiguration of current patterns and scales of economic and social activity" (Bridge et al. 2013).

While geography and space are increasingly used as *entry points* for analysis, there has not been a fundamental conceptual shift in the field of transition studies. Despite a more explicit concern with the spatial dimensions of transition, according to Hansen and Coenen, there has been "an emphasis on understanding the importance of place-specificity at the *local* level" (2014: 2; emphasis added). What is notable is that to date, there is relatively little consensus on *how* exactly spatial dimensions shape transitions (Smith et al. 2010: 443–4; Hansen and Coenen 2014). In response, the authors (Hansen and Coenen 2014: 2) propose to stimulate a more advanced debate around quintessentially geographical questions: "How do transitions unfold across different geographical contexts? What are the importance and role of relations at different spatial scales for transition processes?". Building on this growing awareness of the importance spatiality in transitions, this chapter introduces a 'relational' understanding of space to argue in favour of a greater acknowledgment of the spatial complexity of sustainability transitions. After a brief exposition of the conceptual thinking behind spatial complexity from a relational perspective, the chapter mobilises a series of spatial concepts to capture sustainability transition processes in the Cities of the East.

In general, relational approaches make sense of the world by focusing on relationships *between* entities, as opposed to trying to understand them as self-contained wholes endowed with essential attributes. Applied to space, this signals a rejection of taking "the boundaries that organize our world as given and natural" for granted (Ollman 1993: 38). Space, just like other attributes, is understood as emergent, and as a result its constitution is treated as a topic in its own right. A spatial analysis, typical of human geography, uses spatial concepts as analytical devices to "establish, clarify and analyse connections, comparisons and meaning… to unsettle the dominant binaries and master narratives" (Howitt 1998: 49–50). Applying this type of spatial sensitivity to transition frameworks such as the multi-level perspective enables the surfacing of spatial 'master concepts' (Leitner et al. 2008) that have dominated in transition scholarship: across approaches, the prevailing (even if implicit) spatial forms that have received most attention are 'territorial' (the nation, the region, the city) and 'networks' (actors making up the make-up of 'niches' and 'regimes'). While there have been some attempts at 'unpicking' and 'unpacking' networks of actors at niche and regime levels (as noted by Genus and Coles (2008)), there has been little methodical examination of how these two spatial forms – networks and territories – may in fact be co-constitutively tied up with one another in practice.

In contrast, relational approaches to space explicitly deal with the relationship between different spatial forms. In particular, actor-network theory (ANT) (e.g., Law 1992; Mol and Law 1994; Law and Singleton 2003) has shown a specific concern with theorising the relationship between territories and networks (Law 1986 [2001]). Accordingly, the seeming coherence of territories – as places which are demarcated from others by relatively clear boundaries – is emergent. Territories such as cities and nations are understood as the products of less immediately visible networked relationships. For instance, infrastructural networks (such as electricity and water systems) may integrate cities, regions and nations into a seamless singular unit served by a seemingly homogenous infrastructure provision model (Maassen 2012). Beyond interrogating the relationship between territories and their underlying networks, the notion of 'scale' has been used by geographers to refer to spatial relations consisting of "a hierarchical scaffolding of nested territorial units stretching from the global, the supranational, and the national downwards to the regional, the metropolitan, the urban, the local" (Marston et al. 2005: 416). Similarly to networks, scale is thus understood as integrating territory, however it does so in a hierarchical rather than 'flat' manner (Marston et al. 2005; Jones et al. 2007).

At its most basic, therefore, the significance of relational thinking for understanding transition processes is that space ceases to be a passive backdrop of the analysis. This implies that spatial complexity may be mobilised as a *means for explaining* transitions. What is more, rather than debating the 'right' spatial lens through which to analyse transitions, a relational approach to space offers the possibility that different kinds of spatial relations (such as territories and networks) may in fact *coexist, overlap* and *intersect* (Mol and Law 1994: 641). This way of mobilising spatial complexity in an analytical manner has been used to understand, amongst others, diseases (Law and Singleton 2003; Mol 2002), natural resource management (Bear and Eden 2008; Kortelainen 2010; Medd and Marvin 2008), the social and spatial organisation of hospital wards (Middleton and Brown 2002; Moreira 2004), and car traffic (Kullman 2009). For instance, in relation to water governance in the UK, Medd and Marvin (2008: 297), seek to uncover "the multiplicity of relations that differentiate as much as integrate the regional space".

Understanding transition processes as spatially complex opens up a fruitful avenue for extending current conceptualisations of transition processes to other, less well-studied cases, such as urban sustainability transitions in the Cities of the East. Besides destabilising spatial master narratives, an important consequence of treating spatial complexity as constitutive of transition processes is that our attention is drawn to those processes and entities that are critical for integrating otherwise separate territorial, scalar and networked relationships. In the literature, this 'patchwork' has been conceptualised as 'strategic intermediation' (e.g., Medd and Marvin 2008; Hodson and Marvin 2009a, 2009b; Moss 2009). Accordingly, the fluid work of intermediaries involves deliberate processes of translating between (sometimes competing, and potentially conflicting) visions, priorities, and organisational realities, across and beyond formal institutional structures, and at different scales of government and stakeholder groups. Crucially, intermediation seeks to account for the micropolitics and power distributions at play in change processes, by revealing how elites (urban, or other) may 'speak on behalf of the city' at the expense of other, more marginal voices (Hodson and Marvin 2012).

As will be seen in the remainder of this chapter, understanding how sustainability transitions are unfolding in the Cities of the East requires sensitivity to both the spatial complexity of transitions, as well as to the processes and devices of trans-spatial intermediation. Having briefly and selectively explored the conceptual implications of spatial complexity for understanding unfolding sustainability transitions, the chapter now proceeds to trace the origins of the need for transformation in the Cities of the East.

The Scalar Origins of Urban Unsustainability in the East

As in many places across the world, there is no question that sustainability challenges in the East have a distinctly urban dimension. As elsewhere, the common denominator for addressing sustainability are infrastructure systems: urban areas are the physical locations of most key resource intensive infrastructure (in particular power, heat and water) and urbanisation and urban population growth are placing increasing pressures on systems of provision. For instance, in Kazakhstan up to 66% of the population will be urban by 2030, with clusters around Almaty, Astana and Shymkent, where urbanisation rates between 2004 and 2009 exceeded 35% (NAC and Centennial Group 2014). Similarly, during the last 20 years the share of urban population in Uzbekistan increased by 10.2% (Center for Economic Research 2013) – this is particularly significant given that the population has more than doubled, from 14 to 30 million, since the last major investments in infrastructure (WRI 2003). While the region is diverse in terms of economy, climate and resource endowments, this section describes the striking commonality in terms of the urban sustainability challenges facing urban settlements across the region, which stems from their embeddedness in scalar relationships that have mediated infrastructure planning for decades.

The contemporary character of urban infrastructures in the post-socialist East is strongly shaped by historical relationships that placed Soviet cities into a scalar subordination to the centralised control of Moscow. Today's vital infrastructures – power, heat, energy, water –are relics of Soviet-era infrastructure development, shaped by a region-wide 'urban infrastructure regime' (Monstadt 2009; Bulkeley et al. 2014): leaky district heating systems and thermally highly inefficient public, commercial and in particular residential buildings are ubiquitous features across the Cities of the East. For instance, the so-called residential Khrushevki[1] in the Russian Federation account for about 45% of total heat consumption (EBRD-GEF 2008). In Moldova, the building sector accounts for approximately half of the country's entire final energy consumption (EuropeAid 2012). In Kazakhstan, approximately 70% of buildings have very low thermal performance, in particular those constructed between 1950 and 1980, and average technical losses in communal infrastructures are estimated at around 16% in power distribution, 20% in heat supply and up to 60% in water supply. Reflecting the Soviet planning rationality of the time, the majority of the building stock across the region dates back to a period during which the energy performance of buildings was not codified in national law – the period of mass construction between 1960 and 1980 (EuropeAid 2012; BPIE 2011; EuropeAid 2012; EBRD-GEF 2008).

In the Cities of the East, the challenge of sustainability transition is intricately tied up with historical path dependencies (e.g., Unruh 2000; Del Rio and Unruh 2007), as well the post-independence decade, which similarly affected many of the transition economies' national and urban governments. The dissolution of the Soviet Union in December 1991 was accompanied by the dismantling of its centralised provision model, by which budget subsidies cascaded from the centre of power (Moscow) to governments, cities and municipalities. The withdrawal of funds upon which infrastructure planning in the Soviet model relied left many in a financially precarious situation precisely at a time when infrastructures were reaching the end of their lives. As a result, today in relatively higher income countries, such as in the energy-rich Russian Federation, the economic costs of energy intensity are staggering – wasted energy is estimated to cost the economy US$ 84 billion to US $112 billion in lost export revenues and US $3 billion to US $5 billion in federal and municipal spending on energy subsidies (IFC 2013). Energy inefficiency is even more of an issue in countries such as Belarus and Ukraine, which suffer from unstable, inflationary economies partly because their poor energy resource endowments make them dependent on (mostly Russian) energy imports. In the West-facing Eastern European countries (Bulgaria, Czech Republic, Hungary, Moldova, Poland, and Romania), EU accession (or prospects thereof) imply the costly alignment of energy and production infrastructure with European environmental directives and the Energy and Climate policy package (IFC 2013).

Mobilising the capacity to respond to deepening infrastructural unsustainability is a profound challenge. While capital investment needs in many cities are high, institutional and economic structures that could leverage financial and technical capacity are largely lacking. Neither the technical expertise for improved infrastructure nor the substantial financial funds needed are readily available. For most municipalities, finance for upgrading buildings, which was traditionally channelled by the central Soviet state to the Soviet regions and provinces (and from there to the municipalities), is either very low or in some cases even decreasing. While there are nuances across the region in extent and severity, in general the state's prominence in service provision is associated with features such as the lack of cost recovery in public services (related to utilities' historical dependence on centralized subsidies for their operations) and ill-defined contracting and procurement legislation, including, for instance, the limited fiscal autonomy of municipalities (which affects their legal right to borrow). On the one hand, dedicated earmarked funds, where these exist, tend to support current expenditure rather than capital investments (such as upgrading and new construction) (OECD 2011). On the other hand, borrowing for infrastructural renewal is challenging, as traditionally municipalities had limited legal and technical capacity for catalysing private sector investments. Resource efficiency codes and standards (e.g., for buildings, cars and appliances) are often low, only inconsistently enforced or entirely absent; and there is usually a general lack of awareness by the population of resource efficiency issues.

Owing to the historically prominent role of the Soviet state in the economy, the Cities of the East were embedded into the lowest level of a scalar infrastructure regime. At present, post-independence neglect and obsolescence coupled with growing pressures on systems of provision converge to create a profoundly challenging prospect for urban sustainability transitions in the East. The historical legacy of state planning results in a situation where today, potential borrowers (e.g., business and municipal enterprises) have poorly developed investment planning capacities, and domestic financing institutions typically provide loans with unfavourable terms (high rates with short tenors), which are mostly incompatible with the longer-term character of energy efficiency investments. Across the region, common emerging priorities resemble an undifferentiated laundry list of resource efficiency technologies: thermal insulation and high efficiency technical building equipment, modernising district heating systems, cleaner decentralised energy technologies and improved municipal water management (UNFCCC 2014a; 2014b). However, while the technical solutions are largely known and available, viable infrastructure financing models – for example, where semi-public or private housing associations (rather than the state or the local government) commission upgrades – have been slow to emerge.

Having traced the scalar origins of unsustainabilities, the remainder of this chapter traces the emergence and character of the emerging attempts at sustainability transitions by examining one key aspect of current developments: the "climate aid network", in terms of its importance for urban sustainability transitions and the impact of its main intermediary processes and entities on the trajectory of transitions in the urban East. Just like their shared past is defined through scalar integration under a common infrastructure logic, in the post-independence decades another set of common extra-urban relationships have become strong determinants of transition potential in the Cities of the East: the multilateral 'climate aid' network. Neither local, national, nor Soviet, the climate aid network consists of a range of actors involved in channelling international development assistance that targets the mitigation of the causes and adaptation to the impacts of climate change. Evidence presented in the following section suggests that international (as opposed to local or national) funds and expertise have become a firmly established and growing aspect of the response to climate change and other unsustainabilities in the East.

A Networked Response through the Multilateral 'Climate Aid' Network

The emergence of a networked response to urban unsustainabilities in the post-Socialist East can be traced back to the mid-1990s, in relation to international agreements to address climate change. Around that time, multilateral processes gradually elevated climate change from a purely environmental to a human rights issue for the millions of people and communities around the world affected by climate impacts, rising sea levels, increasingly severe floods and storms, and health impacts (OHCHR 2009; Johl and Lador 2012). Substantial growth in bi- and multilateral financial commitments resulted fromthe first Meeting of the Parties in Montreal (Canada) in 2005 and the entry into force of the Kyoto Protocol. Since then, development leaders have made climate change a "top priority" (UN Secretary General in 2013) and declaring the "Year of Climate Change Action" (World Bank's President in 2014). Beyond multilateral rhetoric, climate aid now mobilizes over US $20 million annually worldwide in bilateral funds alone (OECD 2013). In Eastern Europe and Central Asia, over US$ 1 billion have been channelled through the climate aid network to date (Climate Funds Update 2013).

Crucially, linking climate change to poverty and human development issues at the highest multilateral levels had the effect of extending the structures and processes of the well-established international aid system to address climate change issues in the developing world. As is typical of other areas of development aid, climate aid brings three principal actors into a networked relationship: 'donors' (often multilateral trust funds), 'recipients' of climate aid (often national governments of developing countries) and multilateral development banks (MDBs) and development agencies (which manage the disbursements of climate aid funds). The evolution of the specific climate aid network for the East is abstracted in Figure 11.1, illustrating how it expanded over time in terms of both actors and the number of individual interventions (called 'projects') enabled through the network. For the sake of simplicity, Figure 1. only refers to the region's major donor in absolute terms, the Global Environment Facility (GEF), the financial mechanism for the UNFCCC (United Nations Framework Convention on Climate Change)[2]. The period 1992–2012 in Figure 11.1 is divided into four phases, reflecting the times at which the GEF received bilateral financial injections from over 40 governments worldwide (totalling over US$ 3.5 billion for the entire period depicted; over US$ 420 million for Eastern Europe and Central Asia). Between the last two periods depicted, a large injection of donor funding into the GEF for its fifth replenishment took place, following the coming into force of the Kyoto Protocol and increasing international focus on climate change (while the relative decrease indicates the fund's gradual exhaustion leading up to its recent replenishment).

Considering climate aid as a networked response makes it possible to understand the network as a whole and its effectiveness in channelling funds to the urban scale. Specific to the GEF's climate aid network, the central nodes through which financial resources flow and through which expertise is mobilized are the GEF, recipient countries, and multilateral development banks, who are the mediators of the flow of resources – the World Bank/International Finance Corporation (IFC) and the European Bank for Reconstruction and Development (EBRD); as well as the UN agencies (UNDP, UNEP, UNIDO). The relationship between these entities can be understood as a quasi-triangular

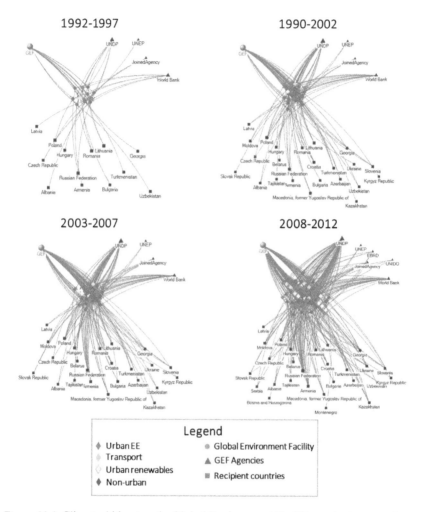

Figure 11.1 Climate Aid network: Global Environment Facility project approval
(by GEF Agency and recipient country). Created with NodeXL (http://
nodexl.codeplex.com) based on source material from the GEF project
database (http://www.thegef.org/gef/project_list *'Joined agency' refers to
projects that are led by two GEF Agencies

configuration: donors provide funds that are tied to specific objectives (e.g.,
related to climate mitigation and adaptation), agencies create proposals and
leverage additional funds (often but not exclusively concessional loans), and
recipients (typically national governments) provide political support to projects that are aligned with their needs. In sum, interventions take shape at
the intersection of donors' funds, agencies' mandates and climate aid recipients' need for financial resources and expertise. This configuration, which
transcends both territorial and scalar spaces, effectively enables recipients

(in the GEF's case national governments) to access finance and expertise that would otherwise be beyond their reach.

The network graphs in Figure 11.1 highlight those projects with a specific focus on urban interventions (red for urban energy efficiency, green for transport and yellow for urban renewables). The trend in urban projects largely mirrors that of the GEF climate aid network as a whole, namely its growth in size and 'wealth' (in terms of monetary resources that flow through it) over the last decades. At the centre of Figure 11.1 is the increasingly dense 'project space', which is made up of a total of 123 (urban and non-urban) projects at a total cumulative value of over $3 billion (this includes GEF trust fund financing as well as the 'co-finance' mobilised by development agencies). Over half the funds for the region have been committed to specifically urban interventions, including energy efficiency in buildings and district heating systems (90%), followed by low-carbon urban transport (7%), and urban renewables (mostly biomass for heating, accounting for 3% of urban interventions). The GEF's first replenishment period (1992–1997) saw six projects focusing specifically on urban sustainability issues across six countries and led by only three GEF implementing agencies (UNDP, UNEP, and the World Bank) totalling a mere US$ 65 million of total project value. By the end of the 2008–2012 period, a total of 54 urban-focused projects were approved (out of a total of 123 in Eastern Europe and Central Asia). The value of these projects exceeds US$ 1.4 billion (including GEF finance and co-financing) and implementation is taking place across 20 countries and led by five GEF Agencies (the EBRD and UNIDO in addition to the original three).

What is remarkable about the structure of the climate aid network is its 'non-local' character – the key nodes in the climate aid network are spatially distant donors, development banks and agencies and national governments. In contrast, local governments, the domestic private sector (where it exists), and civil society are far less integrated into the network than is the case with more familiar transition processes in the West. In this context of spatial complexity – where multilateral networks are blended with territorial imperatives and scales of governance – the non-local character of resource mobilisation questions the nature of those critical entities and the intermediary processes that enable financial and technical resources to flow to urban areas.

Once again, the fabric of the multilateral climate aid network closely reflects the international aid regime, in which so-called programming is an integral process by which a diversity of actors are bound into strategic and commercial relationships that enable specific interventions – climate aid projects – to take place. Programming acts as a form of strategic alignment that is achieved through the production of a range of documentation that rhetorically and strategically aligns local needs (typically framed as economic growth) with global imperatives (expressed as resource efficiency using the language of global climate change). The most high-profile programmatic documents include, among others, UNFCCC National Communications, Technology Needs Assessments, Biennial Update Reports and Nationally

Appropriate Mitigation Actions (NAMAs). That such devices are critical for enabling the flow of resources through climate aid is suggested by the fact that substantial funds (over US $14 million from the GEF in Eastern Europe and Central Asia alone) are spent on supporting their production, typically with the involvement of international experts from within the broad climate aid network. Analogous programmatic devices, which typically have a shelf life of several years, exist amongst development agencies and banks and recipient countries in the form of 'country strategies' and 'partnership frameworks'.

What is remarkable about programmatic intermediation as an intermediary process is how it serves to mediate between the economic and political interests of donors, agencies and recipients. Programming effectively sets out the conditions by which climate aid projects take place – defining the access of funds by recipients and the modalities of development agencies' involvement. For instance, GEF funds may be used solely under the banner of one of the strategic 'focal areas' (amongst others, 'Low-carbon Technology Transfer', 'Renewable Energy', 'Energy Efficiency', 'Low Carbon Urban Systems' (GEF 2010)). Significantly, climate aid funds are allocated on a national basis. Given that national governments' 'endorsement' is required on a project-by-project basis, this may limit non-governmental actors' access to finance and expertise. Even GEF agencies' access to funds is codified (Chong and Gradstein 2008; Halimanjaya 2013), as agencies are requested to act according to their respective "comparative advantage" (GEF 2007: i). In practice, this means that UN agencies usually undertake technical assistance for capacity and institution building whilethe MDBs are the preferred vehicles for public and private sector investment lending.

At the end of this lengthy chain of translation, characterised by multilateral programmatic alignment processes, climate aid projects come into being, which include interventions such as infrastructure investments and upgrades and building code reforms. Projects take shape at the intersection of the needs, capacities and mandates of donors, agencies and recipients and effectively act as specific, localised entry points for engendering transformation. Projects are geographically situated (on one or several locations and/or industry) and time-limited (lasting usually no longer than 5 years), such as the "Demand-side Energy Efficiency in Public Buildings, Lodz" project (GEF# 1445). Notwithstanding the diversity of donors, recipients and implementing agencies, any specific project typically has a specific objective, desired outcomes and concrete outputs. The relatively formalised structure of projects, which mirrors the interventions in the international aid system, consists of main (one or several) 'components': investment components (with a focus on infrastructure financing of pilots, demonstration projects or scaling up investment facilities), legal and regulatory reform components (e.g., of building codes, procurement and contracting legislation), capacity building components (e.g., of government officials and technical professionals), and awareness raising (of all stakeholders, and often specifically the public). The non-financial components often fall under the banner of 'technical assistance', designed to support the climate aid recipients' 'readiness' for using investment finance (UNDP 2012; RISE).

In this way, through intermediated and formalised networked relationships, which are neither determined through a strict scalar nesting, nor along territorial boundaries, climate aid effectively ties the local level of the unstainable city of the East into a global network of finance and expertise. However, while the climate aid network grows in extent, density and wealth, its effectiveness in achieving sustainable transitions in systems of provisions remains open to question. While in the Eastern European cities in the region, there is more conclusive evidence of the emergence of markets for energy efficiency in buildings through the proliferation of Energy Services Companies (ESCOs), in the Russian Federation MDBs such as the EBRD and IFC are at a stage of promoting policy reform efforts at the same time as trying to develop viable transactions, for instance, with local housing management companies for building energy upgrades (e.g., UNECE 2013; Bertoldi et al. 2006; EBRD-GEF 2013; EBRD/IFC GEF 2013; COMO 2014). In stark contrast, in the Central Asian Republics the baseline against which relative successes are measured can be much lower – for example, in Turkmenistan and Uzbekistan, projects have solely consisted of technical assistance focusing on a range of enabling activities, such as capacity building, policy advice on building codes and the setting up of dedicated national state structures (UNDP-GEF 2009; UNDP-GEF 2008). On the whole, the question of impact remains a topic of much debate in the climate aid community, with discussions revolving around questions of quantifiable change, timescales and the relative contribution and attribution to individual efforts (e.g., Climate Eval 2012).

Conclusion

This chapter explored the understudied case of urban sustainability transitions in the Cities of the post-socialist East. The contemporary situation of high inertia and poor domestic capacity was traced to how urban settlements were historically nested at the bottom of a scalar urban infrastructure planning regime. Unsettling these highly obdurate scalar legacies, responses have emerged from extra-local networks that channel financial and technical resources under the banner of climate aid – development assistance for climate change mitigation and adaptation. While distinctly extra-local, the chapter situated climate aid as intra-systemic to the broader international aid system. The relational constitution of climate aid is defined by the well-established triangular relationship between donors, recipients, and development agencies that manage the implementation of climate aid–funded interventions. Programming and the project-based approach are the key intermediary processes by which alignments between local needs and extra-local capacity are achieved. In this set-up, typical of other areas of development, interventions take shape as financial capital made available by bi- or multilateral 'donors' (often trust funds) is converted into situated interventions based on recipient need, and according to the capacities and mandates of development agencies. In the process, the unsustainable and ill-resourced Cities of the East are becoming embedded into a global network of finance and expertise that reaches far beyond the urban boundary.

Arguably, transition thinking has much to gain from a greater appreciation of the spatial complexity of, and a sharper focus on, the intermediary fabric of transition processes. Applied to the cities of the East, an expanded spatial register opens up the possibility to account for the scalar legacies of the Soviet planning regime, as well as to conceptualise how, from a shared legacy, contemporary trajectories are differently shaped across the regions, depending on climate aid resource flows. Sensitivity to spatial complexity enables us to portray a situation in which unsustainabilities are urban in effect, scalar in terms of origin, and networked in terms of prospects for change. As such, the ingredients for urban sustainability transitions extend far beyond the urban boundary, consisting of international flows of financial, technical and human capital that are being channelled into the countries and cities of the East through the multilateral climate aid network. An examination of the intermediary fabric of the climate aid network hints at unequal power relations – as a result, those endowed with resources are strong determinants of the urban sustainability agenda, while urban actors often have only a marginal say on how sustainability challenges will be addressed. Fruitful avenues of future inquiry could include, for instance, revisiting well-studied interventions with a specific focus on the multiplicity of scales, networks and territories involved in innovative processes, and on the factors that shape the effectiveness of intermediary translation processes in achieving common definitions of the domains and modes through which transition is attempted.

As the climate network expands in reach, density and wealth, several important questions arise in relation to the governance of urban sustainability through the climate aid network. While the potential impacts of climate aid–enabled interventions across the cities of the East remain latent in still unfolding interventions and future promises of development assistance, salient questions emerge in relation to the effectiveness of climate aid interventions. Significantly, assessing the impacts of interventions is much less straightforward than simply considering the magnitudes of inputs, and there is little consensus on understanding relative achievements in relation to specific starting points. Multilateral structures fostering transparency and accountability have not emerged at the same pace as the boom of climate finance and the number of specific interventions. With respect to the urban dimension of sustainability transitions, a further question emerges in relation to the often poor integration of urban actors into a system dominated by extra-local resources and sovereign state channels for accessing funds. In the process, Eastern cities and their representatives risk remaining marginal in shaping the urban sustainability agenda – an issue that also relates more broadly to the nature of unequal power relations between key nodes in the climate aid network. Involving urban decision makers and urban constituencies further upstream in climate aid programming consultations and project preparation may provide an important way forward in the absence of alternative avenues for resource mobilization in the Cities of the East. While the climate aid network provides important channels for the much needed finance and expertise, it may not provide definitive solutions to suitably addressing challenges as profound as in the Cities of the East.

Notes

1 Low-cost, concrete or brick, three- to five-level apartment building developed during the early 1960s while Nikita Khrushchev led the Soviet government.
2 Other multilateral donors to the region include EuropeAid (over US$ 350 million) and the Climate Investment Funds (at over US$ 110 million to date). While the Climate Investment Funds are currently the largest trust fund dedicated solely to climate mitigation and adaptation, it is still marginal for the Eastern Europe and Central Asia compared to the Global Environment Facility's historical contributions. In addition, the Clean Technology Fund (which channels sustainable energy investments) focuses on middle-income countries, and covers only Kazakhstan and Ukraine in Eastern Europe and Central Asia.

Bibliography

Bear, C. and Eden, S. (2008) Making space for fish: The regional, network and fluid spaces of fisheries certification. *Social & Cultural Geography* 9(5): 487–504.
Bertoldi et al. 2006; http://www.sciencedirect.com/science/article/pii/S0301421505000303 Bertoldi, P, Rezessy, S and Vine, E (2006) "Energy Service companies in European countries: current status and a strategy to foster their development", Energy policy, 34 (14): 1818–32.
Binz, C. and Truffer, B. (2011) Technological innovation systems in multi-scalar space: Analyzing an emerging water recycling industry with social network analysis. *Geographica Helvetica*, 66 (4): 254–260.
BPIE (2011) Europe's buildings under the microscope: A country-by-country review of the energy performance of buildings. Buildings Performance Institute Europe. [Available from: http://www.europeanclimate.org/documents/LR_%20CbC_study. pdf; accessed March 2014]
Bridge, G., Bouzarovski, S., Bradshaw, M., and Eyre N. (2013) Geographies of energy transition: space, place and the low-carbon economy. *Energy Policy* (53): 331–340.
Bulkeley, H., Castán Broto, V., and Maassen A. (2014) Low-carbon transitions and the reconfiguration of urban infrastructure. *Urban Studies* 51(7): 1471–1486.
Castán Broto, V. and Bulkeley, H. (2012) A survey of urban climate change experiments in 100 cities. *Global Environmental Change* (23): 92–102.
Center for Economic Research (2013) Urbanization in Central Asia: Challenges, Issues and Prospects. Analytical Report 2013/03. [Available from: http://www.unescap.org/sites/default/files/Urbanization%20in%20Central%20Asia_ENG_0.pdf; accessed 21 March 2014].
Chong, A. and Gradstein, M. (2008) What determines foreign aid? The donors' perspective. *Journal of Development Economics*, 87: 1–13.
Climate Funds Update (2013) http://www.climatefundsupdate.org/data [Accessed: 21 March 2014].

Collier, S. (2011) *Post-Soviet Social: Neoliberalism, Social Modernity, Biopolitics.* Princeton, NJ: Princeton University Press.

COMO (2014) Covenant of Mayors in post-Soviet countries: Why and how? [Available from: http://www.eumayors.eu/news_en.html?id_news=399; accessed December 2013].

DECC (2009) The UK Low Carbon Transition Plan: National Strategy for Climate and Energy (London: Department for Energy and Climate Change. [Available from: http://www.official-documents.gov.uk/document/other/9780108508394/9780 108508394.asp; accessed December 2013].

Del Rio, P. and Unruh, G. C. (2007) Overcoming the lock-out of renewable energy technologies in Spain: The cases of wind and solar electricity. *Renewable and Sustainable Energy Reviews* 11: 1498–1513.

EBRD (2011) The Low Carbon Transition. Special Report on Climate Change. Available from: http://www.ebrd.com/downloads/research/transition/trsp.pdf. [Accessed March 2013].

EBRD (2013) Sustainable Energy Initiative. Financing Sustainable Energy: EBRD in action and results [Available from: http://www.ebrd.com/downloads/research/ brochures/sei.pdf; accessed December 2013].

EBRD/IFC-GEF (2013) Midterm Review of the EBRD-IFC GEF Project, Improving Urban Housing Efficiency in the Russian Federation, 17 June 2013. [not publicly available].

EBRD-GEF (2008) Improving Efficiency in Public Buildings in the Russian Federation. Project Identification Form (PIF) [Available from: http://www.thegef .org/gef/gef_projects_funding; accessed December 2013].

EBRD-GEF (2010) Increasing Climate Resilience through Drinking Water Rehabilitation in North Tajikistan. Project Identification Form (PIF) for Full-size projects of the Special Climate Change Fund (SCCF). [Available from: http://www .thegef.org/gef/gef_projects_funding; accessed December 2013].

EBRD-GEF (2013) Mid-Term Review of the EBRD-GEF Project, Improving Energy Efficiency in Public Buildings in the Russian Federation. 13 December 2013 [not publicly available].

EC (2008) Commission of the European Communities, Green Paper Towards a Secure, Sustainable and Competitive European Energy Network. COM (2008) 782. Brussels, 7.1.2009. [Available from: http://eur-lex.europa.eu/LexUriServ/ LexUriServ.do?uri=CELEX:DKEY=483121:EN:NOT; accessed December 2013].

EuropeAid (2012) Final Task Report B 2.2: Setting up the standards (passports) for buildings, stating their level/classes of effectiveness of energy utilisation/production linked to international benchmarks. Support to the Implementation of a Comprehensive Energy Policy for the Republic of Belarus. EuropeAid/129710/C/ SER/BY [not publicly available].

GEF (2007) Comparative advantages of the GEF agencies. Global Environment Facility. [Available from: http://www.thegef.org/gef/node/427; accessed March 2014].

GEF (2010) GEF-5 Climate Change Mitigation Focal Area Strategy Document. [Available from: http://www.thegef.org/; accessed December 2013].

Genus, A. and Coles, A.-M. (2008) Rethinking the multi-level perspective of technological transitions. *Research Policy* 37(9): 1436–1445.

Guy, S., Marvin, S., Medd W., and Moss, T. (Eds.) (2010) *Shaping Urban Infrastructures: Intermediaries and the Governance of Socio-Technical Networks.* London: Routledge.

Halimanjaya A. (2013) Climate finance across developing countries: What are the major determinants?, Working Paper 45, DEV Working Paper Series, The School of International Development, University of East Anglia, UK.

Hansen T. and Coenen L. (2014) The geography of sustainability transitions: Review, synthesis and reflections on an emergent research field. Forthcoming in *Environmental Innovation and Societal Transition* (Elsevier).

Hodson, M. and Marvin, S. (2012) Mediating low-carbon urban transitions? Forms of organisation, knowledge and action. *European Planning Studies* 20(2): 421–439.

Hodson, M. and Marvin, S. (2009a) Cities mediating technological transitions: Understanding visions, intermediation and consequences. *Technology Analysis & Strategic Management* 21(4): 515–534.

Hodson, M. and Marvin, S. (2009b) 'Urban ecological security': A new urban paradigm? *International Journal of Urban and Regional Research* 33(1): 193–215.

Hodson, M. and Marvin, S. (2010) Can cities shape socio-technical transitions and how would we know if they were? *Research Policy* 39(4): 477–485.

Howitt, R. (1998) Scale as relation: Musical metaphors of geographical scale. *Area* 30(1): 49–58. [Available from: http://www.green-alliance.org.uk/aboutus/]. http://www.climate-eval.org/. Sharing good practices on climate change and development evaluation.

Huffington Post (2013) UN Climate Change Action Is a Major Goal for Secretary-General Ban Ki-Moon in 2013. [Available from: http://www.huffingtonpost.com/2013/01/22/ban-ki-moon-climate-change-un_n_2523928.html; accessed March 2014].

IFC (2013) Climate-Smart Business: Investment Potential in EMENA: Mapping investment potential in renewable energy, resource efficiency, and water in Emerging Europe, Central Asia, and the Middle East and North Africa. [Available from: http://www.ifc.org/wps/wcm/connect/f9d1938041aa9f1f8e23bf8d8e2dafd4/Investment+Potential+in+EMENA.pdf?MOD=AJPERES; accessed March 2014].

International Crisis Group (2011) Central Asia: Decay and Decline. Asia Report N°201 – 3 February 2011. [Available from: http://www.crisisgroup.org/~/media/Files/asia/central-asia/201%20Central%20Asia%20-%20Decay%20and%20Decline.pdf; accessed 21 March 2014].

Johl, A. and Lador, Y. (2012) A Human Rights-based Approach to Climate Finance. The Friedrich-Ebert-Stiftung – Dialogue on Globalization. [Available from: http://library.fes.de/pdf-files/iez/global/08933.pdf; accessed 21 March 2014].

Jones, J. P., III, Woodward, K. and Marston, S. A. (2007) Situating flatness. *Transactions of the Institute of British Geographers* 32: 264–276.

Kortelainen, J. (2010) Old-growth forests as objects in complex spatialities. *Area* 42: 494–501.

Lane, D. (2006) Post-state socialism: A diversity of capitalisms? In D.L. Myant (Ed.), *Varieties of Capitalism in Post-Communist Countries*, pp. 1–12. New York: Palgrave Macmillan.

Law, J. (1986 [2001]) *On the Methods of Long Distance Control: Vessels, Navigation, and the Portuguese Route to India. Power, Action and Belief: A New Sociology of Knowledge?* London: Routledge. [Web version. Available from: http://www.lancs.ac.uk/fass/sociology/papers/lawmethods-of-long-distance-control.pdf].

Law, J. (1992) *Notes on the Theory of the Actor Network: Ordering, Strategy and Heterogeneity.* Centre for Science Studies, Lancaster University, Lancaster LA1 4YN, UK. [Available from: http://www.comp.lancs.ac.uk/sociology/papers/Law-Notes-on-ANT.pdf.]

Law, J. and Singleton, V. (2003) *Object Lessons.* Centre for Science Studies, Lancaster University, Lancaster LA1 4YN, UK. [Available from: http://www.comp.lancs.ac.uk/sociology/papers/Law-Singleton-Object-Lessons.pdf].

Leitner, H., Sheppard, E. and Sziarto, K. M. (2008) The spatialities of contentious politics. *Transactions of the Institute of British Geographers* 33: 157–172.

Maassen, A. (2012) Solar cities in Europe: a material semiotic analysis of innovation in urban photovoltaics. Durham theses, Durham University. Available at Durham E-Theses Online: http://etheses.dur.ac.uk/3592/

Markard J., Raven R. and Truffer B., (2012) Sustainability transitions: An emerging field of research and its prospects. *Research Policy* (41), 955–967.

Marston, S. A., Jones, J. P., III and Woodward, K. (2005) Human geography without scale. *Transactions of the Institute of British Geographers* 30: 416–432.

Medd, W. and Marvin, S. (2008) Making water work: Intermediating between regional strategy and local practice. *Environment and Planning D* 26: 280–299.

Middleton, D. and Brown, S. (2002) The baby as a virtual object: Agency and stability in a neonatal care unit. *Athenea Digital* 1.

Mol, A. (2002) *The Body Multiple: Ontology in Medical Practice*. Durham, N.C., and London: Duke University Press.

Mol, A. and Law, J. (1994) Regions, networks and fluids: Anaemia and social topology. *Social Studies of Science* 24(4): 641–671.

Monstadt, J. (2009) Conceptualizing the political ecology of urban infrastructures: Insights from technology and urban studies. *Environment and Planning A* 41(8): 1924–1942.

Moreira, T. (2004) Surgical monads: A social topology of the operating room. *Environment and Planning D* 22: 53–69.

Moss, T. (2009) Intermediaries and the governance of sociotechnical networks in transition. *Environment and Planning A* 41(6): 1480–1495.

Naakhooda, S., Norman, M. (2014) Climate Aid: Is It Making a Difference? A Review of the Effectiveness of Multilateral Climate Funds. London: Overseas Development Institute.

NAC and Centennial Group (2014) *Kazakhstan 2050: Toward a Modern Society for All*. Oxford: National Analytical Center and The Centennial Group; Oxford: Oxford University Press.

OECD (2011) Greening Public Budgets in Eastern Europe, Caucasus and Central Asia; Greening Public Budgets in Eastern Europe, Caucasus and Central Asia. Organisation for Economic Co-operation and Development [Available from: http://www.keepeek.com/Digital-Asset-Management/oecd/governance/greening-public-budgets-in-eastern-europe-caucasus-and-central-asia_9789264118331-en#page62 accessed December 2013]

OECD (2013) OECD-DAC Statistics Climate-Related Aid. Organisation for Economic Co-operation and Development-Development Assistance Committee [Available from: http://www.oecd.org/dac/stats/Climate%20change-related%20 Aid%20Flyer%20-%20November%202013.pdf; accessed March 2014]

OHCHR (2009) Report of the Office of the United Nations High Commissioner for Human Rights (OHCHR) on the relationship between climate change and human rights. Document No: A/HRC/10/61, Jan. 15. [Available from: http://daccess-dds-ny.un.org/doc/UNDOC/GEN/G09/103/44/PDF/G0910344.pdf?OpenElement; accessed 21 March 2014]

Ollman, B. (1993) *Dialectical Investigations*. London and New York: Routledge.

Pertoldi, P., Hinnells, M., and Rezessy, S. (2006) Liberating the power of Energy Services and ESCOs in a liberalised energy market. European Commission DG JRC, University of Oxford and Central European University. [Available from: http://www.eci.ox.ac.uk/research/energy/downloads/bmt-report3.pdf   accessed December 2013]

Rotmans, J., Kemp, R. and van Asselt, M. (2001) More evolution than revolution. Transition management in public policy. *Foresight* 3(1): 15–31.

Schot, J. (1998) Processes of niche formation: The approach of strategic niche management. *Technology Analysis & Strategic Management* 10(2): 175–195.

Schot, J. and Geels, F. W. (2008) Strategic niche management and sustainable innovation journeys: Theory, findings, research agenda, and policy. *Technology Analysis & Strategic Management* 20(5): 537–554.

Seyfang, G. and Smith, A. (2007) Grassroots innovations for sustainable development: Towards a new research and policy agenda. *Environmental Politics* 16(4): 584–603.

Seyfang, G., Hielscher, S., Hargreaves, T., Martiskainen, M. and Smith, A. (2014) A grassroots sustainable energy niche? Reflections on community energy in the UK. *Journal of Environmental Innovation and Societal Transitions*, 13: 21–44.

Shirokanova, A. (2010) Making sense of the post-Soviet capital: Politics of identity in the City of Minsk. *Anthropology of East Europe Review* (28)1: 355–387.

Smith et al. 2010 https://lowcarbonpolitics.files.wordpress.com/2013/05/smith-et-al-2010-innovation-studies-and-sustainability-transitions.pdf Innovation studies and sustainability transitions: The allure of the multi-level perspective and its challenges Adrian Smitha,*, Jan-Peter Voßb, John Grinc; Research Policy 39 (2010) 435–448.

Smith, A. (2011) Community-led urban transitions and resilience: Performing transition towns in a city. In H. Bulkeley, V. Castán Broto, M. Hodson and S. Marvin (ed.), *Cities and Low Carbon Transitions*. New York and London: Routledge: 159–177.

Späth P. and Rohracher H., (2012) Local demonstrations for global transitions: Dynamics across governance levels fostering socio-technical regime change towards sustainability, *European Planning Studies*, 20(3): 461–479.

Späth, P. and Rohracher, H. (2010) The 'eco-cities' Freiburg and Graz: The social dynamics of pioneering urban energy and climate governance. In H. Bulkeley, V. Castán Broto, M. Hodson and S. Marvin (ed.), *Cities and Low Carbon Transitions*. London and New York: Routledge.

Sýkora, L. and Bouzarovski, S. (2011) Multiple transformations: Conceptualising the post-communist urban transition. *Urban Studies* 49(1): 43–60.

Truffer, B. and Coenen, L. (2012) Environmental innovation and sustainability transitions in regional studies. *Regional Studies* 46(1): 1–21.

UNDP (2012) Readiness for Climate Finance: A framework for understanding what it means to be ready to use climate finance. United Nations Development Programme. [Available from: http://www.undp.org/content/dam/undp/library/ Environment%20and%20Energy/Climate%20Strategies/Readiness%20for%20 Climate%20Finance_12April2012.pdf; accessed March 2014]

UNDP (2013) Human Development Report 2013 – The Rise of the South: Human Progress in a Diverse World. United Nations Development Programme. [Available from: http://hdr.undp.org/en/2013-report; accessed March 2014]

UNDP-GEF (2008) Promoting Energy Efficiency in Public Buildings in Uzbekistan. Project Identification Form (PIF) for Full-size projects of the GEF Trust Fund [Available from: http://www.thegef.org/gef/gef_projects_funding; accessed December 2013]

UNDP-GEF (2009) Improving Energy Efficiency in the Residential Buildings Sector of Turkmenistan. Project Identification Form (PIF) for Full-size projects of the GEF Trust Fund. [Available from: http://www.thegef.org/gef/gef_projects_funding; accessed December 2013]

UNECE (2011) Strengthening Water Management and Transboundary Water Cooperation in Central Asia: the Role of UNECE Environmental Conventions. United Nations Economic Commission for Europe (UNECE) [Available from: http://www.unece.org/index.php?id=28204; accessed 21 March 2014]

UNECE (2013) Twenty-fourth session of the Steering Committee of the Energy Efficiency 21 Programme. The UN Economic Commission for Europe Committee on Sustainable Energy. Geneva, 17 April 2013 [Available from: http://www.unece. org/fileadmin/DAM/energy/se/pdfs/eneff/eneff_sc_24_Nov.13/ECE_ENERGY_ WP.4_2013_1.rev.pdf; accessed December 2013]

UNFCCC (2014a) National Communications to the UNFCCC. United Nations Framework Convention on Climate Change. [Available from: http://unfccc.int/national_reports/non-annex_i_natcom/items/2979.php; accessed March 2014]

UNFCCC (2014b) – Technology Needs Assessments (TNAs). United Nations Framework Convention on Climate Change. [Available from: http://unfccc.int/ttclear/templates/render_cms_page?TNA_home; accessed March 2014]

Unruh, G. C. (2000) Understanding carbon lock-in. *Energy Policy* 28(12): 817–830.

Van Driel, H. and Schot, J. (2005) Radical innovation as a multi-level process: Introducing floating grain elevators in the Port of Rotterdam. *Technology and Culture* 46(1): 51–76.

Verbong, G. and Geels, F. (2007) The ongoing energy transition: Lessons from a socio-technical, multilevel analysis of the Dutch electricity system (1960–2004). *Energy Policy* 35(2): 1025–1037.

World Bank (2012) Investments in ECA's Energy Efficiency are Paying Off.... ECA energy efficiency. [Available from: http://siteresources.worldbank.org/ECAEXT/Resources/258598-1357934047604/EnergyEfficiencyFactSheet101212.pdf; accessed March 2014]

World Bank (2014) World Bank Group President: This Is the Year of Climate Action. [Available from: http://www.worldbank.org/en/news/feature/2014/01/23/davos-world-bank-president-carbon-pricing; accessed March 2014]

WRI (2003) Earth Trends 2003 Country Profiles. [Available from: http://earthtrends.wri.org; accessed 21 March 2014]

WRI (2014) Aqueduct Atlas – Measuring and Mapping Water Risk. World Resource Institute [Available from: http://www.wri.org/our-work/project/aqueduct/aqueduct-atlas; accessed 21 March 2014]

12   From Building Small Urban Spaces for a Car-Free Life to Challenging the Global Regime of Automobility

Cases from Vienna and Freiburg

Philipp Späth and Michael Ornetzeder

Introduction

Mobility systems have often been studied as prime examples of socio-technical systems in which material elements, such as road infrastructures, and social elements, such as routinized mobility patterns, interplay and stabilize each other (Cohen 2012; Geels et al. 2012). The built environment brings significant inertia to these systems, for example, through the spatial relationships between office, commercial, recreational and residential areas. At a smaller scale, specific designs and arrangements within single neighbourhoods, like the distance between apartments and the car park, may influence individual patterns significantly.

In the mid 1990s, several European cities launched first experiments with radical new combinations of designs and institutional arrangements that placed individual cars in less privileged positions than they had long enjoyed in the planning of new districts or neighbourhoods. In this chapter, we discuss two early initiatives aimed at creating urban environments especially suited for a car-free life – one in the Austrian capital Vienna, and another in the southern German city of Freiburg. We do so in order to explore the ways in which such initiatives aimed at shaping specific, *local* environments to potentially contribute to broader *sustainability transitions*.

Both initiatives are distinctively urban in the sense that they are focused on a clearly delimited urban territory in which novel institutional arrangements, attractive architectural designs and mobility infrastructure solutions were developed. Together, these elements were meant to enable city dwellers to live an almost car-free life.

As the second part of this book explores the role of experimentation in urban sustainability transitions – that is, its drivers, different forms, prerequisites, outcomes, impacts and limitations – we examine our two cases with regard to these aspects: What objectives drove these initiatives, how did they work and what wider impacts have they had? Did they really bring about more sustainable mobility practices? What has been learned in these environments? And, most importantly, what role do these spatially confined initiatives play against the background of a larger transition towards more sustainable urban mobility?

To this end, we build on earlier research dealing with the Vauban model district (Späth 2013) and the car-free housing project in Vienna (Ornetzeder et al. 2008), examining these cases through the use of quantitative data and qualitative interviews with initiators and participants of the initiatives, as well as with document analyses of project-related materials and various additional studies. Within the limits of this chapter, we aim to provide historical descriptions as well as a brief comparison of the two cases as a basis for discussing the relevance of these locally confined initiatives for larger urban sustainability transitions.

In Section 12.2, we briefly refer to concepts from the multilevel perspective as our main reference framework. This prepares the ground for the description of our examples in Sections 12.3 and 12.4. Section 12.5 contains a table juxtaposing the two cases and a discussion of similarities, differences and the varied success factors identified for the two cases. In our conclusions, we discuss the potential of such urban initiatives to provide transformative momentum and briefly discuss some theoretical implications of our results.

Urban Niches for the Transition of the Mobility System

Initiatives to develop sustainable infrastructure often simultaneously pursue objectives on two spatial levels: they seek to achieve specific and tangible *changes in a place-bound system of provision*, often to the benefit of a clearly defined constituency. At least in their scope and direction, however, the changes relate to a broader vision of regime shift which transgresses the local perspective. The initiators of our case study experiments sought to provide a built and institutional environment favourable to a car-free life specifically to the dwellers of a planned block or district; for example, by keeping some streets free of cars or by relieving certain car-free households of the costs of a parking space. At the same time, these experiments explicitly aimed at revolutionizing the way new blocks and districts are shaped and planned, challenging the regime of 'car dominance' in everyday life as well as in urban planning, hence *contributing to a global struggle* towards 'sustainable mobility'.

As a heuristic for understanding such ambivalences, we refer to concepts developed within the so-called *multilevel perspective* (MLP). This framework is comprised of the concepts of socio-technical regimes, niches and landscape. Our example initiatives strategically engage in the creation of protected spaces – in our terms contextualized and place bound socio-technical *niches* – while at the same time hoping for the concurrence and aggregation of their initiatives' effects with other dynamics, thus building a 'global niche' (Raven and Geels 2010) and a systemic challenge to the global regime of car dominance.

The implicit reference to a generic mobility system, which in terms of our analysis should be considered a socio-technical *regime*, along with the interventions into a routine of urban planning which were intended to also become exemplars for application elsewhere, bring us to the interesting question of whether 'urban transitions' exist at all. The regime of car dominance is clearly ubiquitous in most Western countries, and increasingly so in urban agglomerations of Africa and Asia. The very nature of this system of far-reaching mobility, with its networks of highways, a globalized car industry and a fuel provision infrastructure, makes it apparent that we are dealing with a socio-technical system of global proportions (Urry 2004). At the same time, dynamically developing cities are crucial loci in which decisions are constantly renegotiated over the way and exact manner in which global regimes are 'enacted' (Quitzau et al. 2013), that is, implemented and maintained *locally* (Hodson and Marvin 2010). As scholars from different parts of the world increasingly report of 'cracks' in the regime of automobility, observed particularly in urban contexts (Marletto et al. 2011; Cohen 2012; Geels et al. 2012), we are hence curious to examine the ways in which our case study initiatives may have contributed to this rising challenge that the regime of automobility seems to face.

From a niche-oriented transitions perspective, car-free settlements can be understood as protected spaces for *experimentation* and the emergence of radical social-technical innovations in something like 'test beds' (Hoogma et al. 2002). In order to successfully transform new ideas into working configurations, such niches must also support the articulation of *deviating expectations* and *visions*. This usually involves network-building activities and various learning processes on dimensions such as technical design, user preferences or symbolic meanings (Geels 2011). As Smith and Raven (2012) most explicitly pointed out, niches – in the sense of protected spaces – fulfil different roles in *shielding* innovations from mainstream selection pressures, *nurturing* such innovations and *empowering* them to compete with incumbent practices or even transform existing regimes. In our cases, we may, for example, examine how novel institutional arrangements may shield people and their mobility practices from the prevailing regime of automobility – including its typical influence on the layout of a district and the cost structure behind the purchasing of a private flat.

However, even highly successful niche activities do not guarantee changes within the regime. In this respect Geels and Schot (2007) have reminded us of an original claim of the MLP: without pressure from the wider *landscape*, regimes are very likely to successfully reproduce themselves and to remain relatively stable. As one of us argued in earlier work, it is also important to understand strategic niche activities, particularly in 'model regions' or 'model districts', not only as "experimentation for the sake of *variation*" but often also as "implementation for the sake of *demonstration*" (Späth and Rohracher 2010, 2012). In the field of energy provision, for example, the demonstration of alternative socio-technical configurations – including institutional innovations – is often organized in "model regions", which are then strategically supported and used as exemplars by national or international networks originally formed around the aim of promoting rather generic visions of radical regime shifts (e.g., an energy turnaround). In general, such demonstrations of socio-technical feasibility in specific places can *lend credibility* to a discourse around more abstract visions of a socio-technical future. For example, they may lead to institutionalization processes taking place beyond the "model regions" via their (discursive) influence on national legislation, funding priorities or other institutions that previously supported the entrenched regime.

Seyfang and Haxeltine (2012) have summarized even more ways in which niches can generally influence regimes: by enabling replication of projects within the niche, by bringing about aggregative changes through a growing number of small initiatives, by enabling constituent projects to grow in scale and attract more participants, or by facilitating the translation of niche ideas into mainstream settings. With these approaches and concepts in mind, we present our two case studies in the following sections. We briefly review the historical context and the history of the projects, deal with the institutional innovations involved in them and report on results and effects.

The Car-Free Settlement in Vienna

Vienna is the capital, and with about 1.8 million inhabitants, the largest city of Austria. The city has a long tradition of social housing and urban renewal policies dating back to the 1920s when the Social Democratic Party gained control of the municipal administration for the first time. Whereas initially, the main objective was to provide affordable housing, in the last decades the city has increasingly sought to actively steer urban development as a whole. Even today, the influence of the city on the housing market is enormous. Almost 60 per cent of Viennese housing units belong to the public, subsidised sector. In the 1990s, the city began developing large housing estates around thematic foci responding to the diverging needs of modern urban society (Eigner et al. 1999). Since then, the responsible fund has developed more than 50 large residential housing projects, many of them with a distinctive innovative focus. One of these thematic projects of the early period aimed at car-free living. The city's first residential complex of this kind totalled 244 rental apartments, and opened in 1999. Based on the experiences of this early pilot project, less radical environmental mobility concepts have been taken up by similar residential developments since then. Just recently, the city of Vienna adopted a new urban development plan decidedly advocating for an environmentally friendly transport policy. According to this plan, 80 per cent of all inner-city journeys should be covered by public transport, by bike or on foot by the year 2025 (Vienna City Administration 2014).

A Short History of the "Model Car-Free Housing Project" in Vienna

Inspired by similar projects in Germany – especially a well-known but never-realized project in Bremen, but without any connection to the ongoing developments in Freiburg – the idea of car-free neighbourhoods had been discussed in Vienna in the early 1990s for the first time. City councillor Christoph Chorherr from the Green Party took up the issue and became a particularly strong advocate of the idea of car-free living. Due to his initiative, the Greens filed a petition to launch a car-free housing project under the Viennese social housing scheme in 1992. Two years later, after extensive political negotiations, the concept eventually gained support from the responsible Councillor from the leading Social Democratic Party, as well as from the urban development and housing department. In order to test the demand for this radically new concept, a first call for interested parties (i.e., residents-to-be) was launched in 1995. In the same year a suitable site was selected for the pilot project, which was to be located in the 21st District in a former industrial zone. In 1996, the city solicited proposals for the housing-development while simultaneously amending Viennese garage regulation to allow for a substantial reduction in parking space provided in the context of this pilot project. When the winning team of architects began with the planning process, 550 people had already shown their interest. Consequently, the city administration contracted an external enterprise to facilitate a process to allow interested parties to be involved in the planning from the start. In October 1997, the construction works were launched and at the end of 1999, the first tenants moved into the building (Gutmann and Havel 2000). The drastically reduced car facilities allowed for significant economic savings in comparison to other public housing schemes of the time, which in turn enabled future tenants to successfully demand a number of special features to be paid for, including additional common areas (e.g., roof garden, sauna, areas for children), green-technologies (e.g., PV-systems), an improved building energy standard, a car-sharing station, generous courtyards and ample bicycle parking facilities (Moser and Stocker 2008).

Institutional Innovation in the Viennese Case

As soon as the political decision to support the development of a car-free settlement was made, the involved city councillors urged that the claimed car-free status of the project had to be guaranteed as much as possible from the beginning. The car-free project was expected to become a successful showcase, able to support the authority of policy-makers as well as the innovative image of the municipality. The responsible working group from the city administration decided that the future tenants' car-free status in the planned settlement should be bounded by contract, and based on this, the legally guaranteed absence of private cars should already be actively used in developing the architectural concept of the building. Consequently, it was necessary to reduce parking space to an absolute minimum. However, the Viennese building regulations in vigour at the time prescribed that for each newly constructed dwelling, parking space for one car had to be created. The working group therefore had to obtain a change in the garage regulation in this regard first in order to be able to specify car-free requirements in the tender documents. The required amendment was adopted by the city parliament in June 1996.

Since then, it is generally allowed to put up residential buildings in Vienna with less than one parking lot per dwelling. Although the tender for the architecture competition was launched two months earlier, it already made use of the new parking lot requirements (Gutmann and Havel 2000).

In order to ensure the success of the project and avoid subsequent claims by tenants for parking space, the developer decided that residents had to commit to refrain from owning a private car as long as they lived in the building by signing a special lease agreement (Moser and Stocker 2008). This contractual agreement between the housing company and the tenants helped to legitimise the reallocation of social housing subsidies reserved for the construction of parking space to other facilities, which were abundantly made use of in the model project. Another special feature of the model project was the extraordinary involvement of tenants in the planning process. This was intended from the beginning, but the responsible project team had underestimated the true extent of interest to participate and hence the related work. Gutmann and Havel (2000) report that the negotiations between the architects, the developer and the future tenants were not always easy. On the one hand, the external facilitator was sometimes overwhelmed by the task, and on the other hand, delays in the planning phase and the resulting high turnover among the interested parties made the process difficult to handle. However, a core group of future tenants was able to influence a number of decisions made during the planning process and developed a unique tenants' statute that guaranteed a democratic representation of interests, which served as a legal basis to self-administrate the settlement's community facilities.

Effects of the Viennese Car-Free Housing Project

Since all residents had to contractually commit themselves to not owning a car as long as they lived in the settlement, the Viennese project represents a particularly strict form of car-free living. However, it is interesting to note that most people who moved to the car-free settlement did not have to change their mobility patterns fundamentally. According to Gutmann and Havel (2000), 50 per cent of men and 76 per cent of women tenants had never owned a car before. Evaluation studies show that car-free households in Vienna cover their daily mobility needs largely by means of public transport and cycling. The regular use of bicycles is of particular importance in this case. Moser and Stocker (2008) report that more than 50 per cent of the car-free residents use a bicycle to go to work and to meet daily shopping needs, whereas the average share of bicycle users in Vienna is below 10 per cent. According to Moser and Stocker (2008), planners clearly underestimated the huge importance of cycling in the beginning. However, interested parties successfully called for additional facilities (lockers, repair shop, etc.) in the course of the participation process and achieved several changes from the ideas originally formulated by the responsible architects.

Using a quantitative approach to estimate the environmental impact of consumption, Ornetzeder et al. (2008) came to the conclusion that measured per household, per capita and even per euro spent, the car-free housing settlement had lower carbon dioxide emissions than a neighbourhood reference settlement and significantly lower emissions than the Austrian average. Avoiding car use was the most important reason for reduced emissions, although the use of district heating and the purchase of green electricity were also important. As a side effect, the study by Ornetzeder et al. (2008) uncovered that, after all, there are a few private cars in use in the model project. However, both the total mileage per year and the environmental impact of this usage were negligible.

All sources of available data indicate that a stable car-free life style has been established within the model settlement. The model developed in this case remained the only project of its kind in Vienna. However, in 2008 a housing project of a slightly different type was completed in an inner-city district, which drew heavily on the experiences made in the car-free settlement (Gesiba 2013). This new project is called 'bike city', and it is the first subsidized housing project specifically tailored to the needs of cyclists in Vienna. It offers bicycle garages, large elevators for easy transport, bicycle repair services, a shower for cyclists, an in-house sauna, and a fitness area. Due to the great resonance among their current and potential tenants, various Viennese social housing organizations plan to implement similar schemes in the near future. These and other new developments (e.g., shared spaces, car-free zones) are mainly aimed to improve the building environment for bicycle and pedestrian traffic.

Car-Free Living in the "Model District Vauban"

Freiburg, a university town at the foot of the Black Forest Mountains in the very south-west of Germany, home to roughly 230,000 inhabitants, is widely known as a "green city" and a pioneer in environmental policies. This recognition is largely due to the participatory development of two new city districts in the 1990s: Rieselfeld and Vauban (Buehler and Pucher 2011). Particularly the latter is internationally renowned as a 'sustainability model district' (Scheurer and Newman 2009). Since the first building activities started in 1998, this Vauban model district is not only famous for exclusively passive houses and low energy buildings, around 70 per cent of which were developed by so-called building groups of owner-users, but also for the very active participation of interested citizens in the planning and shaping of the district. A key aspect of the model district's ambitions – as they were articulated very early in the planning process by future inhabitants and citizen experts – was to implement an exemplary mobility concept for the whole district, allowing for a collective demonstration of the feasibility of a car-free live in an urban setting. The institutional arrangements, which were later developed in dialogue with the city administration and city councillors, currently enable a significant share of the district's inhabitants to go about their lives without owning or relying on a private vehicle.

How the Vauban District Became a "Niche" for Car-Free Living

When plans were developed in the mid-1990s to convert the former military area Vauban at the southern fringe of Freiburg into a district for about 5,500 inhabitants, interested future inhabitants and citizen experts joined forces and organized themselves as the "Forum Vauban," lobbying strongly for turning this development into a "model district" for social and environmental sustainability. Next to measures for energy efficiency and participatory planning, provisions for sustainable mobility were at the core of their vision.

In addition to what the municipality had already planned with regard to transportation in the future district – a tram line and the reduction of driving through residential roads by giving them a U-shape – these activists demanded that the urban planning of the district should set an example in many more ways: by significantly reducing parking space provided, which should furthermore be concentrated at the fringes of the district; by allocating the costs of parking spaces only to those households who own a private car; by providing first-class cycling and walking infrastructure by means of off-street cycle lanes, wide and inviting pedestrian routes and comfortably equipped public spaces; and by keeping all residential roads free of parked cars (AK Verkehr et al. 1995). As these activists gained the support of more and more members of the city council and from within the municipal administration, most of their requests were eventually fulfilled (Sperling 1999).

Initially, however, the city administration had been very sceptical about the potential of reducing parking space in the district and insisted that two multistorey parking houses (with 470 spaces) needed to be built just for the first part of the area to be developed in Vauban. But after 147 households had contractually agreed not to frequently use a car (Lange 2009), and when it thus became obvious that only a smaller share of inhabitants of the new district wanted to own a car, the administration had to admit that these two garages were sufficient for quite a large part of the district, which consequently was zoned a parking-free area. For residents of this part of the district (see Figure 12.1 below), parking is limited to parking spaces that can be bought or rented in two parking houses at the fringe of the settlement.

The extension of an existing tramline right through the district had already been envisaged by the municipality from early on and was realized in 2006, replacing the bus services that existed since the late 1990s. Now, a tram ride of just 15 minutes connects the new district with the city centre and the main train station. From the beginning, all residential roads of the district had been declared as play areas (implying walking speed at maximum for vehicles) and designed in such a way that traffic is avoided. Furthermore, bicycle routes link every corner of the district with the high-quality network of cycle routes

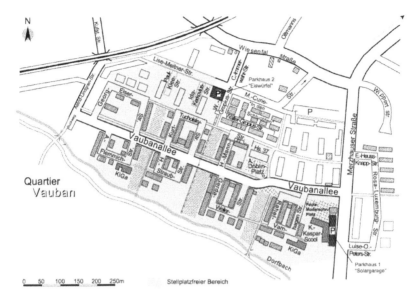

Figure 12.1 The area in light grey is designated "*stellplatzfrei*"; inhabitants must use the two garages (marked in dark grey). Source: Verein für Autofreies Wohnen e.V. (2012). "Jahresbericht für 2011".

in the city and its hinterland. And although the district was designed for a particularly high density of around 130 inhabitants per hectare of settled area (compared with the Freiburg average of 48; Stadt Freiburg 2012: 169; 5) a network of generously large public spaces was set aside for walking.

The planning phase officially started in late 1993 with a decision of the city council to develop the area. In 1994, a competition for urban development plans for the area was announced. Already before that, the administration had negotiated some criteria for this competition with engaged citizens and agreed to constrain the competitors, for example, by ruling out stand-alone family houses and by making the minimisation of on-street parking an obligatory feature (Delleske 2013). Construction works began early in 1998. And in early 1999, the first inhabitants already moved in. By the end of 2006, most construction activities had been completed and the municipal development scheme was officially closed. To date, around 400 jobs have been created within the area and all typically used services are provided in the district, including a great variety of all major health services, etc. Of the 2,300 households registered in the whole district as of the end of 2012 (Stadt Freiburg 2012), roughly 430 participated in the scheme for car-free households, which is approximately 40 per cent of the households living in the area specifically designated for this scheme (Verein für Autofreies Wohnen e.V. 2012).

Institutional Innovation in Vauban

Building legislation in the state of Baden-Württemberg generally requires that for every housing unit, a built parking space for one car needs to be provided. Promoters of the sustainability model district Vauban invented a set of legal instruments which helped detach the costs for parking space from the building costs and hence to enable households to benefit financially from being car-free (Epp 1999; Brohmann et al. 2002; Lange et al. 2003). Within this scheme, households not owning a car can join an association (*Verein für autofreies Wohnen e. V.*) and by providing a deposit of around 3,600 EUR per household the association manages to keep some land at the fringe of the district 'in stock' for the case that members find themselves in need of parking space at some later stage. Only on account of this framework could the city administration be persuaded to allow for fewer parking spaces than housing units to be built. This means that car-free households can save their share of the money usually spent for building an obligatory parking space (i.e., capital costs of roughly 18,000 EUR). By allocating the largest share of these usually hidden costs of car ownership only to those households that own a car, they become visible – and avoidable. Of course, the possibility to avoid these costs also represents a strong temptation for a few of the households who in fact (co-)own and frequently use a car. Some falsely confirm not to do so in order to fully benefit from the scheme for car-free households as well. Such freeriding, however, has always been limited to a small percentage of households, and although the city administration has difficulties with sanctioning it, some households have finally been fined for cheating and forced to accept the costs of their parking.

In the early planning phase, the city administration was very sceptical about the feasibility of a low car ownership rate in the new district and, insisted to experiment with an option for eluding the 1-parking-lot-per-housing-unit-rule in one small block only. The great demand for this scheme, however, soon allowed for an expansion to a larger area, now covering nine residential roads. All households in this area (marked in light blue in Figure 12.1 above) are allowed to freely opt in or out of the "car-free" status. Opting out, for example, means that they must lease or purchase one of the parking lots available in the parking ramps at the fringe of the district. When they quit the association that had reserved some land in case both parking ramps filled up, they receive the 3,600 EUR, which they had to deposit with the association when opting in. Because of this flexibility, this model was ultimately preferred over a model where all households of a defined area have to be car-free households (and remain so as long as they live there). The activists in Freiburg deliberatively deviated from such a strict scheme as prominently debated in relation with the Bremen-Hollerland initiative, not knowing that such an all-and-forever scheme would be realized in Vienna shortly after (Sperling 1999, Ornetzeder et al. 2008). Besides the flexibility for the households involved, another feature of the Vauban model is that it provides the whole population of a larger area (some people owning a car and some not) with the benefits of a very limited presence of cars on the streets.

Effects of the Local Niche for Car-Free Living

In 2012, only 165 privately owned cars per 1,000 inhabitants of Vauban were registered. This is about half of the average in Freiburg (326) (Stadt Freiburg 2012) and only slightly more than a third of the German average (411). Even if we consider that a few cars are frequently used by inhabitants of the district, but not registered there, the absolute number of 937 private cars registered in the district (Stadt Freiburg 2012) is extraordinarily low.

The effects of these measures on mobility practices were first assessed in 2002 by two complementary studies (Brohmann et al. 2002; Lange et al. 2003; Nobis 2003a, b; Nobis and Welsch 2003). This research has shown that a large share of those who moved to the district in that very early phase of development differed quite strongly in their mobility behaviour from the German average, in the sense that they walked and cycled much more for shorter trips. Over the last few years, only qualitative research has been done: Koch, for example, conducted in-depth interviews in 2014 on the motivations and enabling factors behind the decision of households to either relinquish their car or to acquire a car while moving to or living in the district.

While the population of the Vauban district is relatively wealthy (Stadt Freiburg 2012) and may therefore overcompensate for the positive effects of a car-free lifestyle with problematic consumption elsewhere (e.g., long-distance flights for holidays), we can nevertheless state that the intended effects of the particular mobility situation in Vauban have been achieved: car-free mobility practices are clearly more common and perceived as 'normal' in the district than in other parts of the 'green city' Freiburg, let alone other cities of similar size. Walking to shops or to the market and the use of handcarts are very common practices in the district. Even larger items like construction wood or skis are often transported by means of bicycle trailers or the tram. Most interviewees, whether they own a private car or not, stress that they perceive the mostly car-free life in Vauban as something very attractive. Some emphasize they need a car just for their professional life and are looking forward to getting rid of it in the future. Many actually never owned one, even when they lived somewhere else before moving to Vauban (Späth 2013). But all agree that conditions in the car-reduced district are particularly comfortable to live in (Koch 2014).

Case Comparison and Discussion

In the following, we briefly compare the two case study projects and, based on this combined view, we discuss the leading questions of this chapter. In particular, we are interested in understanding our cases as niches for urban mobility innovation and their internal and external dynamics. Table 12.1 gives

Table 12.1 Comparison of the two case studies

	Car-free housing project, Vienna	Model District Vauban, Freiburg
Objectives	Showcase for car-free living	Counter-model to car-oriented urban planning, flexible enough for upscaling
	Additional facilities, state-of-the-art green technologies and common areas owing to reduced parking space	
		Dedication of public space to non-motorized use / community life
	Promotion of new community-oriented lifestyles	Fair allocation of costs for parking space to those who own cars
Size of experimental site	244 apartments, approx. 700 inhabitants	9 residential roads, i.e., large parts of the district for 5,500 inhabitants
Type of settlement	One multistorey residential building (all subsidized rental and ownership)	Many 4-storey, mostly multi-household buildings (mixed rental and self-owned)
Legal approach to car ownership	Car ownership "forbidden" by contract for all inhabitants of the block ("island-solution")	Opt-in/opt-out model: households can opt in (by annually confirming not to own a car) or opt out (than only paying fully for a parking space)
Planning period	1992–1997	1992–1998
Construction period	1997–1999	1998–2006

an overview of the two concurrent but unconnected initiatives and highlights some similarities and differences. Both projects aimed to provide improved conditions for a car free urban life and they shared – as a secondary agenda – the ambition to set an example and to thereby contribute to an expected shift away from car-oriented towards more sustainability-oriented urban planning.

Interestingly, in both cases existing rules first had to be changed or options for circumvention had to be developed to enable settlements with less parking space. This institutional work made it possible to create cost effective solutions, enabling additional green technologies and attractive common facilities in Vienna and significantly lower costs for tenants in Vauban. In both cases, pressure on the building code regime stemmed from the wish to implement model projects and played out due to very high demand for buying into or renting in car-free environments. But the strong political engagement of individual actors, motivated to have an impact far beyond the individual housing project, was also key to the final success in circumventing the strict rules concerning the number of parking spaces to be provided per housing unit. In the meantime, this rule has been softened, in Baden-Württemberg as elsewhere, giving municipalities much more flexibility with regard to prescribed parking space rates. We unfortunately have no evidence about the Vauban Model district in Freiburg influencing this higher-level legislative process, but we consider such an influence probable.

Future residents also played an important role in the planning process in both cases, resulting in a high degree of co-determination, emotional relatedness with the projects and their goals and active community-building processes. Not surprisingly, the two initiatives attracted similar target groups. To a large extent, residents did not change their mobility practices fundamentally after they moved to the settlement. Rather, they found largely improved conditions to continue or advance what they had done before. However, what these people did before they moved into the new settlements in an individualized way then became both a social activity offering learning opportunities, and a new practice better visible to others. Furthermore, living in a (largely) car-free urban community led to new behaviours (e.g., year-round cycling) and revealed further needs to support a car-free lifestyle (e.g., facilities for bicycles).

However, the projects aimed to achieve their objectives at different scales. From the beginning, the Viennese initiative was confined to a particular building block of social housing – even if the proponents could also hope to influence the standards of later developments in other parts of the city. The proponents of the Model District Vauban had initially aimed to significantly reduce and centralise parking spaces and provide ideal conditions for car-free households in an entire district of 38 hectares. Today, roughly 430 households in a designated core area of the district have opted into the scheme as car-free households, benefitting financially from this institutional innovation, while the whole population of approximately 2,000 households in the whole district benefit from the advantages of a largely car-free inner district and generously designed public spaces. The Viennese project is not only smaller than the experimental area in Freiburg – it is also stricter in its policy and hence more ambitious. While activists in Freiburg, after intense debates, agreed to provide a scheme with greater flexibility (Lübke 2014), the project in Vienna was planned from the beginning as an offer for an "advanced" target group only, a highly visible car-free "island" among ordinary urban residential areas, and an example which could help developers and the city administration to learn more about car-reduction strategies.

Besides the obviously successful implementation of both initiatives, relevant indicators show that inhabitants unanimously appreciate the car-reduced features of their settlements and the outstanding price-rises in real estate at Vauban would also not be possible if this particular environment would not be highly appreciated. Moreover, all available evaluation studies in congruence with our own observations indicate that both cases have been very successful regarding their original goals so far. The following table summarizes these considerations.

Table 12.2 Comparing innovation, learning and impacts of the two projects

	Car-free housing project, Vienna	Model District Vauban, Freiburg
Institutional novelties	Amendment of the Viennese building regulation regarding mandatory parking space Special lease agreement Unusual extensive participation of future residents Unique tenants statute and self-administration of common facilities	Stay of the execution of the state's building regulation regarding mandatory parking space (one lot per housing unit) on the basis of a contractual commitment not to frequently use a car by members of an association which owns space for extra parking, if required Association ensures additional parking space can be created if needed (owning ground) Contracts between households and association developed in collaboration with municipal building department
Evaluation findings	Private car use at extremely low level Positive ecological effects Stable car-free mobility patterns (cycling, walking, tram) Bicycles most important means of daily transport High emotional relatedness of residents Self-recruitment and ongoing community-building activities in the settlement important factor for success	Car use and car ownership at very low levels Stable car-free mobility patterns (cycling, walking, tram) Positive ecological effects Self-recruitment and ongoing community-building activities important factor for success Car-free spaces greatly appreciated, contributing to immense interest to buy/rent in the district
Interest in learning from the "model"	No distinct "showcase-tourism" but model project is still of interest for architects, journalists and students Car-free community linked with other local eco-villages, but no contact with other car-free projects	Thousands of visitors from all over the world annually to see and experience the "Model District Vauban" High media attention: study tour reports in online blogs and numerous newspaper articles
Wider impact of the model projects	Strict form of car-free living remains singular case in Austria Project was cause for regulatory change, reference project and building block of Vienna's mobility policy Follower projects in Vienna less strict regarding private car ownership but with special focus on needs of cyclists	No replication of the model in Freiburg Adoption of the opt-in/opt-out model in several other German cities in recent years Project may have influenced regulatory change at state level (so far speculative)

But have the two initiatives really contributed to a larger, systemic or cultural change, as their initiators had hoped?

The mere fact that both projects did contribute to a regulatory change at the regional level supports the assumption that our cases have contributed to a change of the mobility regime – at least to a certain extent. However, these new legal opportunities have not resulted in a large number of follow-up developments so far. In Vienna, a few new developments have already benefited from this new legal situation and in a contemporary political debate (January 2015), the complete abolition of parking requirements has been discussed. Regarding our question, however, it is important to note that in both cases an important legal barrier for car-free neighbourhoods has been removed.

Given the international recognition of the 'Freiburg Model' as implemented in Vauban, it is surprising that it has not been implemented or further developed in later developments in Freiburg itself. This fact may be interpreted as an indication for strong inertia of a car-oriented planning culture, which is actually persisting in Freiburg and has been overcome only in one very special historical situation. The urban context of Vienna, in contrast, seems to be better suited for a succession of further projects in the vein of the car-free settlement. Developers in Vienna have also drawn an important conclusion from their experiences and recently started to frame new building project as "bicycle-friendly" instead of "car-free", leading to more flexible and less strict mobility schemes.

Freiburg Vauban, however, is well renowned and visited by thousands of planners, journalists, architects and councillors annually from all over the world as a comprehensive showcase of sustainable urban development (not limited to mobility issues). Particularly the 'up-market' image of the iconic Model District Vauban, with its mostly affluent and educated inhabitants, may contribute to the weakening of the 'they cannot afford it' association with car-less households. Those visitors who come to observe and personally experience the sustainable mobility practices in Vauban may hence turn into multipliers of a new set of social practices of car-free mobility or even of less mobility-intensive, more place-bound lifestyles. Although in different ways, both examples clearly contributed to raising awareness that car averse planning can significantly contribute to the living quality experienced in a block or district.

Conclusions

The exact ecological and institutional effects of these projects are very difficult to quantify. Furthermore, assessing how important the demonstrations of feasibility and attractiveness of car-free settlements were for a discursive shift in urban planning would also require studies of a different scope. However, we were able to show that our cases helped raise awareness about sustainable mobility, offered spaces for learning and experimentation, and challenged and finally contributed to a shift in existing building regulations on a very practical level.

In our cases, support for a car-free life has been approached by means of new institutional arrangements – such as the official status of a 'car-free household' in Vauban. This allowed for a fairer allocation of costs for parking spaces to car users, which again resulted in a financial incentive to join the group of car-free households. Furthermore, sophisticated alternative mobility infrastructure has been provided from the city level (tramline, cycling lanes) to the community level (plentiful parking space for bicycles and trailers, a bicycle workshop, etc.). Generally, a built environment has been provided which is not only supportive of alternative lifestyles but also highly attractive in many more aspects. As we have seen, the planning of such environments has been a highly contested process in both cases. Both processes were largely determined by local windows of opportunities and power configurations, and hence followed place-specific trajectories. However, the initiatives were similarly influenced by and are manifestations of (a) a trans-local movement in search for sustainable lifestyles and (b) a trans-local movement towards more inclusive and less car-dominated urban planning.

Both cases qualify as socio-technical niches and continuously provide a space for the further development and stabilization of alternative social practices and the demonstration of their attractiveness. Experimentation with emerging socio-technical configurations has been rather limited in both cases, since the hybrids of material-institutional components (such as generous facilities for cyclists, nearby car-sharing locations, central parking houses, and collectively owned spare ground to ensure the option of returning to higher car rates) worked quite well from the beginning and never had to be substantially modified.

With regard to the notion of urban sustainability transitions and the MLP, we state that both were useful as a heuristic for describing attempts to demonstrate deliberate deviations from a dominant regime in urban contexts. In order to get a full picture of the transformative dynamics, however, we learned that we need to study not only material and institutional changes, but also shifts in discourse and social practices. These have been brought about very strategically and far-sightedly by supposed 'niche actors' and it seems feasible that they – again in the language of the MLP – can aggregate and contribute to significant changes at the 'landscape level'.

Provided with similar adaptive approaches and comprehensive mixes of policy and institutional strategies, it is likely that future initiatives for car-free or car-reduced urban areas would succeed in any other European city as well, as every urban environment above a certain size will provide enough interested parties to realize at least one such project. This reflects a raising awareness among a sufficiently large share of (at least Western European) populations that car-free urban environments of certain types can be conducive to a very high quality of life. And, as we have shown in this chapter, these two ambitious initiatives clearly have contributed to this situation.

With regard to the scope for governance towards transitions at the urban level, we may conclude that it needs local knowledge and savvy to make use of particular opportunities as they arise. A blueprint approach would not have been successful in either case. However, our cases suggest some possible directions for the future of urban mobility: they point to the importance of community-building activities, stress the importance of personal identification with neighbourhoods, and show the importance of appropriate material conditions provided for pedestrians and cyclists – within the settlement, but also regarding the connection to the wider bicycle infrastructure and complementary mobility alternatives.

References

AK Verkehr, der erweiterten Bürgerbeteiligung and Forum Vauban (1995). "Modellstadtteil Vauban – Verkehrskonzeption: Auf kurzen Wegen und Autofrei ins nächste Jahrtausend! – Stellungnahme des AK Verkehr der erweiterten Bürgerbeteiligung". Freiburg, Forum Vauban.

Brohmann, B., Fritsche, U., Hartard, S., Schmied, M., Schmitt, B., Schönfelder, C., Schütt, N., Roos, W., Stahl, H., Timpe, C. and Wiegmann, K. (2002). "Nachhaltige Stadtteile auf innerstädtischen Konversionsflächen: Stoffstromanalyse als Bewertungsinstrument – Endbericht". Darmstadt, Freiburg, Berlin.

Buehler, R. and Pucher, J. (2011). "Sustainable transport in Freiburg: lessons from Germany's environmental capital". *International Journal of Sustainable Transportation* **5** (1): 43–70.

Cohen, M. J. (2012). "The future of automobile society: a socio-technical transitions perspective". *Technology Analysis & Strategic Management* **24** (4): 377–390.

Delleske, A. (2013). "Vauban.de – Planung und Daten, Ablauf (Kurzfassung)" online at http://www.vauban.de/themen/planung-daten, accessed 21 Jan. 2015. Retrieved 21.1.2015, 2013.

Eigner, P., Matis, H. and Resch, A. (1999). "Sozialer Wohnbau in Wien. Eine historische Bestandsaufnahme". In: Verein für Geschichte der Stadt Wien. *Studien zur Wiener Geschichte, Jahrbuch des Vereins für Geschichte der Stadt Wien*, Verlag des Vereines für die Geschichte der Stadt Wien. **55**: 49–100.

Epp, C. (1999). "Rechtsformen autofreien Wohnens. – Privatrechtliche und öffentlich-rechtliche Instrumente der Autobeschränkung in Neubaugebieten". Baden-Baden, Nomos-Verl.-Ges.

Geels, F. (2011). "The role of cities in technological transition: analytical clarifications and historical examples". In: H. Bulkeley, V. C. Broto, M. Hudson and S. Marvin. *Cities and Low Carbon Transitions*. London, Routledge: 16 S.

Geels, F. W. & Schot, J. (2007). "Typology of sociotechnical transition pathways." Research Policy **36** (3): 399–417.

Geels, F. W., Kemp, R., Dudley, G. and Lyons, G. (2012). *Automobility in Transition? A Socio-Technical Analysis of Sustainable Transport*. New York, Routledge.

Gesiba. (2013). "project information". from http://www.stadt-wien.at/immobilienwien/immobilien/gesiba.html.

Gutmann, R. and Havel, M. (2000). "Sozialwissenschaftliche Dokumentation & Evaluierung 'Autofreie Mustersiedlung Wien-Floridsdorf', Auftraggeber: Stadt Wien, MA 50, Wohnbauforschung, Endbericht 7/2000". Wien, Wohnbund.

Hodson, M. and Marvin, S. (2010). "Can cities shape socio-technical transitions and how would we know if they were?" *Research Policy* **39**: 477–485.

Hoogma, R., Kemp, R. and Schot, J. (2002). *Experimenting for Sustainable Transport: The Approach of Strategic Niche Management*. London, Spon Press.

Koch, J. (2014). "Car-free living in Vauban, Freiburg – An analysis of decision making and enabling factors". *Umwelt und Natürliche Ressourcen*. Freiburg, ALU Freiburg.

Lange, J. (2009). *Unterstützen Sie unser Verkehrskonzept! – Information – Forderungen – Unterschriftenliste.* Freiburg, AK–Verkehr Vauban.

Lange, J., Heuer, M., Linck, H., Loose, W., Nobis, C., Schieder, A., Sperling, C. and Members of the Mobility Working Group (2003). "Umsetzungsbegleitung des Verkehrskonzeptes im Stadtteil Freiburg-Vauban". Freiburg, Forum Vauban, DLR, Ökoinstitut, DBU.

Lübke, M. M. (2014). Personal communication, e-mail of 21 March 2014.

Marletto, G., Crenos, D., Sassari, U. and Tre, R. (2011). "The city as an environment for radical change: The case of low-carbon urban mobility (Draft!)". *AISRE 2011.* Torino: 15–17.

Moser, P. and Stocker, E. (2008). "Autofreies Wohnen – Evaluierung der Mustersiedlung in Wien Floridsdorf, Stadt und Regionalforschung GmbH, gefördert von der Stadt Wien, MA 50, Wohnbauforschung", Stadt und Regionalforschung GmbH, gefördert von der Stadt Wien.

Nobis, C. (2003a). "Bewohnerbefragung Vauban – Bericht im Rahmen des Projektes "Umsetzungsbegleitung des Verkehrskonzeptes im Stadtteil Freiburg-Vauban". Berlin, DLR.

Nobis, C. (2003b). "The impact of car-free housing districts on mobility behaviour – Case study". *WIT Transactions on Ecology and the Environment 67*: 701–710.

Nobis, C. and Welsch, J. (2003). "Mobility management at district-level –The impact of car-reduced districts on mobility behavior". Proceedings of the 7th European Conference on Mobility Management, Karlstad, Sweden.

Ornetzeder, M., Hertwich, E. G., Hubacek, K., Korytarova, K. and Haas, W. (2008). "The environmental effect of car-free housing: A case in Vienna". *Ecological Economics 65* (3): 516–530.

Quitzau, M.-B., Jensen, J. S., Elle, M. and Hoffmann, B. (2013). "Sustainable urban regime adjustments". *Journal of Cleaner Production 50*: 140–147.

Raven, R. and Geels, F. (2010). "Socio-cognitive evolution in niche development: comparative analysis of biogas development in Denmark and the Netherlands (1973–2004)". *Technovation 30* (2): 87–99.

Scheurer, J. and Newman, P. (2009). "Vauban: A European Model Bridging the Green and Brown Agendas – Case study prepared for Revisiting Urban Planning: UN Habitat: "Planning Sustainable Cities: Global Report on Human Settlements 2009"; https://unhabitat.org/books/global-report-on-human-settlements-2009-planning-sustainable-cities/".

Seyfang, G. and Haxeltine, A. (2012). "Growing grassroots innovations: exploring the role of community-based initiatives in governing sustainable energy transitions". *Environment and Planning C: Government and Policy 30* (3): 381–400.

Smith, A. and Raven, R. (2012). "What is protective space? Reconsidering niches in transitions to sustainability". *Research Policy 41* (6): 1025–1036.

Späth, P. (2013). "How to understand (and support) non-ownership of a car? Reviewing the case of Vauban in Freiburg (Germany): Individual choices versus social practices". *IST 2013 – 4th International Conference on Sustainability Transitions.* Zurich.

Späth, P. and Rohracher, H. (2010). "'Energy regions': the transformative power of regional discourses on socio-technical futures". *Research Policy 39* (4): 449–458.

Späth, P. and Rohracher, H. (2012). "Local demonstrations for global transitions — dynamics across governance levels fostering socio-technical regime change towards sustainability". *European Planning Studies 20* (3): 461–479.

Sperling, C. (1999). "Nachhaltige Stadtentwicklung beginnt im Quartier. Ein Praxis– und Ideenhandbuch für Stadtplaner, Baugemeinschaften, Bürgerinitiativen am Beispiel des sozial-ökologischen Modellstadtteils Freiburg-Vauban". Freiburg, Öko-Institut.

Stadt Freiburg (2012). "Freiburg im Breisgau – Stadtbezirksatlas 2012". Freiburg, Amt für Bürgerservice und Informationsverarbeitung.

Urry, J. (2004). "The 'System' of Automobility". *Theory, Culture & Society* **21** (4/5): 25–39.

Verein für Autofreies Wohnen e.V. (2012). "Jahresbericht für 2011". Freiburg.

Vienna City Administration (2014). "STEP 2025 Urban Development Plan Vienna – Short Report". Vienna, Municipal Department 18.

13 Multiple Transitions

Energy Precariousness and 'Transient' Urban Tenants

Saska Petrova

Introduction

Decision makers and academics alike are becoming increasingly aware of the need to consider issues of distributional and procedural justice in the implementation of urban sustainability transitions (Agyeman and Evans 2004; Linnér and Selin 2013). This is particularly true in the case of policies in the domains of energy, carbon and climate change, which can affect both fuel prices and the energy efficiency of the housing stock. Both the affordability of energy and the ability of the infrastructures of the home – the building materials, appliances and heating systems – are crucial contributors to the rise of domestic energy deprivation: a condition characterised by the inability of a household to secure a socially and materially necessary level of energy services in its residential dwelling (Bouzarovski and Petrova 2015; Bouzarovski et al. 2015). This predicament has been persistently present and expanding in developed and developing countries alike. In the global North, its broader dimensions are often encapsulated under the notion of 'fuel poverty', which is frequently the subject of remedial or preventative measures implemented by the state. The term 'energy poverty' – traditionally used in the global South to underscore issues of access to infrastructure that characterize many such states – is now increasingly used across the world to denote the end result of this situation: the lack of adequate energy facilities and functions in the home.

This chapter focuses on energy poverty among young adults (less than 30 years of age) living in the private rented sector. Often termed nontraditional, these household structures usually include individuals living alone, cohabiting or married couples without children, and flat-sharers (Buzar et al. 2007). As such, they do not conform to the home-owning nuclear family form, whose normativities have been embedded in urban planning, housing and energy efficiency policies (Cutas and Chan 2012; Myers 1990). The relative neglect of nontraditional households in decision-making contexts has persisted despite their rapid increase in developed countries, particularly within urban areas. The demographically and spatially fluid nature of such groups has often led to lower levels of political visibility. Thus, young and 'transient' urban dwellers (Goodman 1999; Haase, Grossmann, and Steinführer 2012; Sage, Smith, and Hubbard 2012) have also been marginalised in mainstream understandings of energy poverty. This situation poses major challenges for sustainability transitions focusing on, inter alia, the decarbonisation of urban energy policies.

The relevance of nontraditional households to urban sustainability transitions in the energy domain can be seen via two dimensions:

- First, there is a need to offer a nuanced perspective on the societal context in which end-use energy demand is generated and articulated in everyday life among such groups, including issues such as the specific use of information and digital technology, as well as the portfolios of household energy-related social practices as they vary across the temporal and spatial fabric of society. The fact that nontraditional households are disproportionately concentrated in urban areas while moving through the housing stock further complicates efforts to target environmentally unsustainable infrastructures and practices within this context.
- Second, young people who are moving into independent accommodation for the first time in their lives can potentially constitute a prime target for interventions aimed at addressing energy end-use attitudes, behaviours, and social practices. Indeed, it is known that the evolution of consumption practices throughout an individual's life is shaped by the norms, attitudes and conditionings that characterize the environment in which they undertake their transition into adulthood (Grønhøj and Thøgersen 2012; Kleinschafer and Morrison 2014). While teenagers and children have frequently found themselves the subjects of research and policy aimed at reducing domestic energy use, young adults have received almost no attention in this context. The possible presence of underconsumption among the latter is adding to the complexity of the situation (Bouzarovski et al. 2013).

This chapter uses the notion of 'the energy precariat' to capture the socially and technically fragile underpinnings of energy consumption among transient urban populations in developed countries. In essence, I extend the traditional notion of 'precariat' to the energy domain. The precariat is typically defined by 'short-term employment, persistent marginalisation, and social insecurity – something of a fragmented urban underclass whose precariousness is increasingly evident in traditionally middle-class economic life' (Kautzer and Harvey 2008, 151). In doing this, the paper aims to highlight how the articulation of sustainability transitions (Berkhout, Smith, and Stirling 2004; Frantzeskaki, Loorbach, and Meadowcroft 2012; Markard, Raven, and Truffer 2012) among transient urban dwellers is contingent upon the wider dynamics of infrastructural embeddedness and everyday life that contribute to this group's increasing vulnerability to energy poverty. This highlights the need for integrating energy poverty and sustainability transitions scholarship, by emphasising the policies, procedures, norms and symbolic meanings that underpin the presence of domestic energy deprivation within 'different mutually-related and mutually-influencing life domains' (Ulrich Mayer 2004, 166) undergoing social and technological change.

My overarching aim is to highlight that sustainability transitions themselves cannot be seen in isolation from other processes of systemic change in society: they need to be understood within the context of related demographic, housing and institutional transformations, while considering the inequities that underpin energy use. As such, the chapter addresses two of the general themes of the book, pertaining *(i)* to the difference between urban sustainability transitions and other types of sustainability transitions and *(ii)* to the scale-related conflicts and synergies implicated in such processes.

I support these arguments with findings from on-going research project in Eastern and Central Europe (ECE), focusing on issues of thermal comfort, fuel costs and social practices among urban households in a number of inner-city areas (Bouzarovski 2014; Petrova, Gentile, et al. 2013). The chapter thus commences with a discussion of the multiple transitions that affect young adults across the developed world, with a special focus on the changing nature of housing provision and energy consumption. I then move onto a review of the literature on energy poverty, highlighting both the driving forces and systemic consequences of this form of deprivation. This is followed by an exploration of the sustainability transitions-energy precariousness nexus with the aid of a number of vignettes from ethnographic fieldwork undertaken in Prague during 2013 and 2014[1].

Energy Use and Deprivation among Transient Urban Populations

The geographical and thematic setting of my study implies that the notion of transition has several additional meanings in the chapter, aside from the term 'sustainability transitions':

- Post-communist urban transitions: since the early 1990s, ECE states have been subject to a movement away from the centrally planned economy and a single-party system towards a market-oriented parliamentary democracy. This dynamic has deeply affected the transformation of planning and environmental policies, involving shifts in energy consumption patterns that generally lead to improvements in energy efficiency while increasing overall energy demand and urban mobility – thus affecting sustainability transitions themselves. At the same time, ECE countries are undergoing wider systemic transformations towards low carbon use, despite their different economic and political histories.
- The second demographic transition: this process involves, inter alia, changes away from conventional family structures into a wider array of nontraditional household arrangements, underpinned by the increasing individualisation of society, the decline in fertility rates, and fundamental reconfigurations in ties of kin and friendship. The second demographic

transition has been underway in developed countries since 1970s (Mills and Blossfeld 2013), although its influence is being increasingly felt across ECE states (Hoem et al. 2009; Petrović 2011).

- Housing transitions: one of the consequences of the second demographic transition is accelerated movements between different residential formations, as individuals attempt to embed their life 'into social structures primarily in the form of … partaking in social positions and roles, that is, in regard to their membership in institutional orders' (Ulrich Mayer 2004, 163). Such residential progressions usually involve transitions between different housing types, and as such primarily entail household-level shifts (as opposed to wider societal and economic changes). In the case study context, the most common form of housing transition involves moving away from the parental home or catered student housing into independent living arrangements, primarily in the private rental sector.

It should also be pointed out that the three dynamics described are inter-related: post-communist transition dynamics have facilitated the expansion of the second demographic transition in the ECE setting, as the result of a combination of cultural factors (such as the preference for nontraditional life-styles) and economic circumstances (e.g., the decrease in marriage rates and the decline of fertility due to financial pressure). Nevertheless, the increase in numbers of young adults living in unconventional household configurations is part of the broader dismantling of traditional demographic arrangements across the developed world. This is exemplified by the fact that four out of five households in the UK now see themselves as falling outside the definition of the 'classic' nuclear family (BBC 2010). The influence of the second demographic transition – the postponement and decline of marriage, rising divorce rates, the decline of the nuclear family and an increasing diversity of household formations and stages – means that the statistic of non-nuclear family households generally includes individuals living alone, or in cohabiting or house-sharing arrangements.

The spatial agency of 'nontraditional' households is particularly felt in inner-city areas and urban cores (Buzar et al. 2007) – and there is widespread evidence to suggest that this includes many large- and even medium-sized cities across ECE (Haase et al. 2011). The term 'reurbanisation' has been put forward as a descriptor of the spatial implications stemming from the concentration of particular demographic groups in the residential districts of the inner core. Reurbanisation is relatively well established in major developed-world cities, and is beginning to be felt in lower levels of the urban hierarchy. For example, the latest census results in the UK show that the rising urban core populations of second-tier cities like Manchester, Birmingham, Leeds, Bristol, Nottingham, Sheffield and Glasgow have a markedly different income and educational profile compared to the extant residents of surrounding inner-city areas. This mirrors processes seen in major ECE cities, such as Prague, Budapest, Warsaw and Ljubljana. Reurbanising populations exhibit a tendency to inhabit particular types of housing while being characterised by specific daily mobility and consumption patterns. Their mobility through the housing stock is characterised by relatively fast transitions among 'household events' (Feijten and Mulder 2002). As a whole, their presence has altered the residential and technological characteristics of inner cities, by creating new patterns of mobility and rhythms of everyday life. The housing mix has seen the increased presence of shared and multiple-occupancy housing, as well as private rented dwellings. Such residential models have been largely neglected in the mainstream literature and policy on urban housing demand evolution and management.

The social practices that underpin energy demand are a crucial component of the new political, economic and spatial implications of the second demographic transition and reurbanisation alike. This is underscored, for instance, by claims that rising household numbers lead to higher energy consumption (Liu et al. 2003). There is evidence to suggest that the synergistic effects of end use energy demand associated with the demographic profiles and spatial behaviours of nontraditional households are associated with the cultural expectations and public discourses that influence their everyday lives. However, very little is known about the specific energy consumption features of households in this group, especially when placed in the context of their specific housing requirements and residential features. In particular, there is a need for understanding how the energy consumption practices of urban young adults (either living alone, or in cohabitating or house-sharing arrangements) are related to the broader economic and residential precariousness experienced by such households, within the wider dismantling of traditional notions of 'community' (Petrova 2014).

The residential circumstances and preferences of student populations provide important insights into the energy-housing nexus among nontraditional households at the younger end of the age distribution. In a study of houses in Dunedin, New Zealand, Shannon et al. (2003) have dedicated some discussion to students' perceptions and the behaviours they develop in order to cope with the particularly disadvantaged position they hold: 90 per cent of the surveyed houses were heated below comfort standards, and 70 per cent experienced mould, damp or draughts. Valuing affordability and location over housing quality, most of the interviewees dealt with this situation by leaving the house and studying or socialising elsewhere. The study also revealed the surveyed households' high acceptance levels of their situation, and the reluctance to give up even small portions of their budget for the purpose of housing improvements.

When speaking about energy issues as they relate to transient households, it is important to note that individuals who do not own their homes or who live in impermanent housing or household arrangements, have often found themselves outside the existing support system for energy efficiency investment. In the UK, the legal and policy framework that drives national local action on such issues – epitomised in the government's new programme for energy efficiency action via programmes such as the Energy Company Obligation and the Green Deal – has almost exclusively favoured house-owning households living in individual homes. The implementation of urban regeneration, planning and housing policies has also exhibited a limited understanding of the specific energy needs and functionings of this group. Similar circumstances can be found throughout ECE, where state-led support frameworks for housing investment are poorly developed overall, while private sector finance almost entirely favours home ownership within the context of more 'established' household arrangements (Lux and Mikeszova 2012; Pichler-Milanovich 2001).

Researching Developed-World Energy Poverty in the Context of Sustainability Transitions

Understanding the historical evolution of energy poverty scholarship and policy can provide important insights into the current relationship between sustainability transitions and energy demand among young adults in transient housing arrangements. Domestic energy deprivation policies and research are most advanced in the UK and Ireland, where, following Boardman's (1991) seminal contribution, a distinct group of academics and practitioners sought to highlight the difficulties faced by households who are unable to afford an adequate level of thermal comfort in their homes. Debates on 'fuel poverty' entered the political agenda mainly thanks to the public recognition of the health problems associated with cold homes. These have traditionally been identified as respiratory, rheumatic and heart conditions leading to, inter alia, excessive winter mortality and morbidity (Boardman 1991; Chang et al., 2004; Critchley et al. 2007; Healy and Clinch 2002; Lawlor 2001; The Eurowinter Group 1997 in Watt 1994). Links with mental health problems have also been pointed out (Lawlor 2001; Liddell and Morris 2010) but have been studied in less detail. Poor housing conditions stemming from insufficient heating have also been suggested to entail socio-economic disadvantages with an additional knock-on effect on health (Anderson, White, and Finney 2012; Boardman 1991; Frank et al. 2006; Gibbons and Singler 2008; Lawlor 2001; O'Neill, Jinks, and Squire 2006).

Two demographic groups have been identified as being most vulnerable to these conditions: children and the elderly (Clinch and Healy 2004; Liddell 2008 inter alia). Most research and policy agendas have focused on energy deprivation among the latter, who represent the most visible, distinctive and vulnerable stratum (see, for example Wilkinson et al. 2004). This has resulted in the comparative neglect of other demographic groups suffering from inadequately warm homes. At the same time, households have been categorised and assessed according to the likelihood of suffering from fuel deprivation, whereby mono-parental families under the poverty line and single retired people rank highest (Liddell 2008), again, showing that children and older people are most at risk.

Emphasising the role of energy efficiency and poor housing – which increase the cost of final energy services received by the household – have allowed for a broader understanding of the systemic driving forces of fuel poverty (Clinch and Healy 2004; Rudge 2012; Sefton 2002). The importance of implementing residential retrofits aimed at improving the energy efficiency of the housing stock, appliances and heating system provides an important entry point for clarifying the relationship between domestic energy deprivation and sustainability transitions more generally. Since the mid-2000s, the implementation of measures to tackle fuel poverty by means of residential or infrastructural improvement have prompted the implementation of evaluation studies aimed at, inter alia, pinpointing the health impacts of cold homes. For instance, Critchley et al. (2007) have assessed data coming from the Warm Front Scheme, a programme that provided grants for improving energy efficiency in owner occupier and private rented homes. These authors have identified the older part of the housing stock as most likely to involve deprivation, a situation further worsened by the fact that most residential dwellings in this age bracket are in the rental market, making retrofitting less likely. Their study draws on several other field trials (Chapman et al. 2009; Howden-Chapman et al. 2008; Howden-Chapman et al. 2007 in Howden-Chapman et al. 2012) which have explored the effects of improvement measures – notably investment in insulation or and heating systems – on the housing stock.

Of relevance to the ECE transition context – where energy poverty is particularly widespread due to the combination of significant income disparities, increasing energy prices, and inefficient housing and heating systems as well as a series of political and regulatory circumstances (Bouzarovski 2010; Bouzarovski, Petrova, and Sarlamanov 2012) – is the need for developing more comprehensive detection and measurement frameworks. It has been argued that taking socio-demographic particularities at the household scale into account can provide a better assessment of the population at risk. This is why Khandker et al. (2012) revise different definitions of the threshold at which energy deprivation starts to occur, seeking to more effectively decouple it from strict income poverty (see also Dubois 2012; Palmer, MacInnes, and Kenway 2008). They emphasize the particular context of developing countries where climate, household needs, fuel accessibility and energy markets differ. Reckoning that fuel poverty situations are composed by a host of circumstances – which hinder the necessary task of accurately identifying households at risk – some authors have proposed a wide range of definitions and indicators (see Moore 2012 for a review) in addition to methodologies that regard energy poverty as an integrated problem, including research and policy questions (Dubois 2012; Palmer, MacInnes, and Kenway 2008).

It is also worth mentioning the significant amount of scholarly work on the socio-demographic determinants and economic impact of energy poverty. These contingencies are being increasingly explored within a wider context, beyond the hardship associated with accessing necessary fuel supplies and the health consequences of inadequate energy services. However, the driving forces and consequences of the contextual factors associated with domestic energy deprivation are often difficult to tell apart, as energy poverty is intertwined with wider circumstances such as low incomes, education, behaviour, disabilities, and social exclusion as well as the broader conditions of housing and energy markets (Anderson, White, and Finney 2012, 50). Attitudes and standards towards heating and energy lie at the core of the difficulties associated with quantifying fuel poverty levels (Anderson, White, and Finney 2012; Brunner, Spitzer, and Christanell 2012; Palmer, MacInnes, and Kenway 2008). A number of authors have attempted to establish a typology of households and energy users, so as to create a baseline for assessing the risk of deprivation among different groups (see Healy and Clinch 2002).

Recent research also points to the need for considering energy poverty as a function of cultural and social particularities in households. This leads to empirical and practical definitions that can take into account different levels of risk and vulnerability beyond economic indicators. Along this line, a study made by Barnes et al. (2008) on the effects of 'bad' housing on children breaks down the households according to parents' work status, income, debt, number of children and ethnic origin. One of the criteria they use to assess housing as 'bad' refers to the extent to which it provides a reasonable degree of thermal comfort, assessed in thermal insulation and efficiency terms defined by the standards of the Department for Communities and Local Government (2006 in Barnes, Butt, and Tomaszewski 2008).

Overall, the literature is increasingly challenging traditional conceptions of domestic energy deprivation as being exclusively related to income poverty and health problems, while bringing to light interactions with other types of disadvantage. Nevertheless, very few authors have directly challenged the artificial normativities created by standard definitions of energy poverty, whose underlying assumptions fail to reflect the wide diversity of household formations and conditions associated with the experience of domestic energy deprivation. What is more, the definition of a limited number of assessment and evaluation methods – whereby a number of variables need to remain constant in order to make calculations possible – means that situations that deviate from this standard find themselves excluded from both academic research and policy action. This places severe limitations on the ability of scholarship and practice on sustainability transitions to fully integrate the multiple spatial and social dimensions associated with processes of structural change (Moss, Becker, and Naumann 2014; Petrova, Torres Garcia, and Bouzarovski 2016).

Indeed, the demographic of young adults in inner-city areas – a group that includes mainly students and house shares – has been identified as potentially highly vulnerable to pressing problems of urban energy poverty (Bouzarovski et al. 2013). In addition to some of the issues already discussed in the previous two sections of this chapter, the political marginalisation of this stratum may also be attributed to the wider perception that its members do not face immediate health risks and are not concerned with the quality of living standards.

However, work by authors such as Barnes et al. (2008) connects educational attainment and psychological functioning among young people with energy poverty levels. Their work highlights the obstacles to academic performance endured by secondary school students living in poorly heated homes and lacking adequate study space. This becomes particularly relevant in the current situation of youth unemployment, financial pressure and housing strain faced by many university students and individuals moving out of the parental home.

The National Union of Students and Friends of the Earth (National Union of Students 2013) recently performed a pilot survey about fuel poverty and energy efficiency in some 300 student households in the UK. The preliminary results of this undertaking indicated that over three-quarters of the respondents had felt 'uncomfortably cold at home over the winter'. Its authors liaised with the Lancaster University Student Union to find that high average energy bills may indicate fuel poverty to be widely spread within the student community. A number of more detailed studies have been announced as a result of such findings, accompanied by policy statements emphasising the need for concerted action at the nexus of housing standards in student housing, landlord behaviour and domestic energy deprivation.

Mainstream understandings of energy poverty have also been challenged by work focused on the coping strategies and energy-saving measures implemented by households in, or at risk of, energy poverty. Thus Anderson et al.'s (2012) review escapes rigid definitions of energy poverty related to income, locating the issue in the presence of strategies to reconcile energy needs and budget constraints. Brunner et al. (2012) also support an approach that values the perspectives and strategies of affected households, while considering a wider population beyond the commonly accepted risk groups. Using qualitative and quantitative methods on a range of respondents in Vienna, they have drawn attention to the wide practices associated with the presence of domestic energy deprivation in the home: frugality, modesty, cutting back on activity or lighting, and dealing financially – or even psychologically – with nonpayment and arrears.

Challenging the Canon: Energy Poverty among Young Urban Adults

As was pointed out above, exploring patterns of energy use and deprivation among households who do not conform to the dominant model of energy poverty can help provide insights into the broader driving forces of the condition in urban contexts. In the Czech context, it is well known that households living in the rented sector face disproportionate housing costs, and are more likely to fall into poverty (Jahoda and Špalková 2012). At the same time, the private rental housing stock has been marginalised in policies aimed at improving the sustainability of energy use, mainly due to the legal and ownership complexities associated with interventions in the built environment, and to the almost complete omission of this housing stock in official regulatory frameworks.

My own work in Prague uncovered the presence of highly concentrated and specific patterns of domestic energy deprivation among flat-sharing young people in inner urban areas. The homes of most of the individuals I surveyed in both cities were inadequately heated for prolonged periods of time. A highly erratic pattern of energy services was present in such dwellings, with temperatures widely varying during the day: 'We only really heat the home in the evenings, trying to spend time in work, libraries or other public spaces ... we try to cut back on both gas use and electricity' (Marketa 2014). The primary reason for cutting back on energy use was the high proportion of housing and fuel costs in the household budgets of interviewed households. However, the energy affordability and the poor efficiency of the respondents' homes contributed to this situation – many of them lived in multistorey terraced blocks that had were initially built to low thermal efficiency standards and had seen limited improvements in the meantime, particularly with respect to the thermal efficiency of heating systems and domestic appliances. Thus, the economic and housing precariousness experienced by my respondents also assumed an infrastructural nature, having become embedded in the residential structures of the inner city.

My field research also identified the different institutional and spatial pathways that allowed inner city young adults to become exposed to conditions of energy poverty in the home. In particular, I found that many individuals in this group became vulnerable by means of the specific socio-technical, economic and institutional settings in which they led their everyday lives. They lived in areas of high housing demand, which disincentivised landlords from investing in the energy efficiency of the housing stock as it provided a constant supply of tenants: 'There is fierce competition for good and affordable housing in central Prague, especially in shared flats ... such apartments are generally below standard but the owners know that they can get away with it because they can always find someone else to fill your place' (Pavel 2013). In a number of cases, rental and utility payments were tied up in single contracts, thus increasing costs more than situations where bills were paid separately. The energy efficiency of many rental dwellings was exacerbated by the legacies of the system of regulated rents (Buzar 2005) – and the informal economy it created via the illegal subletting of rent-controlled apartments – as it gave tenants a limited ability to force landlords to improve the quality of housing. However, the abolition of regulated rents has led to an overall rise in rental prices across the city, thus increasing the vulnerability of households in this group.

A large part of the cultural expectations revolved around the belief that young people need not live in adequate housing: there was an overall feeling that they need to move up the 'housing ladder' and earn their status in society before being able to live in adequate housing conditions. As was pointed out by one of my interviewees 'I know that this situation is only temporary

... eventually we will buy our own dwelling and move out to a better home'
(Petr 2013). However, several of the households I interviewed felt that the goal
of a proper home was increasingly distant, as the result of financial strain and
debt that they experience – with youth unemployment constantly increasing
in both countries, the classic housing and career progression model seems
increasingly less plausible. Among flat-sharers, I frequently encountered the
practice of bringing down energy consumption to the level of the person who
could least afford their bills, in a form of intra-household solidarity. This further decreased the quality of energy services received in the home.

The interviewees pointed out that they were not aware of any state-sponsored or private-sector support schemes that they could access in order to
improve the thermal efficiency of the housing stock. This is despite the fact
that sustainability goals are present in a range of official frameworks developed both by the Czech state and the City of Prague, including the 2010
spatial plan (Petrova, Posová, et al. 2013) and strategic plans adopted by
local municipalities, as well as the updated strategic plan at the level of the
entire city (http://www.iprpraha.cz/clanek/83/co-je-strategicky-plan). Both
the regulatory frameworks that I surveyed and the decision-makers whom I
interviewed displayed an inability to grasp the complexities associated with
addressing systemic problems at the nexus of sustainable energy transitions
and poverty as they relate to transient urban populations.

Concluding Thoughts

In this chapter, I have aimed to make a contribution to the understanding
of domestic energy deprivation in transitioning urban contexts, by exploring
the energy consumption and social practices of nontraditional young adult
households in inner-city areas. I have sought to highlight the connections
between energy-related programmes and related housing and planning policies with respect to this group. These processes have influenced the manner
in which energy demand is conditioned, timed and synchronised in the built
environment, as well as the evolution of a specific infrastructural underclass,
whose characteristics match the definition of a social precariat with added
technical constraints and subjectivities influenced by domestic energy deprivation. As such, they exhibit a structural ability to influence the outcomes of
sustainability transitions, by creating vulnerable populations with a limited
ability to influence housing stock transformations despite their significant
social and spatial presence in the city.

When placed in the context of wider research on energy poverty, my findings point to the overarching role of social justice issues in shaping the multiple transitions (Sýkora and Bouzarovski 2012) that intersect in urban spaces.
As such, they match the outcomes of Walker and Day's (2012) price–income–
efficiency triptych, where energy poverty is identified as an issue of distribu-
tive injustice composed by interconnected inequalities in all three domains.
Like them, I would argue in favour of a redefinition of energy poverty so

as to take into account the diversity of energy needs and socially related practices (Buzar 2007). I would also underline the importance of maintaining a multi-scalar understanding of the problem, as energy policy encompasses a wide range of processes between end-users; and sustainability transitions are expressed via a variety of spatial and territorial structures (Coenen, Benneworth, and Truffer 2012).

Returning to the more specific aims of this book, the empirical evidence highlights the embeddedness of urban sustainability transitions in other transformations occurring at this scale – themselves highly contingent upon demographic, regulatory and spatial processes that are specific to the city. What is more, they have also emphasised that as far as the question of energy precariousness is concerned, urban sustainability transitions are endangered by processes occurring deep within the grain of the city, involving cultural change and socio-economic segregation. As such, the multiple transitions that have been described here generate conflicts that can, in the long run, threaten the effectiveness of energy decarbonisation – the more specific form of sustainability transition relevant to the evidence presented in this chapter.

In general terms, this study has prompted me to argue in favour of further multidisciplinary research using mixed methods to adequately combine evidence about the multiple factors involved in driving the rise of domestic energy deprivation within the context of urban sustainability transitions. Such research cannot be strategically undertaken without an identification of the different pathways to deprivation, in the shape of an inclusive typology. There are already instances of work in this direction, categorising fuel poverty as chronic or occasional, as well as a risk that is present at different levels; characterisations of coping strategies rather than household types can also be placed in this trope. Another hurdle to overcome is the issue of scale in studying and identifying populations at risk, as household particularities may make a difference in determining the degree of vulnerability. What is clear is that energy deprivation is no longer understood as an effect of income poverty on age groups with weak health: it can affect all demographic sectors in a variety of ways, and some of these are still unexplored, as are their knock-on effects. Last but not least, I would emphasize the need for continuing to consider the role of energy supply and distribution policies, particularly in terms of the manner in which market regimes can be a determining cause in the systemic expansion and establishment of domestic energy deprivation.

Acknowledgments

The research leading to this paper has received funding from the European Research Council under the European Union's Seventh Framework Programme (FP7/2007–2013)/ERC grant agreement number 313478.

Note

1 Involving 'expert' interviews with 5 decision-makers and ethnographic home-based interviews with 15 flat-sharing households in inner-city Prague.

References

Agyeman, Julian, and Bob Evans. 2004. "'Just Sustainability': The Emerging Discourse of Environmental Justice in Britain?" *Geographical Journal* 170 (2): 155–64. doi:10.1111/j.0016-7398.2004.00117.x.

Anderson, Will, Vicki White, and Andrea Finney. 2012. "Coping with Low Incomes and Cold Homes." *Energy Policy* 49: 40–52.

Barnes, Matt, Sarah Butt, and Wojtek Tomaszewski. 2008. "The Dynamics of Bad Housing: The Impact of Bad Housing on the Living Standards of Children." National Centre for Social Research.

BBC. 2010. "Traditional Family 'in Decline.'" *BBC*, July 2, sec. Education & Family. http://www.bbc.co.uk/news/10487318.

Berkhout, Smith, and Stirling. 2004. "Socio-Technological Regimes and Transition Contexts." In *System Innovation and the Transition to Sustainability: Theory, Evidence and Policy*, edited by Elzen, Geels, and Green, 48–75. Cheltenham: Edward Elgar.

Boardman, Brenda. 1991. *Fuel Poverty: From Cold Homes to Affordable Warmth.* London: Belhaven Press.

Bouzarovski, Stefan. 2010. "Post-Socialist Energy Reforms in Critical Perspective: Entangled Boundaries, Scales and Trajectories of Change." *European Urban and Regional Studies* 17: 167–82.

———. 2014. "Energy Poverty in the European Union: Landscapes of Vulnerability." *Wiley Interdisciplinary Reviews: Energy and Environment* 3 (3): 276–89. doi:10.1002/wene.89.

Bouzarovski, Stefan, and Saska Petrova. 2015. "A Global Perspective on Domestic Energy Deprivation: Overcoming the Energy Poverty–fuel Poverty Binary." *Energy Research & Social Science* 10 (November): 31–40. doi:10.1016/j.erss.2015.06.007.

Bouzarovski, Stefan, Saska Petrova, Matt Kitching, and Josh Baldwick. 2013. "Precarious Domesticities: Energy Vulnerability among Urban Young Adults." In *Energy Justice in a Changing Climate: Social Equity and Low-Carbon Energy*, 30–45. London: Zed Books.

Bouzarovski, Stefan, Saska Petrova, and Robert Sarlamanov. 2012. "Energy Poverty Policies in the EU: A Critical Perspective." *Energy Policy* 49: 76–82.

Bouzarovski, Stefan, Sergio Tirado Herrero, Saska Petrova, and Diana Ürge-Vorsatz. 2015. "Unpacking the Spaces and Politics of Energy Poverty: Path-Dependencies, Deprivation and Fuel Switching in Post-Communist Hungary." *Local Environment*, http://www.tandfonline.com/doi/abs/10.1080/13549839.2015.1075480.

Brunner, Karl-Michael, Markus Spitzer, and Anja Christanell. 2012. "Experiencing Fuel Poverty. Coping Strategies of Low-Income Households in Vienna/Austria." *Energy Policy* 49 (October): 53–59. doi:10.1016/j.enpol.2011.11.076.

Buzar, Stefan. 2005. "The institutional trap in the Czech rental sector: nested circuits of power, space and inequality." *Economic Geography* 82: 381–405.

———. 2007. *Energy Poverty in Eastern Europe: Hidden Geographies of Deprivation.* Aldershot:Ashgate.

———. 2007. "Splintering urban populations: emergent landscapes of reurbanisation in four European cities." *Urban Studies* 44: 651–77.

Chang, Choon Lan, Martin Shipley, Sir Michael Marmot, and Neil Poulter. 2004. "Lower Ambient Temperature Was Associated with an Increased Risk of Hospitalization for Stroke and Acute Myocardial Infarction in Young Women." *Journal of Clinical Epidemiology* 57: 749–57.

Chapman, Howden-Chapman, Viggers, O'Dea, and Kennedy. 2009. "Retrofitting Houses with Insulation: A Cost-Benefit Analysis of a Randomised Community Trial." *Journal of Epidemiology and Community Health* 63 (4): 271–77. doi:10.1136/jech.2007.070037.

Clinch, J. Peter, and John D. Healy. 2004. "Quantifying the Severity of Fuel Poverty, Its Relationship with Poor Housing and Reasons for Non-Investment in Energy-Saving Measures." *Energy Policy* 32 (2): 207–20.

Coenen, Lars, Paul Benneworth, and Bernhard Truffer. 2012. "Toward a Spatial Perspective on Sustainability Transitions." *Research Policy*, Special Section on Sustainability Transitions, 41 (6): 968–79. doi:10.1016/j.respol.2012.02.014.

Critchley, Roger, Jan Gilbertson, Michael Grimsley, Geoff Green, and Warm-Front Study Group. 2007. "Living in Cold Homes after Heating Improvements: Evidence from Warm-Front, England's Home Energy Efficiency Scheme." *Applied Energy* 84: 147–58.

Cutas, Daniela, and Sarah Chan. 2012. *Families – Beyond the Nuclear Ideal*. London and New York: Bloomsbury.

Dubois, Ute. 2012. "From Targeting to Implementation: The Role of Identification of Fuel Poor Households." *Energy Policy* 49 (October): 107–15. doi:10.1016/j.enpol.2011.11.087.

Feijten, and Clara H. Mulder. 2002. "The Timing of Household Events and Housing Events in the Netherlands: A Longitudinal Perspective." *Housing Studies* 17: 773–92.

Nicole B. Neault, Anne Skalicky, John T. Cook, Jacqueline D. Wilson, Suzette Levenson, Alan F. Meyers 2006. "Heat or Eat: The Low Income Home Energy Assistance Program and Nutritional and Health Risks among Children Less Than 3 Years of Age." *Pediatrics* 118 (5): 1293–1302.

Frantzeskaki, Niki, Derk Loorbach, and James Meadowcroft. 2012. "Governing Societal Transitions to Sustainability." *International Journal of Sustainable Development* 15 (1): 19–36. doi:10.1504/IJSD.2012.044032.

Gibbons, Damon, and Rosanna Singler. 2008. "Cold Comfort: A Review of Coping Strategies Employed by Households in Fuel Poverty." CentrInclusion Research Consultancy and Energywatch. http://www.infohub.moneyadvicetrust.org/content_files/files/cesi_cold_comfort_report.pdf.

Goodman, Jack. 1999. "The Changing Demography of Multifamily Rental Housing." *Housing Policy Debate* 10 (1): 31–57. doi:10.1080/10511482.1999.9521326.

Grønhøj, Alice, and John Thøgersen. 2012. "Action Speaks Louder than Words: The Effect of Personal Attitudes and Family Norms on Adolescents' Pro-Environmental Behaviour." *Journal of Economic Psychology* 33 (1): 292–302. doi:10.1016/j.joep.2011.10.001.

Haase, Annegret, Katrin Grossmann, and Annett Steinführer. 2012. "Transitory Urbanites: New Actors of Residential Change in Polish and Czech Inner Cities." *Cities*, Heteropolitanization: Social and Spatial Change in Central and East European Cities, 29 (5): 318–26. doi:10.1016/j.cities.2011.11.006.

Haase, Steinführer, Sigrun Kabisch, Katrin Grossmann, and Ray Hall. 2011. "Introduction: Idea, Premises and Background of This Volume." In *Residential Change and Demographic Challenge: The Inner City of East Central Europe in the 21st Century*, edited by Annegret Haase, Annett Steinführer, Sigrun Kabisch, Katrin Grossmann, and Ray Hall, 3–16. Aldershot:Ashgate.

Healy, John D., and J.Peter Clinch. 2002. "Fuel Poverty, Thermal Comfort and Occupancy: Results of a National Household-Survey in Ireland." *Applied Energy* 73 (3–4): 329–43. doi:10.1016/S0306-2619(02)00115-0.

Hoem, Jan M., Dora Kostova, Aiva Jasilioniene, and Cornelia Mureşan. 2009. "Traces of the Second Demographic Transition in Four Selected Countries in Central and Eastern Europe: Union Formation as a Demographic Manifestation." *European Journal of Population / Revue Européenne de Démographie* 25 (3): 239–55. doi:10.1007/s10680-009-9177-y.

Howden-Chapman, Philippa, Anna Matheson, Julian Crane, Helen Viggers, Malcolm Cunningham, Chris Cunningham, Tony Blakely, et al. 2007. "Effect of Insulating Existing Houses on Health Inequality: Cluster Randomised Study in the Community." *British Medical Journal*, no. 334: 460–64.

Howden-Chapman, Philippa, Pierse, Nicholls, Gillespie-Bennett, Viggers, Cunningham. 2008. "Effects of Improved Home Heating on Asthma in Community Dwelling Children: Randomised Controlled Trial." *BMJ* 337 (1): a1411–a1411. doi:10.1136/bmj.a1411.

Howden-Chapman, Philippa, Viggers, Helen, Chapman, Ralph, O'Sullivan, Kimberly, Telfar Barnard, Lucy and Loyd, Bob. 2012. "Tackling cold housing and fuel poverty in New Zealand: A review of policies, research, and health impacts." *Energy Policy* 49: 134–142.

Jahoda, Robert, and Dagmar Špalková. 2012. "Housing-Induced Poverty and Rent Deregulation: A Case Study of the Czech Republic." *Ekonomický Časopis / Journal of Economics*, 2. http://is.muni.cz/repo/958257/02_12_Jahoda-Spalkova_RS.pdf.

Kautzer, Chad, and David Harvey. 2008. "Class, Crisis, and the City." *Radical Philosophy Review* 11 (2): 151–58. http://www.pdcnet.org/radphilrev/content/radphilrev_2008_0011_0002_0151_0158.

Khandker, Shahidur R., Douglas F. Barnes, and Hussain A. Samad. 2012. "Are the Energy Poor Also Income Poor? Evidence from India." *Energy Policy* 47 (August): 1–12. doi:10.1016/j.enpol.2012.02.028.

Kleinschafer, Jodie, and Mark Morrison. 2014. "Household Norms and Their Role in Reducing Household Electricity Consumption." *International Journal of Consumer Studies* 38 (1): 75–81. doi:10.1111/ijcs.12066.

Lawlor, Debbie A. 2001. "The Health Consequences of Fuel Poverty: What Should the Role of Primary Care Be?" *British Journal of General Practice* 51 (467): 435–36.

Liddell, Christine. 2008. "The Impact of Fuel Poverty on Children." Save the Children.

Liddell, Christine, and Chris Morris. 2010. "Fuel Poverty and Human Health: A Review of Recent Evidence." *Energy Policy* 38: 2987–97.

Linnér, Björn-Ola, and Henrik Selin. 2013. "The United Nations Conference on Sustainable Development: Forty Years in the Making." *Environment and Planning C: Government and Policy* 31 (6): 971–87. doi:10.1068/c12287.

Liu, Jianguo, Gretchen C. Daily, Paul R. Ehrlich, and Gary W. Luck. 2003. "Effects of Household Dynamics on Resource Consumption and Biodiversity." *Nature* 421 (6922): 530–33. doi:10.1038/nature01359.

Lux, Martin, and Martina Mikeszova. 2012. "Property Restitution and Private Rental Housing in Transition: The Case of the Czech Republic." *Housing Studies* 27 (1): 77–96. doi:10.1080/02673037.2012.629643.

Markard, Jochen, Rob Raven, and Bernhard Truffer. 2012. "Sustainability Transitions: An Emerging Field of Research and Its Prospects." *Research Policy*, Special Section on Sustainability Transitions, 41 (6): 955–67. doi:10.1016/j.respol.2012.02.013.

Mills, Melinda, and Hans-Peter Blossfeld. 2013. "The Second Demographic Transition Meets Globalization: A Comprehensive Theory to Understand Changes in Family Formation in an Era of Rising Uncertainty." In *Negotiating the Life Course*, edited by Ann Evans and Janeen Baxter, 9–33. Life Course Research and Social Policies 1. Springer Netherlands. http://link.springer.com/chapter/10.1007/978-90-481-8912-0_2.

Moore, Richard. 2012. "Definitions of Fuel Poverty: Implications for Policy." *Energy Policy* 49 (October): 19–26. doi:10.1016/j.enpol.2012.01.057.

Moss, Timothy, Sören Becker, and Matthias Naumann. 2014. "Whose Energy Transition Is It, Anyway? Organisation and Ownership of the Energiewende in Villages, Cities and Regions." *Local Environment* 0 (0): 1–17. doi:10.1080/135498 39.2014.915799.

Myers, Dowell. 1990. "Introduction." In *Housing Demography: Linking Demographic Structure and Housing Markets*, edited by Dowell Myers, 3–31. University of Wisconsin Press.

National Union of Students. 2013. "Energy Efficiency and Fuel Poverty in Student Homes: Greener Research: Greener Projects: Www.nus.org.uk." http://www.nus .org.uk/cy/greener-projects/greener-research/how-cold-is-your-student-house-/.

O'Neill, Tracy, Clare Jinks, and Anne Squire. 2006. "'Heating Is More Important Than Food': Older Women's Perceptions of Fuel Poverty." *Journal of Housing for the Elderly* 20 (3): 95–108.

Palmer, Guy, Tom MacInnes, and Peter Kenway. 2008. "Cold and Poor: An Analysis of the Link between Fuel Poverty and Low Income." New Policy Institute. http:// www.poverty.org.uk/reports/fuel%20poverty.pdf.

Petrova, Saska. 2014. *Communities in Transition: Protected Nature and Local People in Eastern and Central Europe*. Aldershot: Ashgate.

Petrova, Saska, Michael Gentile, Ilkka Henrik Mäkinen, and Stefan Bouzarovski. 2013. "Perceptions of Thermal Comfort and Housing Quality: Exploring the Microgeographies of Energy Poverty in Stakhanov, Ukraine." *Environment and Planning A* 45 (5): 1240–57. doi:10.1068/a45132.

Petrova, Saska, Darina Posová, Adam House, and Ludek Sýkora. 2013. "Discursive Framings of Low Carbon Urban Transitions: The Contested Geographies of 'Satellite Settlements' in the Czech Republic." *Urban Studies* 50 (7): 1439–55. doi:10.1177/0042098013480964.

Petrova, Saska, Miguel Torres Garcia, and Stefan Bouzarovski. 2016. "Using Action Research to Enhance Learning on End-Use Energy Demand: Lessons from Reflective Practice." *Environmental Education Research*, 1–20. http://www .tandfonline.com/doi/abs/10.1080/13504622.2016.1144177.

Petrović, Mina. 2011. "Changes of Marital Behavior and Family Patterns in Post-Socialist Countries: Delayed, Incomplete or Specific Second Demographic Transition?" *Stanovnistvo* 49 (1): 53–78. doi:10.2298/STNV1101053P.

Pichler-Milanovich, Natasha. 2001. "Urban Housing Markets in Central and Eastern Europe: Convergence, Divergence or Policy 'Collapse.'" *International Journal of Housing Policy* 1 (2): 145–87. doi:10.1080/14616710110083416.

Rudge, Janet. 2012. "Coal Fires, Fresh Air and the Hardy British: A Historical View of Domestic Energy Efficiency and Thermal Comfort in Britain." *Energy Policy* 49 (October): 6–11. doi:10.1016/j.enpol.2011.11.064.

Sage, Joanna, Darren Smith, and Phil Hubbard. 2012. "The Rapidity of Studentification and Population Change: There Goes the (Student)hood." *Population, Space and Place* 18 (5): 597–613. doi:10.1002/psp.690.

Sefton, T. 2002. "Targeting Fuel Poverty in England: Is the Government Getting Warm?" *Fiscal Studies* 23: 369–99.

Shannon, Sarah, Bob Lloyd, Jacob Roos, and Jan Kohlmeyer. 2003. "EVH3 – Impact of Housing on Health in Dunedin NZ." *Dunedin: University of Otago and Dunedin City Council*. http://www2.physics.otago.ac.nz/eman/research/Dunedin_Housing_ Report.pdf.

Sýkora, and Stefan Bouzarovski. 2012. "Multiple transformations: conceptualising the post-communist urban transition." *Urban Studies* 49: 43–60.

Ulrich Mayer, Karl. 2004. "Whose Lives? How History, Societies, and Institutions Define and Shape Life Courses." *Research in Human Development* 1 (3): 161–87. doi:10.1207/s15427617rhd0103_3.

Walker, Gordon, and Rosie Day. 2012. "Fuel Poverty as Injustice: Integrating Distribution, Recognition and Procedure in the Struggle for Affordable Warmth." *Energy Policy* 49 (October): 69–75. doi:10.1016/j.enpol.2012.01.044.

Watt, G.C.M. 1994. "Health Implications of Putting Value Added Tax on Fuel." *British Medical Journal* 309: 1030.

Wilkinson, Pattenden, Armstrong, Fletcher, Kovats, Mangtan, and J. McMichael. 2004. "Vulnerability to winter mortality in elderly people in Britain: population based study." *British Medical Journal* 329: 976–77.

14 *Worth the Trouble?!*

An Evaluative Scheme for Urban Sustainability Transition Labs (USTLs) and an Application to the USTL in Phoenix, Arizona

Arnim Wiek, Braden Kay and Nigel Forrest

Introduction

Cities host the majority of the earth's human population, continue to expand in size and density, and accumulate persistent problems with serious damage potential; yet, cities also offer unique development opportunities emerging from the concentration of capital, social networks, and innovation potential (UN Habitat, 2008; Romero-Lankao and Dodman, 2011; Wiek, Guston, et al., 2013). As cities thus become targets of transition efforts towards sustainability, there are more calls for supporting transition research (Cook and Swyngedouw, 2012; Childers et al., 2014). "Urban transition labs" (or "living laboratories" or "urban laboratories"), or, more precisely, "urban *sustainability* transition labs" (USTLs) do exactly that – they develop, test, and implement interventions and initiatives of significant change aimed at achieving sustainability in and across urban domains ranging from housing, land-use, and transportation to social cohesion and education (Evans and Karvonen, 2011a; Lang and Wiek, 2012; Bulkeley and Castán Broto, 2013; König and Evans, 2013; Nevens et al., 2013; Polk et al., 2013; Karvonen and van Heur, 2014; Ryan, 2013).

However, sustainability transition initiatives in general, and USTLs in particular, face obstacles and challenges that jeopardize their yielding lasting sustainability outcomes (Loorbach and Rotmans, 2010; Evans and Karvonen, 2011b; Lang et al., 2012). In the United States, for example, urban sustainability transition efforts encounter disinterest or resistance in many cities where political contexts and social preferences are adversarial to sustainability (Svara et al., 2013). Phoenix, Arizona, owns an impressive portfolio of infamous examples (Ross, 2011). One just needs to review some of the recent legislative initiatives to get a sense for the obstacles sustainability efforts encounter here: for example, AZ Senate Bill 1070 encourages racial profiling, Arizona Senate Bill 1507 prohibits implementation of the Rio Declaration on Environment and Development, and AZ Senate Bill 1227 bans legal requirements related to energy efficiency.

While these obstacles jeopardize the chances of achieving lasting sustainability outcomes, USTLs require significant efforts to get initialized and maintained (Schliwa, 2013). They require, at a minimum, researchers committed to and competent in conducting collaborative transition research through real-world transition experiments; partners and stakeholders (often pioneers) willing and able to engage in real-world transition experiments; sufficient monetary and in-kind funds; and supporting project management and institutional structures (Nevens et al., 2013).

Considering the urgency of urban sustainability problems, as well as the limited resources at the disposal of researchers and practitioners, the emerging question is, *Are urban sustainability transition labs a promising strategy for making progress towards urban sustainability; or, in short, are the accomplishments worth the trouble?* More constructively, the question is, *How do we need to design urban sustainability transition labs so that they generate insights and experiences that eventually yield lasting sustainability outcomes?*

We reflect on these questions through the lens of the USTL in Phoenix, Arizona, that has carried out six urban sustainability transition projects over the past five years (2009–2014). The projects were undertaken in cooperation between teams from the Sustainability Transition and Intervention Research Lab in the School of Sustainability at Arizona State University, professionals in government agencies, and nonprofit organizations, as well as citizens and community members in Phoenix. The projects entailed both real-world efforts towards sustainability, ranging from housing and mobility to food and public health initiatives, as well as transition research in support of these efforts.

Our critical working hypothesis is that the general design guidelines and best practices for USTLs offered in the literature need to be applied with care and account for the life cycle of a USTL. Based on calls for studying effects and effectiveness of USTLs (Bulkeley and Castán Broto, 2013), we explore in how far the six transition projects in Phoenix allowed for learning that is likely to yield lasting sustainability outcomes in the future. And we attempt an honest account if these effects justify the efforts undertaken. We present here a general evaluative scheme for USTLs and a cautious interpretation of exemplary evaluation results (USTL Phoenix). Eventually, our study intends to support people keen on running USTLs who want to learn from previous experiences. More generally, the chapter expands the set of case studies on urban sustainability transition initiatives (Evans and Karvonen, 2011b; König and Evans, 2013; Bulkeley and Castán Broto, 2013; McCormick et al., 2013; Nevens et al., 2013; Forrest and Wiek, 2014) that steadily broadens and enhances the base for evidence-supported urban sustainability transition efforts.

Evaluative Scheme and Design Guidelines for Urban Sustainability Transition Labs

While the concept of urban laboratories has been around for several decades (Karvonen and van Heur, 2014), that of USTLs is fairly young and still under development (Evans and Karvonen, 2011a; Lang and Wiek, 2012; Bulkeley and Castán Broto, 2013; König and Evans, 2013; Nevens et al., 2013;

Polk et al., 2013; Ryan, 2013). Despite plenty of terminological and few substantive differences, agreement is emerging on the key features of USTLs that can serve as design guidelines or design aspirations. These features differentiate USTLs from conventional urban development and propose "urbanization by significantly different means" (Karvonen and van Heur, 2014, p. 380). Thereby, the concept adopts other paradigms, in particular, socio-technical transitions, sustainability, and transdisciplinarity (Nevens et al., 2013; Polk et al., 2013; Karvonen and van Heur, 2014). While some scholars simply summarize key features (e.g., Karvonen and van Heur, 2014, pp. 385–388; Ryan, 2013), others structure the key features along a procedural template, such as transition management (e.g., Nevens et al., 2013, pp. 115–120).

The evaluative purpose of our study in mind, we structure here the key features of USTLs according to an evaluative logical model with inputs, process, outputs, and outcomes (Forrest and Wiek, 2014). Figure 14.1 illustrates the concept structure and provides guiding questions for the four categories.

In the following, we briefly describe the key features of USTLs as design guidelines, following the evaluative perspective that starts with the immediate outputs (what was generated) and the outcomes (what has been and is expected to get accomplished – in terms of sustainability), and then traces them back to the process (how was it done) and finally to the inputs (what was invested):

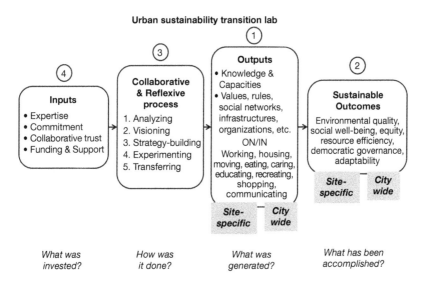

Figure 14.1 Logical model of an ideal-typical USTL with inputs, process, outputs, and outcomes, corresponding to guiding questions. The evaluative process follows the sequence from (1) what was generated and (2) what was accomplished (in terms of sustainability), back to (3) how was it done and (4) what was invested. (Adapted from Forrest and Wiek, 2014, and Wiek, Talwar, et al., 2014.)

(1) *Outputs (What was generated/produced?) – Urban sustainability transition labs ought to generate exemplary knowledge, capacities, rules, infrastructures, technologies, practices, etc. that, if broadly implemented, transferred, and multiplied, lead to a sustainable city.* Different typologies can be used to categorize the outputs generated by USTLs (Forrest and Wiek, 2014; Wiek, Talwar, et al., 2014). USTLs pursue the ultimate objective of a sustainable city less by pure experience, intuition, or accident, but rather by means of action plans and evidence. Thus, a key output that USTLs generate is *knowledge* (generated through research), which distinguishes such labs from conventional urban development projects. Apart from knowledge about the current state (system model) and the desirable state (vision), an important knowledge output is strategic (actionable) knowledge; that is, knowledge on how to effectively and efficiently transition from the current to the desirable state. USTLs produce three different types of strategic knowledge critical for transition efforts: first, a transition strategy that is based on previous evidence of what works and what does not (generalized from other contexts); second, knowledge on what works and what does not work in a specific, small-scale context (testing the transition strategy through experiments, pilots, etc.); and third, knowledge on what works and what does not on the city level (monitoring the broad implementation and transfer of the transition strategy). USTLs themselves are intended to *guide* urban development; they do *not replace* urban development. The generated knowledge needs to be applied. For real-world applications, knowledge needs to be internalized and activated through skills. Thus, USTLs often strive to build *capacities* that allow stakeholders and decision makers to apply the generated knowledge.

Producing knowledge and capacities alludes to complementary outputs that distinguish USTLs from conventional research projects. These outputs are *real-world changes*, including changed or new values, rules, practices, behavior, networks, infrastructures, technologies, organizations, and so forth (Forrest and Wiek, 2014; Wiek, Talwar, et al). USTLs operate through experiments and broader implementation (transfer) of transition strategies – thus, a wide array of real-world changes are an integral output generated. Yet, these changes often have a provisional character (experimental phase) and only later become permanent and might even penetrate the entire city, if successfully tested and multiplied. These larger outputs go beyond the more narrowly defined borders of a USTL as a *laboratory*. Last but not least, an important real-world output is that some graduates receive job offers due to the qualifications obtained in USTL projects (if they involve educational settings).

Building upon previous work, Forrest and Wiek (2014, pp. 73–75) propose to systematically capture these real-world changes through the lens of urban activity domains, including working, housing, moving, eating, caring, educating, recreating, shopping, and communicating (activities and structures in each domain).

(2) *Sustainable Outcomes (What has been accomplished?)* – Urban sustainability transition labs ought to foster a sustainable city. As stated above, USTLs generate insights intended to lead to real-world changes – but not just any. They have "a strong normative aim" – namely, "to create more desirable futures" (Karvonen and van Heur, 2014, p. 387). More specifically, they are being created in order to transition a given city from a currently *unsustainable* development path (or period) to a *sustainable* one. In short, the ultimate objective is creating and maintaining a *sustainable city*.

A sustainable city is a complex network of urban structures and actions (lifestyles); this network is restructured, maintained, and developed in ways that fulfill two conditions: first, they uninterruptedly secure a sufficient level of well-being for all inhabitants; second, they do so without jeopardizing a sufficient level of well-being for the natural environment, as well as for other regions (hinterland) and societies (along global impact chains) affected by the city. Specific sustainability targets – all oriented towards a *sufficient* level of well-being, not a *maximum* level of wealth, consumption, or entertainment – can be defined for and across all urban activity domains, based on sustainability principles (Gibson, 2006; Forrest and Wiek, 2014). According to a widely referenced review by Gibson (2006), sustainability principles can be translated into sufficient levels of environmental quality, social well-being, equity, resource efficiency, democratic governance, and adaptability.

There is broad agreement that the current development path is not only slightly but significantly off from sustainable pathways, with critical tipping points already being passed (Rockström et al., 2009). Thus, USTLs strive to generate transition strategies for significant or even radical change (Nevens et al., 2013; Ryan, 2013). As Karvonen and van Heur (2014, p. 387) put it: "The urban laboratory is conceived for change that is intentionally radical [...] rather than incremental or entropic."

The outcomes perspective critically explores the changes that can reasonably be extrapolated from a USTL. That means the USTL team explores, through the lens of sustainability, what outcomes could result if the outputs would be widely generated or applied. A USTL, while mainly operating on particular sites or in small areas (e.g., neighborhood) or in specific sectors (e.g., food) of a city, aspires to contribute to the sustainability of the city *as a whole*. Therefore, the extrapolated outcomes of a USTL must ultimately be assessed against the (un)sustainability of the entire city. It is thereby important to consider the full range of outputs and outcomes, not only physical or infrastructural ones. Following Bulkeley and Castán Broto (2013), it seems that the most critical effects of USTL experiments pertain to reconfiguring the governance processes in cities.

(3) *Methodical, Collaborative, and Reflexive Process (How was it done?)* – *Urban transition labs ought to apply transformational sustainability*

research frameworks in collaborative and reflexive processes to develop, test, implement, and evaluate transition strategies. Transformational sustainability research frameworks (Wiek and Lang, 2016), such as transition management or integrated planning research, combine problem/system analysis, visioning, strategy building, experimenting (with evaluating), and transferring (with evaluating) – with the objective to generate outputs that lead to sustainable outcomes in a given city (see above). For each step, specific methods are employed that allow developing, testing, and implementing transition strategies in effective, efficient, and transparent ways (Wiek and Lang, in prep). The method-driven development of transition strategies, the experimental testing of these strategies, as well as the careful monitoring and evaluating of strategy implementations distinguish the work in urban sustainability transition *labs* from conventional urban development projects.

Special emphasis is put on the *experimentation* phase that links knowledge production to generating provisional real-world changes. As laboratories, USTLs conduct real-world experiments. It is critical to be clear about what constitutes an *experiment* (and what not). Karvonen and van Heur (2014, p. 387) rightfully take a strong stance on distinguishing experimentation from other types of gathering experiences: "Rather than conflating 'experimentation' with 'change' and claiming that everything is an experiment, we argue that there is a need to adopt a more precise understanding of the practice of experimentation. Returning to the laboratory studies scholarship, it is helpful to understand experimentation as (a) involving a specific set-up of instruments and people that (b) aims for the controlled inducement of changes and (c) the measurement of these changes." Relevant are here conditions (a) and (c), as we have already covered (b) above (1 and 2). First [corresponding to condition (a)], there is the set-up or design of the experiment – without a documented reference state and a basic theory of change, it is very difficult to conduct an experiment and measure any changes and accomplishments (pre- and post design). This does not mean that the design of such experiments requires complete information and endless preparation. Such experiments do not need to be based on fully developed plans (Lang et al., 2012; Nevens et al., 2013). Experiments in USTLs acknowledge the complexity and 'wickedness' of urban sustainability problems, the deficits of the command-and-control approach to problem solving, and the risk of the 'knowledge-first trap'. "Real-world experimentation is founded on the idea that one is compelled to act despite uncertainties and gaps in knowledge" (Karvonen and van Heur, 2014, p. 387); in other words, "unanticipated outcomes are to be expected" (ibid.) and are part of the *adaptive* experimental design (reflexivity). Second [corresponding to condition (c)], monitoring and evaluation is an integral part of USTLs. As König and Evans (2013, p. 2) emphasize: "The purpose of living laboratories is not only to allow novel things to be tried that would not be possible in conventional urban settings, but to also monitor their social and physical impacts in order to provide a robust knowledge base for learning." The objective is to create transition strategies that can be generalized, transferred, and scaled-up elsewhere (under varying contexts) to support the citywide transition towards sustainability. The notion of experiments implies that there is an active experimentation phase that requires careful and adaptive design in small-scale applications; and at a later phase that pertains to transferring and scaling-up of the tested (evidence-supported) transition strategies to the citywide level.

Collaboration across different communities of knowledge (interdisciplinarity) as well as across researchers and stakeholders (transdisciplinarity) are integral part of operating USTLs. A great deal of literature justifies and spells out roles, responsibilities, procedures, and participatory settings for successful collaborations among diverse participants in pursuit of sustainability transitions (Talwar et al., 2011; Lang et al., 2012). Specific concepts such as the *transition arena* that structures the collaboration among various transition agents, or the facilitation through so-called *transacademic interface managers* (TIMs) have been developed in support of collaboration in transition processes (Van den Bosch, 2010; Brundiers et al., 2013; Nevens et al., 2013).

An additional key characteristic of the operating process in USTLs is *reflexivity*, which means routinely reflecting on and adapting the results produced and procedures applied. This is a means to cope with the complexity of the sustainability challenges addressed, which does not permit using simple command-and-control approaches to problem-solving. It also allows taking advantage of new insights. Reflexivity is explicitly built into the process template through several evaluations; yet, it should be a routine procedure after each major module.

Closely linked to reflexivity is an additional feature that is often, yet not always, mentioned as a design aspiration towards USTLs – which is utilizing USTLs as explicit *educational settings for students* pursuing degrees with relevance to sustainability. The real-world experience that can be gained through USTLs offers a prime setting for relevant and impactful sustainability education. If sufficiently combined with review, reflection, and complementary studies, the USTL outmatches classroom-based education by far. Pragmatically, one might argue that USTLs are being undertaken anyway – so, why not utilize them for educational purposes, instead of trying to evoke such experiences in distant classroom settings? Various models have already been developed and implemented (e.g., Lang and Wiek, 2012; König and Evans, 2013; Trencher et al., 2014; Ryan, 2013) that can be used as reference cases.

(4) *Inputs (What was invested?) – Urban sustainability transition labs ought to acquire and invest the necessary expertise, commitment, collaborative trust, and resources necessary for successfully developing, testing, implementing, and evaluating transition strategies.*

Sound methods, procedures, and protocols are critical for achieving both real-world changes and evidence that these changes have lasting positive outcomes and can be reproduced under varying conditions. Yet, pre-requisites are that people are knowledgeable and skilled; that they are visionary and committed, that they trust one another, and that there is sufficient funding and favorable institutional support to conduct transition experiments and transfer activities. The absence of any one of these conditions can jeopardize the entire work of a USTL.

First, there is the issue of *expertise*. On first sight, this is particularly relevant for researchers. Current degree programs rarely train researchers in empirical research that generates evidence on which transition strategies actually work (and which ones don't) – the type of research asked for in USTLs (Wiek et al., 2012). Careful recruitment is necessary to pick the few researchers trained in constructive transition, intervention, program evaluation, and solution-oriented research. But expertise is required not only from researchers. There are analytical and evaluative methods that call for technical expertise, while experimenting and transferring successful strategies in real-world settings requires a great deal of professional experience; then again, visioning requires analytical, creative, and experiential skills. So, a wide range of expertise is necessary as critical ingredients for successful USTLs.

Next, there is the issue of *willingness and commitment*. USTLs are seeking to involve stakeholders willing and committed to explore radical changes towards sustainability. As Karvonen and van Heur (2014, p. 387) put it: "Laboratory advocates express an explicit dissatisfaction with 'urban-development-as-usual' approaches." Visionary, pioneering stakeholders are the type of stakeholders USTLs call for, but this can be a significant stumbling block. For example, municipal professionals may be uncomfortable with the openness of the process and the lack of fixed targets (Nevens and Roorda, 2014), whereas community members happy to commit to radical visions can be much more hesitant when it comes to taking action that may impinge upon lifestyles (Ryan, 2013). Then again, the requirement is mutual – researchers need to be similarly committed to leave their safe spaces and explore new frontiers with all the institutional barriers and career risks involved in such endeavors (Talwar et al., 2011; Polk, Kain and Holmberg, 2013). What this amounts to is a need for USTLs to carefully select stakeholders and to patiently work to assuage concerns and create conditions that are conducive to obtaining the commitment needed (Nevens and Roorda, 2014).

While willingness and commitment primarily pertains to individuals participating in USTLs, the success also depends on mutual *trust in the collaborative effort*. Such trust is a critical interpersonal input that cannot be replaced by advanced facilitation, but requires special attention from the initialization of a USTL onward (Brundiers et al., 2013). Particular effort is needed to enable participants to talk "to each other in a way that both acknowledges and transgresses the potentially incommensurable differences among them" by "reconciling the different ontologies, epistemologies, worldviews and realms of practice that exist within 'issue-driven interdisciplinarity'" (Polk et al., 2013, p. 190). This is more than a technical challenge: it requires a personal approach to overcome these differences and ensure participation takes place on an equal footing and with equal voice (Brundiers et al., 2013).

Finally, *funds and institutional support* are necessary to prepare and execute experiments, transfer successful strategies, and bring the work of USTLs to fruition (Talwar et al., 2011; Farla et al., 2012). Like any project, USTLs require resources – people, facilities, materials, time, and so on – to perform work and produce outputs. But, as Polk et al. (2013, p. 190f.) observe, the "intrinsically different purposes (concrete change *and* scientific output)" (our italics) of experiments mean they "are not as efficient as consultation or discipline-based and applied research". In fact, they take more time and demand more resources. Funding can therefore be problematic due to the lack of fit with traditional funding sources for either research or urban development and due to the novelty of the USTL concept. Even with funding, however, in-kind resources such as utilizing existing capacity or voluntary work are critical, particularly in the preparation and experimentation stages. These stages often lack the concrete outputs often required for an organization, such as a municipality, to commit the necessary resources. But it is equally important to exercise foresight towards the transfer and scaling-up phase, and not to let the transition stumble after successful experimentation. Whether resources are supplied in-kind or are fully funded, it is essential that USTLs receive full institutional support. Participating individuals must "have a formal and practical mandate from within their organizations at all levels to effectively participate in the joint processes. Here there is a risk that practitioner contributions are undervalued and understaffed, since this type of knowledge production does not have a clear position within public bodies" (Polk et al., 2013, p. 190). Such institutional support is not only critical for full participation of individuals, but for building trust in the collaborative effort (see above). It can also provide continuity and stability for transfer and scaling-up of strategies and for participation in further experiments, both of which are essential for broad transition progress.

In view of the following case study section, we translate the design guidelines for urban sustainability transition labs into an evaluative scheme (Table 14.1) that allows us to appraise the projects of the USTL in Phoenix.

The presented evaluative scheme and design guidelines for USTLs are applicable to discrete projects or even individual experiments. However, long-term progress towards sustainability requires cumulative effects of the USTL over multiple such projects and experiments. Meta-evaluative questions therefore

Table 14.1 Evaluative scheme for urban sustainability transition labs (USTL), based on a logical model

Category	Features	Evaluative Question	Pool of Items
(1) Outputs	Urban activity domains	Did the USTL project address and/or impact the most critical urban activity domains, and the problems therein?	Working, housing, moving, eating, caring, educating, recreating, shopping, communicating
	Knowledge	Did the USTL project produce action-able knowledge – did it generate an evidence-supported transition strategy?	Descriptive-analytical (system/problem model), normative (vision; evaluative statements), strategic/instructional (strategy)
	Capacity	Did the USTL project build sufficient capacity?	Systems thinking, anticipating, assessing, strategy-building, collaborating, implementing
	Real-world changes	Did the USTL project generate sufficient real-world changes?	Changed or new (social) values/norms, rules (policies), practices, behavior, social networks (or relationships), infrastructures, technologies, organizations
	Scaling-up	Did the USTL ensure the transfer to the city level?	(All outputs should be evaluated at city level as well as at individual experiment level.)
(2) Outcomes	Sustainability	Can the outputs of the USTL project, when applied or generated widely, be reasonably expected to achieve sustainable outcomes?	Sustainable levels of environmental quality, social well-being, intra- and intergenerational equity, resource efficiency, democratic governance, adaptability
	Scaling-up	Did the USTL ensure the transfer to the city level?	(The above sustainability outcomes should be considered at city level as well as at individual experiment level.)
(3) Process	Methods	Were all critical steps conducted (framework), and what methods were applied in each step?	Problem/system analysis, visioning, strategy building, experimenting (with evaluating), transferring (with evaluating) – and respective methods

Category	Features	Evaluative Question	Pool of Items
	Collaboration	Was the collaboration well organized - who was involved, when, in what setting, and to what degree?	Partners, participants, facilitators (TIMs), participatory settings (expert panel, focus group, workshop, onsite explorations, etc.), level of engagement
	Reflexivity	Were sufficient reflexive activities conducted - who was involved, when, and with what result?	Reflexive activities during the development of the initial strategy (best practices); as part of the experiments; as part of the implementation of the strategy
(4) Inputs	Expertise	Was sufficient expertise acquired for the USTL project?	Expertise to create an evidence-supported transition strategy (research expertise); expertise to execute the real-world components of experiments; facilitation expertise
	Commitment	Was sufficient commitment secured for the USTL project?	Commitment to explore and implement radical change strategies (pioneers); commitment to conduct post-normal transition research
	Collaborative trust	Was collaborative trust built for the USTL project?	Trust in the respective partners; trust in the process; trust in the facilitator(s)
	Funds & Institutional Support	Were sufficient funds and institutional support secured for the USTL project?	Monetary funds; in-kind support; favorable institutional regulations or practices; leadership support

arise, such as what are the cumulative sustainability effects of a USTL? Are they incremental steps to radical change (Grin et al., 2010, p. 145), building on the outcomes of previous steps or synergistically interlocking with other USTL projects in different domains? This integration should not stop with the USTL, but should extend to other projects taking place in the same area. For this to happen the USTL needs to provide the context for long-term change over many projects (Nevens et al., 2013). In another respect, for USTL experiments to contribute to long-term sustainability transition at the city level, they need to be deepened (fully explored in-situ with respect to maximizing outcomes), broadened (transferred to different contexts with suitable variations), and scaled-up (regime level interventions that make conditions more favorable to the desired, on-the-ground change) (Grin et al., 2010, p. 208f.). This suggests it is not enough to carry out a single experiment and then sit back and watch as it takes root and grows; instead, it must be followed up with a translation into 'normal' urban development projects to accelerate the proliferation of the desired change.

The Urban Sustainability Transition Lab in Phoenix

Overview

In this section we sketch out the six projects conducted in the USTL in Phoenix and provide some basic information on how they fare against the design guidelines and design aspirations spelled out in the previous section. For illustrative purposes, we present our last project in more detail (Section 14.3.2) and provide summative information on all projects in Tables 14.2 and 14.3 below.

The USTL in Phoenix was initialized by the Sustainability Transition and Intervention Research Lab, a research group in the School of Sustainability at Arizona State University, in 2009. It displays the following four key features (Lang and Wiek, 2012): it addresses urban sustainability challenges in Phoenix; it employs a transformational sustainability research methodology in order to generate evidence-supported transition and intervention strategies to be tested in real-world experiments; it is based on a strong participatory research approach that employs joint learning and negotiation as key modes of operation in stakeholder workshops and other participatory settings; and finally, it links research and teaching with the aim to build capacity for sustainability transition efforts in students, faculty, and stakeholders.

The City of Phoenix, similar to other metropolitan regions across the US, faces complex sustainability challenges, including the loss of economic opportunities, increasing infrastructure requirements, budgetary deficits, traffic congestion, air pollution, scarcity of natural resources, climate change impacts, poverty, public health issues (e.g., childhood obesity), and social segregation (Ross, 2011; Wiek, Guston, et al., 2013). Conventional research in Phoenix has made some progress in *analyzing* these challenges, but very little progress in *developing and testing strategies to mitigate and solve these problems.* Phoenix is considered an ideal test-bed for sustainability transition research in general and USTLs in particular; as Ross (2011, p. 14) asserts: "If Phoenix could become sustainable, then it could be done anywhere."

All USTL Phoenix projects apply variations of the TRANSFORM framework, a methodological framework for transformational sustainability research that integrates backcasting with foresight and intervention research methods in interactive participatory settings (Wiek, Guston, et al., 2013; Wiek and Lang, 2016). The framework structures research into four modules:

- *Visioning* for crafting a sustainable vision through transfer of knowledge on sustainable systems, application of sustainability principles, and analysis of coherence.
- *Current State / Problem Analysis* for capturing inter-linkages among key actors, activities, constraining/enabling rules and regulations, and impacts on urban environment, economy, and society through system analytical approaches, including structured indicator selection, cause-effect chain analysis, and actor network analysis
- *Scenario Construction* for constructing *non-intervention* scenarios describing the future in contrast to the vision, through consistency and diversity analysis, visualization and translation into narratives
- *Backcasting of Intervention and Transition Strategies* for identifying intervention points and coordinated steps to transition from the currently unsustainable state to its sustainable vision while avoiding undesirable scenarios

While all projects aim to create actionable knowledge, the projects do not follow a conventional participatory action-research approach. Recognizing the needs and capacities of both, stakeholders *and* researchers, the projects facilitate joint learning and negotiations throughout the participatory research process (Talwar et al., 2011; Wiek, 2016). All projects are co-led by researchers from the Sustainability Transition and Intervention Research Lab, and partners from government, administration, nonprofit organizations, and the civil society. In all cases, stakeholders need to express a strong interest in seriously addressing urban sustainability challenges in order to trigger a USTL Phoenix project.

Finally, the USTL Phoenix projects integrate research and learning for sustainability (Wiek and Kay, 2015), as part of the problem- and project-based learning (PPBL) at the School of Sustainability (Wiek et al., 2014). Through the vision of "A New American University," Arizona State University has made a commitment to developing students' capacity to address sustainability challenges; develop and initiate sustainability innovations; and to engage with stakeholders in developing sustainable food, housing, mobility, recreational services, and so forth in Phoenix. The USTL Phoenix projects contribute to these efforts. Similar to other educational initiatives (e.g., Lang and Wiek, 2012; König and Evans, 2013; Trencher et al., 2014; Ryan, 2013), the USTL Phoenix projects use real-world urban settings and experiences to educate students to become agents of change towards sustainability.

Revitalizing Public Spaces for the Public Good in Phoenix

Project Profile

This was a combined teaching and research project with a twofold objective: to educate students in urban sustainability transition work, while fostering social cohesion through positive real-world changes in public spaces in Phoenix, Arizona, and Lüneburg, Germany. The goal was to create exemplary solution cases that could be transferred across both cities and thereby contribute to their respective urban sustainability transition. The project was part of an international educational program called "The Global Classroom" with an array of educational objectives and activities (Wiek, Bernstein, et al., 2013). The project was structured into two sub-projects that were conducted concurrently in Phoenix and Lüneburg (Champagne et al., 2014). We focus here only on the sub-project in Phoenix, which targeted a specific site for the transition experiments, namely Crockett Elementary School in the Gateway district. The experiments aimed at opening up and redesigning part of the school's properties, in order to offer opportunities and space for the community in the Gateway district to congregate, recreate, explore visionary ideas (through art), and produce healthy food. Public spaces in general and such ones catering to the needs of the community in particular are extremely sparse in the Gateway district. Thus, the community is keen on creating such places, recognizing benefits for public health, social cohesion, and educational attainment. The project was a collaboration between faculty and students from different programs at Arizona State University and various external partners, including Crockett Elementary School, Balsz School District, Maricopa County Department of Public Health, and the City of Phoenix's Neighborhood Services Department. The project lasted over two semesters (fall 2013–spring 2014).

Project Outputs

The project outlined a strategy of how stakeholders could transition the Gateway district and Phoenix overall from the current state with a lack of social cohesion and segregation challenges towards a healthy and resilient community. As reference points for the strategy outline, the project produced a pragmatic problem model and a vision of social cohesion that were based on community inputs as well as on evidence from successful cases worldwide (Champagne et al., 2014). Both strategy inputs built on previous research results conducted in other projects of the USTL in Phoenix (e.g., *Reinvent Phoenix*).

The strategy emphasized opening up and redesigning public spaces as a means to achieve the community vision.

In the core of the project, three transition experiments were conducted at Crockett Elementary School in the Gateway district. The first experiment yielded a plan for a community vision mural, which was then created in a public painting event on a wall of Crockett Elementary School visible to the community. The mural provides a public image of what the Gateway district should look like in the future if community needs, desires, and dreams, along with ideas of sustainability were to become real. The second experiment yielded a plan and detailed design (with renderings) of a school orchard and shade trees, which were planted in part in the first implementation phase. The orchard and the shade trees will provide shade for recreational areas; could serve as a natural, permeable buffer between the school properties and the surrounding areas; will grow local food for consumption; and serve as an educational space. The third experiment resulted in a draft joint-use agreement between the school and a consortium of governmental and nonprofit organizations. This contract (with shared liabilities) will turn the school's playground, fields, and gymnasium into a public space after normal closing hours for recreational and other activities.

What distinguishes the three transition experiments from conventional site-specific urban development projects is the intention to create demonstration cases that could be transferred and multiplied within the Gateway district and across Phoenix. The mural experiment was informed by and contributes to citywide collaborative efforts to generate an inspiring vision for a sustainable Phoenix. The orchard experiment was informed by and contributes to ongoing efforts to create a network of green spaces, community gardens, and orchards across Phoenix. The joint-use agreement will be the first of its kind in Phoenix, and all collaborating partners used the experiment to explore the challenges and feasible coping tactics for such an undertaking. If successful, it is likely to be taken up by schools across Phoenix. However, all of these potential transfer and multiplying activities require additional efforts that have not yet been undertaken (see Section 14.3.2.4, below).

Project Outcomes

As the project outputs are either still under development (joint-use agreement; second implementation phase of the orchard) or just completed (mural), there are few demonstrable outcomes realized yet. However, the experiments are intended to demonstrate how to yield sustainable outcomes in the areas of social well-being, intra- and intergenerational equity, and democratic governance. Disenfranchised communities often struggle to collectively envision a sustainable future that could guide real change through policies, initiatives, and projects. The mural experiment is aimed at empowering the community and supporting efforts towards democratic governance. It also is intended to foster intra- and intergenerational equity, as children were part of defining the community vision, which is inspired by ideas of social cohesion across all community groups (and beyond). Social well-being in general and public health in particular are the primary objectives of the orchard and the joint-use agreement experiments – offering accessibility to safe and shaded recreational space and healthy food to residents and children, while enhancing the sense of community as residents and students collaboratively take care of the area.

Project Process

The project combined problem analysis, visioning, strategy building, and experimenting. All parts were fairly strong, applying established transformational research methods, building on previous research results, and utilizing real-world cases for inspiration and support (in the experimentation phase). As an undergraduate research project with significant time constraints, however, there was a lack of in-depth investigation in all stages of the project.

The project was conducted by four bachelor students, coached and supported by a professor, a postdoctoral researcher, and a teaching assistant. This core team collaborated with other faculty (e.g., from ASU's Law School) and graduate students (e.g., from ASU's Design School / Landscape Architecture) through expert interviews in the experimentation phase. The main external partners in the experimentation phase included Crockett Elementary School, Balsz School District, Maricopa County Department of Public Health, City of Phoenix' Neighborhood Services Department, and Artlink – they were involved through individual expert interviews and a collaborative expert panel. Critical for the success of the project, particularly in the stage of experimentation, was the project's transacademic interface manager (TIM), who utilized his existing networks to line up the three experiments. This was a major undertaking, as he had to align several agendas, timelines, and working styles.

As an educational project, plenty of reflexive activities were built into the project. Yet, because of time constraints and the ambitious experimental agenda, the project displays deficits with respect to the evaluative component of the experiments – despite the fact that the experiments were documented, lessons learned were collaboratively drawn from them, and evaluations of long-term impacts are roughly planned as part of the USTL in Phoenix. The team was fully occupied with executing the experiments (transition actions) – so that there was little capacity to observe and document the effects of the experiments in detail. Most of the information provided in the output and outcomes sections above has been reconstructed and lacks nuance and empirical evidence. However, it might be able to make up for this as the project continues.

The orchard experiment is currently continued by one of the undergraduate students. A new team is forming, as several health initiatives in the Gateway district are gaining momentum. This team might take up the planned evaluations as part of an effort to make insights from urban transition experiments accessible to a broader audience (Forrest and Wiek, 2014).

Project Inputs

Sufficient expertise was secured; stronger expertise in intervention research could have been advantageous; excellent 'matchmaking' and facilitation secured favorable conditions for experimentation. Commitment was strong from all collaborating partners; in particular, a good share of pioneering stakeholders got involved. Collaborative trust was built through the project's TIM and through collaborative experiences of the core team prior to the project (faculty and students had worked together before). Funds were provided through the Global Classroom grant for a teaching assistant ($50,000); in-kind support was provided through the School of Sustainability, as the dean was strongly committed to create favorable conditions for PPBL (Wiek, Xiong, et al., 2014).

Discussion – *Worth the Trouble?*

There are subtle and promising hints that Phoenix – infamously granted the distinction of being the "least sustainable city in the world" (Ross, 2011) – is getting more serious on issues of sustainability. The six USTL Phoenix projects outlined above (Tables 14.2 and 14.3) were intended to support these efforts. So, how did they fare? Or, getting back to our more general question: Are urban sustainability transition labs a promising strategy for making progress towards urban sustainability; in short, are the accomplishments worth the trouble?

Referring back to Table 14.3, there are the following accomplishments to account for in the case of the USTL Phoenix:

Over the course of the six transition projects, the USTL Phoenix has secured critical inputs that enable a successful operation:

- *Expertise*. From the start with the *Phoenix General Plan Update* the USTL research team has successively built their *expertise* in sustainability transition research. Considering the fluctuation of team members (because students graduate), the USTL research team has been able to secure 'collective expertise' through publications and internal resources, such as handbooks and templates. In all projects, building expertise has been a primary objective, at times at the expense of implementation and real-world changes (e.g., *SD in Light Rail Districts in Phoenix*). Additional sources of expertise are currently being secured through partnerships with faculty, students, and researchers outside the core team (in particular with intervention and transition researchers). Similarly, the expertise to meaningfully participate in impactful transition research has been built in some of our external partners (terminology, concepts, methods, examples).

Table 14.2 Basic information on the six USTL Phoenix projects

Project Title	Phoenix General Plan Update (PPBL Case Studies I)	Sustainable Development in Light Rail Corridor Districts in Phoenix (PPBL Case Studies II)	Sustainable Solutions for Food, Water, and Accessibility in Phoenix (PPBL Case Studies III)	Integrated Health Care for Communities – Participatory Clinic and Playground Design in Phoenix	Reinvent Phoenix – Transit-Oriented Development in the Light Rail Corridor	Revitalizing Public Spaces for the Public Good in Phoenix
Project Structure and Sequence	1 project	2 sub-projects / concurrent	3 sub-projects / concurrent	2 sub-projects / subsequent	5 sub-projects / concurrent & subsequent	2 sub-projects / concurrent
Topics	Mass transit, city cores, roads, open space, water use, etc.	Working, housing, moving, eating, caring, educating, recreating, shopping, communicating	Accessibility / Mobility Food Water	Community Clinic Playground	Housing Green Infrastructure Health Mobility	Public space Food Art
Level	City	District (Corridor)	District (Corridor) Neighborhood	Site	Corridor (Light Rail)	Site
Locations	Phoenix	Gateway District Uptown District	Gateway District Garfield Neighborhood Sky Harbor Neighborhood	MPHC East Clinic, Gateway District	Gateway, Eastlake Garfield, Midtown, Uptown, Solano Districts	Crockett Elementary School (Gateway District)
Project Duration	Fall 2009–Fall 2010	Fall 2010	Spring 2012	Summer 2012 – Spring 2013	Fall 2012–Spring 2014	Fall 2013–Spring 2014
Project Type	In-kind research project and studio	Course project	Studio	Funded research project	Funded research project and studio	Course project

Project Title	Phoenix General Plan Update (PPBL Case Studies I)	Sustainable Development in Light Rail Corridor Districts in Phoenix (PPBL Case Studies II)	Sustainable Solutions for Food, Water, and Accessibility in Phoenix (PPBL Case Studies III)	Integrated Health Care for Communities – Participatory Clinic and Playground Design in Phoenix	Reinvent Phoenix – Transit-Oriented Development in the Light Rail Corridor	Revitalizing Public Spaces for the Public Good in Phoenix
Budget (no in-kind)	$3,000	$1,000	$1,000	$23,000 (incl. overhead)	$600,000 (incl. overhead)	$50,000
In-Kind Funded Positions [SOS]	2 faculty (part)	1 faculty (part)	1 faculty (part), 1 research assistant (full)	1 faculty (part), 1 postdoc (part)	2 faculty (part)	1 faculty (part), 1 postdoc (part)
Project Core Team	2 faculty, 6 team leaders, 18 doctoral and masters students	1 faculty, 1 assistant, 27 doctoral and masters students	2 faculty, 1 assistant, 10 doctoral, masters, and bachelors students	1 faculty, 1 post-doc, 2 masters students	2 faculty, 1 post-doc, 5 team leaders, 25 doctoral, masters, and bachelors students	1 faculty, 1 post-doc, 1 assistant, 4 bachelors students
Main External Partner(s)	City of Phoenix (Planning)	Mountain Park Health Center, Local Arizona First, property owners, community advocates	City of Phoenix (Neighborhood Services)	Mountain Park Health Center	City of Phoenix (Planning)	Crockett Elementary School Maricopa County (Public Health)
References	Wiek et al., 2010; Wiek et al., 2012	Wiek and Kay, 2011; Wiek and Kay, 2015	Bernstein et al., in press	Xiong et al., 2012	Wiek, Kay, et al., in prep	Wiek, Bernstein, 2013; Champagne et al., 2014

Table 14.3 Evaluative information on the six USTL Phoenix projects

		Phoenix General Plan Update	SD in Light-Rail Districts in Phoenix	Sustainable Solutions for Phoenix	Participatory Clinic and Playground Design in Phoenix	Reinvent Phoenix	Revitalizing Public Spaces for the Public Good in Phoenix
(1) Outputs	Urban activity domains	Working, housing, eating, caring, educating, recreating, shopping, communication	Working, housing, moving, eating, caring, educating, recreating, shopping, communication	Housing, moving, eating, recreating	Moving, eating, caring, educating, recreating	Working, housing, moving, eating, caring, educating, recreating, shopping, communication	Eating, caring, educating, recreating
	Knowledge	System model, vision, scenarios, strategies	System model, evaluative statements, vision	Problem models, visions, strategies	Problem model, vision, strategies	System models, evaluative statements, visions, strategies	System model, vision, strategies
	Capacity	System thinking, anticipating, strategy-building, collaborating	System thinking, assessing, anticipation, collaboration	System thinking, anticipation, strategy-building, collaboration, implementing	System thinking, anticipation, strategy-building, collaboration, implementing	System thinking, assessment, anticipation, strategy-building, collaboration	System thinking, anticipation, strategy-building, collaboration, implementing
	Real-world changes	New professional relationships	New professional relationships	New practices, infrastructures; professional relationships	Changed values; new infrastructures; profess. relationships	New rules (policies), social networks	Changed values, rules; new infrastructures; professional relationships

	Phoenix General Plan Update	SD in Light-Rail Districts in Phoenix	Sustainable Solutions for Phoenix	Participatory Clinic and Playground Design in Phoenix	Reinvent Phoenix	Revitalizing Public Spaces for the Public Good in Phoenix
Scaling-up	(Yes)	No	(Somewhat)	No	(Somewhat)	(Somewhat)
(2) Outcomes Sustainability	No	No	Yes (environ. quality, social well-being, intra- and intergenerational equity)	Yes (social well-being, intra- and intergenerational equity)	Not yet	Yes (environ. quality, social well-being, intra- and intergenerational equity)
Scaling-up	No	No	No	No	No	No
(3) Process Methods	CS analysis, scenario analysis, visioning, strategy building	CS analysis, sustain. assessment, visioning	Problem analysis, visioning, strategy building (intervention); implementation	Problem analysis, visioning, strategy building (intervention); implementation	CS analysis, sustainable assessment, visioning, strategy building	CS analysis, visioning, intervention design; implementation
Collaboration	Expert interviews, workshops	Interviews, workshops	Expert interviews, workshops	Expert interviews, workshops	Expert interviews, surveys, workshops	Expert interviews, workshops

(continued)

Table 14.3 Evaluative information on the six USTL Phoenix projects (*continued*)

		Phoenix General Plan Update	SD in Light-Rail Districts in Phoenix	Sustainable Solutions for Phoenix	Participatory Clinic and Playground Design in Phoenix	Reinvent Phoenix	Revitalizing Public Spaces for the Public Good in Phoenix
	Reflexivity	Part of strategy development Educational setting	Low Educational setting	Part of strategy development Educational setting	Low	Part of strategy development Educational setting	Low Educational setting
(4) Inputs	Expertise	Low	Low/Medium	Medium	High	Medium/High	Low/Medium
	Commitment	Medium (Partners) High (Researchers)	Low (Partners) Low/Medium (Researchers)	Medium (Partners) High (Researchers)	High (Partners) High (Researchers)	Medium (Partners) High (Researchers)	High (Partners) High (Researchers)
	Collabor. trust	Low/Medium	Low	Medium	High	Medium	High
	Funds and support	Low	Low	Medium	Medium	High	Medium

- *Partner Network*. The USTL Phoenix can now rely on a small but strong *network of dedicated and committed external partners* (including some of our graduates) that are excited to participate in transition experiments and use Phoenix in general, and the Gateway district in particular, as a living laboratory for exploring urban sustainability (e.g., *Revitalizing Public Spaces for the Public Good in Phoenix*). Similar to the previous aspect (expertise), the early projects have mainly been used to create this network, at times at the expense of implementation and real-world changes.
- *Institutional Support*. Finally, the USTL Phoenix has secured *long-term institutional support* from the School of Sustainability, which provides funds for the PPBL (Wiek, Xiong, et al., 2014) in support of the USTL and similar projects. Federal, state, and private agencies funding research and education are becoming more willing to provide significant monetary funds for USTL projects (e.g., *Reinvent Phoenix*) – which is particularly critical for the experiment stage of USTL projects.

The USTL Phoenix can now rely on a *robust process template* for developing transition strategies and doing experiments (with evaluation), as the template provides sound instructions on methods, collaboration, and reflexivity (Wiek, Guston, et al., 2013; Wiek and Lang, 2014). This template has been tested and expanded upon over the course of the six projects, with important milestones, for instance, in developing a rigorous visioning methodology (*Phoenix General Plan Update; Reinvent Phoenix*).

The USTL Phoenix has created a *broad knowledge base* of USTL projects, not only the ones conducted in Phoenix (documented in project reports, handbooks, publications, etc.), but also other cases (Lang and Wiek, 2012; Forrest and Wiek, 2014). The USTL team uses these resources for designing and executing future transition projects (as, for example, done in *Revitalizing Public Spaces for the Public Good in Phoenix*).

The USTL Phoenix is able to offer *high-quality educational experiences* to students and capacity-building opportunities to professionals. The six projects have all served as test-beds for innovative pedagogies and educational settings (Wiek and Kay, 2015); for example, for training facilitation of contested issues in *Reinvent Phoenix*. The USTL Phoenix has a track record of providing critical qualifications for the job market in Phoenix and beyond (some graduates have secured prominent sustainability officer or planner positions across the US).

The USTL Phoenix has yielded *real-world changes* beyond professional relationships with some positive sustainability outcomes. For example, *Sustainable Solutions for Phoenix* has led to the implementation of a small tree and shade program in the Sky Harbor Neighborhood in the Gateway district of Phoenix; *Participatory Clinic and Playground Design in Phoenix* has led to the construction of an innovative playground (plus programming) on the Mountain Park Health Center clinic campus in the Gateway district.

Not all projects have yielded such outputs, let alone sustainability outcomes on the city level. Apart from the often-described delays (e.g., between the creation of an urban development plan and its actual implementation – *Reinvent Phoenix*), some projects fulfilled function or focused on a different outcome (e.g., building a network of partners in *SD in Light Rail Districts in Phoenix*). Our graduates themselves represent a major real-world impact as they collaborate on or continue USTL Phoenix projects in their respective professional positions (this could be regarded a scaling-up effect).

Referring back to Table 14.3, there are also shortcomings in the case of the USTL Phoenix:

- The most significant deficit of the USTL Phoenix is the lack of strong evidence on how to yield sustainability outcomes (as defined in the evaluative scheme). All taken into account, half of the projects did not produce any, and the remaining ones struggled with exemplarily achieving *broad* sustainability outcomes. A particular challenge was the scaling-up of outcomes from the neighborhood to the city level. Links to existing initiatives were attempted at times, for instance, in *Sustainable Solutions for Phoenix* with an explicit connection to the citywide tree and shade program. Yet, on balance, only marginal outcomes can be traced back to the USTL Phoenix (yet).

- The lack of sustainability outcomes can in part be explained by a lack of substantive outputs. Some of the USTL Phoenix did not even create actionable knowledge (strategies), for instance, *SD in Light Rail Districts in Phoenix*. While only half of the projects reached the implementation stage, none of the projects completed full experiments (as defined in the evaluative scheme), and therefore did not generate fully evidence-supported transition strategies. This limited the chances to achieve real-world changes such as modified behavior, new infrastructures, or novel governance schemes; in particular changes beyond the local scale (site or neighborhood).

- The process, despite the overall robust template, displayed deficits in some projects. Apart from some methodological deficits (e.g., the current state analysis in *Reinvent Phoenix*, or the strategy building in *Revitalizing Public Spaces for the Public Good in Phoenix*), the main shortcomings pertain to the stages of experimenting (with evaluation) and transferring (with evaluation). If the implementation stage was reached (e.g., *Revitalizing Public Spaces for the Public Good in Phoenix*), systematic evaluations were missing. Although some implementations led to recommendations and attempts to support stakeholders in continuing transition efforts, the overall approach was sporadic and the experimentation stage (with evaluation and learning) remained underdeveloped in all cases. Some projects struggled with stakeholder fatigue and unequal participation of stakeholders (e.g., *Reinvent Phoenix*). Finally, despite a strong educational approach in almost all USTL Phoenix projects, reflexive activities, in particular for stakeholders, were missing at times.

- The USTL Phoenix did not always succeed in securing sufficient expertise, commitment, trust, or resources. In each case, the lack of paying attention to these critical ingredients struck back and eventually led to flawed processes, deficient outputs, and little impact, described above. An example was the lack of commitment from both researchers and partners in one of the sub-projects of *Sustainable Solutions for Phoenix*, which required additional coaching and mediating efforts with little to no substantial outputs. Similarly, the lack of collaborative trust in some phases of *Reinvent Phoenix* burdened the collaborating teams, required inefficient iterations, and led to suboptimal outputs. A good share of the projects struggled with the pertinent culture of 'business-as-usual' in Phoenix and a lack of visionary and pioneering spirit on the part of the partners (*Reinvent Phoenix*), which resulted in overly focusing on incremental changes. Finally, the early USTL Phoenix also suffered from a lack of intervention and transition research experience as well as insufficient funding and institutional support (due to the pertinent culture of supporting descriptive-analytical / problem-focused research). The indicated process deficits were in part caused by the limited duration of all projects and a lack of available funds to carry out transition experiments (e.g., *SD in Light Rail Districts in Phoenix*).

It seems that, despite its shortcomings, the USTL in Phoenix has developed a promising pathway to making contributions to the sustainability transition in Phoenix. The jury is still out on *how significant* these contributions will be. In our study, we respond to Bulkeley and Castán Broto (2013), who called for studies that "consider the effects of experimentation". They proposed: "Such research might consider the effectiveness of experiments – their role in achieving climate and other urban goals. [...] Research in this area will also need to consider the effect that experiments have in relation to the reconfiguration of urban socio-technical systems and whether they may lead to broader processes of transition and change in the city." We would suggest here that this question should rather be applied to the overall USTL (its collective impact) than the individual experiment. When considering the effects of a USTL, we argue that it would not do all projects full justice if they *all* would *equally* be assessed against the evaluative scheme presented. This can be illustrated with the USTL in Phoenix. From a life-cycle perspective, the early USTL Phoenix projects fulfilled functions of 'breaking ground' (e.g., initial capacity building and creating a network of partners) and thereby compensated for a lack of substantive outputs and outcomes. Yet, while this would suggest a strategic agenda in selecting and conducting experiments with specific functions, we have to admit that a good share of the USTL Phoenix projects emerged in some, if not all, components rather accidentally and opportunistically. This led to barriers and frictions in the collaborative arrangements and ultimately to suboptimal results and little demonstrable impact. Despite some common threads, the six projects did not fully build upon one another and systematically take full advantage of lessons learned and insights gained. In retrospect, perhaps the *Phoenix General Plan Update* was too ambitious, large-scale, and at too high a level at this early stage in the USTL Phoenix. So, it is a fine line to walk – getting a USTL started by establishing a network and taking advantage of opportunities, while not getting stuck in the early stages. It is critical to keep the eyes on the prize: conducting impactful transition experiments that allow for scaling them up and transferring them. While the described detours might be acceptable for a USTL of the first generation, it might not be necessary to make the same detours when creating USTLs in the future. This is why we close the chapter with recommendations based on the experiences gained in the USTL Phoenix.

Recommendations

We draw conclusions from the evaluative account presented above and provide some recommendations for people keen on running USTLs and who want to learn from previous experiences. So, how do we need to design urban sustainability transition labs so that they yield lasting sustainability outcomes?

Based on the USTL Phoenix experiences, we would recommend the following:

- Overcome as soon as possible the opportunistic and reactive mode of operation, and move towards strategic choices. Select strategically: amenable intervention points, 'hot' (but not *too* hot) topics that receive public attention; committed and pioneering partners, collaborators experienced in transition and/or intervention research, a skilled transacademic interface manager, funding opportunities with reasonable demands, and so forth.
- Consider the running of a USTL as a transition process itself, with initialization, take-off, acceleration, and stabilization phases. Select strategically what is needed to succeed in the different stages. Make sure not to get stuck in the early phases, and move fast into the stage of strategically designed full transition experiments and scaling-up efforts (sustainability outcomes) – to demonstrate success and motivate collaborators and partners.
- Create a simple (maybe distributed) USTL infrastructure that allows for easy connection to and among (potential) partners and collaborators. The infrastructure includes physical (notice board, office, room in a community location, etc.), online (working platform, website, etc.), other media (e.g., newsletter). Design it so that it allows for various forms of gathering, exchange, exploration, and so forth – building community and identity of change agents across the city.
- Become aware of *where* (what stage) in the transition process the city stands, and anticipate different transition path opportunities. Timing and design of transition efforts are critical, as the transition process requires

different activities and support at different stages. In return, the same activity or support can be useless if timing and design are off or inappropriate. Certain domains or stakeholders might be closer to readiness for takeoff (or whatever other stage). In these cases, the effort should be to identify promising initiatives and to subsequently deepen, broaden, and scale them up.

- Focus on establishing a long-term transition partnership in one neighborhood or small urban area (e.g., Gateway district), to provide continuity and coherence across transition efforts and experiments as well as to link to other initiatives in the area. Such a focal area could motivate sustained efforts that would make it less likely to have the starts, stops, and lack of continuity that can be observed in current USTLs.
- Balance working on the local *and* the city level. While projects on the local level often yield more quickly more significant results (if pioneers are involved), changes on the city level, even if delayed, can have broader and longer-lasting effects (e.g., crafting legally binding urban development plans in *Reinvent Phoenix*). Thereby, revisit the multilevel transition perspective and different transition path opportunities (interplay between local and city level).
- Build the capacity for sustainability-oriented transition efforts in your collaborators and external partners. Excitement and commitment are very important. But there is nothing more powerful as 'partners in crime' who are knowledgeable and skilled about transition experiments and other transition efforts.
- Monitor and evaluate as systematically and continuously as possible. Craft experimental settings and develop clear rationales for the assessment of outputs and outcomes, considering the experimental character of the projects (what demonstrates effectiveness). Use the lessons learned for future design of USTL projects and experiments. Carefully assess what kind of research is needed in support of transition efforts and balance research activities with other transition activities (networking, negotiating, exploring, etc.). This is essential not only for internal learning and moving the transition forward, but also for generating evidence needed to support scaling-up and securing funds.
- Stay in contact with other USTLs; coordinate schemes and experiments in order to learn from each other and together.

Acknowledgments

The authors would like to thank an anonymous reviewer for helpful comments on an earlier version of this chapter. We also would like to thank the editors Niki Frantzeskaki, Lars Coenen, Vanesa Castán Broto, and Derk Loorbach for their leadership and patience in putting this book together and providing helpful comments on earlier versions of this chapter.

References

Bernstein, M.J., Wiek, A., Brundiers, K., Pearson, K., Minowitz, A., Kay, B., and Golub, B. (2014). Mitigating urban sprawl effects – a collaborative tree and shade intervention in Phoenix, Arizona, USA. *Local Environment*, 2016, 21(4), 414–431.

Brundiers, K., Wiek, A., and Kay, K. (2013). The role of transacademic interface managers in transformational sustainability research and education. *Sustainability*, 5, 4614–4636.

Bulkeley, H., and Castán Broto, V. (2013). Government by experiment? Global cities and the governing of climate change. *Transactions of the Institute of British Geographers*, 38(3), 361–375.

Champagne, E., Dorsch, L., Falk, A., Keeve, T., Quinn, J., Spears, B., VanOrden, M., Wiek, A., and John, B. (2014). Revitalizing Public Spaces for the Public Good – Strategies to Enhance Social Cohesion and Overcome Segregation. Project Report. Arizona State University, Tempe, AZ, and Leuphana University of Lüneburg.

Childers, D.L., Pickett, S.T., Grove, J. M., Ogden, L., and Whitmer, A. (2014). Advancing urban sustainability theory and action: challenges and opportunities. *Landscape and Urban Planning*, 125, 320–328.

Cook, I.R., and Swyngedouw, E. (2012). Cities, social cohesion and the environment: towards a future research agenda. *Urban Studies*, 49(9), 1959–1979.

Evans, J., and Karvonen, A. (2011a). Living Laboratories for Sustainability: Exploring the Politics and Epistemology of Urban Transition. In: Bulkeley, H., Castán Broto, V., Hodson, M., and Marvin, S. (Eds). *Cities and Low Carbon Transitions*. London: Routledge, pp. 126–141.

Evans, J., and Karvonen, A. (2011b). 'Give me a laboratory and I will lower your carbon footprint!' Urban laboratories and the pursuit of low carbon futures. *International Journal of Urban and Regional Research*, 38(2), 413–430.

Farla, J., Markard, J., Raven, R., and Coenen, L. (2012). Sustainability transitions in the making: A closer look at actors, strategies and resources. *Technological Forecasting and Social Change*, 79(6), 991–998.

Forrest, N., and Wiek, A. (2014). Learning from success – Towards evidence-informed sustainability transitions in communities. *Environmental Innovation and Societal Transitions*, 12, 66–88.

Gibson, R.B. (2006). Sustainability assessment: basic components of a practical approach. *Impact Assessment and Project Appraisal*, 24, pp. 170–182.

Grin, J., Rotmans, J., and Schot, J. (2010). *Transitions to Sustainable Development – New Directions in the Study of Long Term Transformative Change*. London: Routledge, New York; Abingdon, UK.

Karvonen, A., and van Heur, B. (2014). Urban laboratories: experiments in reworking cities. *International Journal of Urban and Regional Research*, 38(2), 379–392.

König, A., and Evans, J. (2013). Experimenting for sustainable development? Living laboratories, social learning, and the role of the university. In: König, A. (Ed.) (2013). *Regenerative Sustainable Development of Universities and Cities – The Role of Living Laboratories*. Cheltenham, UK: Edward Elgar. pp. 1–24.

Lang, D.J., and Wiek, A. (2012). The role of universities in fostering urban and regional sustainability. In: Mieg, H.A., and Töpfer, K. (Eds.) Institutional and Social Innovation for Sustainable Urban Development. Earthscan: London, pp. 393–411.

Lang, D.J., Wiek, A., Bergmann, M., Stauffacher, M., Martens, P., Moll, P., Swilling, M., and Thomas, C. (2012). Transdisciplinary research in sustainability science – Practice, principles and challenges. *Sustainability Science*, 7 (Supplement 1), 25–43.

Loorbach, D., and Rotmans, J. (2010). The practice of transition management: examples and lessons from four distinct cases. *Futures*, 42(3), 237–246.

McCormick, K., Anderberg, S., Coenen, L., and Neij, L. (2013). Advancing sustainable urban transformation. *Journal of Cleaner Production*, 50, 1–11.

Nevens, F., and Roorda, C. (2014). A climate of change: a transition approach for climate neutrality in the city of Ghent (Belgium). *Sustainable Cities and Society*, 10, 112–121.

Nevens, F., Frantzeskaki, N., Gorissen, L., and Loorbach, D. (2013). Urban Transition Labs: co-creating transformative action for sustainable cities. *Journal of Cleaner Production*, 50, 111–122.

Polk, M., Kain, J.-H., and Holmberg, J. (2013). Mistra Urban Futures: A living laboratory for urban transformations. In: König, A. (Ed.) (2013). *Regenerative Sustainable Development of Universities and Cities – The Role of Living Laboratories*. Cheltenham, UK: Edward Elgar. pp. 173–193.

Rockström, J., Steffen, W., Noone, K., Persson, Å, Chapin, F. S., III, Lambin, E. F., Lenton, T. M., Scheffer, M., Folke, C., Schellnhuber, H. J., Nykvist, B., de Wit, C. A., Hughes, T., van der Leeuw, S., Rodhe, H., Sörlin, S., Snyder, P. K., Costanza, R., Svedin, U., Falkenmark, M., Karlberg, L., Corell, R. W., Fabry, V. J., Hansen, J., Walker, B., Liverman, D., Richardson, K., Crutzen, P., Foley, J. A. (2009). A safe operating space for humanity. *Nature*, 461, 472–475.

Romero-Lankao, P., and Dodman, D. (2011). Cities in transition: transforming urban centers from hotbeds of GHG emissions and vulnerability to seedbeds of sustainability and resilience. *Current Opinion in Environmental Sustainability*, 3(3), 113–120.

Ross, A. (2011) *Bird on Fire: Lessons from the World's Least Sustainable City*. Oxford: Oxford University Press.

Ryan, C. (2013). Eco-Acupuncture: designing and facilitating pathways for urban transformation, for a resilient low-carbon future. *Journal of Cleaner Production*, 50, 189–199.

Schliwa, G. (2013) Exploring Living Labs through Transition Management: Challenges and Opportunities for Sustainable Urban Transitions. MSc. Thesis, Lund University, Sweden.

Svara, J.H., Watt, T.C., and Jang, H.S. (2013). How are US cities doing sustainability? Who is getting on the sustainability train, and why? *Cityscape*, 15, 9–44.

Talwar, S., Wiek, A., and Robinson, J. (2011). User engagement in sustainability research. *Science and Public Policy*, 38(5), 379–390.

Trencher, G., Yarime, M., McCormick, K.B., Doll, C.N.H., and Kraines, S.B. (2014). Beyond the third mission: Exploring the emerging university function of co-creation for sustainability. *Science and Public Policy*, 41(2), 151–179.

UN Habitat (2008). State of the World's Cities 2008/2009 – Harmonious Cities. London: Earthscan.

Van den Bosch, S.J.M. (2010). Transition Experiments – Exploring Societal Changes towards Sustainability. Doctoral Thesis. Erasmus University Rotterdam: Dutch Research Institute for Transitions (DRIFT).

Wiek, A., Selin, C., and Johnson, C. (Eds.). (2010). The Future of Phoenix, Arizona – Crafting Sustainable Development Strategies. Project Report. School of Sustainability, Arizona State University.

Wiek, A., and Kay, B. (2011). Community-Focused Sustainability Assessment and Visioning of Light Rail Corridor Districts in Phoenix. Project Report. School of Sustainability, Arizona State University.

Wiek, A., Ness, B., Brand, F.S., Schweizer-Ries, P., and Farioli, F. (2012). From complex systems analysis to transformational change: a comparative appraisal of sustainability science projects. *Sustainability Science*, 7 (Supplement 1), 5–24.

Wiek, A., Bernstein, M., Laubichler, M., Caniglia, G., Minteer, B., and Lang, D.J. (2013). A global classroom for international sustainability education. *Creative Education*, 4, 19–28.

Wiek, A., Guston, D.H., van der Leeuw, S., Selin, C., and Shapira, P. (2013). Nanotechnology in the city: sustainability challenges and anticipatory governance. *Journal of Urban Technology*, 20(2), 45–62.

Wiek, A., Talwar, S., O'Shea, M., and Robinson, J. (2014). Towards a methodological scheme for capturing societal effects of participatory sustainability research. *Research Evaluation*, 23(2), 117–132.

Wiek, A., and Lang, D.J. (2016). Transformational sustainability research methodology. In: Heinrichs, H., Martens, P., Michelsen, G., and Wiek, A. (Eds.). *Sustainability Science – An Introduction*. Berlin, New York: Springer. pp. 31–41

Wiek, A., Xiong, A., Brundiers, K., and van der Leeuw, S. (2014). Integrating problem- and project-based learning into sustainability programs – a case study on the School of Sustainability at Arizona State University. *International Journal of Sustainability in Higher Education*, 15(4), 431–449.

Wiek, A., and Kay, B. (2015). Learning while transforming – solution-oriented learning for urban sustainability in Phoenix, Arizona. *Current Opinion in Environmental Sustainability*, 16, 29–36.

Wiek, A., Kay, B., Golub, A., and Harlow, J. (in prep). From business-as-usual to transformational planning – two steps forward, one step back on the way towards sustainable urban development.

Xiong, A., Talbot, K., Wiek, A., and Kay, B. (2012). Integrated Health Care for Communities – Participatory Visioning and Strategy Building for a New Mountain Park Health Center Clinic in Phoenix. Project Report. School of Sustainability, Arizona State University.

15 Change and Persistency

Understanding Social-Ecological Transition in a Post-Socialist City – the Example of Leipzig, Germany

Dagmar Haase, Annegret Haase and Dieter Rink

Introduction

When large cities in state socialist Europe entered the era of political change in 1989, they did not only witness a change in their political, institutional and economic foundations. They also experienced a fundamental change of their socio-environmental situation in the course of deindustrialization, changes in economic and labour market trends as well as socio-spatial differentiation. Environmental quality became of increasing importance for residential areas. Environmental degradation caused by industry declined. At the same time, increasing motorization led to new pollution. Additionally, many post-socialist cities underwent population decline in the 1990s and 2000s. While some of them have stabilized or even seen regrowth over the last few years, others continue losing population. The co-evolution of political and economic change and socio-ecological transition in a short period of time has thus produced specific results in terms of change and persistency as well as their imprints on urban space.

Set against this background, this chapter analyses the development and specifics of socio-ecological transformations in the city of Leipzig, eastern Germany. This city represents a case in point to illustrate the context mentioned above because of two reasons: firstly, it has experience fundamental change in various steps over a short period of time (two decades). Secondly, it shows how political and economic turnaround and the transition of socio-ecological structures happened at the same time and interfered each other. Thirdly, this development places Leipzig, despite all its particularities, in the context of several former industrial cities in post-socialist Europe.

Leipzig represents a city and an urban region which has been fundamentally transformed by post-socialist change after 1989. This change affected almost all sectors of the socio-environmental system of the city. At the time of the political turnaround, the city had suffered from far-reaching environmental degradation of both urban nature and the ecosystems of Leipzig's surroundings, through destructive exploitation of soft coal sediments in the south of the city accompanied by heavy coal and chemical industries and the resulting air and water pollution that were intolerable for a large urban population of about

500,000 people. Leipzig's residents were protesting against this destruction of their environment and thus initiated early protests in 1988 which ended up in the manifestations for political change in 1989. Thus, although this political and societal transition turn was rather socio-economic nature, it was initiated by the unacceptable environmental situation. After the reunification of Germany, new terms describing the situation in the city of Leipzig, the whole urban region and its environment were born: terms such as "shrinking city" (referring to the 1990s) or "regrowing city" (referring to the 2000s and 2010s) highlighted the predominant trends of population development and labour market as well as economic development. Terms such as "water city" or "Leipzig's green belt" described visions of what Leipzig should be after the regreening of its large lignite coal production sites and the waterway system in its industrial districts. Within the last few years, Leipzig has undergone vibrant regrowth and a gradual improvement of its environmental situation. However, regrowth, which concentrates in the inner city, endangers environmental quality through densification and growth in vehicle use and transit.

Approach and Research Objectives

As this book is on sustainability transitions, we define for this chapter "transitions" as fundamental, far-reaching changes in development patterns that affect many fields of socio-ecological development, leading to new or distinct goals and transforming urban space and society in a qualitative way. However, we decided to use the term of "paradigms" for analysing changes and persistencies in space and over time in our discussion of the example of Leipzig. We define a paradigm change as a change of visions and long-term goals through acting and decision-making by policymakers, planners and wider urban society. We hypothesise that paradigm changes as we understand them better cover the processes after 1989 in this case, whereas the political turnaround might have more to do with a transition.

In our paper, we aim to answer the following questions:

1   How did the socio-ecological system of the city and its environment change since 1990?
2   Which predominant qualities of change and persistency do we find over this period of 25 years?
3   How can we detect these changes and continuities in space, and how do these transitions unfold over time and space?
4   To what extent can we speak of a "Leipzig case" in terms of transition, and what are transition potentials with particular emphasis on sustainability?

Using site-specific broad and long-term empirical evidence, we analyse how change over time in Leipzig since 1990 can be described, understood and explained. In particular, we look at features of transformation/transition, adaptation and persistency as qualities with which to assess the multidimensional change of an urban system. In our analysis, we will focus on the following investigation perspectives: environment and ecosystems, land-use, governance and planning policy and, last but not least, the residents of Leipzig.

Research Design – A Mix of Methods to Empirically and Conceptually Capture Emerging Patterns of Urban Transitions

Covering an issue as complex as city paradigms, changes, continuities and transition potential requires a broad range of different research material and methods. The key issues that enabled the authors intend to draw a complex story of the city of Leipzig are (a) the interdisciplinary background of the team – sociology, cultural sciences, land system sciences and ecology – and the mutual acceptance and inclusion of methods from these different backgrounds into one path of research, and (b) a long-term research expertise on Leipzig and its urban region. Investigating the city of Leipzig has a long history since the foundation of the Helmholtz Centre for Environmental Research–UFZ in 1991. Thus, shortly after the aforementioned systemic change, the study of the demographic, social, economic, housing market, land-use planning/ governance and ecological processes and patterns has begun and has been carried through to the present. Therefore, any ideas and findings presented here were conceptually developed, empirically underpinned, reworked and, in some cases, even discarded.

What is more, we learned that although a single pattern shows interesting trends, only bringing together all the different aspects of the system allows identifying changes and persistencies in one paradigm and its transition towards another. The material and data to embed and to feed the story told above is multiple and rich: it ranges from more qualitative information such as a photo documentary, an extensive literature review about Leipzig, many reviews of urban plans and planning documents since 1991, a wide range of meetings and workshops with many different stakeholder groups and on a diversity of topics and, last but not least, more quantitative information such as statistical and census data and mappings about population segregation and surveys about life satisfaction as well as land-use change maps and ecosystem services calculations (Haase, D. et al., 2014; Haase, D. et al., 2012; Rink et al., 2012; Bauer et al., 2012).

How Did the Socio-Ecological System of the City and Its Environment Change since 1990?

Leipzig's socio-ecological system (i.e., the social and ecological conditions that shape the local context and the development of the city) is basically and structurally similar to that of many other large Central European cities founded in the Middle Ages. However, it experienced a somewhat specific, more recent history since its integration into state socialist Europe from 1945 to 1989. After 1989, the post-socialist transition led, again, to fundamental changes in the political, institutional and economic framework, which largely impacted the social and ecological situation as well. Thus, we can observe a specific sequential change of leading paradigms in urban policymaking in Leipzig, which stands, however, in the context of a larger group of cities in the post-socialist realm.

As already reported in the literature, the ecological/environmental situation in most of the GDR cities in 1989 was, on a large scale, disastrously devastated urban ecosystems; enormous air and groundwater pollution; destroyed soil due to soft coal mining; and more. These extreme environmental conditions became a real threat to public health and caused ongoing emigration. Despite the suppression of opposition "elements" (individuals, actions) by the GDR government, this situation evoked and strengthened societal opposition where environmental and health issues became a central topic (e.g., a movement using the slogan "Can Leipzig still be saved?"; in German, *Ist Leipzig noch zu retten?*). Protests developed into a massive democratic movement in 1989–90, which resulted in the collapse of the GDR state and German reunification. In this sense, the 1989 revolution in the GDR has close relations to the disastrous environmental situation. Environmental groups and initiatives belonged to the first protesters, and the environmental issue figured at the so-called Monday demonstrations in 1989 and 1990 (Rink, 2002). Thus, Leipzig's protests also had a clear environmental dimension. The post-socialist transition to come radically changed all land-use policies in a wider sense: opencast soft coal mining was stopped, and most of the coal-based industries were closed in summer 1990. Insofar as deindustrialisation brought most environmental pollution to an end in the first half of the 1990s, one could say that civil society and the political turnaround in 1989 initiated an ecological paradigm shift, which was enforced and completed by deindustrialisation.

After the reunification in 1990, all the political and economic structures of the former GDR were almost automatically adapted to the western German system and to EU norms. Additionally, many lead functions within the new administration were taken over by policymakers and planners with a western German education and background that decisively determined further discussions, vision creation and decision-making. From 1990 onwards, as already reported, the ecological conditions improved as coal mines were closed, soil and wetlands revitalised and most of the coal-based heating systems replaced by modern oil and gas heating. In addition, due to the closing down of almost all industrial production in the city, water pollution could be stopped and former rivers, streams and wetlands restored (Haase, 2003; Haase and Gläser, 2009).

In the early 1990s, the ecological revitalisation of the urban landscape was one of the central goals of policy as well as a civil society project after German unification. It was supported by federal policy and programs. Within the overarching vision of the harmonisation of living conditions in the western and eastern parts of Germany, and catch-up modernisation in eastern

Germany, large revitalisation projects were also initiated in Leipzig, often with the participation of civil society and funded by federal money stemming from subsidies to the labour market. Thus, ecological transition became part of a welfare policy. At this time, several paradigmatic projects aimed at transforming the urban landscape took place. First of all, in the so-called *Südraum* (southern area of mining), large former opencast mines were transformed into lakes and the area itself into a new "lake district". In the eastern part of Leipzig, the so-called *Ostraum* (eastern territory) project was conducted by a range of civic initiatives and intermediate actors with the aim of creating a green connection between the city of Leipzig and its surrounding regions in the east. In the inner city of Leipzig, the revitalization of the Pleiße river and a constructed channel (*Karl-Heine-Kanal*) was conducted, bringing about enormous improvements in the urban environmental situation. What is more, these improvements were supported by so-called ecological gratis effects of deindustrialisation, leading to the decrease in air, water and soil pollution.

Around the year 2000, the ecological system had been completely transformed into a healthier urban environment, but started to suffer from considerable particle emissions and noise pollution by car transportation; the number of cars from pre-1990 increased by almost 400% (Haase, 1997). Having escaped the ecological crisis, Leipzig entered a job and social crisis with a massive elimination of jobs and subsequent emigration to western Germany (Kabisch et al., 2008). On the housing market, the social crisis found its most extreme expression in high flat vacancy rates in Leipzig shortly after 2000 (about 20% of the housing stock; Stadt Leipzig, 2012). Thus, a new paradigm shift happened because the city firstly realized and secondly tried to manage urban shrinkage by applying different strategies of urban restructuring and right-sizing. Shrinkage management became the new paradigm itself: landscape design was embedded into the new integrated master plan of urban restructuring in 2000 under the new vision "less density, more green".

After having established an environmental governance structure after 1990 to manage the ecological crisis, the city administration collaborated with several groups of stakeholders to develop a range of policies and projects counteracting shrinkage and to keep the city liveable despite population loss after 2000 (Rink et al., 2012). Establishing the approach of "perforation" (Lüdke-Daldrup, 2001), that is, the development of urban space through concentration of uses and enlargement of green areas in between, and developing policy instruments such as interim use agreements (in German *Gestattungsvereinbarung*; Rall and Haase, 2011) or urban forest areas (Rink and Arndt, 2011), the city became a prominent case in how to deal with urban shrinkage innovatively over the past 15 years. The spatial extent of the new paradigm "less density more green", however, was much smaller and more specific compared to that of the remedial actions in the 1990s; as a result, we find many different uses side by side: revitalised brownfields, small parks, interim-use sites, urban gardens, many urban forests and other "experimental sites". At the same time, numerous neighbourhoods were upgraded by the renovation of building stock (using various attractive schemes for tenants or owner-occupiers) and also by the enlargement or new establishment of parks and other green areas. In a way, Leipzig has become a laboratory for urban landscape planning. Again, civil society played an important role as initiator and co-designer of this revitalisation and the design of land-use perforation; for example, through opposing the demolition of the old built-up housing structures in the inner city, or as users of urban gardens and interim use plots. Because of upgrading by revitalisation, the city became more and more attractive in the late 2000s. Apart from other factors such as housing quality, culture and jobs, the "new urban landscape" also substantially contributed to Leipzig's regrowth or reurbanisation: that is, the influx of new populations into the inner city and a substantial yearly population growth rate since the late 2010s (Rink et al., 2012; Rink, 2014).

Regrowth or reurbanisation caused new changes and probably initiated a shift to another paradigm quite recently. After 2010, the development of the urban landscape has been embedded into a framework of regrowth and (new) competition for land. The revitalisation of brownfields has predominantly encouraged upgrading and partial gentrification of housing stock in the inner city. Examples can be found in the so-called waterfront-development in the western part of Leipzig, or the port of Lindenau where several thousand new houses will be built exclusively for the upper-price segment and for middle class families (Rink et al., 2014a). Thus, the so-called *Wasserstadt* (water city) Leipzig can be seen as a paradigmatic project, and civil society often finds itself in the role of being the opponent to gentrification (ibid.). The new growth strategy and the related construction boom in the city has caused a number of (land-use) conflicts, since interim uses like urban gardens have been threatened by exclusion from their locations. In addition, the orientation towards mass tourism in Leipzig has been leading to conflicts between designed places and floodplain forests conservation.

Implementing new green infrastructure, transforming brown- and greyfield sites into parks and developing attractive housing units in the inner city helped change Leipzig into a "comeback city", which currently exhibits one of the highest growth rates compared to the overall city and population size in all of Germany (Rink, 2014). But in terms of overall environmental and social justice –. the extent to which all city residents are able to benefit from clean air, more green and water quality after 1990 – the number of beneficiaries of the new green infrastructure is limited, since as many of the new housing units and green spaces built or implemented after 2000 are mainly located in "better-off" parts of the city (Rink et al., 2014b).

Figure 15.1 summarizes this development by showing an overview of the paradigm changes impacting Leipzig's socio-ecological development and its triggers.

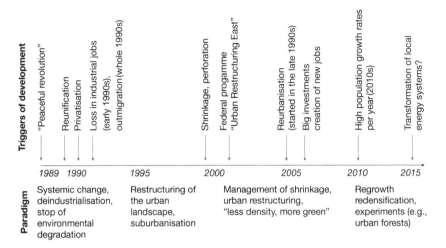

Figure 15.1 Paradigm changes and their triggers in Leipzig's socio-ecological development since 1989. (Source: Authors.)

Which Predominant Qualities of Change and Persistency Do We Find over this Period of 25 Years?

The term "change" is used here to detect qualitative and structural distinctiveness, or structures or processes that are qualitatively or structurally distinctive compared to their former appearance or former point in time, respectively. Since 1990, there have been a large number of such changes in the socio-ecological system of Leipzig: first and foremost, the political and institutional system, and the rules in which the city had been embedded, changed. In addition, entering a social market economy changed all prevailing market rules typical of a socialist economy. Next to the change in the political and economic systems, most remarkable were the changes in the social make-up of the city (socio-demographic composition of the residential population) and its increasing differentiation until today. In GDR times, the social differentiation within the housing stock of Leipzig was very low compared to a market-based housing pattern typical of the West (Kindler et al., 1997). There were also a number of demographic changes which included features of post-transition processes, such as massive emigration due to a lack of jobs on the one hand, and features of a more general Europe-wide demographic turn – the so-called second demographic transition, including low fertility, postponement of childbearing, childlessness, individualisation and decline of the household size (Kabisch et al., 2008) – on the other. Last but not least, the entire housing market also included patterns of residential segregation changed according to income differences that emerged and developed after 1990 (Grossmann et. al., 2015, Rink et al., 2014a,b).

Compared to GDR times, but also during the first 25 years after the political change, a multitude of visions for the city's future have developed – discussed as paradigms in this chapter. The role of governance and government, as well as that of the participation and enrolment of different actors, changed several times due to and along with the changing paradigms. Governance as a form of interaction in the city emerged in 1990. In a more technical sense, almost all networks of urban infrastructure – transport, social, educational, water supply, power supply and health – changed in quantitative and qualitative terms (Kabisch et al., 2010).

We also observe considerable changes in the environmental dimension of our socio-ecological system: the former soft coal mining area, the *Südraum Leipzig*, was completely transformed from a mining area into a new lake and recreation district, with a large supply of recreational infrastructure and accommodation. In inner parts of the city, land-use patterns also changed: former industrial areas became large grey- and brownfields (Rink et al., 2011). There were also changes in the perception of the urban environment: whereas in GDR-times the resource-use aspect clearly dominated, urban nature is now understood as a key aspect for the urban quality of life (Haase et al., 2014). Moreover, we observe a change in the types of environmental impacts, particularly with respect to air pollution, which completely changed from soft coal-heating particle dust in 1990 into noise and NO_x pollution from high traffic volumes today (Weber et al., 2014).

Next to change, persistency also belongs to a socio-ecological system in transition. In this chapter, persistency is understood as structures, patterns or mechanisms that were retained, remained, stayed more or less stable or did not undergo major/substantial changes as they were defined above. There might not be less persistency than change, but change is less noticeable, or one could say that it is more noiseless. Some parts of the residential make-up of the city remained consistent until today, but we observe an "ageing in place" in some of the GDR-time built areas, while some "better-off" areas around the city centre (e.g., the area around the *Waldstraße*) and the settlement of *Markkleeberg* (south of Leipzig) remained high-class and high-income areas. In addition, other "low-end" parts of the city did not evolve, such as the "poor Leipzig-East" (Schetke and Haase, 2008). Overall, and typically for most types of settlements, main parts of the housing estates and the urban fabric did not change substantially despite the new construction and demolition of housing stock after 1990. The area and the shape of Leipzig's largest recreation area, the floodplain forests, also remained stable (Haase, 2003). The same is true of the function and shape of allotment gardens, whereas the owner and user structure changed considerably. Interestingly, the image of Leipzig as the prototype of the Eastern German city after 1990 kept stable over the entire post-socialist period until today.

Generally, one can say that Leipzig represents a prominent example of the rupture that took place after the breakdown of state socialism. Change was fundamental and affected all spheres of economic and social life. In contrast to other former state socialist countries, in eastern Germany the political and institutional structures of western Germany were installed from one day to another. There was no gradual change but a sudden and total one. This also affected the type and speed of all the paradigmatic changes mentioned above in the socio-environmental sphere. This makes change in cities such as Leipzig different from what we know from most western European cities, which saw more gradual change over the last decades, or at least no change resulting from total systemic turnaround. Apart from the predominating changes, there is persistency, too. In most cases, we observe a kind of simultaneous change and persistency, in which structures survived but underwent changes, such as a large housing estate from state socialist times that still exists but has undergone a change of residents and image. The floodplain forest and allotment gardens still exist but equally saw a change of their use or owners/users.

How Can We Detect Changes and Persistencies in Space? What Are Meaningful *Indicators*[1]?

As a result of our long-term research in Leipzig, we elaborated a range of indicators that we found most meaningful in terms of identifying how the aforementioned changes and persistencies unfold in space and over time.

Demographic Change

Leipzig's demographic make-up changed considerably and in various ways after 1990: we observe a breakdown in *birth rates* after 1990 with the lowest rate of birth worldwide in eastern Germany in 1995 (0.77; Kabisch et al., 2008), massive *emigration* after 1990 (about 100,000 people for the period 1990–1999, or 20% of the total population until 1998), as well as suburbanization that roared in the mid-1990s. Since population losses were age-selective, they resulted in a massive ageing of the population (with the *ageing index* more than doubling between 1990 and the late 2000s). Since the late 1990s, we observe the opposite population movement: Leipzig has experienced reurbanisation with new, young immigrants moving to the city. In the last years, the ageing process has been attenuated by (a) recent *young immigration* of about 10,000 people per year and (b) increasing birth rates. While younger people concentrate in the inner city, the outer districts are still rapidly ageing.

Socio-Spatial Differentiation

Residential segregation exists in Leipzig according to different dimensions: socio-economic (*unemployment rate*), *age* (younger and older people), *ethnic* (migrants, see Figure 15.2). Segregation patterns have evolved and changed various times since 1990. We identified three phases after 1990: the phase of resolving socialist *segregation* (in the first half of 1990s), the phase of initial new segregation (in the second half of 1990s) and the phase of consolidation

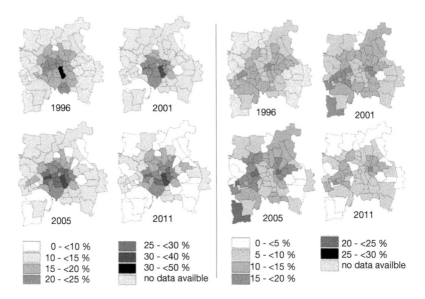

Figure 15.2 (left) Concentration of young (<40 years) and (right) unemployed population in Leipzig – change over time. (Modified after: Grossmann et al.,
2015, Arndt, Haase, A., Rink, Steinführer, 2013.)

of the new segregation patterns (in the first half of 2000s). Today, we are
maybe entering the next phase, with rising differences between urban neighbourhoods and increasing gentrification and exclusionary displacement
(Grossmann et al., 2014, Grossmann et al. 2015).

Housing Market

Leipzig's housing market has undergone various changes, too. In the first half
of the 1990s, housing vacancies began to emerge as a result of the emigration mentioned above. By 2000, they reached peak values of about 20% of
the whole stock, due to the overlap of different, simultaneously happening
processes: population emigration, *suburbanization, new construction* and *renovation of the old building stock*. After 2001, surplus housing was demolished
mainly in the large housing estates from state socialist times, and to a lesser
degree in the inner-city areas, where it reached its highest rates. At the same
time, new people moved into the renovated inner-city housing stock, which
made *vacancy rates* decrease there. In the large housing estate, demolition also
brought about a decrease in vacancies. Within the last years, Leipzig's housing
market went from vacancy towards a new boom due to regrowth of about 2%
per year. There are new constructions, mostly in the upper market segments
(Rink et al., 2014a and b). Related to this new situation, there are rising *housing costs* and increasing differences between housing market segments as well.

Greening strategies mainly benefited more attractive areas and made ground rents rise there. Re-densification is now taking place in some inner-city areas, and even in large housing estates de-densification and initial perforation were taking place some 15 years before (Figure 15.3).

Figure 15.3 Housing vacancies and demolition of housing stock in Leipzig. (Source: A. Haase, M. Bernt.)

Economy and Labour Market

As a result of deindustrialization, Leipzig experienced massive losses in *industrial jobs* in the first half of the 1990s: about 80,000 jobs. This led to high unemployment over a long period of time, which at times even exceeded this job loss. Only since the mid-2000s has Leipzig's job situation started to improve. Some major investments happened with the help of massive *public financial support*, and some 50,000 new jobs were created since then, not least in new industries. As a result, unemployment rates have more than halved and the general investment climate has improved (this is seen as an important source of Leipzig's regrowth story).

Land Use

The number and areas of brown- and greyfields massively increased. After the development of new green spaces in 1995, predominantly at the brownfields, high-quality *green space* development ended when Leipzig resumed growth after 2005. Good indicators for quality of green space are their structural properties (Voigt et al., 2014), their number of trees and sanitary infrastructure. Soft-coal mining areas were largely restored, which can be measured by land-use change (Larondelle and Haase, 2012; Haase and Nuissl, 2007). Current regrowth will possibly lead to an increasing *reuse of brownfield sites* as business/housing sites, competing with alternative green reuses (e.g., in the case of the so-called *Jahrtausendfeld* in Plagwitz, a large vacant plot in Leipzig's inner west which was used as an interim greenfield).

Environmental Pollution

Noise pollution changed from being no problem to the major source of air pollution in Leipzig – we detected this using noise maps (Weber et al., 2014). Here, unintended effects of the change from the GDR to the western city emerged. At the same time, air pollution declined in terms of coal-heating *particle dust* and SO_2, but, with an increasing number of cars, *ultrafine particles, NO_x and O_3* pollution have been affecting residents' health in Leipzig. Thus, bringing noise and air pollution together, the urban climate situation did not change in quantity but in quality. The health of the residents – regardless of whether we look at the GDR or post-socialist period – is of secondary importance for public policy and policy maker who seek for economic prosperity primarily.

Conclusions: To What Extent Can We Speak of a Leipzig Case of Transition, and What Are Its Sustainability Transition Potentials?

In this chapter, we used paradigms and paradigm change to analyse Leipzig's development pathway over the past 25 years. What is the relation between transition and paradigm change? Transition includes both emergent and planning or policy-based changes, while paradigms describe changes resulting from the latter only. Leipzig saw a political/systemic transition in 1989, later followed by paradigm changes taking place within the same general framework, which is democracy and market economy. Leipzig experienced massive changes due to its population development within the last 25 years. After it had lost 100,000 inhabitants in the 1990s, it jumped back to being one of the large cities in all of Germany with one of the most dynamic rates of regrowth (2 and more per cent per year since 2012 until today [spring 2017]). These extreme and opposite dynamics have been reflected in manifold ways with respect to land use, housing, infrastructure and more, as well as in changes of policy responses. However, despite the dramatic decline mentioned above, Leipzig never gave up its growth orientation in terms of policymaking. As shown in this paper, in the 1990s and first half of the 2000s, it officially went for growth, but in reality it managed to decline (Rink et al., 2012). It is therefore difficult to classify policy changes or paradigm changes in policymaking as a response towards shrinkage or regrowth as transitions. In this vein, city planners developed green infrastructure strategies in order to face shrinkage in the short term while making the city attractive for further growth in the longer term (Haase, 2008). Our case study therefore shows that both policy and paradigm changes operate and act at different spatio-temporal scales, producing trade-offs – socio-demographic segregation, gentrification and exclusionary displacement – and synergies such as new and more green space in many parts of the city.

To a certain extent, the transitions of Leipzig's urban space discussed in this chapter catalysed transformative change in the urban landscape of Germany, insofar that the city has been acting as a pioneer in terms of how to deal with shrinkage and the corresponding land management and organisation of the housing market. Leipzig's land-use planners developed instruments for interim uses of vacant land and buildings, and it was here where the term "land use perforation" was shaped. It introduced a new concept of loose patterns of built and open spaces in the inner city, breaking with the prevailing ideal of the compact city to face enormous housing vacancies and to develop greyfields and brownfields in a sustainable (green) way (Lütke-Daldrup, 2001). Land use perforation as a concept entered the national and international discourse of urban shrinkage but lost its importance in Leipzig in the mid- 2000s.

Currently (spring 2017), as the city is planning for further dynamic growth (as a paradigm); some of the positive aspects of the past period of shrinkage mentioned above, such as low-density developments and green spaces, might come under increasing pressure. Processes of increased inner-city segregation and even polarisation may occur, with negative consequences first and foremost for the large share of poor households in the city. At the same time, the city's facilities to respond to such challenges are considerably limited, due to its scarce budget and austerity goals (Rink and Bernt, 2010). Leipzig's future will decisively depend on how the city and its actors will manage to steer further regrowth within the given context. To what extent a transition towards more sustainability within the given conditions has a chance to happen remains a question that cannot be answered today. Last but not least, Leipzig's local pathway also depends on national developments such as the consequences of the German "*Energiewende*" (new energy policy after the Fukushima catastrophe in 2012 that focusses on renewable energies), which might have larger impacts on the entire urban system and its spatial patterns, including positive ones in terms of a decreasing emissions footprint, but also negative ones in terms of increasing residential segregation through thermal insulation, an increase in rents, or on land use through more use of urban land for local energy production. But this new paradigm is in its infancy, and its consequences are still unclear. The same holds true for the above-mentioned austerity policy framework in the aftermath of Europe's various crises after 2008, which are likely to determine the fates of all German cities within the next years, if not decades.

Note

1   Meaningful indicators are given in *italics*.

References

Bauer, A, Röh,l D, Haase, D, Schwarz, N (2012): Ecosystem services in a stagnating urban region in Eastern Germany. In: Nilsson, K, Pauleit, S, Bell, S, Aalbers, C, Sick Nielsen, Th A (Eds.). *Peri-Urban Futures: Scenarios and Models for Land Use Change in Europe*. Springer Dordrecht, New York: pp 209–240.

Grossmann, K, Haase, A, Arndt, T, Cortese, C, Rumpel, P, Rink, D, Slach, O, Ticha, I, Violante, A (2014): How urban shrinkage impacts on patterns of socio-spatial segregation: the cases of Leipzig, Ostrava, and Genoa. In: Yeakey, CC, Thompson, VS, Wells, A (Eds.): *Urban Ills: Post Recession Complexities to Urban Living in Global Contexts*. Lexington Books: New York, London, Boston, pp 241–268.

Grossmann, K, Arndt, T, Haase, A, Rink, D, Steinführer, A (2015): The influence of housing oversupply on residential segregation: exploring the post-socialist city of Leipzig, In: *Urban Geography* 36 (4), 550–577. doi: 10.1080/02723638.2015.1014672.

Haase D, Haase A, Rink D 2014. Conceptualising the nexus between urban shrinkage and ecosystem services. *Landscape and Urban Planning* 132, 159–169.

Haase D, Kabisch N, Haase A, Kabisch S, Rink D (2012): Actors and factors in land use simulation – the challenge of urban shrinkage. *Environmental Modelling and Software* 35, 92–103. doi:10.1016/j.envsoft.2012.02.012.

Haase D 1997. Urban ecology in the new federal countries of Germany. Contamination of upper soil and urban atmosphere with heavy metals in Leipzig. Archive for Nature 37, 1–11.

Haase D 2003. Holocene floodplains and their distribution in urban areas – functionality indicators for their retention potentials. *Landscape & Urban Planning* 66, 5–18.

Haase, D (2008): Urban ecology of shrinking cities: an unrecognised opportunity? *Nature and Culture* 3, 1–8.

Haase D, Gläser J 2009. Determinants of floodplain forest development illustrated by the example of the floodplain forest in the District of Leipzig. Forest Ecol. Manage. 258, 887–894, doi:10.1016/j.foreco.2009.03.025.

Haase, D, Nuissl, H (2007): Does urban sprawl drive changes in the water balance and policy? The case of Leipzig (Germany) 1870–2003. *Landscape and Urban Planning* 80, 1–13.

Kabisch N, Haase D, Haase A 2010. Evolving reurbanisation? Spatio-temporal dynamics exemplified at the eastern German city of Leipzig. Urban Studies 47(5) 967–990.

Kabisch, S, Steinführer, A, Haase, A, Grossmann, K, Peter, A, Maas, A (2008): Demographic change and its impact on housing. Final report for the EUROCITIES network, Brussels and Leipzig.

Kindler, A, Kabisch, S, Rink, D (1997): Sozialatlas der Stadt Leipzig, Leipzig, Umweltforschungszentrum GmbH.

Larondelle, N, Haase, D (2012): Valuing post-mining landscapes using the ecosystem services approach – an example from Germany. *Ecological Indicators* 18, 567–574.

Lütke-Daldrup, E (2001): Die perforierte Stadt. Eine Versuchsanordnung. *Bauwelt* 24, 40–42.

Rall E D, Haase D 2011. Creative Intervention in a Dynamic City: a Sustainability Assessment of an Interim Use Strategy for Brownfields in Leipzig, Germany. *Landscape and Urban Planning* 100, 189–201.

Rink, D (2002): Environmental policy and the environmental movement in Eastern Germany. *Socialism – Nature – Capitalism*, 51, 9, 73–91.

Rink, D (2014): Auferstanden aus Ruinen. *Kreuzer*, February 2014, 18–20.

Rink, D, Bernt, M (2010): "Not relevant for the system": the crisis in the backyards. *International Journal for Urban and Regional Research* 34, 678–685.

Rink, D, Haase, A, Grossmann, K, Couch, C, Cocks, M (2012): From long-term shrinkage to re-growth? A comparative study of urban development trajectories of Liverpool and Leipzig. *Built Environment* 38, 2, 162–178.

Rink, D, Haase, A, Bernt, M, Arndt, T, Ludwig, J (2011): Urban shrinkage in Leipzig, Germany. Research Report, EU 7 FP Project Shrink Smart (contract no. 225193), WP2. UFZ report 01/2011, Helmholtz Centre for Environmental Research–UFZ, Leipzig.

Rink, D, Rumpel, P, Slach, O, Cortese, C, Violante, A, Calza Bini, P, Haase, A, Mykhnenko, V, Nadolu, B, Couch, C, Cocks, M, Krzystofik, R (2012): Governance of shrinkage – Lessons learnt from analysis for urban planning and policy (WP7 D13-15), EU 7FP project Shrink Smart – Governance of Shrinkage within a European Context (No. 225193), Helmholtz Centre for Environmental Research–UFZ, Leipzig, unpublished typescript, 48 pp.

Rink, D, Haase, A, Schneider, A (2014a): Vom Leerstand zum Bauboom? Zur Entwicklung des Leipziger Wohnungsmarkts, in: *Stadt Leipzig, Amt für Statistik und Wahlen: Statistischer Quartalsbericht* I/2014, 25–28.

Rink, D, Schneider, A, Haase, A (2014b): Das gehobene Wohnsegment, in: *Stadt Leipzig, Amt für Statistik und Wahlen: Statistischer Quartalsbericht* II/2014, 25–30.

Rink, D., Arndt, T. (2016): Investigating perception of green structure configuration for afforestation in urban brownfield development by visual methods—A case study in Leipzig, Germany, in: Urban Forestry & Urban Greening 15, 65–74.

Schetke S, Haase D 2008. Multi-criteria assessment of socio-environmental aspects in shrinking cities. Experiences from Eastern Germany. Environmental Impact Assessment Review 28, 483-503.

Voigt A, Kabisch N, Wurster D, Haase D, Breuste J 2014. Structural diversity as a key factor for the provision of recreational services in urban parks – a new and straight-forward method for assessment. AMBIO 43(4), 480–491.

Voigt A, Kabisch N, Wurster D, Haase D, Breuste J (2014): Structural diversity as a key factor for the provision of recreational services in urban parks – a new and straightforward method for assessment. *AMBIO* 43(4), 480–491.

Weber N, Haase D, Franck U A (2014): Assessing traffic-induced noise and air pollution in urban structures using the concept of landscape metrics. *Landscape and Urban Planning* 125, 105–116.

INTERLUDE

16 A Multi-Actor Perspective on Urban Sustainability Transitions

Flor Avelino and Julia Wittmayer

Introduction

Transitions as long-term processes of change are understood as involving a broad range of heterogeneous actors (Markard et al. 2012, Farla et al. 2012, Grin et al. 2010) and as involving shifts in power (Rotmans and Loorbach 2010, Avelino 2011). Given this inherent 'multi-actor' nature of transitions, it is important to understand the specifics of multi-actor power relations in order to study transitions (Avelino and Wittmayer 2016).

One could argue that an understanding of multi-actor power relations is particularly relevant for the urban context and for experimentation. The multi-actor nature of the latter is emphasized in literature (cf. Castán Broto and Bulkeley 2013, van den Bosch 2010). It can take the form of partnerships (Castán Broto and Bulkeley 2013, Frantzeskaki et al. 2014, Wittmayer et al. 2015) but can also be a site of contestation, struggle and conflict (Hodson and Marvin 2010, Wittmayer et al. 2014). This puts power relations under the magnifying glass and makes an understanding of current or envisaged power relations and their shifts an important analytical angle. We see increasing attention to cities as places for experimentation (this volume, Sengers et al. 2014, Castán Broto and Bulkeley 2013). In cities understood as loci of transitions, politics and power are not something 'out there'. They manifest in different ways: for example, in the personal sphere, in the relation between neighbours or with policymakers. Moreover, at an institutional level, the city government has the potential to be far less anonymous and distant than other governance levels – possibly adding to a sense of identity and community, but also making the government and its policies the target of possible conflicts of interest and lobbying activities of different local actors. Cities are nested in and linked with other governance levels and networks at regional, national or international scales (Nevens et al. 2013). Cities are autonomous to take up specific topics and combine their forces as initiatives, as demonstrated by the examples of Local Agenda 21 movement (ICLEI 2012) or the Covenant of Mayors[1]. As such, they actively construct relevant scales and interact with these in ways that support them in achieving their goals (cf. Coenen et al. 2012). Combining this with multi-domain interactions, the fact that cities are loci where developments in different domains (e.g., energy, mobility, healthcare, welfare) quite literally 'take place' (Nevens et al. 2013) makes cities interesting places for experimentation.

Thus, experimenting cities take full advantage of socially embedded relations, geographical proximity as well as multi-scalar and multi-domain interactions to develop alternative ideas, practices and social relations which address current unsustainabilities (cf. Boschma 2005, Wittmayer and Loorbach forthcoming). Our focus in this Interlude is on the socio-political dimensions of experimenting cities: "*Accomplishing urban low carbon transitions becomes a matter not only of policy, or of 'niche' experimentation, but of the reconfiguration of socio-technical networks – a process that is at once highly political and open to contestation and disruption*" (Bulkeley et al. 2011:30). It is this socio-political dimension that we put centre-stage in this interlude chapter by applying a Multi-Actor Perspective to discuss the previous chapters on "experimentation and urban sustainability transitions" in terms of multi-actor roles and relations. By doing so, this interlude aims to highlight how the previous chapters demonstrate transitions as being multi-actor processes.

Introducing the Multi-Actor Perspective

The Multi-Actor Perspective (MLP) is based on the 'Welfare Mix' scheme by Evers and Laville (2004:1740) and Pestoff (1992:2537) (see Figure 16.1). This scheme distinguishes between actor categories along three axes, namely (1) informal–formal, (2) for profit–non-profit and (3) public–private. The state is characterized as non-profit, formal and public; the market as also formal, but private and for-profit; and the community as private, informal and non-profit. Finally, the Third Sector is conceptualised as an intermediary sector in between the three others. It includes the 'non-profit sector' that is formalized in private, but also many intermediary organisations that cross and/or merge the boundaries between profit and non-profit, private and public, formal and informal (e.g., 'not-for-profit' social enterprises, universities, or cooperatives).

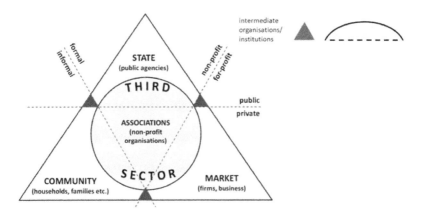

Figure 16.1 Welfare Mix scheme. (Avelino and Wittmayer 2015, adapted from Evers and Laville 2004, Pestoff 1992:25.)

This Welfare Mix scheme provides a richer alternative for the common distinction between 'market', 'state' and 'civil society', which is often used in transition studies (cf. Durrant 2014), sometimes also including science as a separate category (cf. Grin et al. 2011, Farla et al. 2012, Pesch 2014). We argue that the broad category of 'civil society' is problematic in the sense that it includes both formal entities such as trade unions or informal entities such as families, which all get generalised for civil society as a whole. This leads to an underestimation or overestimation of the relative power of these sectors vis-à-vis state and market. What makes the Welfare Mix apt as a basis for an MLP on transitions is that it acknowledges an important differentiation between the formalised 'Third Sector' and the informal 'community'. Such a differentiation allows for specifying the kind of power of the Third Sector (towards state and market) as a significantly different one than that of informal community. As such, it allows for a more adequate estimation of the relative power of these sectors vis-à-vis state and market.

We have taken the Welfare Mix model and developed it further into the MLP as a heuristic for analysing and discussing multi-actor dynamics in transitions (Avelino and Wittmayer 2015). What we have added to the Welfare Mix scheme is a specification of different levels of aggregation: (1) sectors, (2) organisational roles and (3) individual roles. At the level of sectors, the distinction is based on the general characteristics and 'logic' of a sector (i.e., formal vs. informal, for-profit vs. non-profit, public vs. private), as laid out in the Welfare Mix scheme (Figure 16.1). While sectors themselves can be viewed as 'actors', they can also be seen as specific 'institutional contexts' or 'discursive fields' in which collective/organisational or individual actors (see Figures 16.2 and 16.3) operate and with which they interact. Moreover, sectors can also be viewed as sites of struggle and/or cooperation between different actors (e.g., the state as interaction among politicians, voters and different departments, the market as interaction between consumers and producers).

In each sector, individual actors tend to be constructed in a different manner following the specific sector logic, ranging from 'resident' or 'neighbour' to 'citizen' or 'consumer'. One single individual is constructed differently in different sector logics; for example, a policymaker is also a neighbour, consumer and possible a volunteer in his free time – this is why we speak of individual *roles* (see Figure 16.2). In this understanding, individual actors are performing different social roles (Turner 1990). They are typically expected to perform a set of agreed-upon activities, rights and responsibilities that are part of a particular sector logic and as such reproduce that logic. While this implies a certain level of structurization, a focus on change and shifting power relations acknowledges that both the boundaries between the sectors as well as the construction of roles are continuously contested (see Avelino and Wittmayer 2015).

Besides individual actors roles, there are also organizational actors (roles) such as organizations, social entities, groups or networks, that may also operate in different sector logics simultaneously: for example, a cooperative can combine the logic of the market, the Third Sector and the community within its organizational fabric (see Figure 16.3).

Figure 16.2 Multi-Actor Perspective: individual roles. (Source: Avelino and Wittmayer 2015.)

Figure 16.3 Multi-Actor Perspective: organisational roles. (Source: Avelino and Wittmayer 2015.)

The Case-Studies from a Multi-Actor Perspective

Applying this Multi-Actor Perspective to analyse the case-studies in the previous chapters enables us to unravel the actor dynamics and power relations in the respective case-studies. While the chapters display a rich diversity of urban contexts and very different challenges, one of the things they have in common is that they demonstrate sustainability transition dynamics as multi-actor processes. We used the MLP to review the chapters, and then to summarise and specify the case-studies in terms of multi-actor processes. Therein we focused on answering the following three questions: (1) which actors are involved in the case-descriptions, (2) how can these actors be positioned in the different sectors/ institutional contexts, and (3) what are the interactions and (power) relations between those actors?

Chapter 10 by Timothy Moss (see figure 16.4), "The rise, fall and re-emergence of waste-to-energy technologies in Berlin's infrastructure history", addresses waste-to-energy technologies applied in Berlin, focusing on the interwar period (1920–1939). The chapter analyses the emergence, disappearance, persistence and re-emergence of these technologies in terms of "a combination of political pressures, economic incentives, market opportunities and environmental sensitivities". In terms of actor dynamics, the chapter analyses the tendency of professional actors – engineers, planners and companies – to adapt to the political ideology of incumbent political regimes. Certain waste-to-energy technologies that were pushed during the Nazi regime were thereafter disassociated from by professionals, not primarily for technological arguments, but rather due to the negative political associations. At a more epistemological level, Moss also comments on the selective construction of the past, present and future by engineers and researchers: the waste-to-energy technologies applied in Berlin during the interwar period have been historically neglected or even "written out of history". As such, the case-study demonstrates (1) how agency manifested in (individual) actor roles can be both promoting as well as hindering and overlooking regarding socio-technical innovation, and (2) the deeply and inextricably political nature of (the history of) urban infrastructure.

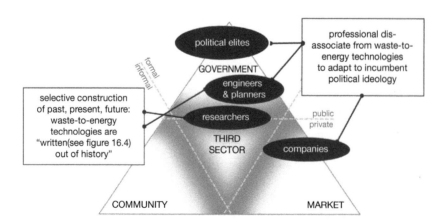

Figure 16.4 Multi-actor characterization of Chapter 10: "The rise, fall and re-emergence of waste-to-energy technologies in Berlin's infrastructure history".

Chapter 11 by Anne Maassen (see figure 16.5) addresses 'Climate Aid' in the Cities of the East. These cities have specific characteristics, as a result of a shared legacy of centrally planned Soviet-era infrastructure in heat, energy, water and transport. In such a context, the author argues that "state-driven technological niching" or "grassroots innovation" (e.g., Seyfang and Smith 2007, Aiken 2012) are less appropriate or likely. Instead, Climate Aid has a particular important role to play, as the "spatial-temporal unit of the [Climate Aid] 'project' becomes salient as a means of – at least temporarily – aligning otherwise potentially misaligned actors". A challenge, however, lies in the subsequent high dependence of recipient governments on the Climate Aid system (i.e., donors and development agencies), which poses a risk for the resilience and long-term continuity of local climate programs.

Chapter 12 by Philipp Späth and Michael Ornetzeder (see figure 16.6) discusses urban niches for car-free life and the regime of automobility in urban planning, through two case-studies in Vienna and in Freiburg respectively. These cases demonstrate how "niches" were able to change the rules and place persistent pressure on "regimes". In more specific actor terms, resident groups were able to 'amend' and 'tweak' parking and building regulations rules to enable car-free/low-car pilot areas by smartly cooperating and/or lobbying with architects, developers, national governments and municipalities. This ability was for a great part driven by the strong interests and political engagement of future residents and their strong participation and involvement in the planning process. The authors emphasize the importance of a combination of community building, personal identification and material conditions to enable such community-led infrastructure change.

Chapter 13 by Saska Petrova (see figure 16.7) addresses energy poverty among transient urban populations and coin the concept of a "socio-technical precariat". Transient urban populations (e.g., singles, youngsters, unemployed, flat-sharers) tend to be excluded in energy poverty discussions,

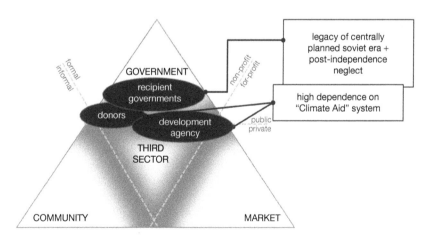

Figure 16.5 Multi-actor characterization of Chapter 11: Characterization of Climate Aid in the 'Cities of the East'.

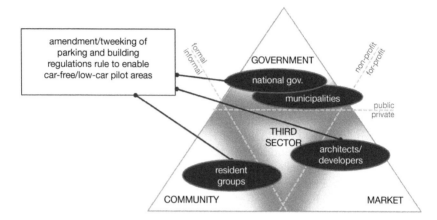

Figure 16.6 Multi-actor characterization of Chapter 12: Car-free initiatives in
         Vienna and Freiburg.

because the "normativities of the nuclear family form" have been "embedded in urban planning, housing and energy efficiency policies". The authors
argue that policymakers and researchers need to be critically aware of how
they construct population groups along traditional lines, and that they need
to reconsider their focus on 'household types' and 'demographic groups' (in
terms of, e.g., age or health). Rather, they propose "a redefinition of energy
poverty so as to take into account the diversity of energy needs and socially
related practices".

Chapter 14 by Arnim Wiek, Braden Kay and Nigel Forrest (see figure 16.8)
describes and evaluates the promises of the Phoenix Urban Sustainability
Transition Lab (USTL) at Arizona State University in six distinct transition
projects. Based on this, the authors draw lessons and recommendations for the
design of USTLs in other places. The Sustainability Transition and Intervention
Research Lab, a research group at the School of Sustainability of Arizona State
University, is the most prominent actor and driver of the USTL and the associated experiments and projects. Together with others (stakeholders or partners)
from "government, administration, non-profit organizations and the civil society" (Wiek et al. this volume), it co-leads the projects. Zooming in on one of
the projects, the revitalization of urban spaces in the Gateway district, the overwhelming majority of actors seems framed from a governmental/ Third Sector
logic. This is especially interesting, and is a challenge to multi-actor dynamics,
because this partnership acts in the context of a 'disenfranchised community',
while no community actors are mentioned in the article (which still might mean
that they played a role). In terms of actor dynamics, these transition projects led
to the creation of a strong overall partner network for (the work of) the USTL
Phoenix. As educational projects, the USTLs also contribute to the problem-
solving capacities of their graduates, which continue to be part of the USTL
network in their professional lives.

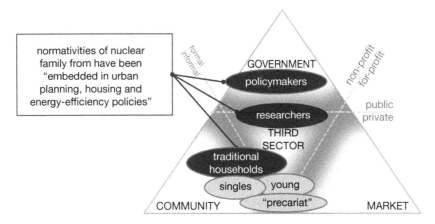

Figure 16.7 Multi-Actor Perspective characterization of Chapter 13: "Multiple transitions: Energy precariousness and 'transient' urban tenants".

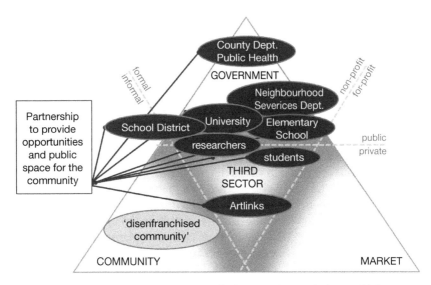

Figure 16.8 Multi-actor characterization of Chapter 14: Worth the trouble? Transition project for the revitalization of urban spaces of the Gateway district, Phoenix.

In Chapter 15, Dagmar Haase, Annegret Haase and Dieter Rink (see figure 16.9) analyse the socio-ecological transformations undergone by the city of Leipzig, Germany, starting with reunification in 1989. Different development phases are distinguished, which can all be related to different actor constellations. The first developments leading to reunification were driven by the residents of Leipzig and environmental groups and initiatives, whereas in

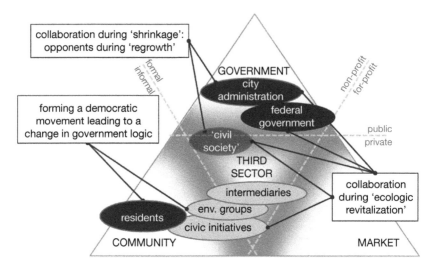

Figure 16.9 Multi-Actor Perspective on the socio-ecological transformation of
Leipzig – Chapter 15.

the following ecologic revitalization, it was a collaboration between the new
federal government and what the authors refer to as 'civil society' actors,
including civic initiatives and intermediary actors. During both phases, that
is, a period of shrinkage of the city as well as its re-growth, the municipal
government was initiating activities and taking responsibility. While this happened in close collaboration with 'civil society' and 'stakeholder groups' during the shrinkage phase, the same actors actually opposed the gentrification
of the last years as part of the re-growth or re-urbanization of the city. It was
during the shrinkage phase in which different actors of the urban society were
collaborating that Leipzig was described as a "laboratory of urban landscape
planning" (Haase et al. this volume) resulting in a diversity of different side by
side land uses (e.g., parks, interim-use sites, urban gardens). This chapter is an
example where the use of the catchphrase 'civil society' disguises who actually
takes action, how formalized these actors are and what kind of power they use.

Discussion and Conclusion

When we compare the multi-actor perspectives in the different chapters and
case-studies, there are a few common threads. First, each case-studies can be
read as a narrative about urban (un)sustainability *as a result of power relations, negotiations and dependencies between different actors*, among different
urban actors, but also among urban, national and international actors. Even
if the case-study is originally not focused on multi-actor power dynamics,
the Multi-Actor Perspective helps to specify the multi-actor power dynamics underlying the case-study. For instance, Chapter 11 on the rise, fall and

re-emergence of waste-to-energy technologies in Berlin during the interwar period can be summarized from an MLP in terms of a power narrative on how engineers disassociated from particular technologies, not for any technical reasons, but primarily to adapt to the dominant ideology of political elites and – in relation to that – how selectively the past, present and future of technology is constructed as the waste-to-energy technologies applied in Berlin during the interwar period have been historically neglected or even "written out of history" by both engineers and researchers.

A second cross-case commonality is that many of the case-studies demonstrate a strong focus on the public sector. This is of course not surprising, as municipalities play an important role in urban experimentation (Castán Broto and Bulkeley 2013). Nevertheless, it does raise the question if and to what extent the dominance of the public sector might be (1) a researcher bias in the selection of case studies and (2) a selective (mis)representation of urban multi-actor dynamics. Could it be that recent and ongoing urban transition processes are much more dominated by market actors, 'social entrepreneurs' and citizens than is currently acknowledged? Strictly speaking, the MLP does not predefine which type of sectors or actors are situated in 'niches' or 'regimes'. However, there is a tendency in empirical analyses and in management applications to equate the regime with 'government and big business', while associating niches with 'small entrepreneurs and/or civil society' (Avelino and Wittmayer 2015). This is partly a result of the inherent conceptual premise in the MLP that regimes have 'more power' than niches (Avelino 2011). The MLP helps to specify and question such underlying assumptions, and to analyse the complex diversity of the (ascribed/ constructed) roles of different sectors and actors in multi-level transition dynamics. An important element for doing so is the unpacking of 'civil society'. In much of the transitions literature so far, 'civil society' is mostly characterized in terms of 'grassroots innovation' and/or 'niche-activities'. The MLP helps us to see civil society beyond such niche-focus, as it also acknowledges the Third Sector as "a different articulation of the social into economic life by often powerful socioeconomic organizations and not only the petty under-scaled or undercapitalised local initiatives of moaning communities" (Moulaert and Ailenei 2005:2043–2044). While explicitly acknowledging the significant contribution of grassroots community activism, it is also important to recognize that the Third Sector encompasses more than that, including – in fact – rather powerful regime structures such as labour unions, large cooperatives and religious networks. This is nicely illustrated by Chapter 12 on the high dependence of some governments on international climate aid systems, in which the Third Sector (i.e., development agencies) plays a pivotal and powerful role.

As an insight for future research, the Multi-Actor Perspective serves to specify urban sustainability transitions as not only socio-technical but also socio-political processes. There is an increasing attention to the role politics and power relations play in urban transitions, also within this book.

However, the *object* of transition still often has a socio-technical focus: that which is subject to change and sustainability consists of socio-*technical* structures and practices. The 'socio-political' is often seen as one *dimension* of socio-technical transition, rather than as the object of transition itself. If we want to take the socio-political perspective on transitions further than a dimension of socio-technical change, the question becomes, what is the object of a *socio-political* transition? What changes in an urban *socio-political* transition? We argue that the main object of change therein consists of actor relations and actor roles.

As such, it is not simply a matter of asking what the roles of different actors and related actor constellations in urban sustainability transitions are. Rather, urban sustainability transitions *in themselves* consist of changing actor roles and relations, and of shifting boundaries among sectors. Thus, relevant questions for future research are, how are the boundaries and relations between sectors shifting in the urban domain (between public and private, for-profit and non-profit, formal and informal)? Which (new) actor roles are (re-)emerging in the urban context? For instance, Chapter 13 on car-free initiatives in Vienna and Freiburg, as well as Chapter 16 on socio-ecological transformations, demonstrate a strong role for resident groups and community-based initiatives. Not only do such dynamics imply new relations among the community, the market and the government, these also lead to new roles within each of these sectors – for example, 'social entrepreneurs' or 'prosumers' – in which the roles of residents, consumers and activists are combined with those of entrepreneurs and producers. This blurs the very distinction between for-profit and non-profit, market and community, and raises questions on the (new) roles of the public sector and intermediary Third Sector organizations in dealing with these new 'in-between' roles in both community and market logics.

Note

1   See the website: http://www.covenantofmayors.eu (accessed 19 December 2014).

References

Avelino, F. (2011) *Power in Transition: Empowering Discourses on Sustainability Transitions*. PhD-Thesis. Erasmus University Rotterdam.

Avelino, F. and Wittmayer, J.M. (2016) "Shifting Power Relations in Sustainability Transitions: A Multi-actor Perspective", *Journal of Environmental Policy and Planning*, 18(5), 628-649

Avelino, F., Wittmayer, J.M., Pel, B., Weaver, P., Dumitru, A., Haxeltine, A., Kemp, R., Jørgensen, M.S., Bauler, T., Ruijsink, S. and O'Riordan, T. (submitted) Transformative social innovation and (dis)empowerment: Towards a heuristic, submitted to *Technological Forecasting and Social Change*.

Boschma, R.A. (2005) Proximity and innovation: A critical assessment. *Regional Studies* 39(1): 61–74.

Bulkeley, H., Castán Broto, V., Hodson, M. and Marvin S. (eds.) (2011) *Cities and Low Carbon Transitions*. London: Hoboken, Routledge.

Castán Broto, V. and Bulkeley, H. (2013) A survey of urban climate change experiments in 100 cities. *Global Environmental Change* 23: 92–102.

Coenen, L., Benneworth, P. and Truffer, B. (2012) Toward a spatial perspective on sustainability transitions. *Research Policy* 41: 968–979.

Durrant, R.A. (2014) Civil society roles in transition: Towards sustainable food? PhD Thesis, University of Sussex, UK.

Evers, A., and Laville, J. L. (eds.) (2004) The third sector in Europe. Cheltenham, Cheltenham UK: Edward Elgar Publishing.

Farla, J., Markard, J., Raven, R., and Coenen, L. (2012) Sustainability transitions in the making: A closer look at actors, strategies and resources, *Technological Forecasting and Social Change* 79(6): 991–998.

Frantzeskaki, N., Wittmayer, J. and Loorbach. D. (2014) The role of partnerships in 'realizing' urban sustainability in Rotterdam's City Ports Area, the Netherlands. *Journal of Cleaner Production* 65: 406–417.

Grin, J., Rotmans, J., & Schot, J. (2011). On patterns and agency in transition dynamics: Some key insights from the KSI programme. Environmental Innovation and Societal Transitions, 1(1), 76–81.

Grin, J., Rotmans, J., Schot, J., icw. Loorbach, D., and Geels, F.W. (2010) *Transitions to Sustainable Development: New Directions in the Study of Long Term Transformative Change*. New York, Routledge.

Hodson, M. and Marvin, S. (2010) Can cities shape socio-technical transitions and how would we know if they were? *Research Policy* 39: 477–485.

ICLEI (2012) Local Sustainability 2012: Taking Stock and Moving Forward. Global Review, ICLEI Global Report. Freiburg: ICLEI.

Markard, J., Raven, R. and Truffer, B. (2012). Sustainability transitions: An emerging field of research and its prospects. *Research Policy* 41(6): 955–967.

Moulaert, F. and Ailenei, O. (2005) Social economy, third sector and solidarity relations: A conceptual synthesis from history to present, *Urban Studies* 42(11): 2037–2053.

Nevens, F., Frantzeskaki, N., Loorbach, D., and Gorissen, L. (2013) Urban transition labs: co-creating transformative action for sustainable cities. *Journal of Cleaner Production* 50: 111–122.

Pesch, U. (2014) Sustainable development and institutional boundaries. *Journal of Integrative Environmental Sciences* 11(1): 39–54.

Pestoff, V. (1992) Third sector and co-operative services – an alternative to privatization. *Journal of Consumer Policy* 15: 21–45.

Rotmans, J. and Loorbach, D. (2010), Towards a better understanding of transitions and their governance: a systemic and reflexive approach, part II in: Grin, J., Rotmans, J. and Schot, J. (eds.) *Transitions to Sustainable Development: New Directions in the Study of Long Term Transformative Change*. New York, Routledge.

Turner, R.H. (1990) Role change. *Annual Review of Sociology* 16: 87–110.

Sengers, F. Wieczorek, A.J., Raven, R. (2016) Experimenting for sustainability transitions: A systematic literature review. Technological Forecasting & Social Change. Online first. http://dx.doi.org/10.1016/j.techfore.2016.08.031

Seyfang, G. and Smith, A. (2007) 'Grassroots Innovations for Sustainable Development: towards a new research and policy agenda' in Environmental Politics Vol 16(4) pp. 584-603

van den Bosch, S. (2010) Transition Experiments: Exploring Societal Changes Towards Sustainability. PhD thesis. Erasmus University, Rotterdam.

Wittmayer, J.M. and Loorbach, D. (forthcoming) Governing transitions in cities: Focusing alternative ideas, practices and social relations through transition management. In Loorbach, D., Wittmayer, J.M., Shiroyama, H., Fujino, J. and Mizuguchi, S. (eds.) *Governance of Urban Sustainability Transitions: European and Asian Experiences*. Springer, Tokyo.

Wittmayer, J.M., Schäpke, N., van Steenbergen, F. and Omann, I. (2014) Making sense of sustainability transitions locally: How action research contributes to addressing societal challenges. *Critical Policy Studies.* 8 (4): 465–485.

Wittmayer, J.M., Rok, A., Roorda, C. and van Steenbergen, F. (2015) Governing sustainability: a dialogue between Local Agenda 21 and transition management. *Local Environment: The International Journal of Justice and Sustainability.* http://dx.doi.org/10.1080/13549839.2015.1050658

Part III

Politics of Urban Space and of Urban Sustainability Transitions

17 Cities as Arenas of Low-Carbon Transitions

Friction Zones in the Negotiation of Low-Carbon Futures

Harald Rohracher and Philipp Späth

Introduction

The idea of a 'low-carbon transition' as a fundamental change in our way of producing and consuming is increasingly taking hold in policy circles and the wider public. Conceptually, such questions of long-term, transformative change towards greater sustainability have been taken up in diverse research communities, such as industrial ecology, ecological economics or science, technology and innovation studies. The study of 'sustainability transitions' – that is, the understanding and shaping of radical, goal-oriented and long-term change processes towards more sustainable systems of energy, mobility, food or housing – is attracting a growing group of researchers from a wide range of disciplines (Markard et al., 2012).

Although the growth of this research field has led to conceptual diversity and a huge variety of empirical case studies, by far the most analyses of low-carbon transitions have either focused on particular governance levels (e.g., national energy policy), particular sectors (e.g., the electricity system) or particular actor perspectives (e.g., supply- *or* demand-side perspectives) (see, e.g., the structure of the earlier books of the series 'Routledge Studies in Sustainability Transitions'; Geels et al., 2012; Grin et al., 2010; Spaargaren et al., 2012; Verbong and Loorbach, 2012). However, attempts to manage the transition of such partial systems (such as the national electricity system) tend to underestimate the complexity and interrelatedness of these change processes and draw too optimistic a picture of the capacity to induce and shape radical change through policy interventions. Also at a conceptual level, critical discussions are questioning the appropriateness of capturing the dynamics of change through a multilevel perspective of interactions between socio-technical niches, regimes and landscapes – a perspective which informs the majority of transition studies. In this chapter, we will discuss how shifting the focus from rather homogeneous socio-technical systems to cities as heterogeneous arenas for sustainability transitions may help us address some of these problems. Not only is such an arena located at the intersection of various types of socio-technical regimes and emerging niches, but also cities are 'hotspots' for socio-economic and socio-political changes. Such a perspective thus rather emphasizes the inherent partiality of transition approaches, the importance of bottom-up or 'inside-out' (Smith and Stirling, 2007) processes of sense-making about transitions, and their dependence on other social and political dynamics.

Politically, cities have long been important sites for actions to combat climate change or create more sustainable alternatives in energy, transport or the built environment – and they are increasingly put centre stage along with an (at least perceived) incapacity of national governments to take decisive measures for change (see, e.g., Betsill and Bulkeley, 2004; Hakelberg, 2014; Taylor, 2012 on the role of green city networks). However, it is not only that municipalities are increasingly recognised as important actors and that cities are studied increasingly as particular arenas for new governance configurations, which is of interest to us. We also consider the conceptual implications of giving cities more space in our thinking about transformative change towards sustainability. Bringing together transition concepts and urban studies puts questions of how socio-technical configurations such as niches and regimes are embedded in broader socio-political dynamics and how they are connected with each other to the foreground. Cities are arenas where the above-mentioned levels (e.g., urban–global), functional subsystems (e.g., transport–energy) and actor constituencies (e.g., suppliers–users) meet and intersect. Cities are not only sites of niche–regime–landscape interactions – for example, regarding systems of mobility – but they are simultaneously following other logics of action, whether as tourist cities, sites of economic production and competition for national and multinational companies, sites of knowledge and cultural production or simply the recreation and wellbeing of its inhabitants (see Rohracher and Späth, 2014). Anchoring interrelations of emerging niches (such as new forms of renewable energy generation), regimes (the fossil-fuel-based centralised energy system) and landscapes (deeply entrenched values and institutions, such as neo-liberal governance ideals) in localised contexts of cities directs our view to the embedding of, for example, energy generation and use in wider social practices beyond the energy system, and to potential clashes of energy system change with other logics and fields of action.

In this chapter, we will apply such a bottom-up perspective of 'transitions in the making' and 'cities as contested arenas' for such processes of change to two exemplary case studies in Graz, Austria, and Freiburg, Germany. The Graz case is about the conflicts and reframings taking place in an attempt to construct new hydropower stations (seen as a move to extend the basis of urban renewable electricity generation or as a destruction of a particular habitat), while the Freiburg case is about heat supply options for a low-energy-building district (seen as an opportunity to extend the sustainable district heating system or as a disincentive for the construction of energy-efficient passive houses). Both cases share the characteristic that these change processes towards sustainability also create new zones of friction, pitch different actor worlds against each other and reframe visions of more sustainable cities. To some extent, these visions become an emergent property of situated socio-technical constellations and actor configurations. Moreover, different levels of governance are mobilised in this process, just as new social groups and interests are drawn into the arena. Due to their social and spatial density, we believe that cities are particular microcosms for such intersections of different life-worlds and socio-technical systems, which makes them a privileged place to study the dynamics of transition processes and their embedding in wider socio-political contexts.

In the next section, we will give a short introduction to conceptual approaches to understand socio-technical transitions and recent conceptual developments emphasising the role of space, and the emergent and conflictual character of transitions in the making, which are not given appropriate conceptual weight in a multilevel perspective on transitions. We will then apply these perspectives to our two cases in Graz and Freiburg, and will finally draw some conclusions on how the study of such examples may help us further develop transition concepts.

Urban Transitions in the Making

What makes urban sustainability transitions special? Let us first take stock of current transition studies. Sustainability transitions are long-term, systemic innovation processes towards more sustainable socio-technical configurations of, for example, energy or transport systems. The dominant approach to understanding such transformations is the multilevel perspective, which distinguishes different levels of structuration (see, e.g., Geels, 2005b; Rip and Kemp, 1998): the central level and focus of interest are socio-technical regimes, stable structures of e.g. energy production and consumption where technologies, institutional arrangements (e.g., regulation, norms), social practices and actor constellations (user-producer relations and interactions, intermediary organisations, public authorities etc.) mutually reinforce each other. A regime is usually defined by the fulfilment of a societal function, such as transport, communication or housing, and thus puts more emphasis on aspects of use and functionality than economics of innovation approaches (Geels, 2004). By contrast, niches are much less structured than the emerging socio-technical configurations such as new energy technologies and the new competences, networks of actors, use practices or institutions that take shape around them. Niches can thus be seen as test beds for new innovations, which create new variety and potentially change existing dominant regime structures – sometimes in a fundamental way. Recent work has focused on niche-internal processes such as the formation of social networks, the shaping of expectations and learning processes (Schot and Geels, 2008; Verbong et al., 2010), or on different strategies of shielding and empowering in niche-growth processes (Smith and Raven, 2012). The third level concerns socio-technical landscapes, as the broader structures regimes are embedded in, for example, cultural norms, values and other slowly changing structures beyond the reach of regime actors (Geels, 2005b; Rip and Kemp, 1998). The creation of novel technologies and radical change is thus brought about not only by bottom-up processes, but also by the interactions of multiple levels: niche innovations building up momentum, destabilised regimes creating windows of opportunity for niche innovations, and changes at the macro-level of socio-technical landscapes creating pressure on the regime (Schot and Geels, 2008). Transition management is therefore about governance strategies to shape and support regime transitions towards long-term aims such as sustainability, and is well aware of the limitations inherent to steering such processes or strictly defining transition goals in advance (see, e.g., Loorbach, 2007). Emphasis is put on interactive processes of envisioning, the creation of transition arenas and transition projects as well as constant processes of monitoring and goal-oriented adaptation.

As various studies have shown, this conceptual framework works very well in a hindsight perspective to analyse, for example, historic transitions in modes of transport or types of energy carriers (see, e.g., Geels, 2002; Geels, 2005a). Moreover, typical transition studies focus on infrastructure systems (e.g., the electricity system) at a national level and analyse, for example, already visible structural changes, emerging niches or the formation of new discourses and visions (see, e.g., Kern et al., 2014; Verhees et al., 2013). Transition management projects are more normative in their orientation and aim at vision-building, creating platforms for interaction between a broad range of stakeholders or the mapping and collective creation of possible pathways of change (see Loorbach, 2007).

Dealing with transitions in an urban context – for example, efforts in cities to make the local energy system more sustainable – raises a number of questions and problems that the multilevel transition framework is struggling with. Analysing low-carbon transition attempts in the eco-cities of Freiburg and Graz, we have made several observations which call for a modification or at least diversification of our understanding of sustainability transitions (Rohracher and Späth, 2014):

- One issue which has already gained increasing prominence among transition scholars, is the need to draw more attention to the role of space in transition processes (see, e.g., Coenen et al., 2012; Hodson and Marvin, 2009; Raven et al., 2012). Analysing urban change processes shows how malleable and heterogeneous regimes are. Different spatial and socio-economic contexts in cities create a broad range of regime variations and allow for 'showcases' or 'proofs of principle' in cities, demonstrating the viability of (limited) regime transformations (Späth and Rohracher, 2012). Spatial aspects are also of importance for the interplay of discourses and institutions of different spatial reach and the 'scaling' of infrastructural decisions across urban, regional, national and transnational governance levels (Späth and Rohracher, 2014). Cities and regions can thus be an important arena of struggles about the development and change of socio-technical regimes and partial implementation of systemic alternatives.

- A second key point is the understanding that cities are arenas cross-cutting through niche and regime structures. They are certainly also places where niche experiments are carried out, and they are part of broader socio-technical regimes, but cities are also places where new networks and alliances across niche and regime structures are formed, partly through the influence of spatial proximity. An example is municipal utilities becoming drivers of change towards sustainability while being part of the incumbent actor structure of the dominant energy regime. Such examples show how hard it is to define boundaries between niches and regimes and how such boundaries can be shifted by municipal governance efforts.
- A third crucial point is the importance of urban socio-political dynamics reaching beyond the logics of regimes and niches. Changes in the energy or transport system are often strongly shaped by such discourses and dynamics – e.g. of cities positioning themselves in global economic competition, dealing with social problems or trying to attract a young and educated population – and not by urban energy plans, transition targets or the aim to learn about new technologies. This observation points to the conceptual weakness of 'socio-technical landscapes' as an embedding of regimes – socio-political dynamics beyond the control of regime actors are much more actively involved in shaping the regime change than through 'external pressures', and call for a much more differentiated understanding of how regime structures are interrelated with their societal (e.g., urban) environment.

Ongoing urban transition processes are therefore much more messy and partial than a focus on national infrastructure change and sustainability visions would suggest. At the same time, they are more integrated in socio-political dynamics and conflicts beyond the logic of niche development and regime transformation. As pointed out above, the hierarchically structured analytical levels of niche–regime–landscape are of limited help in understanding these ongoing processes of change.

Recent actor-network-theory-inspired approaches, such as 'navigational governance' (Jørgensen, 2012), 'transition mediators' (Jensen et al., 2015) or 'urban green assemblages' (Blok, 2013), hence adopt a more conflict-oriented and actor-based view and conceive of transition strategies not so much as the (participatory) development of transition pathways, but rather take a bottom-up-oriented perspective organized around different social arenas in which problems of change are interpreted and framed differently and conflicting perspectives hence come to the fore. While such an approach also provides only partial perspectives, this (unavoidable) partiality is made an explicit starting point for the conception of change strategies towards sustainability.

As Jørgenson (2012) puts it, "the parallel existence of several regimes and niches opens for multiple directions of change, as do different visions and interests of actors assigned to socio-technical configurations. It is the very understanding of the problems and responses that are contested, which leads to multiple interpretations of how regimes and actions can be described" (p. 999). Similarly, the concept of 'urban assemblages' introduces an actor-network view on "how urban green knowledge is produced, translated and contested across specific urban sites, scales and relations" (Blok, 2013, p. 6). As Farías and Bender (2010, p. 2) put it, cities are being assembled at concrete sites of urban practice, as a "multiplicity of processes of becoming, affixing socio-technical networks, hybrid collectives and alternative topologies." Jensen et al. (2015) add the concept of 'junctions' which often serve as 'transition mediators' to these bottom-up oriented concepts that conceive of urban transitions as conflictual processes of sense-making. In their example of the opening of the Copenhagen harbour to bathing, Jensen et al. (2015) understand this development not merely as a niche in which new (and potentially more sustainable) socio-technical configurations are tested and stabilised. Such projects, they claim, often rather mediate between different infrastructure systems, different logics of demand and supply, and between social groups with particular interests. They hence form intersections at which different visions and perspectives of urban change are confronted with one another and are negotiated, and may eventually lead to the emergence of new socio-technical configurations (e.g., through repercussions of harbour bathing on the wastewater infrastructure) which stretch far beyond limited socio-technical niches and cannot be fully understood within the multilevel change logics of, for example, the water infrastructure alone. The authors introduce the notion of 'junction' for such place-specific catalysts or mediators of far-reaching change processes (Jensen et al., 2015). The identification of such junctions and intersections where tensions and conflicts arise and which open up new opportunities for negotiations and change becomes a crucial issue for the assessment of transformative dynamics and identification of promising strategies to support transition processes. In our analysis, we will adopt this emphasis on conflict-oriented, knowledge-in-the-making perspectives and will analyse two cases of new junctions as 'issues of concern' that mediate change processes and around which new hybrid collectives with their respective notions of urban sustainability are created.

In these empirical cases, we build on our earlier analysis of urban low-carbon transitions (Rohracher and Späth, 2014), which emphasises the entanglement of sense-making processes about sustainable urban change in local conflicts and socio-political discourses, and directs our attention to two exemplary arenas where such negotiations and controversies about problem-definitions are taking place. The cases of urban hydropower generation in Graz and the heat supply of passive houses in Freiburg show how measures for making energy systems more sustainable also create new zones of friction and inconsistency within existing socio-technical regimes and between different sectors. Different groups of (urban) actors frame the problem of low-carbon transitions differently and embed it into different types of socio-political discourse, which in turn may also result in conflicts and 'trials of force' between different actor perspectives.

The Sustainability of Urban Hydropower in Graz

Our first case concerns the planned construction of a series of hydropower stations along the river Mur in the Austrian city of Graz, which became an arena for controversies about concepts and visions of sustainability. Graz has a population of about 250.000 and has received wide international and national attention for its attempts to become an eco-city. It has been awarded a series of prizes for its activities and achievements in energy, transport and climate change mitigation, such as the Greenpeace Climate Protection Award in 1993 or the Sustainable Energy Europe Award in 2008. Though transformation activities towards a more sustainable city have lost momentum during the past decade (for more details, see Rohracher and Späth, 2014), environmental issues have remained high on the agenda, particularly with the participation of the Green Party in the municipal government. However, the ambition to revive old plans to build hydropower stations along the river Mur, which cuts through the centre of Graz, has become a stumbling block for Green and Conservative coalition partners and has been one of the reasons for the break-up of the coalition.

Hydroelectric power stations have a long and conflict-ridden history in Austria – from post-war projects as key elements of a modernisation strategy for the country to social movements to block the building of new dams in the 1980s and '90s, which in the case of a planned and prevented hydropower dam near Vienna gave birth to the Green Party in Austria. Close to 2.600 hydropower plants in Austria provide a total capacity of 12.920 megawatts, adding up to about 60% of Austrian electricity generation (Klinglmair and Bliem, 2012). Civil-society resistance to most new hydropower projects since the last decades of the 20th century more or less stalled the further development of large-scale hydropower in Austria, mostly based on arguments of nature conservation.

Nevertheless, the prominence of discourses around climate change and the need to increase renewable energy generation appeared to create a new window of opportunity, at least for smaller or medium-scale hydropower dams. The municipal and regional (Styrian) utilities were, moreover, interested in a stronger electricity generation basis within their own company, and linked the plan for new hydropower stations to urban low-carbon strategies in Graz. The core project within the city limits of Graz was a hydropower station in Graz-Puntigam, not far downstream from the city centre, with a planned capacity of 16 MW or a capacity to supply about 20.000 households with green electricity. While the project received strong support from the mayor and his Conservative party, it was fiercely opposed by a citizens platform, 'Save the River Mur', which was supported by various environmental and nature conservation NGOs and the Green Party. The platform enjoyed wide popularity and argued for the conservation of one of the few remaining unregulated parts of the river. Its proponents also enrolled a number of scientists to provide additional arguments for the detrimental effects of the dam on the ecosystem and air quality in Graz, and on alternative means to achieve similar impacts on CO_2 emissions and energy consumption reduction. The pro side also invoked visions of urban sustainability with renewable energy generation in the city and the long-term aim to achieve energy autarky, by linking the hydropower dam to visions of the recreational and touristic value of the park areas supposed to be created along the river. The Green-Conservative party coalition finally broke up over a conflict about a public referendum on the power station (in particular about the timing and the questions to be asked). After a series of lawsuits, the project received clearance from the authorities, though construction has not started to date and the future of the urban hydropower station is still unclear.

Such a conflict is certainly not unique and analogous examples can be found in other cities. What makes the case interesting for urban low-carbon transitions is the fact that such projects create urban arenas where visions of sustainability are negotiated and reframed – in this case with the Conservative Party and incumbent utilities obviously fighting for the increase of urban renewable energy generation and the Green Party and environmental initiatives against it. These are processes of sense-making about sustainability, not at an abstract level, but mediated by concrete cases and their entanglement in other urban questions such as tourism or recreation. Even if visions of sustainable futures and pathways of change have been negotiated and mapped out in advance – for example, in the participative energy and climate protection plan in Graz – they are in practice rather created along with the conflictual implementation of new concrete socio-technical configurations within the city, such as the plan to build a new hydropower dam in Graz. The new junction between urban energy production, nature conservation and socio-political visions of urban development (e.g., inner-city recreation) gives rise to competing hybrid collectives of actors and their socio-material entanglements, interests, discourses and visions. Those 'trials of force' (Latour, 1987) create a much more emergent and 'unmanageable' dynamic of socio-technical transformation than transition theories suggest.

Heating Futures for an Energy-Efficient Housing Stock in Freiburg

The second case we are looking at is located in the sustainability 'model district' of Freiburg-Vauban in Germany and concerns conflicts between the development of district heating and the dissemination of highly energy-efficient passive houses – both key strategies in making infrastructures more sustainable. The case has been described in more detail in Späth and Rohracher (2015).

Providing heat for buildings and households through district heating infrastructures is promoted by many cities as a more sustainable option compared to decentralised space heating based on fossil fuels or electricity. As a result of this measure, local emission levels are reduced, centrally provided heat can be generated more efficiently, and it is usually co-generated with electricity. Moreover, it is easier to switch to renewable energy carriers. Once district heating networks are in place, it also makes economic sense to connect as many heat loads as possible to the system, and cities adopt various strategies – from financial incentives to zoning laws which make the connection to the district heating grid obligatory. This has also become the strategy of Freiburg municipality, one of the ecological forerunner cities in Germany, and particularly so in the Vauban ecological model district which was developed during the 1990s. Freiburg also has a long tradition of enforcing low energy standards for buildings, such as the 'Freiburg low energy building standard' enacted by the city council in 1992 and continuously developed since, always staying far ahead of national standards. Making buildings more energy efficient and transforming the building stock towards low energy consumption is another infrastructure transition, regarded as essential to achieving greenhouse gas emission reductions targets and mitigating resource depletion. One of the most advanced low-energy building standards is the passive house standard, which reduces heat demand of buildings to about 10% or less of average buildings. The low level of heat demand can easily and efficiently be supplied by heat pumps or small pellet ovens. Thus, ambitions for the Freiburg-Vauban were high in terms of achieving passive housing standards for a certain share of new buildings in the area.

The conflict that subsequently arose in Vauban concerned the requirement to connect those passive houses to the district heating system. Essentially, this was a conflict about two different logics of infrastructure change. The tariff households had to pay for their connection to the heat network which reflected the cost structure of the infrastructure: high investment costs (laying the pipes into the ground, maintenance) and small marginal costs per unit of heat consumed (due to efficient generation in semi-centralized stations). While households with higher energy consumption could recover the high connection costs through lower energy costs, passive houses were also characterised by somewhat higher upfront investments which would soon pay off through a very low heating demand. Being forced to connect to district heating thus resulted in high financial burdens with little additional gain (also in environmental terms). Despite resistance from passive house owners supported by citizens organisations, municipal utilities and parts of the municipal administration had a strong interest in maintaining a situation which obliged building owners to connect to the district heating grid (since any exemption from the obligation would have worsened its economic performance) and to maintain the citywide standard tariff (which arguably reflects the cost structure of the network adequately). Despite some sort of compromise – exemptions to connect under specific conditions (e.g., no electricity-based heating) – the position of the municipal utilities prevailed, and most passive house households were forced to connect to the district heating system. Nevertheless, with very low-energy buildings increasingly becoming standard practice, these frictions between centralised heat infrastructures and energy-efficient building stock are bound to flare up again.

Just like the hydropower dam in Graz created a junction between renewable urban energy generation, nature conservation and visions of urban development, the (participatory) development of a new city district in Vauban created unexpected conflicts between heat-supply infrastructures, improved energy efficiency of the building stock and the role of municipal public utilities. In a sense, different socio-technical configurations and visions of urban sustainability and infrastructure development 'rubbed' against each other in Freiburg, and resulted in conflicts around the distribution of infrastructure investment costs and regulatory structures governing infrastructure use by households. Households found themselves at the intersection of different logics of infrastructure change, each connected to different municipal or corporate actors and their particular interests and visions of sustainable infrastructure. And just like in Graz, plans and strategies of urban development were only one side of the coin. More than by plans and strategies (two of which came in conflict here), the actual urban transformation process was shaped by a conflict and a 'trial of force' which unexpectedly emerged in a new arena: the participatory planning process for a new district in Freiburg-Vauban. What was decisive for the ways in which actors redefined and renegotiated their visions of a sustainable energy system were the very particular and place-bound characteristics of an unanticipated conflict that had emerged in a new arena.

Conclusions

While most transition studies are interested in the transformation of large-scale infrastructure systems, we have shifted our focus to the ongoing negotiation and reframing of such transition processes in an urban context. The commonly used multilevel perspective on transitions draws attention to the logic of niche–regime–landscape interactions, to emerging technologies and their interrelation with stable meso-level regime structures and external factors exerting pressures of change on these regimes. Guided by this logic, transition management aims at a long-term, goal-oriented modulation of change processes by developing visions of sustainable futures, mapping out transition paths, creating actor alliances and establishing accompanying processes of monitoring and adaptation.

And indeed, the cities we have studied have put substantial efforts and material investments in developing such plans and action strategies for creating more sustainable energy or transport systems. However, these maps and plans were only one factor among others in shaping ongoing change processes around, for example, renewable energy generation, heating infrastructures or the energy efficiency of buildings. As it turned out, these change processes often created new junctions between initially rather separate issues, which then resulted in unanticipated conflicts, controversies and negotiation. In these conflict zones, ideas of sustainability were situatively renegotiated (usually paying mere lip service to existing plans and visions), were confronted with the affordances of existing socio-material practices and were linked to other discourses and socio-political change processes in their urban context. What we observed were not transitions 'according to plan' or other forms of coordinated transformation processes; such paths and plans were just one element of intervention in a constant process of renegotiating what sustainability could mean *in concreto*, and to what extent these normative orientations could accommodate various actors' interests, power structures and political strategies in cities. As Jørgensen (2012) rightly points out, there is no 'outside position' to such changes that would allow for coordination, map-making or privileged forms of knowing. Researchers and politicians alike are part of these ongoing collective processes of sense-making and alliance-building.

This does not mean that ideas of transition management based on an underlying multilevel perspective are irrelevant for urban sustainability transitions. The cases of Graz and Freiburg in particular have also shown how sustainability visions and projects can at least temporarily mutually reinforce each other and have impacts on other governance levels; for example, by legitimising action and strategies at the national level (Späth and Rohracher, 2012; Rohracher and Späth, 2014). However, as our cases and other studies of urban transitions demonstrate, this is only half the story. At least as important are types of change, which are much less planned, more situational and partial. As our cases of heat supply and urban electricity generation have shown, there are place-bound 'hotspots' and particular phases in these change processes, where conflicting understandings of sustainability and underlying interests come to the fore and unexpected connections between initially separate issues (district heating and building quality, renewable energy and 'urban nature') are established. In such 'hot situations', future enactments of sustainability are decided and further directions of urban sustainability transitions become stabilised. These hot situations thus potentially create opportunities for new forms of situated sustainability governance. They offer chances for municipal actors to 'govern from within', to be more sensitive to the fluidity created by such situations and to more consciously participate in collective sense-making processes about sustainable urban futures instead of siding with powerful plans of urban infrastructure development too quickly, as in the case of heating network extension of in Freiburg or urban renewable energy generation development in Graz. Studying further urban sustainability projects in more depth will improve our understanding and empirical knowledge basis for such attempts to combine a long-term perspective and situational flexibility in the governance of sustainability-oriented urban change.

References

Betsill, M.M. and Bulkeley, H. (2004), 'Transnational Networks and Global Environmental Governance: The Cities for Climate Protection Program', *International Studies Quarterly* 48(2): 471–93.

Blok, A. (2013), 'Urban Green Assemblages: An ANT View On Sustainable City Building Projects', *Science & Technology Studies* 26(1): 5–24.

Coenen, L., Benneworth, P. and Truffer, B. (2012), 'Toward a spatial perspective on sustainability transitions', *Research Policy* 41(6): 968–79.

Farias, I. and Bender, T. (2010), 'Introduction: Decentring the object of urban studies', in I. Farias and T. Bender (eds), *Urban Assemblages – How Actor Network Theory Changes Urban Studies* (London: Routledge): 1–24.

Geels, F.W. (2002), 'Technological transitions as evolutionary reconfiguration processes: a multi-level perspective and a case-study', *Research Policy* 31: 1257–74.

Geels, F.W. (2004), 'From sectoral systems of innovation to socio-technical systems: Insights about dynamics and change from sociology and institutional theory', *Research Policy* 33: 897–920.

Geels, F.W. (2005a), 'The dynamics of transitions in socio-technical systems: A multi-level analysis of the transition pathway from horse-drawn carriages to automobiles (1860–1930)', *Technology Analysis & Strategic Management* 17(4): 445–76.

Geels, F.W. (2005b), *Technological Transitions and System Innovations: A Co-Evolutionary and Socio-Technical Analysis* (Cheltenham: Edward Elgar).

Geels, F.W., Kemp, R., Dudley, G. and Lyons, G. (2012), *Automobility in Transition? A Socio-Technical Analysis of Sustainable Transport* (New York: Routledge).

Grin, J., Rotmans, J. and Schot, J.W. (2010), *Transitions to Sustainable Development: New Directions in the Study of Long Term Transformative Change* (London: Routledge).

Hakelberg, L. (2014), 'Governance by diffusion: Transnational municipal networks and the spread of local climate strategies in Europe', *Global Environmental Politics* 14(1): 107–29.

Hodson, M. and Marvin, S. (2009), 'Cities mediating technological transitions: Understanding visions, intermediation and consequences', *Technology Analysis & Strategic Management* 21(4): 515–34.

Jensen, J.S., Lauridsen, E.H., Fratini, C.F. and Hoffmann, B. (2015), 'Harbour bathing and the urban transition of water in Copenhagen: junctions, mediators, and urban navigations', *Environment and Planning A* 47(3): 554–70.

Jørgensen, U. (2012), 'Mapping and navigating transitions – the multi-level perspective compared with arenas of development', *Research Policy* 41(6): 996–1010.

Kern, F., Smith, A., Shaw, C., Raven, R. and Verhees, B. (2014), 'From laggard to leader: Explaining offshore wind developments in the UK', *Energy Policy* 69(0): 635–46.

Klinglmair, A. and Bliem, M.G. (2012), 'Evaluation of Households' Preferences for the Planned Hydropower Station in Graz-Puntigam Using a Choice Experiment', in, *12. Symposium Energieinnovation* (Graz: TU Graz).

Latour, B. (1987), *Science in Action: How to Follow Scientists and Engineers through Society* (Cambridge, MA: Harvard University Press).

Loorbach, D. (2007), *Transition Management: New Mode of Governance for Sustainable Development* (Utrecht: International Books).

Markard, J., Raven, R. and Truffer, B. (2012), 'Sustainability transitions: An emerging field of research and its prospects', *Research Policy* 41(6): 955–67.

Raven, R., Schot, J. and Berkhout, F. (2012), 'Space and scale in socio-technical transitions', *Environmental Innovation and Societal Transitions* 4(0): 63–78.

Rip, A. and Kemp, R. (1998), 'Technological change', in S. Rayner and E.L. Malone (eds), *Human Choice and Climate Change: Resources and Technology* (Columbus, Ohio: Batelle Press): 327–99.

Rohracher, H. and Späth, P. (2014), 'The interplay of urban energy policy and socio-technical transitions: The eco-cities of Graz and Freiburg in retrospect', *Urban Studies* 51(7): 1413–29.

Schot, J. and Geels, F.W. (2008), 'Strategic niche management and sustainable innovation journeys: theory, findings, research agenda, and policy', *Technology Analysis & Strategic Management* 20(5): 537–54.

Smith, A. and Raven, R. (2012), 'What is protective space? Reconsidering niches in transitions to sustainability', *Research Policy* 41(6): 1025–36.

Smith, A. and Stirling, A. (2007), 'Moving outside or inside? Objectification and reflexivity in the governance of socio-technical systems', *Journal of Environmental Policy & Planning* 9(3): 351–73.

Spaargaren, G., Oosterveer, P. and Loeber, A. (2012), *Food Practices in Transition: Changing Food Consumption, Retail and Production in the Age of Reflexive Modernity* (New York: Routledge).

Späth, P. and Rohracher, H. (2012), 'Local demonstrations for global transitions – dynamics across governance levels fostering socio-technical regime change towards sustainability', *European Planning Studies* 20(3): 461–79.

Späth, P. and Rohracher, H. (2014), 'Beyond localism: The spatial scale and scaling in energy transitions', in F.J.G. Padt, P.F.M. Opdam, N.B.P. Polman and C.J.A.M. Termeer (eds), *Scale-Sensitive Governance of the Environment* (Oxford: John Wiley & Sons, Ltd): 106–21.

Späth, P. and Rohracher, H. (2015), 'Conflicting strategies towards sustainable heating at an urban junction of heat infrastructure and building standards', *Energy Policy* 78: 273–80.

Taylor, P.J. (2012), 'Transition towns and world cities: towards green networks of cities', *Local Environment* 17(4): 495–508.

Verbong, G. and Loorbach, D. (2012), *Governing the Energy Transition: Reality, Illusion or Necessity?* (New York: Routledge).

Verbong, G.P.J., Christiaens, W., Raven, R.P.J.M. and Balkema, A. (2010), 'Strategic Niche Management in an unstable regime: Biomass gasification in India', *Environmental Science & Policy* 13(4): 272–81.

Verhees, B., Raven, R., Veraart, F., Smith, A. and Kern, F. (2013), 'The development of solar PV in The Netherlands: A case of survival in unfriendly contexts', *Renewable and Sustainable Energy Reviews* 19(0): 275–89.

18 Mediators Acting in Urban Transition Processes

Carlsberg City District and Cycle Superhighways

Andrés Felipe Valderrama Pineda,
Anne Katrine Braagaard Harders and Morten Elle

Introduction

The questions to be addressed in this chapter are, How and why are urban sustainability transitions different from other types of transitions? And how do urban transitions unfold over time and space? We will discuss these questions through two case studies: one is the Carlsberg City District urban development project in the City of Copenhagen (the municipality being a part of the urban fabric of Copenhagen); the other is the Cycle Superhighways project, coordinated by an independent secretariat and developed with the involvement of various municipalities from the Greater Copenhagen area, the regional authority and the Danish Road Directorate.

We assume that transitions are actually happening in cities. Whether these transitions are sustainable is difficult to assess (Hodson and Marvin 2010). However, in the two cases we draw upon we can verify two things: first is that there are explicit ambitions to make both projects sustainable; and second, in both cases there is a declared alignment of the City of Copenhagen's and the Danish government's ambitions to become CO_2-neutral and fossil free (Danish Government 2013; Københavns Kommune 2012). This means that although we do not know with certainty if actual transitions are happening, we can at least verify that there are intentions of contributing to a transition to sustainability.

The way in which we address our research questions is inspired by Arenas of Development Theory (AoD). One of the basic principles of this theory is that no single actor in a transition process has complete knowledge of what is happening. All actors have only partial views and incomplete knowledge. As a project unfolds, actors invest a lot of work in somehow understanding what is going on. This has serious implications according to different actors' capacities, ambitions and the observed mismatch between what they claim to be doing and what they actually do. Additionally, actors also invest a lot of work in understanding other actors' partial views and the ways in which they can be aligned, negotiated, or not negotiated at all. Moreover, the complex dynamics of this process produce changes in the composition of the actors that are actually part of the project and, thus, the content of the project (Jørgensen 2012; Jørgensen and Strunge, 2002; Valderrama and Jørgensen 2015).

This chapter is a product of two research projects conducted at the centre for Design and Innovation for Sustainable Transitions (DIST) at the Copenhagen campus of Aalborg University. One is the "Enabling and Governing Transitions to a Low Carbon Society" project funded by the Danish Research Council. The other is the "Urban Initiatives towards Sustainability in the Greater Copenhagen Area" project.

This chapter is organized as follows. First, we present the main theoretical concepts we use for our analysis. We then analyze the Carlsberg City case, in which we focus on how the transition unfolds over time. This is followed by our analysis of the Cycle Superhighway case, where we pay special attention to how the transition unfolds in space. Based on these two cases, we conclude that we are not only able to describe how transitions unfold over time and space, but also we can explain how and why sustainable urban transitions are different from other transitions.

Theoretical Framework: Mediators and Navigational Processes

The AoD approach to transitions focuses on what actors involved in a change process actually do, intend to do, claim or fail to do. It builds on a tradition of science and technology studies based on the principle stating that the contents of a scientific theory or a technology are intimately related to the social context in which they are developed and used. Several theories within this field also claim that the actual scientific content of a theory or the design and technical workings of a technology intimately depend on the network of actors that supports its existence. As a consequence, the dynamics of including and excluding actors from a development process (of a theory, a technology, or a sustainable transitions project) is essential (see Sismondo 2011 for an overview of the field).

A key characteristic of a development process is that no single actor has complete knowledge and control over what is happening. Some actors may have more knowledge and control over the process than others, but this is a dynamic development. In fact, actors invest a lot of work in negotiating knowledge and power as part of the process. In doing so, they configure and reconfigure the content (vision and actual outcomes) of a transition project. Therefore, actors do partial mappings and navigate according to their immediate knowledge about themselves and about other actors (Jørgensen 2012).

The navigational process in a transition project is, therefore, not the result of a single actor's manoeuvres. We use 'mediator' to denote the navigating entity in relation to a given transition project at a given time and place. All those actors who have managed to be part of a specific project constitute the mediator. In every project, the constitution of the mediator will vary vis à vis the content of the project in time. The mediator is thus not a consistent actor with special abilities and a stable identity, but a constellation of actors that negotiate, disagree, conflict, align or any combination of these sociotechnical dynamics (Valderrama and Jørgensen 2015; Jensen et al. 2015). Moreover, a mediator *mediates* between an existing situation and a desired situation, bearing in mind that both the existing and the desired are also subject to multiple interpretations among actors included by and excluded from the mediation. Our two cases will demonstrate the dynamics of mediators and relate them to sustainable urban transitions.

The meaning of 'mediator' is therefore in line with that forwarded by Guy et al. (2011) in their analysis of urban transformations. They relate to the same intellectual background, and more explicitly to Latour's definition of 'mediator', as "actors endowed with the capacity to translate what they transport, to redefine it, redeploy it, and also to betray it" (Latour 2005: 39). However, the actual cases they compile all relate to specially designed organizations that mediate between different established organizations. They choose to call them intermediaries, although they assert their relational character. In this chapter, we want to contribute by showing how mediators change in time as the content of the projects they bear also evolves; and how they are distributed in space, thereby producing a configuration of place-specific translations that also modify the content of the projects. The first case, Carlsberg City, will place emphasis on variations in time and the second, Cycle Superhighways, will illustrate spatial variations.

Carlsberg City District

The development of Carlsberg City District was initiated in 2006, as the brewery production was relocated, leaving behind an area of 33 hectares to be developed for commercial and residential use. Carlsberg City District constitutes a relevant case, as the vision for the project was (and still is) to create a sustainable urban district. The empirical study behind this chapter was carried throughout the initial steps of the actual building process (Harders 2014). The focal point of this study is to investigate how 'sustainability' as a concept has been translated through the process of realizing the vision for the urban development project. To frame the case study, we found the decision of the car-parking norm an exemplary element of this realization process. We regard the Carlsberg project itself as a mediator, in the sense that the aim of the project is to make a difference compared to more traditional urban development projects, and in this case a transition to a more sustainable situation. The mediator is constituted by constantly changing actors along the way that all bring in different perspectives, interests, expertise, knowledge and frameworks. Thus, the case not only reveals how the mediator dealt with the existing reality, but also how the mediator changes along the way, along with its actors and their actions. Some actors are allowed influence at some stages, but not at others. These changes are situated. Hence, it is in these various situations that the mediator's strength is constantly challenged and established. In the following section, we will outline a number of concrete situations with relevance to sustainable transition – or why it is left out.

At the early stages of the Carlsberg project in 2006, when the vision was still to be formulated, the mediator was constituted by the top management of Carlsberg (the brewery) and political leaders of City of Copenhagen – the first constellation of the mediator. Together, they formulated and agreed on a vision for Carlsberg City District to be sustainable. At this point, they did not define how sustainability was to be realized, but they did define sustainability as being a situation where environmental, social and economic factors are all included in one way or another, in order to encourage a holistic approach to sustainability. In the ensuing process, buzzwords such as "car free" and "CO_2 neutral" came into play as elements of the sustainable solution, but did not lead to specific formulations or commitments as such. Some of these elements, however, reveal an understanding of car traffic as being unsustainable, and thus something that should be reduced.

The first vision evolved as an open architectural competition was initiated starting from 1 November 2006 (Carlsberg and City of Copenhagen 2006). It was an open competition in the sense that all professions and nationalities could submit an entry. It was also open in terms of how sustainability could be interpreted and conceptualized in a visualization of the future urban district. Despite the fact that the competition was 'open' to various professions, it presented numerous parallels to traditional architectural competitions: five international architectural firms were invited beforehand; the material to hand in was solely composed of illustrations, while renderings and long written accounts were not allowed; and finally the professional jury consisted only of architects. The jury played a decisive role in this second constellation of the mediator. Furthermore, the competition was anonymous, and the only relation between the participants and the jury was the actual entries.

At this point, the mediator was abstracted from the physical situation of Carlsberg City District and from those actors who would later on decide. This phase is focused on the ideas, the visualization of a future situation and characterized by painting a rather radical picture of the future with limited car traffic and urban spaces for non-motorized transport and social activities. The winner of the competition was announced in May 2007. The winning entry master plan was designed by the small Copenhagen-based firm Entasis (Carlsberg and City of Copenhagen 2007). The firm suggested reducing car traffic by at least half of the City of Copenhagen's average, and to further require 50% of traffic to be based on a car-share system. Thus, car parking was suggested to be rather limited, with the purpose of discouraging car use without prohibiting it directly. At this stage, the idea of a car-free sustainable area was still present, but in the following phases the vision as visualized by the master plan had to be translated into a formal district plan set up for political evaluation. The following phase thus represents a change in the constellation of the mediator – the third constellation.

The decisions made for the formal district plan were not only based on the master plan, but also and in relation to the surrounding and existing city's infrastructures and practices, including the City of Copenhagen's norms for car-parking. The development of the district plan began in late 2007 and was approved in early 2009. The actors involved in the mediator at this point were developers (a sub company owned by Carlsberg), the municipality (respectively representing the traffic engineering, urban design, and economics departments), engineering consultants, and architects. These actors all brought new perspectives and interests into play, which did not necessarily accord with those of the master plan developed by Entasis.

The developer stated a wish for a high car-parking norm in order to meet what they considered a need or requirement, or indeed a foundation for selling property at all – according to the developer's assumptions. The municipality opposed this objective in line with its interest in a lower norm aiming at decreasing car traffic for the city as a whole. The vision about sustainability and the master plan itself no longer played explicit roles as change-drivers at this point, whereas the norm for car-parking had suddenly become central in an intense, almost conflict-like discussion between the developer and the municipality. The discussion was based on previous experience and the present problems at hand relative to dealing with (existing) car traffic. The final norm was decided upon as a result of negotiations between the top management from the developers and leading politicians – indicating that it had a very high priority. The solution allowed for car sharing of twice the amount of what the master plan suggested, which required expanding infrastructure within and outside the district.

In the early phase of the project, the mediator had a constellation setting out an ambitious course for sustainable transition. The constellation of the mediator changed, and a much less ambitious course was taken. What remained was the illusion of a car-free area, obtained primarily by building car parking facilities underground. The Carlsberg City District will appear almost car-free, but residents will be able to park their cars close to their new homes – which in the developer's perspective makes it possible to sell the properties. A truly car-free Carlsberg City District would have contributed to less car traffic in Copenhagen. The chosen parking solution will make car traffic in Copenhagen increase, which is normally not considered as a part of a sustainable transition. Figure 18.1 below visualizes how the parking solution was presented at two different points in time.

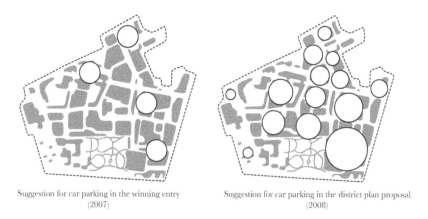

Suggestion for car parking in the winning entry (2007)

Suggestion for car parking in the district plan proposal (2008)

Figure 18.1 Underground car-parking facilities in the original master-plan and in the final proposal. The number of circles indicates the number of underground parking lots. The size of the circles are in proportion to the capacity of each parking lot. (Source: Harders 2014.)

The translation and interpretation of sustainability depend on the actors involved and the situated actions. In other words, the constellation of the mediator changed dramatically over time, which was decisive for the navigational processes. The initial vision was solely a statement, but no commitments were made by the actors involved at this stage or further in the process. There were no consequences caused by the translations, as the role of the early constellation of the mediator was outplayed along the way. Ideas and visions were modified to fit into existing practices and structures rather than changing them. Instead of a transition away from an unsustainable situation, unsustainable structures and practices were actually enhanced. The dynamic development of the constellation of the mediator over time is decisive for how the urban transition unfolds over time. An apparently sustainable vision in the early phase of the project did not lead to a sustainable urban transition.

Cycle Superhighways

The Cycle Superhighway project (*Supercykelstier* in Danish) is a collaborative cross-municipal endeavour in Copenhagen. In the Greater Copenhagen Area, cycling has traditionally been considered a mode of transport for short (intra-municipal) trips. Cycling in central Copenhagen has been developing since the early 1970s (Knudsen, Krag, and Forbund 2005). For longer distances, however, the tendency has been a reduction of bicycle use and an increase in motorized transport, especially car use (Næss and Jensen, 2005). Therefore, the Cycle Superhighway project is a direct attempt to change this tendency by supporting non-motorized transportation, thereby improving health and reducing emissions. In this sense, the Cycle Superhighway project can be seen as an attempt to contribute to a sustainable urban transition. The City of Copenhagen has been eager to promote inter-municipal bicycle commuting in the Greater Copenhagen Area in order to achieve more bicycle commuter traffic in the city, which is part of the City of Copenhagen's visions for a CO_2-neutral city.

The continuous urban fabric of Copenhagen is larger than the City of Copenhagen (the municipality). The Danish urban planner Steen Eiler Rasmussen described these municipal borders as 'fatal lines' dividing the city into different administrative units that were resistant to collaboration (Rasmussen, 1994), thereby creating tensions. This damage was enhanced by the municipal reform of 2007, which reduced regions to precarious political units predominantly running hospitals (Bundgaard and Vrangbæk 2007). If the regional authority had been powerful in relation to transport planning, one could have imagined that the Cycle Superhighway project had been run by this authority with little municipality involvement. The lack of a strong regional authority was decisive in relation to how the urban transition unfolded in space.

The Cycle Superhighway is coordinated by an independent secretariat, funded by the participating municipalities, the Capital Region and the Road

Directorate of Denmark. Some 20 regional municipalities are participating in the project. Its objective is to build 467 kilometres of high-quality cycling paths to provide citizens with the possibility of cycling across the city. In order to understand the development of the project, it is important to recognize that the project consists of a number of sub-projects. Every sub-project has its own mediator, constituted of different local actors, supplemented by some regional and national actors. The navigational processes are different from subproject to subproject. We will demonstrate this with examples from two different municipalities.

In the Municipality of Ballerup, one of the challenges was navigating between cyclists' new and old perceptions. Most Danish bicyclists travel for shorter distances. If the distance is shorter than 5 km, 59% of individuals going to work or study in Copenhagen choose a bicycle. For distances longer than 5 km, only 20% use a bicycle. Speed is not considered crucial for cycling short distances – this is the 'old' way of perceiving bicyclists. Speed is, however, decisive for the new type of cyclists commuting longer distances. The constellation of the mediator in Ballerup included both local actors with a traditional view of cyclists and actors with new perceptions. Thus, some of the tensions related to slow, local routes, improved intra-municipality connections versus faster, more direct routes. According to old perceptions of cyclists, designing infrastructure in such a way that forces cyclists to stop often and dismount from their bicycle is not a problem. Traditional ideas on how to make a bicycle route safe for cyclists often entail a number of obstacles that reduce speed, manifesting tensions at a physical level (Vejdirektoratet-Vejregeludvalget 1981). An early suggestion for a route through Ballerup required cyclists to dismount from their bicycles and walk with them through the railway station. However, intense negotiations in the mediator eventually led to the recognition of the need for a cycle superhighway allowing constant speed – and the suggested route through the stations was no longer considered a part of the project, but a strictly local solution. In relation to the project in Ballerup, it was decisive that not only local actors were included in the mediator – the constellation with regional and national actors helped to navigate towards a sustainable transition.

In the Municipality of Furesoe, most of the cycling infrastructure existed prior to the project (as was the case in most municipalities). In local projects, there has been a specific focus on removing some obstacles and adding comfort to the route, for instance with improved signage and bicycle pumping stations along the path. There are, however, economic limits for added comfort – there are tensions between different perceptions of how much should be spent on bicycles. This can be illustrated by our second example: in the Municipality of Furesoe, a bicycle path suitable for integration into the Farum-Copenhagen cycle superhighway existed. This route did, however, include some 3 km through a forest. The local actors considered this an obstacle. They feared that cyclists would not use the route when it was dark. Hence, they proposed improved illumination along the path. This solution was considered too expensive by the national and regional actors, who refused to finance it. The local municipality then invented a low-budget solution: LED-lights supplied by photovoltaic batteries. Navigating the sea of solutions considered possible, the mediator found a solution. Another example relative to the Farum-Copenhagen route and economic tensions is a missing bridge. In a place where the cycle superhighway runs parallel to the highway for cars, they both cross a road. The highway for cars crosses on a bridge. Cyclists, however, have to stop and wait for a green light – a bridge for bicyclists was considered too expensive also. In this case, there was no easy, well-functioning, innovative way of solving the problem. A recent evaluation of the Farum-Copenhagen cycle superhighway shows an increase of 52% in the number of cyclists. The missing bridge is pointed out as being the most serious problem (COWI 2014).

The Cycle Superhighway case demonstrates how the urban transition unfolds in different ways in different places. The transition taking place is not the result of the work of one mediator, but of a number of mediators with different constellations and navigating in relation to both specific local conditions and more general regional and national conditions. The navigational processes of the mediators are situated actions in an existing urban fabric. By situated actions, we mean that actors take a number of actions, depending on the configuration of actions and visions at a specific point in time and space, that is, a specific situation.

Conclusion

If we consider sustainable urban transitions as a navigational process, one may ask: Who is the navigator? In this chapter, we have introduced the *mediator* as the entity that navigates in urban transitions. We have used two specific examples from Copenhagen to demonstrate two important characteristics of mediators.

The Carlsberg City District project demonstrates that *time* is an essential factor: the mediator changes over time, and new constellations replace old constellations. This results in an evolving project trajectory, which we have illustrated with the issue of car-parking. In the early days of the project, the visions were almost car-free. Gradually, through changes in the constellation of the mediator, more and more car-parking was included in the project. Despite its intention of being a sustainable urban project, the Carlsberg City District project was progressively navigated onto a car-dependent course, betraying its initially ambitious sustainability targets. Underground parking facilities will, however, make it possible to keep the illusion of a car-free neighbourhood, while the district will contribute to more car traffic on the neighbouring roads in Copenhagen.

The Cycle Superhighway project demonstrates that *space* is an essential factor. No single actor creates an urban transition; it is a number of actors related to specific spatially defined parts of the routes, each with different configurations and with specific challenges relating to the specific material character of a given space. In one place, it is the navigation between providing infrastructure for local bicycle traffic and inter-municipal commuter traffic on bicycles that are essential for the Cycle Superhighway project. In another place, it is the navigation between removing obstacles for bicyclists – like darkness and crossing roads – that is fundamental in relation to the Cycle Superhighway. The combined effect of all these actors explains the strength of the mediator in achieving the desired objectives: as actors succeed in aligning materials, objectives and each other, the project becomes a success. If they fail to align, then the project is weakened.

Summing up, in order to understand how sustainable urban transitions unfold over time and space, we can state that it is important to identify the mediators of the transition processes and be aware that these actor constellations may develop over time and that the mediators may be spatially distributed.

At the very start of this chapter we raised the question: How and why are urban sustainability transitions different from other types of transitions? Based on our analysis, we claim that urban transitions are different from technology-centred system transition because urban transitions relate to a specific place. When Frank Geels (2005) describes the transition from horse-drawn carriages to automobiles, the analysis centred around the technology, not a specific urban context. The relation to a specific urban context is important when studying urban transitions. In our study of the Cycle Superhighways, we had to relate to the different spatial parts of the project in order to understand the specific navigational processes. If we understand urban as in opposition to rural, it is the value of space that enters the picture. It will most likely be difficult to find a developer who insists on spending a fortune on providing underground parking for her/his rural development project.

In the Carlsberg City District case, we have seen how the intention of being sustainable does not necessarily make a project a part of a sustainable transition. Ultimately, the developer's assumption that more car-parking would considerably increase the value of the real-estate eventually marginalized the vision of a car-free city, reducing it to a question of underground parking. We claim that this development of the course of the project can be understood by tracing how the constellation of actors that constitute the mediator changes in time.

Two reflections follow from the analysis above in relation to other questions addressed in this book. One is, how do urban transitions fit into multiple scales and levels? From our analysis we consider that there are no fits. That is the problem of using multiple scales and levels in the analysis of urban transition. What makes sense at one level (the vision outline by the directors of Carlsberg or the planners of Copenhagen) rapidly conflicts with developers' and municipal planners' practices. There is a need to create alignment between different actors. Sometimes, this alignment requires a change of competencies, skills and practices that has not been properly anticipated.

The other question is, how can urban transitions catalyze and/or leapfrog transformative change on a national or global scale? We have developed a knowledge base that allows us to say that the cases we discuss are specifically urban. They can inform and inspire other similar projects in other urban contexts, with respect to the complex navigational processes in the mediator: it is not the actual infrastructure, but the hard work of navigating in the different mediators, that makes a project succeed.

Additionally, we can verify that the scale of interaction among disconnected socio-technical systems in urban projects requires the development of new expertise. In order to navigate sustainable urban transitions, the next generation of urban planners must learn how to act in spatially specific, dynamically developing mediators.

References

Bundgaard, U., and Vrangbæk, K. (2007). Reform by coincidence? Explaining the policy process of structural reform in Denmark. *Scandinavian Political Studies*, 30(4), 491–520.

Carlsberg City of Copenhagen (2006). *Vores By – Konkurrenceprogram*, Copenhagen.

Carlsberg City of Copenhagen (2007). *Vores By – Dommerbetænkning*, Copenhagen.

COWI (2014): *Farumruten – Evaluering*, Copenhagen.

Danish Government, The (2013) The Danish Climate Policy Plan: Towards a Low Carbon Society, The Ministry of Climate, Energy and Building, Denmark.

Farias, I., and Bender, T. (2012). *Urban Assemblages: How Actor-Network Theory Changes Urban Studies*. Routledge, Oxon, UK..

Geels, F. W. (2005). The dynamics of transitions in socio-technical systems: a multi-level analysis of the transition pathway from horse-drawn carriages to automobiles (1860–1930). *Technology analysis & strategic management*, 17(4), 445–476.

Guy, S., Marvin, S., Medd, W. and Moss, T. (Eds.). (2011). *Shaping Urban Infrastructures: Intermediaries and the Governance of Socio-Technical Networks*. Routledge, London, UK.

Harders, A. K. B. (2014). *Stædige infrastrukturer and genstridige praksisser - et praksisteoretisk studie af byudviklingsprojekter mellem vision og realitet*, Ph.D. thesis, Aalborg University, Copenhagen.

Harders, Anne Katrine Braagaard (2014) Stædige infrastrukturer og genstridige praksisser: Et praksisteoretisk studie af byudviklingsprojekter mellem vision og realitet. PhD Dissertation. Institute for Development and Planning. Aalborg University. Copenhagen. Denmark.

Hodson, M., and Marvin, S. (2010). Can cities shape socio-technical transitions and how would we know if they were? *Research Policy 39*(4), 477–485.

Jensen, J. S., Lauridsen, E. H., Fratini, C. F., and Hoffmann, B. (2015). Harbour bathing and the urban transition of water in Copenhagen: junctions, mediators, and urban navigations. *Environment and Planning A Abstract*, 47(3), 554–570.

Jørgensen, U. (2012). Mapping and navigating transitions – The multi-level perspective compared with arenas of development. *Research Policy, 41*(6), 996–1010.

Jørgensen, U., and Strunge, L. (2002). Restructuring the power arena in denmark: Shaping markets, technologies and environmental priorities. *Shaping Technology, Guiding Policy: Concepts, Spaces and Tools*, , 286–318.

Knudsen, W. B., Krag, T., and Forbund, D. C. (2005). *På cykel i 100 år: Dansk cyklist forbund 1905–2005* Dansk Cyklist Forbund.

Københavns Kommune (2012). *KBH 2025: Klimaplanen*, København.

Latour, B. (2005). *Reassembling the Social – An Introduction to Actor-Network-Theory*. Oxford University Press, Oxford, UK.

Næss, P., and Jensen, O. B. (2005). Bilringene og cykelnavet: Boliglokalisering, bilaf- hængighed og transportadfærd i Hovedstadsområdet. Aalborg Universitetsforlag, Aalborg, Denmark.

Rasmussen, S. E. (1994) *København: Et bysamfunds særpræg og udvikling gennem tiderne.* Gads Forlag. Copenhagen. Denmark.

Sismondo, S. (2011). *An introduction to science and technology studies.* John Wiley & Sons. Oxford. UK.

Valderrama, A., and Jørgensen, U. (2015). Creating Copenhagen's Metro – on the role of protected spaces in arenas of development. *Environmental Innovation and Societal Transitions*, forthcoming.

Vejdirektoratet-Vejregeludvalget. (1981). *Cykel-og knallerttrafik*. København.

19 Flows, Infrastructures and the African Urban Transition

Mark Swilling, Josephine Musango, Blake Robinson and Camaren Peter

Introduction

Africa's growing cities face an opportunity to affect a sustainability transition. Unencumbered by large-scale, resource-hungry fixed infrastructure systems, the continent's cities will need to grow in a manner that frees their inhabitants from resource dependence, maximizes their adaptive capacities and minimises their impact on climate change. The multilevel perspective (MLP) is useful for understanding societal transitions toward sustainability, but requires adaptation to deal with the challenges of Africa's unique urbanization processes.

In this chapter, we consider African cities as spaces where challenges meet opportunities, and where innovative transitions could take place if an appropriate set of assumptions about the nature of urban development replace conventional paradigms. Following an introduction to the scale of African urbanization, we consider the impact of the 'resource curse' on African countries, and the need for structural transformation to break free of it. We then focus on cities as the spaces in which structural transformation will need to take place, and propose a combination of the MLP with urban metabolism measurements as a way to structure sustainable urban transitions. The chapter concludes with an overview of a new approach to resource-efficient cities that is of relevance to the African context.

African Urban Realities

The first urbanization wave took place between 1750 and 1950, and resulted in the urbanization of about 400 million people in what is now the developed world. The second urbanization wave between 1950 and 2030 is expected to result in the urbanization of close to 4 billion people in the developing world in less than a century. Based on UN population data for 1950–2050 (Department of Economic and Social Affairs, United Nations 2012), the total global urban population is expected to increase from 3.5 billion in 2010 (of which 73% were in cities in developing countries) to 7.3 billion in 2050 (by which time 83% of the urban population will be living in cities in developing countries).

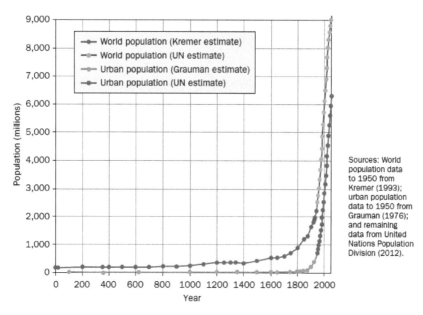

Figure 19.1 World population and urban population growth trends. (Source: Angel, 2012.)

This means that by 2010 the global process of urbanization that began in earnest in 1800 (see Figure 19.1) had resulted in the urbanization of only 48% of the estimated urban population by 2050.

Furthermore, according to the ground breaking UN Habitat report *Challenge of Slums* (United Nations Human Settlement Programme, 2003), of the 3.5 billion who were living in cities by 2010, 1 billion lived in slums. In other words, 210 years of urbanization had created a decent quality of life for only two-thirds of all urban dwellers. Resolving this problem must, therefore, be seen as integral to a just urban transition by 2050. Of the 52% that must still be urbanized over the next four decades to 2050, most will end up in developing country cities, in particular Asian and African cities. If we include the 1 billion slum-dwellers, material infrastructures of one kind or another will need to be assembled for an additional 5 billion new urban dwellers by 2050.

This raises an obvious and vitally important question from a sustainability transition perspective: what will the resource requirements of future urbanization? Are there more resource-efficient alternatives? No-one has attempted to answer these questions yet, which is why they have become the focus of our new research initiative for the International Resource Panel. Until then, the African case may well be instructive because, unlike other world regions, Africa has yet to sink in concrete the socio-technical systems required by contemporary urbanism.

Significantly, although half of all slum-dwellers are in Asian cities, it is only in sub-Saharan Africa that one finds cities where the majority of the population live in slums. Around 62% of all urban dwellers live in slums, compared to Asia where it varies from 43% (Southern Asia) to 24% (Western Asia), and in Latin America and the Caribbean where slums make up 27% of the urban population (UN Habitat, 2008b). Given the fact that urbanization rates in Africa are the highest in the world at 3.3% (UN Habitat, 2008a:4), the slum cities of Sub-Saharan Africa will be with us for the foreseeable decades. Africa is now 40% urbanized and is projected to be 60% urbanized by 2050, which translates into an increase in the *urban* population from the 2007 estimate of 373 million to 1,2 billion by 2050 (UN Habitat, 2008a:5). If Africa's governments continue to ignore this problem (by stubbornly insisting that slum-dwellers must go back to the rural areas), the additional 800 million urban dwellers will land up in Africa's mushrooming slums.

Africa is becoming a continent of slum cities and, in so doing, it is transforming entirely what we mean when we use the word 'city' to describe quite a unique set of urban dynamics and modalities (Pieterse, 2008; Simone, 2004; Simone, 2001; Swilling et al., 2003; Parnell and Pieterse, 2014; Buckley and Kallergis, 2014). Indeed, for many analysts and policymakers, African cities don't deserve to be called cities at all – a position that is tenable only if you assume that the 'Western City' is the only legitimate template for defining the city. Maybe it is time to realise that the iconic image of the Western City that emerged from the specificities of the first urbanization wave (1750–1950) has become little more than a mirage from an African perspective. Maybe it is time

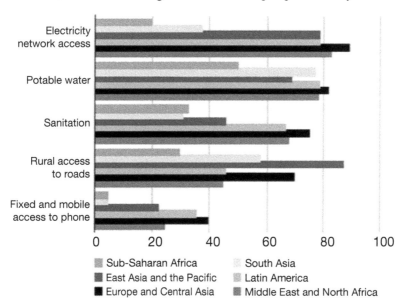

Figure 19.2 Percentage of population with access to infrastructure services, per region. (Source: Ajulu & Motsamai, 2008.)

to find non-Western reference points for rethinking our deepest assumptions about the purpose, meaning and impact of the city (Malik, 2001; Swilling et al., 2003). This will mean recognising that industrialisation, modernisation, and (from the late 1980s onwards) high-tech informationalism have not been the primary driving forces of African urbanization.

But this is starting to change in light of rapid economic growth of many African economies since 2000 and the resultant focus on 'structural transformation'. The key question becomes, Are traditional urban socio-technical regimes appropriate for an African information-based industrialization pathway within a resource- and climate-constrained world? A key driver of both economic growth and the demand for urban development is the rapidly expanding African middle class. Although a small part of a continent with over a billion people, it is a class that comprises of a rapidly expanding number of increasingly better educated younger people, with enormous potential for rapid improvements in productivity through education, health and functional urban systems. It has emerged from adversity and its strengths are adaptability, flexibility and high levels of ICT-based interconnectivity. It is primarily urban-based, and the annual growth of its consumption expenditure is over 3% (McKinsey, 2010).

African urban planning (to the extent that it exists) tends to merge a colonial cognitive model with an idealised conception of urban modernity and conventional socio-technical regimes to deliver the false promise that African cities can replicate what has been achieved elsewhere (Pieterse, 2014). For those interested in sustainability transitions using the MLP this is a new kind of challenge: the challenge here is not about the path dependency of existing 'sunk in concrete' socio-technical systems, but rather it is about replacing this unrealised idealised false promise with an alternative vision of what is possible that could potentially be a more equitable and ecologically sustainable.

To achieve a more sustainable future for African cities, it will be necessary to address two key challenges: what the African discourse refers to as 'structural transformation' to overcome the so-called resource curse, and spatial transformation to foster the emergence of a unique mode of African urbanism. These are not unrelated: the human and institutional capabilities that many in Africa regard as essential preconditions for structural transformation do not emerge in a spatial vacuum, and yet discussion of these capabilities hardly ever refers to these spatial conditions. At the same time, the discussion about an appropriate mode of African urbanism needs to interface more coherently with the dominant discussion of structural transformation.

Overcoming the Resource Curse: The Need for Structural Transformation

The Economist magazine in 2000 depicted Africa as the 'the hopeless continent', very different to its December 2011 front cover depicting Africa as 'the hopeful continent'. For 8 out of the 10 years to 2011 economic growth rates in sub-Saharan Africa were higher than in East Asia, and 6 of the 10 fastest-growing economies by 2012 were African. Upbeat hype about African growth was reinforced by consulting companies (Ernst and Young, 2011; McKinsey Global Institute, 2010; *Monitor*, 2009) and financial institutions (World Bank, 2011; International Monetary Fund, 2011).

However, at an African Union summit of Ministers of Finance and Economics in Abuja, March 2014, Ministers repeatedly warned that economic growth is too dependent on the extraction and export of primary resources.[1] Primary resources still made up 86% of exports into non-African markets in 2013 (United Nations Economic Commission for Africa & African Union, 2014:17). There seemed to be complete consensus that unless Africa implements what was repeatedly referred to as 'structural transformation', the economic fortunes of African economies will be determined by the notoriously unstable global commodity markets. Furthermore, extractive industries were seen to benefit only a narrow band of employees and shareholders, with limited domestic backward and forward linkages.

The challenge, therefore, is to ensure that resource rents from the extractive sector are reinvested in the diversification of African economies to ensure sustained long-term economic growth. It is this process of change that is referred to in African discussions as 'structural transformation'. However, as Paul Collier has argued, the more dependent an economy becomes on the exploitation of natural endowments, the less incentive it has to diversify (Collier, 2010). This, in essence, is what the 'resource curse' is all about. Key consequences are state failure and resource wars resulting from entrenched corporate and elite practices that prevent the reinvestment of resource rents (Swilling, 2013).

Three recent reports address directly the challenge of structural transformation. The first two are highly influential (and frequently cited at the AU Summit referred to on p. 000): the 2014 United Nations Economic Commission for Africa (UNECA) report entitled *Dynamic Industrial Policy in Africa* (United Nations Economic Commission for Africa, 2014) and the *2014 African Transformation Report* by the Accra-based African Center for Economic Transformation (ACET) (African Center for Economic Transformation, 2014). The third report – which is hardly ever referred to – is UNCTAD's 2012 Economic Development in Africa Report that was subtitled *Structural Transformation and Sustainable Development in Africa*. Unlike the first two reports, the UNCTAD report calls for '*sustainable* structural transformation' with special reference to the need to decouple economic growth rates from rates of resource use (UNCTAD, 2012, emphasis added).

The UNECA report argues that Africa's average annual growth of 3.6% during 2009–2013 was 0.6% below its growth potential of 4.2% per annum. The key to higher and more inclusive growth, the report argues, is to reverse the stagnation/decline of the African manufacturing sector. This, in turn, "calls for industrial policies ... that address constraints to economic diversification and development." (United Nations Economic Commission for Africa

& African Union, 2014:29). In line with the new institutional economics, the state is seen as leading this change strategy: "Institutions and policies are the key instruments for increasing productivity, growth and structural transformation" (United Nations Economic Commission for Africa & African Union, 2014:31). A key conclusion is that a "well-crafted growth and transformation strategy that enhances the productive capacities ... tends to reduce inequality.... Economic transformation strategies should thus ... promote high-quality education and health services, powering greater productivity and more inclusive growth" (United Nations Economic Commission for Africa & African Union, 2014:29).

Remarkably, the UNECA report says nothing about the 'where' of all this: by not contextualising this modernist vision within a particular conception of urban space, the UNECA report fails to identify how urban space will need to be transformed. In short, it is incorrectly assumed by omission that institution building and inclusive growth are spatially decontextualized processes, and, unlike the UNCTAD report, sustainability is ignored.

The ACET report redefines African progress by proposing what it calls a Transformation Index that includes, but goes beyond, GDP. Sadly though, it fails to explicitly acknowledge the spatial preconditions for transformation and the wider sustainability challenge. To compile its comprehensive index, ACET takes into account improvements in GDP per capita growth, diversification of productive activities, diversification of exports away from just primary materials, export competitiveness, productivity in manufacturing, productivity in agriculture, technological upgrading and human well-being (primarily social factors, including the proportion of people in formal employment) (African Center for Economic Transformation, 2014:25–35). It then uses these factors to analyse 21 African economies over two 3-year periods (1999–2001 and 2009–11). Two realities emerged: improvements or not between the two periods indicated by the positive/negative numbers on the left, and where these economies were as at 2011 as reflected in the index along the horizontal axis.

ACET's aim is to influence the *direction* of structural transformation. When it comes to the key agent of change, ACET shares UNECA's institutional economics: a new generation of institutions must be created by governments to drive industrial policies that will lead to diversification through manufacturing and the modernization of agriculture. And like the UNECA report, it ignores the 'where' question: remarkably, there is no acknowledgement at all that key factors like productivity, technological upgrading and human well-being are inseparable from their urban spatial contexts. Dysfunctional spaces will inevitably subvert productivity, innovation and well-being.

Significantly, the UNCTAD report goes beyond institutional economics by integrating material flow analysis that has emerged in recent years from the work of leading ecological economists and also the work of the International Resource Panel (Fischer-Kowalski and Haberl, 2007; Fischer-Kowalski and Swilling, 2011) into an understanding of structural transformation.

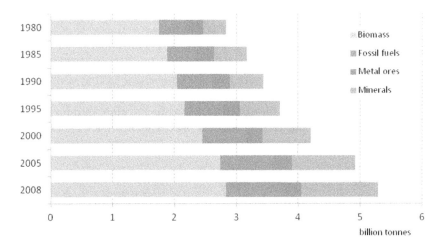

Figure 19.3 Domestic Material Extraction in Africa, 1980–2008. (From *Economic Development in Africa Report 2012: Structural Transformation, Decoupling and Sustainable Development in Africa*, by United Nations Conference on Trade and Development.© 2012 United Nations. Reprinted with the permission of the United Nations.)

Figure 19.3 demonstrates that total domestic material extraction increased by 87% between 1980 and 2008, from 2.8 bt to 5.3 bt, with fossil fuels and minerals extraction increasing faster than the other sectors. Figure 19.4 and 19.5 reveal that Africa is a net exporter of non-renewable resources (fossil fuels and minerals) and a net importer of biomass (renewables). Africa exported 500 Mt of unrefined fossil fuels and imported 100 Mt of refined fuels. And contrary to the popular image that Africa is the producer of mainly agricultural exports, only 14.5Mt of largely unprocessed agricultural materials were exported, while 95.8 Mt of mainly processed biomass was imported (mainly cereals followed by vegetable fats and oils, timber and sugar crops).

Compared to the rest of the world, resource productivity (i.e., purchasing power parity in US$/per ton of resources) in Africa by 2008 was the lowest by a factor of 4 compared to Europe and by a factor of 0.5 compared to Latin America and Asia. This improved by 33% over the period 1980–2008, but off such a low base that Africa remained with the lowest resource productivity levels in 2008.

It was this resource perspective on Africa's development trajectory that led UNCTAD to call for

a strategy of sustainable structural transformation (SST). This is a development strategy which promotes structural transformation but which adopts deliberate, concerted and proactive measures to improve resource efficiency and mitigate environmental impacts of the growth process. In short, they should promote sustainable structural transformation, which will be defined here as structural transformation accompanied by the relative decoupling of resource use and environmental impact from the economic growth process. (UNCTAD, 2012:26).

Energy provision is an excellent candidate for this kind of decoupling. Given that the installed electricity capacity of Africa is equal to that which exists in France, and given that many African economies are growing at 5–7% per annum, for this rate of growth to persist Africa has to embark on a massive electrification programme. If this is done using fossil-fuel-based technologies, all the global climate targets will be breached. The world, in short, has an

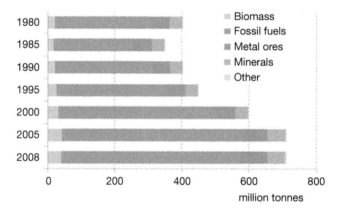

Figure 19.4 Africa's Physical Exports (Mt), 1980–2008. (From *Economic Development in Africa Report 2012: Structural Transformation, Decoupling and Sustainable Development in Africa*, by United Nations Conference on Trade and Development.© 2012 United Nations. Reprinted with the permission of the United Nations.)

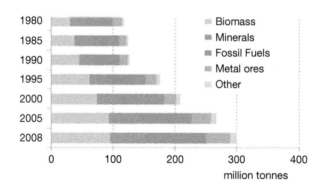

Figure 19.5 Africa's Physical Imports (Mt), 1980–2008. (From *Economic Development in Africa Report 2012: Structural Transformation, Decoupling and Sustainable Development in Africa*, by United Nations Conference on Trade and Development.© 2012 United Nations. Reprinted with the permission of the United Nations.)

interest in African economies investing in renewable energy. Fortunately, this is technically and economically feasible. The International Renewable Energy Agency has developed a detailed feasibility assessment for what they call the Africa Clean Energy Corridor that stretches from the radiation-rich south west, to the hydro reserves of the Congo River, to the geothermal potential of the Rift Valley and the windswept expanses of North Africa (International Renewable Energy Agency, 2014). This feasible alternative would contribute substantially to what UNCTAD has in mind, including reducing the cost of electrification over the 20-year life cycle.

However, it is not just a matter of making the energy source sustainable; as important is the question of spatial transformation that envisages an agglomeration of energy-efficient end-users. Structural transformation – whether it is sustainable or not – will depend on how functional African cities become as they emerge as the economic centres of accelerated economic growth and development. The only significant African Report to address this is the UN Habitat State of African Cities 2014 Report, which was subtitled "re-imagining sustainable urban transitions".

On the 'Where' of African Structural Transformation

Although the absence of coherent urban development policies in Africa reflects the fact that geography has yet to be recognised as significant in mainstream African economic thinking (Pieterse, 2014); by contrast there is now a widely held assumption in global mainstream thinking that functional spaces really do positively affect economic growth (see World Bank 2009; *Monitor*, 2009). From this perspective, urbanization in Africa is presented as a panacea, with cities providing the platforms for economic growth and development. However, as Turok (2014) demonstrates, the empirical evidence that urbanization has positive effects on economic development is by no means conclusive. The mounting evidence from the African context suggests that what matters is not just agglomeration per se, but in particular the quality and efficiency of the urban environments that urbanization makes possible within particular contexts (Turok, 2014). This, in turn, is dependent on the evolution of a set of developmental institutions mandated to govern cities in ways that engage and include the urban poor in programmes that are designed for particular contexts with each characterised by unique economic dynamics (Pieterse, 2014). However, following Buckley and Kallergis (2014), the combined effect of Africa's unique urbanization patterns and historically weak (and in many cases non-existent) urban governance institutions means that African cities are currently in reality 'binding constraints' to – rather than potential enablers of – conventionally defined structural transformation as envisaged by the UNECA, ACET and UNCTAD reports.

However, a focus only on 'binding constraints' to conventionally conceived structural transformation will fail to address the challenge of *sustainable* structural transformation as articulated by the UNCTAD Report. To this end, the recently released State of the African Cities Report 2014 highlights the need for structural transformation of resource-intensive, extractive and agricultural economies in Africa, and the role that African cities and their growth trajectories can play in this respect. It emphasizes both the role of cities in Africa as (1) binding constraints on growth, as well as (2) the existing and emerging potentials within African cities to contribute to sustainable, macroeconomic structural transformation. It argues that recognising both the constraints and potentials within a 'sustainability' perspective sheds light on the key factors that could bring about more sustainable urban growth trajectories on the continent, and proposes that a 're-imagining' (UN-Habitat, 2014: 1) of sustainable urban transitions in Africa is necessary.

The report proposes that this 'reimagining' of African urbanism is contingent on some key socio-economic, technical and spatial factors that can be taken into account when formulating strategies for transition to sustainability in Africa. These are briefly summarised below:

Spatial Factors

- The bulk of urban population growth is occurring in secondary and smaller cities rather than the large primary cities (UN-Habitat, 2014:7). The emergence of satellite cities is also important in this regard (UN-Habitat, 2014:6).
- Regional corridors that connect primate cities are experiencing significant growth of secondary and smaller cities, presenting a key opportunity for linking economic growth of cities to each other within and across national boundaries, and driving transboundary regional growth strategies (UN-Habitat, 2014:7).
- Urban sprawl is a key contributing factor to the 'un-sustainability' of African cities and presents a severe limiting factor to economic growth due to the urban economic inefficiencies that sprawl induces (UN-Habitat, 2014:11, 13, 33).

Socio-Economic Factors

- Emerging socio-economic activities in African cities should be acknowledged and harnessed when formulating growth trajectories. Examples include creative industries (e.g., in music, advertising and film), educational institutions (e.g., colleges, schools, universities), as well as ICT developments (e.g., financial services, mobile micro-credit, loans and savings, urban management and citizen participation systems,) (UN-Habitat, 2014: 38–39) and green economic activities (e.g., solar, wind, hydropower, urban agriculture and permaculture) (UN-Habitat, 2014:42).
- The African middle class (McKinsey Global Institute, 2010) is highly vulnerable to food–water–energy transport linkages that impact African urban households. The African middle class is defined as those earning

between USD 2–20 per day, but 81.72% lived on less than USD 4 per day in 2010 (AfDB, 2011). Improving the resilience of these households to exogenous pressures and shocks that significantly impact on household budgets is hence a critical requirement for stabilising the African 'middle class', and for enabling local governments to stabilise revenue collection, as well as stabilising growth and foreign investment (UN-Habitat, 2014:9).

- The African 'youth bulge' is at the same time a potentially important labour and consumption pool and transformative, innovative force for change; as well as a potential force for socio-political unrest, due to their prevailing low skills levels, high unemployment rates, and social marginalisation (UN-Habitat, 2014:38–39).
- Any sustainable urban or macroeconomic growth trajectory will likely depend on their ability to accommodate the high levels of informal trade, service provision, land, housing and rental markets in most (especially sub-Saharan) African cities. Inhabitants of slums and informal settlements often pay much higher prices for service delivery through private and informal sector providers, than those who have access to centralised public infrastructure and service provisions (UN-Habitat, 2014: 42–44).

Technical Factors

- The dearth of infrastructure and service provision in African cities is at the same time a constraint to growth, as well as a key opportunity to leapfrog to more sustainable urban resource and ecological footprints and regimes. Systems, technology and infrastructure choices that are made today in African cities, have large potential to influence the levels of sustainability (or, alternatively, unsustainability) that African cities will enjoy in the medium to long term future (UN-Habitat, 2014:42). The same logic is applied to the need for infrastructures that link cities to each other, across regional and national boundaries.
- There is a large opportunity to engender higher levels of sustainability through the absorption of decentralised and semi-decentralised infrastructure and technology offerings such as solar water heaters, bio-digesters, smart grids, wind power, mobile technologies, rainwater capture, water recycling and grey-water recycling systems, urban agro-ecological activities, urban ecosystem management activities and so forth (UN-Habitat, 2014:42).

Ensuring resource security and resilience to climate change effects are regarded as critical components of achieving city-level and macroeconomic transitions to sustainability in African regions (UN-Habitat, 2014:33–34, 46–50). To this end, economic diversification requires the careful consideration of all the technology and urban infrastructure options that are available to them, as well as emerging and new economic activity areas and niches that are less resource-intensive, before commitments are made; so that countries can avoid locking themselves into investment patterns that exacerbate resource depletion and ecological degradation (UN-Habitat, 2014:20).

African cities are able to influence their environmental footprints with dense built environments, the design of spaces and the management of urban material flows (UN-Habitat, 2014:47). Whereas cities in developed countries typically have sufficient infrastructure to meet their inhabitants' needs and limited scope to change the technologies that service them, many cities in Africa lack adequate service provision. In upgrading and expanding African cities, there is an opportunity to "leapfrog" ahead of their more established counterparts by implementing sustainable and resource-efficient urban designs, infrastructures, technologies and services from the start (UN-Habitat, 2014:47). In many cases, low-tech interventions that are cheap and easy to maintain may be more appropriate for diversifying local economies than are imported high-tech solutions (UN-Habitat, 2014:20).

It follows, therefore, that the African urban transition must recognize that the dysfunctional geographies and governance dynamics of cities are in fact 'binding constraints' on structural transformation, while at the same time they also hold the key to sustainability transitions. A theory of urban transition that is appropriate to the African context must, therefore, conceive of a set of urban regimes that respond to these twin landscape imperatives of a spatially conscious structural transformation that also recognizes the significance of sustainable resource use over the long term.

Thinking through the potential for "bio-regional economic diversification" (Swilling and Annecke, 2012) through embracing non-resource-intensive economic activities and niches as well as systems design, infrastructure and technology choices is hence key to enabling city-level and macroeconomic transitions to sustainability in Africa. Fortunately, our work has revealed that there are significant numbers of niche innovations that confirm that it may well be possible to leapfrog the kinds of unsustainable socio-technical urban regimes that have been consolidated in cities across both the developed and developing world. Examples include the BRT-Lite public transport model in Lagos, the closed-loop landfill site in Durban, and the "Skyloo" EcoSan solution in Lilongwe (see UN-Habitat, 2012; Swilling et al., 2013; UN-Habitat, 2014).

Frameworks for Understanding Urban Transitions

Given the potential of African cities to lead sustainability transitions, the question arises as to how to achieve a favourable transition from slum cities to models of sustainability where both social and environmental needs are balanced. By combining the MLP with an urban metabolism view of cities, a new understanding of urban transitions in the context of African urban realities can be achieved. Currently, the two frameworks are utilised in isolation, but together they offer huge potential for improving urban transition analysis. As highlighted in the City-Level Decoupling report (Swilling et al.,

2013), the "empirical analysis of flows highlights the dependence of cities on specific sinks for resources they require [urban metabolism], while analysis of socio-technical systems addresses the regulatory, institutional and knowledge systems that conduct these flows [MLP]". The two frameworks are thus relevant from a policy perspective in providing more insights on how to deal with increasing urban challenges, yet few studies have connected the concepts.

Hodson et al. (2012) were the first to explore the value of connecting the MLP with an understanding of urban metabolism. On the one hand, they identified an increasing application of both frameworks in (1) urban contexts, (2) analysing infrastructure and flows and (3) answering normative questions with regard to systematic and purposeful changes occurring in urban contexts. On the other hand, they highlighted the differences in the frameworks in terms of their disciplinary origin, conceptual framing and methodological approaches. By reconciling these two frameworks, the empirical analysis of urban transition can be improved. An elaboration of these differences and the potential added benefits of linking the two frameworks is discussed in Section 19.5.1.

The Sociotechnical Approach and Material Flows

MLP is associated with a sociotechnical approach, differentiating three levels of analytical concepts, namely niche-innovations, regimes and landscapes (Geels and Schot, 2007). It is a very useful framework for analysing complex dynamics and explaining systemic change. Moreover, it can help in identifying diverse factors that affect sustainable transitions such as resource availability, key actors or pressures to create change. On the other hand, the MLP is not useful for understanding metabolic flows or how they might be altered to support sustainability (Hodson et al., 2012). The socio-technical systems are viewed as just systems, rather than conductors of resource flows through urban systems. This is one of the major connections that urban metabolism finds with MLP. Urban metabolism aims to understand the 'flows of resources in an urban environment, and of the influences of economic, political, regulatory, and social factors on the flow, use, and transformation of those resources' (Graedel, 1999). Hence, the socio-technical systems are to be viewed as conductors of material flows required to service the urban economy and satisfying social functions. Such perspective would be of particular importance in understanding how the critical infrastructure in Africa can be provided to meet the growing and expected growth in urbanization, while at the same ensuring it is a 'sustainable structural transformation' that is called for in UNCTAD report (see Section 19.3).

Cities as Spaces for Socio-Technical Transitions

There has been a tendency to conflate the three MLP levels with specific territorial boundaries, where regimes describe national features, landscapes depict international features and niches describe local features such as cities (Raven et al., 2012). As a result, many socio-technical transitions case studies implicitly assume the national level as the appropriate representation for transformative change (Dixon and Eames, 2014) and cities or urban areas only act as niches or seedbeds for experiments. From a theoretical perspective, there is no clear justification for associating MLP levels with specific territorial boundaries (Raven et al., 2012).

As earlier indicated, African cities are recognised as vital in shaping the direction in which structural transformation may take place. On the other hand, cities are most likely the binding constraints to Africa's 'sustainable structural transformation'. Theoretical frameworks for urban transition that may be relevant in Africa context then need to account for cities as spaces for socio-technical transitions.

The urban metabolism framework has a strong focus on cities and can add value to the MLP by facilitating the reconceptualization of cities as spaces for sociotechnical transitions where the three levels of MPL interact (Hodson and Marvin, 2010). A focus on cities further helps in locating MLP in space, and may improve the analytical assessment of urban transitions. The analytical assessment may give insights on how the much needed structural transformation in African cities should be facilitated.

Multisegmented and Dysfunctional Regimes

Studies that have utilised MLP to analyse urban transition (e.g., Næss and Vogel, 2012; Eames et al., 2013) already recognise the challenge of conceptualising regimes. In urban environments, particularly in the African context, there exists 'multisegmented and dysfunctional regimes' which are integrated across multiple spatial scales, as well as technological, cultural and environmental domains. The discussion of African realities further highlights how difficult it is to envisage that urban transition can result in massive, rigid and homogenous solutions, given that a heterogenous mix of socio-technical systems is part of everyday life (Jaglin, 2014). This makes it challenging to specify regimes as if they can only be understood as single functional technological solutions.

Urban metabolism provides a range of assessment tools to quantitatively assess metabolic flows through and within urban areas and estimate various sustainability indictors. It therefore adds value to the MLP by allowing for progress toward sustainability to be monitored, and by supporting policy- and decision-making on the structural transformations that are deemed necessary.

A Framework for Structural Transformation

Combining the MLP with an urban metabolism view of cities is a novel concept that is yet to be piloted. There are many ways in which metabolic flows can be assessed, but few of them are designed specifically for cities, and as a result they are limited in their ability to assist with structural decisions required for sustainable transitions at the city scale (UNEP, 2013).

Existing metabolic flow assessment methodologies have limitations in terms of their ability to assist with city decision-making. For example, approaches such as Economy-Wide Material Flow Analysis (EW-MFA) can depict sectoral flows, but fail to take externalities like waste and pollution into account (Hammer et al., 2003; Ramaswami et al., 2012). Alternatives such as the Ecological Footprinting Assessment (EFA) method can be used to evaluate the ecological sustainability of a whole system (Zhang, 2013), but the manner in which data is aggregated limits its usefulness in identifying the reasons behind sustainability problems, or determining appropriate solutions (Rapport, 2000). Many of these limitations can be addressed by hybridising complementary methodologies to suit the needs of city decision makers (UNEP, 2013: 31).

Analyses of urban material flows currently do not have as much influence on urban decisions as they could. Marcotullio and Boyle (2003) are critical of MFA and ecological footprint analysis, saying that they "have provided excellent critiques of the impact of cities on the environment, but have been weaker on providing solutions that city managers can use in their daily work". Zborel et al. (2012) reveal that the reasons for the findings of urban metabolism assessments not being more widely used by urban policymakers include (1) the sophistication of metabolic flow methodologies, (2) the unclear and confusing manner in which the findings are communicated by experts, and (3) various conflicts between the realities of planning and investment cycles and the time requirements of data collection.

One of the most critical issues preventing metabolic flow analysis from being implemented in a more systematic manner is that of data collection. This is especially problematic in less developed cities that do not have the technologies and expertise required to collect regular and accurate data, and where many of the systems that conduct flows are informal. Data problems include a lack of city-level data, unsuitable data formats, incompatible demarcation of boundaries, data confidentiality, inadequate data on informal sectors and locations, and insufficient capacity to capture data. To get around this, national or regional level data is often downscaled, but this is seldom insightful due to the heterogeneity of human settlements (UNEP, 2013:43–46).

Given that (1) existing methodologies need to be hybridised and adapted to meet the needs of the city, (2) the data produced is difficult to translate into action and (3) data collection is a challenge in developing countries, it is evident that the application of a material flows perspective to the transitions of cities of the developing world will require a new approach. Such an approach will need to combine existing approaches that capture the essence of the urban metabolism perspective, whilst remaining sufficiently easy to use in data scarce environments and flexible enough to support change on multiple levels.

One attempt to achieve this is the *Toolkit for Resource Efficient Cities* (UNEP, 2013) that is currently being developed under the auspices of the

Global Initiative for Resource Efficient Cities (GI-REC) – an initiative led by the United Nations Environment Programme (UNEP) and launched in Rio in June 2012. The toolkit is one of the first set of projects undertaken by the GI-REC, and aims to help cities with limited capacity to formulate their own locally relevant strategies for infrastructure investments that will help them to make best use of their locally available resources, and reduce wasteful resource use over time.

The Toolkit for Resource Efficient Cities aims to incorporate the logic of urban metabolisms into a set of learning tools that are easy to implement and sufficiently flexible to be useful in data-scarce contexts. It does not prescribe implementation agents, which allows role players at the landscape, regime and niche level to formulate a plan for urban resource efficiency based on the power relations in each urban area. The toolkit follows a basic logic that supports strategy formulation, and currently consists of the following six proposed steps (UNEP, 2013):

- **STEP 1:** Understand the city's resource profile
  The 'City Resource Profile Tool' would allow for similar cities to be clustered, making it easier for them to find relevant points of comparison in the setting of goals (Step 3) and the scoping of infrastructure options (Step 4). Ratings of 'low', 'medium' and 'high' across categories like population density, rainfall and access to infrastructural services could be used as classification.
- **STEP 2:** Establish a resource-efficiency baseline
  The 'Resource Efficiency Baseline Assessment Tool' would establish a resource efficiency baseline to give direction to cities wishing to set resource efficiency goals (in Step 3). This would allow cities to compare their resource efficiency with similar cities and identify where they can make improvements over time.
- **STEP 3:** Set resource-efficiency goals with timelines
  Cities should set their own goals based on their context, challenges and opportunities, but at the same time those resource efficiency targets need to work within planetary boundaries. The 'Goal Setting Tool' would help cities to set 5- and 10-year resource use targets within an acceptable range between a minimum 'social foundation' and an 'environmental ceiling' to ensure that both human and environmental needs are met.
- **STEP 4:** Identify possible infrastructural approaches
  In order to ensure that cities are considering innovative infrastructure approaches, the 'Infrastructure Option Scoping Tool' would consist of a database of options, including the latest technologies, ecosystem services and social interventions that improve resource efficiency. Categorisation of examples (in line with Step 1) could help cities identify options better suited to each context.
- **STEP 5:** Identify best infrastructure approaches

The 'Infrastructure Strategy Selection Tool' would use a hybrid simulation model to anticipate the likely impacts of various interventions (identified in Step 4) on resource flows in the longer term. This would be combined with qualitative judgments to select the most promising interventions.

- **STEP 6:** Monitor progress
  In order to ensure that consistent improvements in resource efficiency are made over time, the 'Resource Efficiency Performance Assessment Tool' provides a framework for regular monitoring of city performance relative to goals.

The tools within the toolkit need not all be adhered to in strict sequence, and are intended to serve as learning tools where required to fill gaps in knowledge and add rigour to infrastructure strategy formation processes. Weak regimes in many African countries are likely to act as an impediment to change, so the toolkit will be made widely available to allow both regimes and niches to play leading roles in transition. The toolkit is currently being refined so that it can be pilot-tested on cities around the world.

An example of how this toolkit might be used is the innovative approach to sanitation developed in the informal settlements of Lilongwe, Malawi. The "Skyloo" waterless toilets consist of an elevated squat toilet atop an above-ground chamber that holds separate storage tanks for urine and faeces. These tanks are emptied every few months, and the contents can be used to enrich the soil for agriculture. The Malawian Homeless Peoples' Federation's (MHPF) Centre for Community Organisation and Development (CCODE) developed the toilets as an alternative to the widely used pit latrines, using a combination of Internet research and trial and error. Pit latrines were problematic, as they not only took up precious space whilst in use and once decommissioned, but also were contaminating groundwater – the only source of water for residents who could not afford to purchase bottled water (UN-Habitat, 2012).

In a case like this, the city of Lilongwe could have used the *City Profile Tool* to identify that it is in a water scarce area, and that inadequate water and sanitation infrastructure in informal settlements was leading to health issues. It could have calculated the city's overall water efficiency using the *Resource Efficiency Baseline Assessment Tool*, and used the *Goal Setting Tool* to set the goal of a 50% improvement in access to decent sanitation services whilst keeping overall water demand within 10% of current demand in the next 5 years. The *Infrastructure Option Scoping Tool* would have allowed them to investigate a wide range of innovative water-saving and sanitation options from around the world, and the *Infrastructure Strategy Selection Tool* could have been used to reduce the most promising options down to those that were affordable and had the least impact on scarce resources. Once the roll-out of the toilets had commenced, the *Resource Efficiency Performance Assessment Tool* could have been used to track the city's water consumption over time so assess whether the roll-out of waterless sanitation services was helping the city to keep the growth in demand for fresh water services within the target range whilst improving sanitation. In turn, this could have helped them to modify their approach to better reach their water-saving and sanitation goals.

Conclusion

The rapid growth of African cities provides an opportunity to reshape what urbanization means in the 21st century, and for the continent to lead sustainability transitions on an unprecedented scale. If structural transformation is to take place, cities need to be recognised not as binding constraints, but rather as catalysts of the kind of sustainable structural transformation advocated by the likes of UNCTAD. The MLP could play a role in helping conceptualise this transition, but a new approach would be required that connects an MLP perspective on infrastructure transitions to an urban metabolism perspective that analyses the flows through these infrastructures. This would allow African cities to set and pursue quantitative goals for resource consumption, and develop strategies for infrastructure roll-out that will help them to grow in a more sustainable manner than their predecessors in the global North.

Note

1   Personal observations by Mark Swilling, who attended the AU Summit.

References

African Center for Economic Transformation. (2014). *2014 African Transformation Report: Growth with Depth*. Accra: African Center for Economic Transformation.

AfDB (African Development Bank). (2011). *The Middle of the Pyramid: Dynamics of the Middle Class in Africa*. Available online: http://www.afdb.org/fileadmin/uploads/afdb/Documents/Publications/The%20Middle%20of%20the%20Pyramid_The%20Middle%20of%20the%20Pyramid.pdf [Accessed May 14, 2011].

Ajulu, C. and Motsamai, D. (2008). *The Pan-African Infrastructure Development Fund (PAIDF): Towards an African Agenda*. Global Insight 76. Johannesburg: Institute for Global Dialogue.

Angel, S. (2012). *Planet of Cities*. Hollis, NH: Puritan Press.

Buckley, R. and Kallergis, A. (2014). Does Africa urban policy provide a platform for sustained economic growth? In: Parnell, S. and Oldfield, S. (Ed.). *The Routledge Handbook on Cities of the Global South*. New York and London: Routledge.

Collier, P. (2010). The political economy of natural resources. *Social Research*, 77(4):1105–1132.

Department of Economic and Social Affairs, United Nations. (2012). *World Urbanization Prospects: The 2011 Revision*. New York: United Nations.

Dixon, T. and Eames, M. (2014). Sustainable urban development to 2015: complex transitions in the built environment of cities. In: Dixon, T., Eames, M., Hunt, M. and Lannon, S. (Ed.) *Urban Retrofitting for Sustainability: Mapping the Transition to 2050*. London and New York: Routledge.

Eames, M., Dixon, T., May, T. and Hunt, M. (2013). City futures: exploring urban retrofit and sustainable transitions. *Building Research & Information*, 41, 504–516.

Ernst & Young. (2011). *It's Time for Africa: Ernst & Young's 2011 Africa Attractiveness Survey*. London: Ernst & Young.

Fischer-Kowalski, M. and Haberl, H. (2007). *Socioecological Transitions and Global Change: Trajectories of Social Metabolism and Land Use*. Cheltenham, U.K.: Edward Elgar.

Fischer-Kowalski, M. and Swilling, M. (2011). *Decoupling Natural Resource Use and Environmental Impacts from Economic Growth*. Report for the International Resource Panel. Paris: United Nations Environment Programme.

Geels, F. W. and Schot, J. (2007). Typology of sociotechnical transition pathways. *Research Policy*, 36, 399–417.

Graedel, T. (1999). Industrial ecology and the ecocity. *The Bridge*, 29, 10–14.

Hammer, M., Giljum, S., Bargigli, S. and Hinterberger, F. 2003. *Material flow analysis on the regional level: Questions, problems, solutions*. NEDS Working Paper 2, Hamburg. Available online: http://seri.at/wp-content/uploads/2009/09/Material-flow-analysis-on-the-regional-level1.pdf [Accessed October 20, 2011].

Hodson, M. and Marvin, S. (2010) Can cities shape socio-technical transitions and how would we know if they were? *Research Policy*, 39, 477–485.

Hodson, M., Marvin, S., Robinson, B. and Swilling, M. (2012). Reshaping urban infrastructure. *Journal of Industrial Ecology*, 16, 789–800.

International Monetary Fund. (2011). *World Economic and Financial Surveys: Regional Economic Outlook: Sub-Saharan Africa*. Washington, D.C.: International Monetary Fund.

International Renewable Energy Agency. (2014). Africa Clean Energy Corridor: Analysis of Infrastructure for Renewable Power in Southern Africa. Abu Dhabi: International Renewable Energy Agency.

Jaglin, S. (2014) Regulating service delivery in Southern cities. In: Parnell, S. and Oldfield, S. (Eds.) *The Routledge Handbook on Cities of the Global South*. New York : Routledge, pp. 434–447.

Marcotullio, P. J. and G. Boyle. 2003. *Defining an Ecosystem Approach to Urban Management and Policy Development*. Tokyo: United Nations University Institute of Advanced Studies (2003:15).

Malik, A. (2001). After modernity: contemporary non-Western cities and architecture. *Futures*, 33, 873–882.

McKinsey Global Institute. (2010). *Lions on the Move: The Progress and Potential of African Economies*: McKinsey Global Institute. Available online: www.mckinsey.com/mgi.

Monitor (2009). Africa: From the Bottom Up: Cities, Economic Growth, and Prosperity in Sub-Saharan Africa. Houghton, South Africa: Monitor Group.

Næss, P. and Vogel, N. (2012) Sustainable urban development and the multi-level transition perspective. *Environmental Innovation and Societal Transitions*, 4, 36–50.

Parnell, S. and Pieterse, E. (Ed.) (2014). *Africa's Urban Revolution*. Cape Town: UCT Press.

Pieterse, E. (2008). *City Futures*. Cape Town: Juta.

Pieterse, E. (2014). Filling the void: an agenda for tackling African urbanisation. In: Parnell, S. and Pieterse, E. (Ed.). *Africa's Urban Revolution*. Cape Town: UCT Press.

Ramaswami, A., Chavez, A. and Chertow, M. (2012). Carbon footprinting of cities and implications for analysis of urban material and energy flows. *Journal of Industrial Ecology*, DOI: 10.1111/j.1530- 9290.2012.00569.x

Rapport, D. J. (2000). Ecological footprints and ecosystem health: complementary approaches to a sustainable future. *Ecological Economics*, 32, 381–383.

Raven, R., Schot, J. and Berkhout, F. (2012). Space and scale in socio-technical transitions. *Environmental Innovation and Societal Transitions*, 4, 63–78.

Simone, A. (2001). Between ghetto and globe: remaking urban life in Africa. In: Tostensen, A., Tvedten, I. and and Vaa, M. (Ed.). *Associational Life in African Cities: Popular Responses to the Urban Crisis*. Stockholm: Elanders Gotab.

Simone, A. (2004). *For the City Yet to Come: Changing African Life in Four Cities*. Durham NC and London: Duke University Press.

Swilling, M. (2013). Beyond the resource curse: from resource wars to sustainable resource management in Africa. In: Minderman, G., Raman, V., Cloete, F. and Woods, G. (Ed.). *Good, Bad and Next in Public Governance*. The Hague: Elevent International Publishing.

Swilling, M. and Annecke, E. (2012). *Just Transitions: Explorations of Sustainability in an Unfair World*. Cape Town: UCT Press & Tokyo: United Nations University Press.

Swilling, M., Khan, F. and Simone, A. (2003). 'My soul I can see': the limits of governing African cities in a context of globalisation and complexity. In: McCarney, P. and Stren, R. (Ed.). *Governance on the Ground: Innovations and Discontinuities in Cities of the Developing World*. Baltimore and Washington D.C.: Woodrow Wilson Centre Press and Johns Hopkins University Press.

Swilling, M., Robinson, B., Marvin, S. and Hodson, M. (2013). City-level decoupling: urban resource flows and the governance of infrastructure transitions. Report for Cities Working Group of the International Resource Panel, United Nations Environment Program. Available online: http://www.unep.org/resourcepanel/portals/24102/Decoupling/City-Level_Decoupling_Summary.pdf [accessed 15 May 2014].

Turok, I. (2014). Linking urbanisation and development in Africa's economic revival. In: Parnell, S. and Pieterse, E. (Ed.). *Africa's Urban Revolution*. Cape Town: UCT Press.

UNCTAD (United Nations Conference on Trade and Development). (2012). *Economic Development in Africa Report 2012: Structural Transformation, Decoupling and Sustainable Development in Africa*. Geneva: United Nations Conference on Trade and Development.

Robinson, B., Musango, J.K., Swilling, M., Joss, S. and Mentz Lagrange, S. (2013). Urban metabolism assessment tools for resource efficient urban infrastructure. Report prepared for the Global Initiative for Resource Efficient Cities (GI-REC). Paris, France.

UN-Habitat. (2008a). *The State of African Cities 2008: A Framework for Addressing Urban Challenges in Africa*. Nairobi: United Nations Human Settlements Programme (UN-Habitat).

UN-Habitat. (2008b). *State of the World's Cities 2008/2009: Harmonious Cities*. London: Earthscan.

UN-Habitat. (2012). *Urban Patterns for a Green Economy: Optimising Infrastructure*. Nairobi: UNON. 42–46.

UN-Habitat. (2014). *The State of African Cities 2014: Re-imagining Sustainable Urban Transitions*. Nairobi: UNON.

United Nations Economic Commission for Africa & African Union. (2014). *Dynamic Industrial Policy in Africa*. Addis Ababa: United Nations Commission for Africa.

United Nations Human Settlements Programme. (2003). *The Challenge of Slums: Global Report on Human Settlements*. London: Earthscan.

World Bank. (2009). *World Development Report 2009: Reshaping Economic Geography*. Washington D.C.: World Bank.

World Bank. (2011). *Africa's Future and the World Bank's Support to It*. Washington, D.C.: World Bank.

Zborel, T., Holland, G., Thomas, G., Baker, L. Calhoun, K. and Ramaswami, A. (2012). Translating research to policy for sustainable cities: What works and what doesn't? *Journal of Industrial Ecology*, 16(6): 786–788.

Zhang, Y. (2013). Urban metabolism: A review of research methodologies. *Environmental Pollution*, 178, 463–473.

20 Focusing on Ecosystem Services in the Multiple Social-Ecological Transitions of Lodz

Jakub Kronenberg, Kinga Krauze and Iwona Wagner

Introduction

Linking urban sustainability transitions and ecosystem services, Pincetl (2010) described how cities changed since the 19th century, following the modernist sanitary city idea, and then – since the 1970s – how cities further evolved to incorporate the new environmentalist approach. The latter involved paying attention to issues such as air and water pollution, toxic substances, greenhouse gas emissions, and finally ecosystem services. Now, in some cities, large-scale urban greening programs are crowning these transitions. The above well describes what happened in the Western world, but cities in Central and Eastern Europe (CEE) partly followed a different transition path.

Interestingly, greenery played a much more important role in the socialist version of a modernist city, especially compared to the previously densely built-up capitalist central districts (Staniszkis 2012). Since the beginning of the 1990s, cities in CEE have experienced a rapid socio-economic transition from a centrally planned to a market economy. With the new, liberal system in the 1990s came the appropriation of public space for private uses. Many green areas were lost because of so-called construction terrorism, based on exploiting the neoliberal economic system, combined with poor legal protection of green areas and the abuse of numerous legal loopholes (Szulczewska and Kaliszuk 2003, Hirt 2012). Currently, 25 years after the socio-economic transition started, urban green areas in CEE are scarcer than in Western and Northern Europe (Fuller and Gaston 2009) and they continue to shrink (Kabisch and Haase 2013).

Recently, the authorities of many cities in the region began to realise that environmental change (both global and local) affects or is likely to affect quality of life and economic prospects. Environmental awareness, or perhaps rather the awareness of the need to pay more attention to environmental issues, is slowly increasing. Membership in the European Union (EU) and the transposition of EU regulations into national legal systems, combined with growing bottom-up pressure, resulted in the introduction of new local and regional instruments. As a result, CEE cities may finally enter a delayed sustainability transition. However, they still face many challenges, such as urban sprawl and the sealing of surfaces due to the development of new infrastructure.

To study the above processes, we follow the approach of social-ecological transitions. This approach highlights that whatever change we address, it boils down to changes in complex and coevolving social and ecological systems. In this way, questions typically asked within the sustainability transitions debate, such as who governs and whose system framings are considered and prioritized, ultimately refer to social-ecological systems and their evolution (Smith and Stirling 2010). Interestingly, ecological issues have been left out of most sustainability transitions research carried out so far (c.f. Grin et al. 2010), except for specific environmental challenges, such as climate change (c.f. Bulkeley et al. 2014), water (Jefferies and Duffy 2011) and waste management (McCormick et al. 2013). Here, we look at ecological issues through the lens of ecosystem services and how they have been incorporated in urban development planning (c.f. Piwowarczyk et al. 2013, Wilkinson et al. 2013).

Lodz (Łódź), the third largest city in Poland, serves as an illustration of such multiple transitions and their drivers and challenges. The city developed rapidly in the 19th century as one of the largest textile manufacturers in Europe. One of the reasons for the development of the city was a network of streams and wood resources that supplied industry. Specific economic situation of the socialist period did not stop the physical growth of the city. However, the economic crisis of the early 1990s put the city through particularly strong economic and social transformations, the results of which still challenge the city today. By the time of the crisis, however, the city's natural resources had already been largely diminished and degraded. Although the city grew because of ecosystem services, the latter per se have never been on the city authorities' and inhabitants' priority lists. Today, there is an increasing urgency to put them on this list, and the sustainability transition that the city finally seems to be embracing provides the ultimate opportunity to do so.

Lodz in Transition

Lodz has been going through multiple transitions over the last 200 years. From a small town with 428 inhabitants in 1800, it became a CEE capital of the textile industry in the 19th century, with 100,000 inhabitants in 1872, and 500,000 in 1914. After the First World War, the city became part of independent Poland, and after the Second World War, Poland fell under the Soviet Union's influence. The fall of the Soviet Union and the resultant economic crisis initiated yet another phase of socio-economic transition, during which the population of Lodz declined (Figure 20.1).

Rapid development of the city was possible thanks to abundant natural resources (forests and 18 watercourses), its geopolitical location and state ownership of land. Natural resources provided both the energy and water required by the industry and the town community to develop. The city organisation, which developed at the time of the Industrial Revolution, reflected

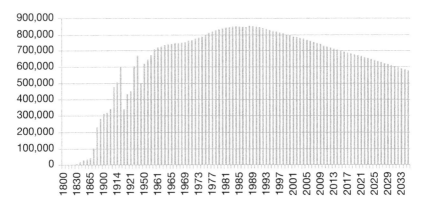

Figure 20.1 Population of Lodz (including a forecast from 2012 to 2035).

a highly diversified class structure in the community. Several factory and workers housing complexes were concentrated around the palaces of factory owners. The surrounding remnants of the forests that had previously covered these areas were transformed into scarce private and public green areas. Rapid growth and industrialisation in the second half of the 19th century resulted in dense development, air, soil and water pollution, and the canalisation of watercourses, which were incorporated into the sewer system of the city. By 1920 the city reached an area of 58.75 km² while green areas constituted only 3.77 km² (i.e., 6.3% of urban area) (c.f. Figure 20.2).

After the Second World War, 19th-century wild capitalism was replaced by socialism. Central planning led to accommodating an increasingly homogenous society in blocks of flats, which kept the city structure relatively compact and functionally organised. In principle, the new spatial planning model favoured the development of green areas and used many of their ecosystem services, as a result of which green areas per capita increased significantly (Figure 20.3). However, this was mainly caused by the continued physical growth of city area and the incorporation of previously agricultural and forested land (cf. Figure 20.2). During the period of socio-economic development in the 1960s and 1970s, the city became a flagship communist industrial success, again at an environmental cost, primarily in terms of pollution, but also cutting down 20% of street trees considered an obstacle to city development.

The economic and social transition initiated in 1989 brought about an economic depression with very high unemployment rates (up to 21.3% in Lodz in 1993), soaring inflation (351% in 1989, 686% in 1990, 170% in 1991) and a significant decrease of GDP (Polish GDP decreased by 11.6% in 1990, and by 7% in 1991). Subsequent developments resulted in an improvement of socio-economic (wealth, happiness) and environmental (e.g., emissions of pollutants from industry, share of treated wastewater) indicators in many Polish cities. Attention was also paid to protecting selected green areas, primarily for

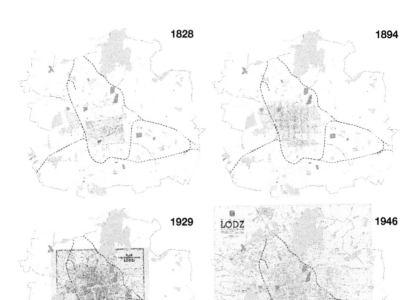

Figure 20.2 Changes in the area of Lodz, as illustrated by the maps of the relevant
years contrasted with the ca. 20 km wide modern contour of the city.
(Courtesy of the State Archive in Lodz – cartographic collection Lodz
1600–2012.)

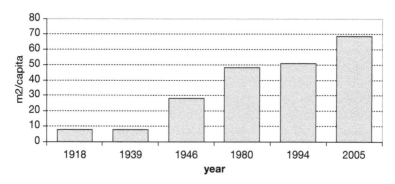

Figure 20.3 Green areas per capita from 1918 to 2005. (Source: Lodz City Office.)

their cultural significance. At the same time, other problems emerged or intensified (e.g., increased generation of waste and traffic). Increased affluence and
new socio-cultural patterns have also led to further urbanisation and urban
sprawl (Kronenberg and Bergier 2012, Wagner and Breil 2013).

Despite a recent reduction of Lodz's population which should remove some pressure on nature in the city, the results of past and current spatial management efforts have strengthened the typical negative effects of urbanisation: urban heat island effect and increased risk of pluvial flooding, decreased ecological and recreational value of watercourses, decreasing connectivity and quality of green spaces (Wagner and Zalewski 2009). Disturbed water cycling and retention have led to an increased occurrence of heat waves and lower humidity, high concentrations of air pollution, thus increasing the prevalence of asthma for both adults and children as well as seasonal rhinitis for children in the city centre, compared to the outskirts (Bergier et al. 2014). All of these changes are part of a reinforcing feedback loop, imposing further stress on green infrastructure, and limiting the delivery of ecosystem services, especially in the city centre.

The above changes are also linked with the migration of the upper and middle classes from the central district of Lodz to the suburbs, in search of a better quality of life. Despite its decreasing population, the city continues to sprawl over the city borders, endangering its green ring and undermining the flow of ecosystem services in the future. The central district's population, which has the lowest quality of life, has halved between 1960 and 2011, hampering the centre's economic development, social and cultural life and attractiveness. In other districts with a better living environment and a higher proportion of green spaces, the number of inhabitants increased at the same time by up to 61% (Szukalski 2012). There is a growing discrepancy not only in the socio-economic status between those living in the city centre and in the suburbs, but even in the related morphological parameters of children, such as BMI, body mass and body height, which are significantly lower in the city centre (Rosset et al. 2012). Thus, the interplay between environmental quality and welfare and their changes over time again resulted in a diversification and stratification of the social-ecological system of Lodz. In this way, ongoing socio-economic changes have also acquired an environmental justice dimension.

The historical perspective makes it possible to distinguish different types of social-ecological transitions in Lodz (Figure 20.4), reflecting the changing dynamics of the social-ecological system and the different types of forces affecting these dynamics (Frantzeskaki 2011). This history can also be seen through the lens of the resilience approach, with a series of regime shifts (occurring in 1820, 1945 and 1989). The most recent phase of socio-economic changes initiated by the economic crisis led to a regime shift and involved a number of technological and institutional changes. Indeed, over time, the socialist system had become vulnerable to change. Conversely, the new socio-economic setting has been more resilient so far, and the upcoming disturbances, such as EU accession in 2004, brought about "the opportunity for doing new things, for innovation and for development" (Folke 2006, p. 253). New planning documents increasingly paid attention to the broader context of socio-economic changes, which have been the primary focus of decision makers during the 1990s (Figure 20.4). This has become especially evident

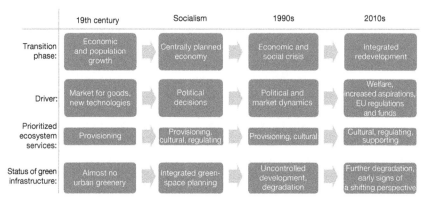

Figure 20.4 Four major transition phases experienced by Lodz (note that the final integrated redevelopment is only a hypothesis investigated in this chapter).

in the 2010s, with the prime example of the *Integrated Development Strategy for Lodz 2020+* adopted in 2012. Has the city finally entered a new integrated redevelopment or a sustainability transition?

Challenges of the 21st-Century Sustainability Transition

One indicator of the modern sustainability transition is the inclusion of ecosystem services into urban development discourse (Ernstson et al. 2010, Elmqvist et al. 2013). In the following subsections, we analyse how ecosystem services have been treated in Lodz's modern development documents, investigating the main challenges involved in transitioning towards sustainability.

Balancing Greater and Inner City Development

The recent creation of a network of 19 new protected areas within the city borders probably provides the best example of what has been achieved in terms of ecosystem services management in Lodz. The network was created to maintain or restore habitats, green corridors, and biodiversity (supporting ecosystem services) and to protect landscape beauty (a cultural service). This network, called the Green Treasures of Lodz (*Zielone Skarby Łodzi*), was established pursuant to the process of 'natural-ecological valorisation' of the city carried out by a team of researchers in 2007 (Ratajczyk et al. 2010). However, all of these areas are located at the outskirts of the city, lacking a comprehensive system of green infrastructure which would link them with the centre, where nature is most scarce and needed.

A comprehensive system connecting the dispersed green and blue areas in Lodz and its surroundings was proposed as the Blue-Green Network within the SWITCH EU project (Zalewski et al. 2012). The concept of the Blue-Green Network focuses on cultural services (recreation, non-motorised transport corridors, revitalisation of cultural heritage), regulating services (stormwater management, regulating humidity, air quality and microclimate) and supporting services (ecological corridors). Although the concept has gained much interest in the city, it has been only partially included into the subsequent Spatial Development Masterplans and other planning documents. This seems insufficient to support ecosystem services in the city especially under increasing development pressure on remnants of green areas (e.g., from housing, road network, commercial, industrial, logistic centres).

A decreasing population and changing management goals as a result of population ageing and evolving needs should be perceived as an opportunity for the city to reuse brownfields within the built-up area, rather than further facilitating sprawl. Such an approach of integrated revitalisation merges environmental issues with social goals and economic realms (Ratajczyk and Drzazga 2005). Without such a systems perspective, environmental issues tend to be neglected. For example, real-estate companies prefer to locate new housing projects outside of the inner city, where they can easily promise the share of green areas desired by future inhabitants, rather than buy expensive land in the city centre and set part of it aside for greenery. Recent changes in the Act on protection of agricultural and forest land make the protection of agricultural land within urban borders more challenging. Formerly, interested parties had to seek agreement from the Ministry of Environment to change land-use patterns. Now, this obligation has been repealed, keeping the responsibility for land-use patterns in the hands of local administrators, who adopt local spatial development plans. Furthermore, there is an ongoing discussion about the introduction of a cadastral tax, which may increase real-estate costs beyond the level affordable for many landowners. This may force them to move from more expensive centres of cities to their surroundings. Thus, the most important supporting services of ecosystems around the city are not properly protected.

Balanced Perspectives on Different Urban Ecosystems

Some ecosystems attract more attention than others. This can also be seen in Lodz, in the case of the large Lagiewniki forest (ca. 1200 ha) which attracts most attention in discussions on urban ecosystems (Krauze et al. 2010). Although one should not underestimate the services provided by this forest, more recognition should be given in official documents and research to other urban ecosystems, including agricultural land (the available space to secure ecosystem services for the future), allotment gardens and cemeteries, which are only briefly mentioned in planning documents. Other green infrastructure components, such as green wedges, are not discussed at all. Information on street greenery is at best restricted to the affirmation that "street greenery is very important in an urban context", followed by a succinct observation that the number of trees and bushes planted in Lodz is constantly decreasing (Wysmyk-Lamprecht et al. 2007, p. 80). Moreover, there is no inventory of urban trees and their health, which makes the management of such dispersed green infrastructure components particularly challenging. However, such small and dispersed natural elements increase inhabitants' quality of life in the more central parts of the city (c.f. Wysmyk-Lamprecht et al. 2007).

Only high diversity of green infrastructure components may provide a variety ecosystem services which are best suited to different parts of the city.

Focus on the Future

Until recently, the documents that guided the decisions of Lodz authorities with regard to environmental issues (Diehl 1997, Wysmyk-Lamprecht et al. 2007, Dalman et al. 2010) contained relatively little focus on the future. Instead, they paid much attention to the past. Most of these documents recycled the same historical information, leaving little space for emerging topics (e.g., Diehl 1997, Wysmyk-Lamprecht et al. 2007). As long as city funds are spent on repeating and recycling that knowledge instead of on sensitivity and vulnerability assessments and modern ecosystem management, critical knowledge gaps, such as those related to ecosystem services, continue to grow.

What raises even more concern is the lack of reliable cause–effect analysis and risk analysis based on a deep understanding of the consequences of socio-economic transformations for environmental quality and vice versa. Such analyses should include learning from long-term observations and forecasting of the consequences of current policies and neglects (e.g., the effects of increasing impermeable surfaces or fragmentation of city green spaces, future climate changes).

Integrated Approaches to Policymaking

In 2012, the Lodz authorities adopted the *Integrated Development Strategy for Lodz 2020+* (City of Lodz Office 2012) and a set of accompanying sectoral policies. Although environmental issues were almost completely absent from the initial version of the strategy, a bottom-up movement of local NGOs, environmental experts and other stakeholders highlighted the importance of ecosystem services which, following public consultations, were included in the strategy (Giergiczny and Kronenberg 2014). Now, Lodz places the environment as one of the three pillars of development and explicitly refers to "the skilful use of ecosystem services and nature's potential for sustainable development of Lodz as a compact city". The new strategy calls for an "improvement of the quality of life of Lodz citizens and enhancement of attractiveness of the city, by exploiting the potential of the environment, by preserving and ordering the biologically active spaces and areas intended for recreation, and for establishing a healthy lifestyle."

One sectoral policy (*Municipal management and environmental protection policy of the City of Lodz 2020+* (City of Lodz Office 2013a) begins with a reference to ecosystem services and the benefits that we can obtain from ecosystems if sound ecosystem management is ensured. Interestingly, in other cities in Poland, including those where linkages to ecosystems might seem much more obvious (e.g., coastal cities), ecosystem services have not been explicitly included in official documents (Piwowarczyk et al. 2013). Another sectoral policy (*Spatial development strategy for the City of Lodz 2020+* (City of Lodz Office 2013b) focuses on the idea of a compact city and on making the city centre more attractive. However, it does not refer to environmental issues, clearly indicating insufficient coordination between different policies and the challenges awaiting the *integrated* development of the city.

Although there is still a long way from strategy to implementation, and although many sectoral strategies still do not contain enough or any references to ecosystem services, the adoption of the main strategy provided an important impulse for putting the concept of ecosystem services on the agenda of local stakeholders. The operationalisation of this concept remains a challenge, further complicated by poor awareness of the importance of nature among decision-makers and within society, a lack of relevant tools and procedures, the persistence of old habits and of the general business-as-usual approach.

Coordinated Management

In recent years, local authorities in Lodz have attempted several times to improve the management of urban ecosystems and integrate them into overall urban management.

Since October 2012, different units responsible for urban greenery, previously operating within different departments of the city office, have been consolidated within the Urban Greenery Maintenance Authority (*Zarząd Zieleni Miejskiej*). This was an important step towards integrating competences related to the management of urban greenery, but interestingly (at least according to the official statements), better coordination was not the main motivation for the new structure. Instead, the main motivation was cutting costs.

In January 2014, a Greenery Task Force (*Zespół ds. Zieleni*) was established, composed of senior managers from the different departments of the city office. Its role is to coordinate different activities related to urban greenery. Moreover, recent discussions indicate that in the near future, the authorities might reinstall the post of an urban gardener, whose tasks would include the coordination of different issues related to greening the city.

Local authorities have recently started to exhibit some openness to new ideas coming from expert NGOs active in Lodz. For example, cooperation among city authorities, scientists, NGOs and water services providers within the European SWITCH project resulted in the formulation of a water vision for the city (*Łódź 2038*) (Wagner et al. 2011), and two sets of recommendations on the implementation of best stormwater management practices and the Blue-Green Network into the Masterplan. More recently, the Phenomenon (of) the Normal City Foundation initiated a joint action involving different departments of the city office, NGOs and researchers to create *woonerfs* in the centre of Lodz (woonerf is a "living street", a concept that originates from the Netherlands and Flanders and involves traffic-calming and creating shared space to be used by the people, similar to home zones in the UK). The Sendzimir Foundation has been helping the city office to develop standards for public procurement, and investment planning and supervision which would incorporate tree-protection issues. Finally, Lodz has the biggest participatory budget in Poland, which the inhabitants create and select projects they consider important. It provides the largest funds for green space in the history of the city, covering investment, improvement and restoration.

Nevertheless, these efforts have not brought any breakthrough in thinking about environmental issues in the city. Many other bodies, such as the City Council's Environmental Commission, have barely been active and reluctant to adopt new governance or management approaches, or to take more determined steps to protect urban greenery. This is due to various institutional failures, such as the incompleteness and inconsistency of regulations which hinder collaborative action, limited funding and a lack of long-term planning, inconsistencies in the decisions made at different levels of decision-making and a limited sense of responsibility (c.f. Kronenberg 2015). Moreover, some additional initiatives have already failed, such as the Consultative Council on Nature (*Rada Konsultacyjna ds. Przyrody*) created in 2011. From the very beginning, it was perceived as an artificial body without any significance, and its importance dwindled as members external to the authorities gradually retired from this body. The main reason for such initiatives to fail seems to have been poor collaboration among the different stakeholders in the area of environmental protection, as indicated by a recent social network analysis carried out in Lodz (Kronenberg et al. 2016).

Discussion and Conclusions

The history of Lodz illustrates a co-evolution of natural and human-made systems which act as one entity going through adaptive cycles. Consequently, traditional approaches to knowledge gathering and environmental management, which focused mainly on assessing state of the environment, should be complemented with an understanding of societal and economic pressures on environment and the feedbacks to society and economy they produce (Fischer-Kowalski and Weisz 1999, Haberl et al. 2006). This is even more relevant as we can talk of transitions within other broader transitions here – the beginning of an urban sustainability transition within a broader national sustainability transition, and a social system in transition within a broader ecological system in transition (multilevel perspective on transitions). Social changes resulted in a more polarised society and new needs, while EU membership brought about new pressures and new funding opportunities, and global changes and global political decisions increasingly spilled over to national, regional and local decisions.

Nevertheless, the key issue here is to demonstrate the importance of a social-ecological approach to transitions, which is of particular importance from the point of view of sustainability (Mirtl and Krauze 2007). The social-ecological transition can be contrasted with a more traditional socio-technical approach to transitions (Smith and Stirling 2010). Lodz shifted from a complete neglect of environmental issues in the 19th century, to a sanitary city model during the socialist period, and eventually to a more integrative approach gradually adopting a social-ecological perspective. While urban green infrastructure was initially seen as a resource to be exploited for urban development, we are now moving to a system that can hopefully consider ecosystem services and natural capital. The concept of ecosystem services provides a useful framework to study those processes; for example, the extent to which the different dimensions of our reliance on nature have been incorporated into city planning over time. It also facilitates the inclusion of various interests of different stakeholders into these plans and concepts.

Taking the perspective of classical four phases of transition (Rotmans et al. 2001), it seems that Lodz is now in the take-off phase with regard to sustainability transition (especially with regard to urban green space and water governance). Depending on how the most important issues summarised in Box 20.1 are addressed, the city can move to the acceleration phase or the transition may fail, eventually bringing about a system breakdown (Grin et al. 2010). We have already witnessed many positive changes in the way in which local authorities in Lodz approach ecosystems, and there are many opportunities to accelerate this important aspect of the sustainability transition:

1 Pressure from the EU, with its political objectives set in the Green Infrastructure Strategy (European Commission 2013) and other documents related to urban nature, and with its funding mechanisms, provides an important context for all decisions made in an EU city.

2 The Blue-Green Network is very slowly being incorporated into operational urban management. Translating big concepts into operational management takes time.

3 Cooperation between the authorities and researchers and expert NGOs has increased in recent years and, while there is still much neglect, the authorities seem to be increasingly open to such collaboration.

4 Pressure from bottom-up movements, including NGOs and members of society protesting against unfavourable decisions, is becoming more commonplace, speeding up the sustainability transition process. This is increasingly important, in spite of the still rather poor social capital in Poland and other social empowerment failures.

5 In light of institutional failures, such as inconsistent regulations or regulations that downplay the importance of urban greenery, the innovativeness and determination of public authorities become a particularly important

Box 20.1 Lessons learnt from the Lodz case, highlighting the needs and priorities with regard to integrating ecosystem services into urban sustainable development.

---

1   Balance greater and inner city ecosystem considerations.
2   Enhance the protection of urban green infrastructure (new protected areas are not yet sufficient to control urban sprawl, at least in the most important ecological areas).
3   Prioritise urban sprawl restriction and restoration of the water cycle, along with ecological connectedness aimed at maintaining urban green infrastructure and securing the delivery of ecosystem services.
4   Focus on systems to link various aspects of urban planning (social and health issues, economic development, nature).
5   Pay more attention to ecosystems other than forests and parks.
6   Consider other, complementary green infrastructure components that would improve urban resilience and adaptive capacity, especially in the inner city.
7   Draw conclusions from history and current trends to properly address emerging and future problems.
8   Perform modern ecosystem assessments, including from the perspective of ecosystem services.
9   Consider environmental issues in all sectoral policies and develop human and institutional capacity for their understanding and implementation.
10 Integrate competences related to the management of urban ecosystems.
11 Facilitate collaboration between the authorities and various stakeholders.
12 Ensure a more open and determined approach to the implementation of local regulations.

---

driver in the transition process. Revitalisation, which is going to be the most important area of spending EU funds in Poland in the coming years, provides ample opportunities for considering the environment.

Some bottom-up movements along with some representatives of local authorities have become "the carriers of system change" (Frantzeskaki 2011, p. 117). However, their involvement might not have brought the same result without additional exogenous drivers in the form of EU membership and pressure on Polish government and local authorities to consider the environment in the planning documents. Even though the authorities were rather reluctant to do so, the two factors combined (bottom-up movements and the EU) have eventually succeeded in initiating the transition. Over time, the authorities in Lodz have gradually started to adapt to these pressures. Still, there are many challenges ahead, particularly with regard to institutional change – institutions play a key role in social-ecological transitions, and they have performed poorly with regard to urban greenery in Poland so far (Kronenberg 2015, Kronenberg et al. 2016).

Acknowledgements

The study described in this chapter was conducted within the GREEN SURGE EU FP7 collaborative project, FP7-ENV.2013.6.2-5-603567.

References

Bergier, T., Kronenberg, J., and Wagner, I., eds., 2014. *Water in the city*. Krakow: Sendzimir Foundation.

Bulkeley, H.A., Broto, V.C., and Edwards, G.A.S., 2014. *An urban politics of climate change: experimentation and the governing of socio-technical transitions*. London and New York: Routledge.

City of Lodz Office, 2012. *Integrated Development Strategy for Lodz 2020+*. Lodz: City of Lodz Office.

City of Lodz Office, 2013a. *Polityka komunalna i ochrony środowiska Miasta Łodzi 2020+*. Lodz: City of Lodz Office.

City of Lodz Office, 2013b. *Strategia przestrzennego rozwoju Łodzi 2020+*. Lodz: City of Lodz Office.

Dalman, J., Muszyński, K., Pistelok, F., and Polek, A., 2010. *Program ochrony środowiska dla miasta Łodzi na lata 2011–2014 z perspektywą na lata 2015–2018*. Kraków: Lemtech Konsulting.

Diehl, J., 1997. *Ecological policy for the city of Łódź*. Łódź: Łódź City Office, Department of Environmental Protection.

Elmqvist, T., Fragkias, M., Goodness, J., Güneralp, B., Marcotullio, P.J., McDonald, R.I., Parnell, S., Schewenius, M., Sendstad, M., Seto, K.C., and Wilkinson, C., eds., 2013. *Urbanization, biodiversity and ecosystem services: challenges and opportunities*. Dordrecht: Springer.

Ernstson, H., Leeuw, S.E. van der, Redman, C.L., Meffert, D.J., Davis, G., Alfsen, C., and Elmqvist, T., 2010. Urban transitions: on urban resilience and human-dominated ecosystems. *AMBIO: A Journal of the Human Environment*, 39 (8), 531–545.

European Commission, 2013. *Green Infrastructure (GI) — Enhancing Europe's Natural Capital*. Brussels: Communication from the Commission to the European Parliament, The Council, the European Economic and Social Committee and the Committee of the Regions (COM(2013) 249 final).

Fischer-Kowalski, M. and Weisz, H., 1999. Society as hybrid between material and symbolic realms: Toward a theoretical framework of society-nature interaction. *Advances in Human Ecology*, 8, 215–252.

Folke, C., 2006. Resilience: The emergence of a perspective for social–ecological systems analyses. *Global Environmental Change*, 16 (3), 253–267.

Frantzeskaki, N., 2011. *Dynamics of societal transitions: driving forces and feedback loops*. Delft: Delft University of Technology.

Fuller, R.A. and Gaston, K.J., 2009. The scaling of green space coverage in European cities. *Biology Letters*, 5 (3), 352–355.

Giergiczny, M. and Kronenberg, J., 2014. From valuation to governance: using choice experiment to value street trees. *AMBIO: A Journal of the Human Environment*, 43 (4), 492–501.

Grin, J., Rotmans, J., and Schot, J., eds., 2010. *Transitions to sustainable development: New directions in the study of long term transformative change*. London and New York: Routledge.

Haberl, H., Winiwarter, V., Andersson, K., Ayres, R.U., Boone, C., Castillo, A., Cunfer, G., Fischer-Kowalski, M., Freudenburg, W.R., Furman, E., Kaufmann, R.,

Langthaler, E., Lotze-Campen, H., Mirtl, M., Redman, C.L., Reenberg, A., Wardell, A., Warr, B., and Zechmeister, H., 2006. From LTER to LTSER: conceptualizing the socioeconomic dimension of long-term socioecological research. *Ecology & Society*, 11 (2), art. 13.

Hirt, S.A., 2012. *Iron curtains: Gates, suburbs and privatization of space in the postsocialist city*. Chichester: Wiley.

Jefferies, C. and Duffy, A., 2011. *The SWITCH transitioning manual: managing water for the city of the future*. Dundee: University of Abertay.

Kabisch, N. and Haase, D., 2013. Green spaces of European cities revisited for 1990–2006. *Landscape and Urban Planning*, 110, 113–122.

Krauze, K., Żelewski, Ł., and Włodarczyk, R., 2010. Rola zieleni miejskiej w mieście przyszłości – Błękitno-Zielona Sieć Łodzi. *Acta Universitatis Lodziensis – Folia Biologica et Oecologica*, Supplementum, 6–27.

Kronenberg, J., 2015. Why not to green a city? Institutional barriers to preserving urban ecosystem services. *Ecosystem Services*, 12, 218–227.

Kronenberg, J. and Bergier, T., 2012. Sustainable development in a transition economy: business case studies from Poland. *Journal of Cleaner Production*, 26, 18–27.

Kronenberg, J., Pietrzyk-Kaszyńska, A., Zbieg, A., and Żak, B., 2016. Wasting collaboration potential: a study in urban green space governance in a post-transition country. *Environmental Science and Policy*, 62, 69–78.

McCormick, K., Anderberg, S., Coenen, L., and Neij, L., 2013. Advancing sustainable urban transformation. *Journal of Cleaner Production*, 50, 1–11.

Mirtl, M. and Krauze, K., 2007. Developing a new strategy for environmental research, monitoring and management: The European Long-Term Ecological Research Network´s (LTER-Europe's) role and perspectives. *In*: T. Chmielewski, K. Krauze, E. Furman and S. Flemming, eds. *Nature conservation management: from idea to practical results*. Lublin: Akademia Rolnicza w Lublinie.

Pincetl, S., 2010. From the sanitary city to the sustainable city: challenges to institutionalising biogenic (nature's services) infrastructure. *Local Environment*, 15 (1), 43–58.

Piwowarczyk, J., Kronenberg, J., and Dereniowska, M., 2013. Marine ecosystem services in urban areas: do the strategic documents of Polish coastal municipalities reflect their importance? *Landscape and Urban Planning*, 109 (1), 85–93.

Ratajczyk, N. and Drzazga, D., 2005. Rewitalizacja przyrodnicza a procesy zarządzania rozwojem miasta na przykładzie Łodzi. *Teka Komisji Architektury, Urbanistyki i Studiów Krajobrazowych – OL PAN*, (1), 135–148.

Ratajczyk, N., Wolańska-Kamińska, A., and Kopeć, D., 2010. Problemy realizacji systemu przyrodniczego miasta na przykładzie Łodzi. *In*: M. Burchard-Dziubińska and A. Rzeńca, eds. *Zrównoważony rozwój na poziomie lokalnym i regionalnym: Wyzwania dla miast i obszarów wiejskich*. Łódź: Wydawnictwo Uniwersytetu Łódzkiego, 78–97.

Rosset, I., Żądzińska, E., Wagner, I., Borowska-Strugińska, B., Lorkiewicz, W., Sitek, A., and Śmiszkiewicz-Skwarska, A., 2012. Badania pilotażowe związku środowiska urbanizacyjnego Łodzi ze statusem społeczno-ekonomicznym rodzin w aspekcie oddziaływania na wybrane parametry morfologiczne dzieci. *Przeglad Pediatryczny*, 42 (3), 133–140.

Rotmans, J., Kemp, R., and van Asselt, M., 2001. More evolution than revolution: transition management in public policy. *Foresight*, 3 (1), 15–31.

Smith, A. and Stirling, A., 2010. The politics of social-ecological resilience and sustainable socio-technical transitions. *Ecology and Society*, 15 (1), art. 11.

Staniszkis, M., 2012. Continuity of change vs. change of continuity: a diagnosis and evaluation of Warsaw's urban transformation. *In*: M. Grubbauer and J. Kusiak, eds. *Chasing Warsaw: socio-material dynamics of urban change since 1990*. Frankfurt-on-Main: Campus, 81–108.

Szukalski, P., 2012. *Sytuacja demograficzna Łodzi*. Lodz: Biblioteka.

Szulczewska, B. and Kaliszuk, E., 2003. Challenges in the planning and management of 'Greenstructure' in Warsaw, Poland. *Built Environment*, 29 (2), 144–156.

Wagner, I. and Breil, P., 2013. The role of ecohydrology in creating more resilient cities. *Ecohydrology & Hydrobiology*, 13 (2), 113–134.

Wagner, I., da Silva Wells, C., Butterworth, J., and Dziegielewska-Geitz, M., 2011. Lodz: city of water. *In*: J. Butterworth, P. McIntyre, and C. da S. Wells, eds. *SWITCH in the city: putting urban water management to the test*. The Hague: IRC International Water and Sanitation Centre, 210–221.

Wagner, I. and Zalewski, M., 2009. Ecohydrology as a basis for the sustainable city strategic planning: focus on Lodz, Poland. *Reviews in Environmental Science and Bio/Technology*, 8 (3), 209–217.

Wilkinson, C., Saarne, T., Peterson, G.D., and Colding, J., 2013. Strategic spatial planning and the ecosystem services concept – an historical exploration. *Ecology and Society*, 18 (1), art. 37.

Wysmyk-Lamprecht, B., Stobińska, A., Jach, K., and Miłosz, M., 2007. *Opracowanie ekofizjograficzne sporządzone na potrzeby Studium uwarunkowań i kierunków zagospodarowania przestrzennego miasta Łodzi*. Łódź.

Zalewski, M., Wagner, I., Frątczak, W., Mankiewicz-Boczek, J., and Parniewski, P., 2012. Blue-green city for compensating global climate change. *Parliament Magazine*, 350, 2–3.

INTERLUDE

21 The Politics of Urban Sustainability Transitions

Thaddeus R. Miller and Anthony M. Levenda

Introduction

Sustainability transitions present obvious engineering and policy challenges to urban governance regimes (Bulkeley et al. 2010, Makard et al. 2012, Meadowcroft 2011). The increasing salience of sustainability discourse and policies in cities across the globe has resulted in the proliferation of sustainability bureaus and agencies, large-scale public deliberations over sustainability goals, and changes in infrastructure planning and design (Bulkeley and Betsill 2005, Bäckstrand 2003). Despite a strong emphasis on the importance of public input and engagement, particularly in the transitions management literature (Kemp and Rotmans 2005), urban sustainability policy and planning are increasingly domains dominated by bureaucratic, scientific and technological expertise (Miller 2015). Urban sustainability is often defined by technological developments, standards and indicators focused on delivering efficiencies or lowering carbon emissions. For example, the Portland Development Commission in Portland, Oregon, US – widely considered one of the most sustainable cities in North America – *We Build Green Cities* initiative works with the Portland policy and business community to "export our best ideas, products, and services to other cities around the world that aspire to be more sustainable" (PDC 2015). This effort is largely focused on economic development and the development and export of technical products and expertise. Similarly, urban sustainability policies and indicators are often measured by the development and implementation of technical standards for buildings (e.g., LEED in the US), neighborhoods and communities (e.g., LEED ND, EcoDistricts, and the International Standards Organization Sustainable Development in Communities).

Largely ignored in much of the public and policy discourse on urban sustainability, however, are the social and political dimensions of sustainability – how it is interpreted, enrolled and contested by various actors and institutions, and ultimately settled and materialized in infrastructure and technological design. The emphasis on the scientific and technological aspects of sustainability *de*politicizes it – masking the degree to which technological choices are also social and political choices. This serves to black box (Latour 1987) and make invisible the values and implications of policy and design choices. It is precisely because of the relative invisibility and obduracy of past political and technical decisions embedded in our sociotechnical systems that we rarely have political conversations about infrastructure. For example, how might information and communication technologies support or hinder democratic values? How does transportation infrastructure promote or impede social equity? How does water control and delivery enhance or ignore environmental values? How do energy systems foreclose or open opportunities for innovation?

Sustainability transitions have the power to open-up conversations (Stirling 2008) about previously hidden physical systems and their political and ethical implications by engaging decision-makers, experts and publics in discussions about the future and potential transition pathways. Building on theories of the social construction of technological systems, and the larger science and technology studies (STS) literature, we explore the visions of urban sustainability to connect its multiple, shifting understandings and complexities. At the same time, this process of deconstruction and reconstruction opens up areas of political negotiation for further investigation and contestation.

In this chapter, we argue that this can only be done by politicizing sustainability, embracing and exploring the political nature of sustainability discourses (Miller and Lubitow 2014, Moore 2006). Utilizing examples from the contributions in this volume and drawing from insights from STS, we present several critical axes to develop a more robust understanding of how politics operates in urban sustainability transitions (Grin 2012). First, we discuss how power operates across sociotechnical systems, opening-up and closing-down potential pathways for urban transitions. Second, we examine the politics of scientific and technological knowledge and expertise, and the degree to which it has come to define urban sustainability discourse. Finally, we consider the importance of political dynamics in public engagement and deliberation.

Techno-Politics and Power in Sociotechnical Systems

Cities are comprised of sociotechnical systems that are acted upon, manipulated, and reconfigured in transitions to sustainability (Hodson and Marvin 2010). Political, economic, cultural and other urban processes and networks overlap and intersect with sociotechnical systems at various scales which make transitions messy, contested, and difficult (Hodson and Marvin 2009, Monstadt 2009, Lawhon and Murphy 2012). This has led to many reflexive considerations of the multi-level perspective on transitions, fueling alternative frameworks and understandings, and reformulations of the approach (Smith, Voß and Grin 2010, Geels 2011). Späth and Rohracher (this volume) make explicit note of the lack of consideration of urban processes and their impacts on transitions while Elle, Braagaard Harders and Valderrama Pineda (this volume) utilize a "flatter" arenas of development approach that does not assume niche–regime–landscape interactions. In these various approaches, power, as an ability to shape the behavior of people and systems and influence outcomes, needs to be treated as a central concern.

We understand power as it relates to urban transitions processes through political, economic, ideological, and epistemological lenses. Urban political economy is concerned with the shaping of urban infrastructures and industries, the control of labor, and the role of institutions in solidifying existing relations of power (Harvey 2009). Culture and ideology can be manipulated to maintain unequal social structures and provide means of control making particular alternatives less feasible or altogether unrealizable. The power/knowledge relationship finds power in the epistemologies that shape and legitimate particular understandings of a more sustainable and democratic world (Foucault 1980; Jasanoff 2004a,b). Each of these elements of power contributes to the shaping of urban sustainability transitions (Hendriks 2009).

Building on this work and missing from both academic and public discourses around urban sustainability, however, is a thicker conception of techno-politics, that is, how sociotechnical systems come to constitute, embody, and enact political goals (Hecht 1998). Power and politics shape sociotechnical systems, "opening-up" or "closing-down" sustainability pathways (Stirling 2008). These techno-politics then become obdurate as they become physically manifested in the built environment and in governance regimes that maintain and manage it (Hommels 2005).

The chapters in this section begin to point to a path toward this work, but lack the common conceptual and theoretical tools to examine how techno-politics acts to open-up or close-down sustainability pathways. As Späth and Rohracher (this volume) show in Freiburg, Germany, tensions between overlapping technological solutions for energy sustainability in the built environment (district heating and passive houses) illustrate the power of developers in partnership with the city to implement and enact particular projects, even with legitimate contestation. Likewise, in the Carlsberg City District of Copenhagen, Denmark, developers and private investors valued economic interests over environmental concerns in the allowance of parking spaces in the sustainable development area, encouraging increased car traffic in the area (Elle, Braagaard Harders and Valderrama Pineda, this volume). In these cases, powerful actors are able to connect with various interests and mobilize them within and between networks to enact changes in the development of urban sustainability projects, even under conflict or competition.

These chapters also show how power is unevenly distributed in sociotechnical systems. Rohracher and Späth explain how sustainability in different cities' energy projects led to "zones of friction" wherein sociotechnical systems change, or transitions, conflicted in various ways. They use this general critique and framework to analyze "transition in the making" from a bottom-up perspective in Graz, Austria and Freiburg. In both cases, there is a distinct conflict over sustainability projects (hydropower in Graz and district heating/*Passivhaus* in Freiburg) that exemplifies how sustainability-focused change processes are in fact political, altering existing systems while disrupting the potential benefits of others, and reframing visions of sustainable cities.

Meadowcroft (2009, 2011) and Shove and Walker (2007), for instance, argue that power and politics in research on sustainability transitions have been weakly developed and thus need more focus in transitions research. More recent work on sustainability transitions has explicitly focused on power and politics, arguing that existing regimes actively resist change through utilizing various forms of power, and that focus should be paid on destabilizing these incumbent regimes (Geels 2014). Challenging the lock-in and obduracy of these existing networks and regimes is essential for realizing sustainability transitions (Smith and Stirling 2010). Urban sustainability transitions need to confront these various conflicts and power structures to ensure more sustainable, just and democratic outcomes. We begin with an exploration of the politics of knowledge and how it shapes urban sustainability discourse and practice.

Politics of Knowledge

Scientific and technological knowledge and expertise have come to dominate debates over the legitimacy and effectiveness of sustainability pathways (Gieryn 1999, Guy and Marvin 1999, Guy 2006). This mirrors developments in environmental governance where climate science, for instance, has come to define the contours of international discussion over policy responses (Edwards 2010, Jasanoff 2004a, Pielke and Sarewitz 2005). The emergence of smart cities illustrates this dynamic.

Under the rubric of "smart cities", advanced information and communication technology (ICT) systems, including sensor networks and data gathering and analytics, are providing enormous amounts of data to be processed and utilized by cities. The goal is often to ensure more sustainable operations and planning (IBM et al. 2009, Allwinkle and Cruickshank 2011), albeit with some criticism and concern (Crang and Graham 2007, Hollands 2008). These systems are driven by models that make sense of the city in ways that do not rely on social, phenomenological, or affective dimensions, but rather information that is abstracted from the urban context. Alongside this ICT infrastructure, a new "science of cities" is emerging, combining elements of physics, complexity science and urban informatics, with concerns over urban structure and organization (Batty 2012, Bettencourt and West 2010). Data from these systems fuels their analysis and predictions about the future of cities, and further informs visions and actions towards addressing sustainability. This way of studying, sensing, and knowing the city can privilege expert knowledge and top-down strategies for sustainability transitions. For example, Swilling et al. (this volume) demonstrate that information gathering is key to measurement and monitoring for sustainable resource use in cities, but that the context of African cities presents a point of diversion that illustrates the need for embracing alternative notions of urbanism in the sustainable city.

The place of scientific and technological expertise in urban sustainability transitions is of concern for three core reasons. First, scientific research on urban sustainability not only produces knowledge about the city and sustainability transitions but also helps to shape political identities, relationships, institutions, and beliefs about sustainability goals (Miller 2013, 2014). This co-production process can shape the discourse and policy choices around urban sustainability, thereby exercising political power (Jasanoff 2004b; Latour 2004). The implication is not that we should seek to thwart the ability of science and technology to foster sustainability transitions. Instead, this points to an important role for research on transitions – that is, to empirically examine the ways in which science and technology shape sustainability discourses and the social, political and ethical implications of these dynamics.

Second, expert knowledge can lend credibility to both knowledge and value claims about the city or sustainability problems (Gieryn 2006, Miller 2014). As illustrated by Elle, Braagaard Harders, and Valderrama Pineda (this volume), parking space allotments (p-norm) were a point of contention between city officials who advocated for fewer spaces to enhance alternative modes of transit, and developers and business interests who wanted more parking for potential customers and ultimately utilized outside consulting firms who could use "unbiased" expert judgment to calculate the optimal p-norm in the Carlsberg City District. Scientific knowledge affects public deliberation over transitions as knowledge claims lend political credibility, while stakeholders without access to knowledge-generating institutions may have little power (Jasanoff 1999, Miller 2008).

Finally, scientific and technological expertise has increasingly come to shape the terms and foci of urban sustainability discourses on issues such as green buildings, energy efficiency and carbon emissions reductions. While these core issues are central to sustainability transitions, they also rely on technological solutions with little, if any, political contestation or deliberation. Critical issues around social equity and broad-based public participation that may carry more overtly political implications are at risk of being sidelined in the research and practice of urban sustainability transitions.

Politics in Public Participation and Deliberation

The study and practice of sustainability transitions has rightly placed an emphasis on public deliberation over the meaning, goals and pathways of sustainability (Miller 2013, Loorbach 2007, Robinson 2003). This underscores the degree to which sustainability is situated in and emergent from social, ecological, and political contexts (Miller 2014, Norton 2005, Robinson 2003). Yet, largely missing from these efforts is a more critical understanding of how power and politics shape the processes and outcomes of public participation and deliberation. While public engagement is critical to the development of robust and widely shared values, goals and policies, it can also serve to mute political contestation via consensus. A brief case from Portland, Oregon, illustrates the importance of considering politics in participation around sustainability transitions in urban infrastructure.

Miller and Lubitow (2014) explore the evolution of a community controversy over the expansion and redesign of cycling infrastructure along North Williams Avenue, a major commuter route and bustling neighborhood in Portland – a city consistently ranked as the most bike-friendly city in the United States (Dille 2012). In city bicycling and transportation planning documents, N. Williams had been identified in as a major bikeway and earmarked for infrastructure investment, an effort lauded by local cycling advocates. N. Williams is also situated in a historically African American community, which has been consistently marginalized in city planning and development over the last several decades and has more recently dealt with community and economic displacement due to gentrification (Gibson 2007).

At the outset, the North Williams Traffic Safety and Operations Project was defined as a infrastructure project focused on issues of pedestrian and traffic safety and cycling access. This safety and access frame represented the consensus among transportation planners at the City of Portland Bureau of Transportation (PBOT) and cycling advocate groups (Lubitow and Miller 2013). Transportation engineers and planners and cycling advocates have a long history of working together on cycling issues in Portland, and had developed a common understanding of such issues. This dominant framing was upset as a community backlash to the project emerged at several community meetings. Critiques from the African American community targeted the composition of the community Stakeholder Advisory Committee to PBOT on the project and pointed to long-lasting concerns that had remained unaddressed. Additionally, community members cited this project as being the latest in a long line of city planning projects that marginalized the concerns of African Americans and other minorities in Portland.

How did a seemingly benign cycling infrastructure project become such a source of political controversy? More broadly, the settled consensus around cycling infrastructure on N. Williams and Portland, had been developed by transportation experts and cycling advocates, who implicitly shared certain framings and values around transportation planning and the vision of the street (Miller and Lubitow 2014). This expertise and its place in city institutions and governance dominated conversations around transportation and cycling policy and planning. Alternative views around cycling and visions for the street and community were, sometimes unintentionally, shut out by this shared frame. It took a controversy that gained wide coverage in local and national media to upset this status quo. To PBOT's credit, the Stakeholder Advisory Committee was expanded to include a more diverse set of community members and tasked with setting community priorities for the project and developing a new design. This last development shows the power of participation, when broadly inclusive, to shape the physical design of urban sustainability transitions (Miller and Lubitow 2014).

The chapters in this section begin to chart a way to adopt a more careful, bottom-up approach to sustainability transitions that may "open-up" space for a more pluralistic politics. Swilling et al. (this volume) and Rohracher and Späth (this volume) advocate for a bottom-up or grassroots approach to sustainability transitions that takes into account competing conceptualizations and articulations of "the urban" and sustainability in various contexts of transitions (Hendriks and Grin 2007). Developing shared visions (Davies et al. 2012), modes of measurement and monitoring (in sustainability indicators. for example, Miller 2005), and knowledge for addressing sustainability (Miller et al. 2011) are key to the implementation of equitable transitions. However, additional research and actual progress on how to "empower" participation and deliberation are still needed, while preserving the importance of context and history in societal transitions to sustainability. Kronenberg, Krauze and Wagner (this volume) explain that embracing and operationalizing big complex concepts, like transitions to sustainability, takes tremendous democratic collaboration between various groups and sectors. Collaboration fueled by bottom-up movements, including social unrest and protests, are powerful agents of change in sustainability-related urban transition processes. Collectively, these chapters illustrate the central need for broader engagement and deliberation about urban sustainability and ways of achieving it.

Politicizing Sustainability

This chapter has argued for a more political conceptualization of sustainability transitions. While chapters in the volume and elsewhere have begun this work, this chapter is an effort to sharpen some common theoretical and conceptual tools around how politics and power shape urban sustainability transitions. Both the study and practice of sustainability must be *politicized* to avoid limiting the debate over visions, values and goals to those with access and control over the credibility or legitimacy of empirical claims. A political sustainability more openly embraces the normative dimensions of sustainability (Miller 2013, Norton 2005, Wiek et al. 2011) as well as the various forms of power that influence particular conceptualizations and operationalized modes of sustainability.

While transitions researchers and other sustainability scholars often expound on how science and governance for sustainability ought to be reflexive and have explored cases where this occurs (Hendriks and Grin 2007, Miller 2015, Voß and Bornemann 2011, Voß et al. 2006), we also need to be attuned to how the politics of sustainability are shaped in practice. Techno-politics focuses our analyses and perhaps advocacy on how values and politics are *built into* our cities, shape our lives and communities, and become obdurate (Miller and Lubitow 2014; Winner 1986). It also challenges researchers and practitioners to explore how alternative values and politics can be designed into urban infrastructure transitions. Developing a more robust agenda around the politics of sustainability transitions offers several avenues for research and practice that build on the axes discussed in this chapter. First, researchers play a critical role in examining controversies over sustainability transitions in order to uncover how various actors and institutions understand the goals and policies for sustainability, and, more broadly, the future of their communities and cities (Voß and Bornemann 2011). This will contribute to a more diverse and plural understanding of sustainability pathways in both research and practice (Leach et al. 2010, Miller 2014, Muñoz-Erickson 2014). Following this, research on the politics of sustainability transition can explore how values and politics are built into sustainability policy and technology design. This "opening up" of the black box of infrastructure and technology can empower often marginalized groups to contest expert design choices and ultimately shape outcomes. Finally, transitions scholars should continue to build on research on "transition arenas" and participation, with particular attention to how power shapes who is included and how expertise frames the terms of discussion. In addition, research of participatory dynamics can show how meaningful engagement and deliberation influence policy and design choices—and how alternative methods might do so more effectively (Davies et al. 2012).

This volume is a tribute to the dynamic, diverse and thriving research on sustainability transitions. This does not mean there is no room for critique and improvement. The research and practice of sustainability transitions must focus on how power and politics shape transitions pathways and its implications not only for sustainability goals, but also for whose voices and perspectives are included or marginalized.

References

Allwinkle, S., and Cruickshank, P. (2011). Creating smart-er cities: an overview. *Journal of Urban Technology*, *18*(2), 1–16.

Bäckstrand, K. (2003). Civic science for sustainability: reframing the role of experts, policy-makers and citizens in environmental governance. *Global Environmental Politics*, *3*(4), 24–41.

Batty, M. (2012). Building a science of cities. *Cities*, *29*, S9–S16.

Bettencourt, L., and West, G. (2010). A unified theory of urban living. *Nature*, *467*(7318), 912–913.

Bulkeley, H., and Betsill, M. M. (2005). *Cities and climate change: urban sustainability and global environmental governance.* London: Routledge.

Bulkeley, H., Castan-Broto, V., Hodson, M., and Marvin, S. (2010). *Cities and low carbon transitions.* London and New York: Routledge.

Crang, M., and Graham, S. (2007). Sentient cities: ambient intelligence and the politics of urban space. *Information, Communication & Society*, *10*(6), 789–817.

Davies, S. R., Selin, C., Gano, G., and Pereira, Â. G. (2012). Citizen engagement and urban change: Three case studies of material deliberation. *Cities*, *29*(6), 351–357.

Dille, I. (2012, May). America's Top 50 Bike-Friendly Cities. *Bicycling*. Retrieved from http://www.bicycling.com

Dirks, S., and Keeling, M. (2009). A vision of smarter cities: How cities can lead the way into a prosperous and sustainable future. IBM Institute for Business Value.

Edwards, P. N. (2010). *A vast machine: computer models, climate data, and the politics of global warming.* Cambridge, MA: MIT Press.

Foucault, M. 1980. *Power/Knowledge.* Colin Gordon, editor. New York: Vintage Books.

Geels, F. W. (2011). The multi-level perspective on sustainability transitions: responses to seven criticisms. *Environmental Innovation and Societal Transitions*, *1*(1), 24–40.

Geels, F. W. (2014). Regime resistance against low-carbon transitions: introducing politics and power into the multi-level perspective. *Theory, Culture & Society*, 0263276414531627.

Gibson, K. J. (2007). Bleeding Albina: A history of community disinvestment, 1940–2000. *Transforming Anthropology*, *15*(1), 3–25.

Gieryn, T. F. (1999). *Cultural boundaries of science: credibility on the line.* Chicago: University of Chicago Press.

Gieryn, T. F. (2006). City as truth-spot: laboratories and field-sites in urban studies. *Social Studies of Science, 36*(1), 5–38.

Grin, J. (2012). The governance of transitions and its politics. Conceptual lessons from the earlier agricultural transition and implications for transition management. *Int. J. Sustainable Development 15*(1–2), 72–89.

Guy, S. (2006). Designing urban knowledge: competing perspectives on energy and buildings. *Environment and Planning C, 24*(5), 645.

Guy, S., and Marvin, S. (1999). Understanding sustainable cities: competing urban futures. *European Urban and Regional Studies, 6*(3), 268–275.

Harvey, D. (2009). *Social justice and the city*. Athens, GA: University of Georgia Press.

Hecht, G. (1998). The Radiance of France: Nuclear Power and National Identity After World War II. Cambridge: MIT Press.

Hendriks, C. M. (2009). Deliberative governance in the context of power. *Policy and Society 28*(3), 173–184.

Hendriks, C. M., and Grin, J. (2007). Contextualising reflexive governance: the politics of Dutch transitions to sustainability. *Journal of Environmental Policy and Planning 9*(3/4), 333–350.

Hodson, M., and Marvin, S. (2009). Cities mediating technological transitions: understanding visions, intermediation and consequences. *Technology Analysis & Strategic Management, 21*(4), 515–534.

Hodson, M., and Marvin, S. (2010). Can cities shape socio-technical transitions and how would we know if they were? *Research Policy, 39*(4), 477–485.

Hollands, R. G. (2008). Will the real smart city please stand up? Intelligent, progressive or entrepreneurial? *City, 12*(3), 303–320.

Hommels, A. (2005). *Unbuilding cities: Obduracy in urban socio-technical change*. Cambridge, MA: MIT Press.

Jasanoff, S. (1999). The songlines of risk. *Environmental Values*, 135–152.

Jasanoff, S. (2004a). Heaven and earth: the politics of environmental images. In Jasanoff, S., and Martello, M. L. (Eds.). *Earthly politics: local and global in environmental governance*. Cambridge, MA: MIT press.

Jasanoff, S. (2004b). The idiom of co-production. In Jasanoff, S. (Ed.). *States of knowledge: the co-production of science and the social order*. London and New York: Routledge.

Kemp, R., and Rotmans, J. (2005). The management of the co-evolution of technical, environmental and social systems. In Weber, M., and Hemmelskamp, J. (Eds.). *Towards environmental innovation systems* (pp. 33–55). Springer Berlin Heidelberg.

Latour, B. (1987). *Science in action: How to follow scientists and engineers through society*. Cambridge, MA: Harvard University Press.

Latour, B. (2004). *Politics of nature*. Cambridge, MA: Harvard University Press.

Lawhon, M., and Murphy, J. T. (2012). Socio-technical regimes and sustainability transitions: insights from political ecology. *Progress in Human Geography, 36*(3), 354–378.

Leach, M., Scoones, I., & Stirling, A. (2010). *Dynamic sustainabilities: technology, environment, social justice*. London: Earthscan.

Loorbach, D.A. (2007). Governance for sustainability. *Sustainability: Science, Policy & Practice, 3*(2), 1–4.

Lubitow, A., and Miller, T. R. (2013). Contesting Sustainability: Bikes, Race, and Politics in Portlandia. *Environmental Justice, 6*(4), 121–126.

Markard, J., Raven, R., and Truffer, B. (2012). Sustainability transitions: an emerging field of research and its prospects. *Research Policy, 41*(6), 955–967.

Meadowcroft, J. (2009). What about the politics? Sustainable development, transition management, and long term energy transitions. *Policy Sciences, 42*(4), 323–340.

Meadowcroft, J. (2011). Engaging with the 'politics' of sustainability transitions. *Environmental Innovation and Societal Transitions, 1*(1), 70–75.

Miller, C. A. (2005). New civic epistemologies of quantification: making sense of indicators of local and global sustainability. *Science, Technology & Human Values*, *30*(3), 403–432.

Miller, C. A. (2008). Civic epistemologies: constituting knowledge and order in political communities. *Sociology Compass*, *2*(6), 1896–1919.

Miller, T. R. (2013). Constructing sustainability science: emerging perspectives and research trajectories. *Sustainability Science*, *8*(2), 279–293.

Miller, T.R. (2014). *Reconstructing sustainability science: knowledge and action for a sustainable future*. London and New York: Routledge.

Miller, T. R., and Lubitow, A. (2014). The politics of cycling infrastructure: contested urban bikeway development in Portland, Oregon. In Agyeman, J. and Zavestoski, S. (Eds.) *Incomplete Streets*. Equity, Justice and the Sustainable City series. London and New York: Routledge.

Miller, T. R., Muñoz-Erickson, T., and Redman, C. L. (2011). Transforming knowledge for sustainability: towards adaptive academic institutions. *International Journal of Sustainability in Higher Education*, *12*(2), 177–192.

Monstadt, J. (2009). Conceptualizing the political ecology of urban infrastructures: insights from technology and urban studies. *Environment and Planning A*, *41*(8), 1924.

Moore, S. A. (2006). *Alternative routes to the sustainable city: Austin, Curitiba, and Frankfurt*. Lanham: Lexington Books.

Muñoz-Erickson, T. A. (2014). Multiple pathways to sustainability in the city: the case of San Juan, Puerto Rico. *Ecology and Society, 19*(3), 2.

Norton, B. G. (2005). *Sustainability: A philosophy of adaptive ecosystem management*. Chicago: University of Chicago Press.

PDC (Portland Development Commission). (2015). We Build Green Cities. Accessed at http://www.webuildgreencities.com/ [5 May 2015].

Pielke Jr, R. A., and Sarewitz, D. (2005). Bringing society back into the climate debate. *Population and Environment*, *26*(3), 255–268.

Robinson, J. (2003). Future subjunctive: backcasting as social learning. *Futures*, *35*(8), 839–856.

Shove, E., & Walker, G. (2007). CAUTION! Transitions ahead: politics, practice, and sustainable transition management. *Environment and Planning A, 39*(4), 763–770.

Smith, A., and Stirling, A. (2010). The politics of social-ecological resilience and sustainable socio-technical transitions. *Ecology and Society*, *15*(1), 11.

Smith, A., Voß, J. P., and Grin, J. (2010). Innovation studies and sustainability transitions: the allure of the multi-level perspective and its challenges. *Research Policy*, *39*(4), 435–448.

Stirling, A. (2008). "Opening up" and "closing down" power, participation, and pluralism in the social appraisal of technology. *Science, Technology & Human Values*, *33*(2), 262–294.

Voß, J.-P., Bauknecht, D., and Kemp. R. (Eds.). (2006). *Reflexive governance for sustainable development*. Cheltenham, UK: Edward Elgar.

Voß, J.-P., and Bornemann, B. (2011). The politics of reflexive governance: challenges for designing adaptive management and transition management. *Ecology and Society 16*(2), 9. [online] URL: http://www.ecologyandsociety.org/vol16/iss2/art9/

Wiek, A., Withycombe, L., and Redman, C. L. (2011). Key competencies in sustainability: a reference framework for academic program development. *Sustainability Science*, *6*(2), 203–218.

Winner, L. (1986). *The whale and the reactor: a search for limits in an age of high technology*. Chicago: University of Chicago Press.

Part IV

Taking Stock and Connecting with Sustainability Transitions Studies

22 Sustainability Transitions and the City

Linking to Transition Studies and Looking Forward

John Grin, Niki Frantzeskaki, Vanesa Castán Broto and Lars Coenen

Why Are Urban Transitions Different? And How?

Bringing forward the lessons from the collection presented in this volume, the key question that still remains is, why should we focus on urban transitions, particularly? In other words, why are urban transitions different? Such question emerges from within a context in which the urban has not been immediately recognized as the 'natural' context for transition. Instead, much focus has gone into characterizing national-based transitions that relate technological innovation systems with national policies for innovation. The immediate reaction is to think of urban transitions as mediated by a localized form of government. As local governments take interest in innovation and sustainability policy, they should also play a role in bringing about systemic change.

Such explanation completely misses the point about why the urban context has generated particular interest both in relation to what transitions are possible (Droege, 2011) and the forms of sustainability governance that are particularly urban (Bulkeley et al., 2014). Asking why urban transitions are different immediately foregrounds another question that has structured the development of this volume: what specific lessons we can draw out from the dynamics of urban transitions, the conflicts and synergies between spatial scales that are revealed in urban transitions and the potential for cities to foster broader systemic change at a national or trans-national scale.

The distinctiveness of sustainability transitions in cities is reflected in the diverse and complex dynamics present and the unfitness of single frameworks to explain them (Wolfram, 2016). Urban sustainability transitions call for a certain theoretical promiscuity that enables a broader engagement with diverse ways of understanding and approaching the urban. Yet, there are common themes that emerge from a collective reading of the contributions to this book. By summarizing this contribution we aim to elucidate what an urban perspective brings to the broader field of transitions to sustainability.

First, comparing urban transitions with transitions in societal domains like food, health, energy and mobility, to which earlier volumes in this series were devoted (central in transition studies) is that urban transitions require a different *unit of analysis*. As argued elsewhere (Grin, 2008: 55–57), a focus on domains is a valid way to analyse historical transitions so as to understand how regimes are structurally embedded in broader technological systems that shape and structure sectors. Focusing on the city as a unit of analysis, however, enables, a type of analysis that engages with real world contexts and with multiple sectors simultaneously. In the context of contemporary transitions, whose eventual result is unknown, the city may as a unit of analysis may offer better opportunities when it is not (yet) clear what domains are evolving or how they are evolving. Transitions for example, may involve domain recombining, for example, with prosumers tying together the domains of 'living' and 'energy production', or 'waste management' and 'production'. As such, the 'urban' in sustainability transitions offers a ground to go beyond domain-explanations and look at multi-regime, 'drifting transitions' across-domains and regimes (Frantzeskaki et al., 2016).

Second, and even more fundamentally, this unit of analysis is a *place*. We share Coenen et al.'s (2012: 969) perspective on space as a relational, meaning that it is developed in the interstices between different elements and actors as a shared property, a common plane of action (Agnew and Corbridge, 1995). From this perspective, distance cannot be equated to merely physical proximity: places at significant physical distance may be related to each other physically, institutionally or through (social and communicative) networks. Cities are thus both places of physical proximity and generally well 'placed' to enable linkages to other physical spaces. This enables them to be laboratories for novel solutions to societal problem (which also tend to be concentrated in cities), drawing on what we typically find in cities: a vibrant civil society, innovation systems (with access beyond the border), and infrastructures that provide connections to both national and international networks of interest (Hodson and Marvin, 2010). As Coenen et al. (2012) have argued, this may be a self-reinforcing effect: such networks may help support 'remote' relationships, extending the notion of 'proximity.' A similar argument has been made by Smith and Raven (2012: 68), referring to evidence from historical studies on glocalisation. For the most enthusiastic defenders of urban-based governance, cities and regions increasingly replace nation states as the key players economic globalisation (Brenner, 2004), having both creative potential and access to mechanisms for a global scaling up of transitions. If transitions may be understood as a 'trialectics' of creativity, power and societal change (Hoffman, 2013), it is clear that urban transitions may benefit from manifold opportunities to initiate, and upscale transitions.

Altogether, this in a nutshell indicates the a priori reasons to assume that cities may play key roles in transitions – answering *why* they matter and should be considered separately. But if the question of why urban areas should be considered has a clear answer, the questions about how they matter, and how they shape transition, remain largely unanswered. In this volume we have try to focus on providing evidence to support different arguments about how cities matter, including (i) how cities offer opportunities for breeding transition beyond incumbent domains; (ii) what 'proximity' means (physically close, communicatively interconnected or institutionally connected) network; and (iii) the politics, that is, the powering, legitimization, trust-building and participation involved.

Briefly in this chapter, we seek to bring together these insights by focusing on the idea of *cities as relational places*. From the point of the departure, our question becomes normative. It is not about whether cities could possibly influence transitions, but rather, about whether they can promote sustainability transitions. In doing so, we will emphasize agency, that is, the 'capacity to act otherwise'. As argued by Bettini et al. in this volume, "neither a short-term nor an incremental crisis provide an automatic mechanism for opening a system to new directions and opportunities". Transitions are not unfolding processes on the aftermath of the crisis, as previous scholars of transition have argued (Rotmans et al., 2001). Looking closer at the urban context, the crisis may even provide a justification for the continuation of past thinking and solutions. Sometimes urban areas are perceived to be on a continue state of crisis, with shortcomings of infrastructure delivery and maintenance shaping the governance possibilities. Instead, urban areas emerge as spaces of opening, arenas of action which create opportunities for new ideas and solutions that follow the emergence of collective agency in governance. McPhearson and Wijsman point at the interdependencies that need to be investigated from looking at how biophysical and material flows and conditions provided by urban ecosystems relate to ongoing and historical transition dynamics. Bringing an urban ecology perspective to unpack transition dynamics in cities, the biophysical and material conditions come forward that have so far been largely neglected by transition studies of sectoral systems.

In a systematic review of the potential role of cities, Hodson and Marvin (2010: 481–483), informed by exploratory empirical work, have proposed three key contributions. They see cities as the loci for elaborating visions, as places to do transitions, or as the home spaces of potential intermediaries. These three alternative visions of the role of cities have inspired many of the chapters of this book and its very conceptualization. Hence, we use this threefold understanding of the role of cities as a starting point for our discussion.

Cities as Relational Places

First, cities as a place may be the *locus where visions are generated that bring together abstract ideas about innovations with the practices, preferences, protests and possibilities found in a real place*. Such processes are obviously politically laden, as the outcome will depend on the powering, puzzling and participation involved (Hodson and Marvin, 2009, and Rohracher and Späth, 2014, who offer also empirical examples). In cities, local sustainability visions are closer to challenges for social justice, quality of living in cities (e.g., via green spaces and green amenities), as well as on how technological innovations reinforce new lifestyles and practices. Local visions created and stewarded in cities are easier to take up and act as attractors for action and partnerships to be realized (Frantzeskaki et al., 2014). Swilling et al also point at the way socio-economic developments and trends can manifest through new visions for urban development that is inclusive not only socially but also inclusive to transformation pathways for African cities.

Second, cities are places *connected to, and interconnecting, practices and regime elements from a range of societal domains.* As Hodson and Marvin (2010: 482) point out, urban transitions imply a transformation of the relationships between cities and their governance arrangements, and societal domains like the energy sector, the health care system or the mobility system. Here they use a notion of urban regime close to that of urban infrastructure regimes, because they are recognized both because of the role they play in configuring normal socio-technical trajectories on the one hand, and maintaining the urban metabolism on the other (Monstadt, 2009). From a relational perspective, this is a matter of connecting, disconnecting or re-connecting niche practices with each other and with regime practices. It is also a matter of connecting niches practices with elements from knowledge and physical infrastructures, governance arrangements, partnerships, market arrangements and so on, in ways that may develop into niche-regimes (de Haan and Rotmans, 2012. As cities occupy central places in national and transnational arrangements, one might expect that connections made around specific practices may also contribute to broadening, deepening and scaling up transitions.

In line with this, the contribution of Binz and Truffer showcase that cities are the fertile grounds that new technologies, new practices and new narratives arrive to be tested, embedded and upscaled. Local actors play a catalytic role in creating agency via establishing and seeking connections for embedding and locally translating new innovations that will benefit sustainability transitions in the city context. Bettini et al argue that politics for transitions in cities needed to be considered more at heart. Specifically, they call for attention to legacy issues as "critical for progressing a transitions" especially related to planning practices and traditions that need to be reflected upon and renewed for transformative ideas and practices to appeal viable. In their suggestions, they position the role of experiments as setting the scene for "an evidence base – political, economic and moral – for change agenda".

Fratini and Jensen argue that different meanings of urban elements such as urban water allow for contradictions and conflicts to be addressed and in this way to redefine assumptions and boundaries of meanings that in turn allow for transformations in ways of thinking and doing to be realized. Wiek et al, with their Phoenix case in the US show how an urban sustainability transition experiment in a public urban space took place and unfolded, explicating the way interventions can inflict sustainability in practice. Despite the fact that not all the experiments in the Phoenix lab were completed, the case shows the effort and operational design needed to start a process of experimentation – an insightful analysis of the 'soft part' of experimentation: setting up the process and create a new narrative explanation of the desired transformative intervention. Wiek et al., Späth and Ortnerzeder and Caprotti and Hammer posit experimenting as a way to intervene and contribute to urban transitions in the making. They all look and posit cities as the places to learn from, and realize sustainability transitions.

Third, *cities are homes to intermediaries*. Hodson and Marvin (2010: 482–483; also, 2009) pay ample attention to the role of intermediaries in processes of visioning and 'doing' transition. In relation terms, they may mediate (and thus help connect) between production and consumption, between different actors (from different domains, and between actors from domain and from urban arrangements) – and, we add, last but not least between practices and (changing) regimes, so as to make dynamics at these different levels productive interact with each other (Grin et al., 2010: 265–266, 279–284). Binz and Truffer identify not only that local actors are active intermediaries of new innovation systems but also conceptualise that this geographical embedding of external knowledge and practice happens via the mechanism of anchoring. As such, the success of the establishment of a new technological system relies on the institutional work on the city ground that active intermediaries realize. In short they argue and show in the case study that active local intermediaries catalyse build-up processes for new local niches to become stabilized, accepted and, in this way, embedded socially and institutionally.

Wolfram also points that intermediaries in Seoul's program on social innovation play an important role and appear to diversify and multiply over time mimicking the multiplying number of urban grassroots. In Seoul different forms of intermediaries coexist and coevolve, taking up roles of knowledge aggregation, coordination and capacity building. As Wolfram also states, "Urban grassroots initiatives may in principle exert pressures on multiple systems of provision (e.g., 'roof gardens': energy, water, construction, green infrastructure, food), but their integrated approach is at odds with the differentiated institutional logic of the regimes concerned. This requires distinct forms of intermediation that are able to connect individual initiatives with various niche formation processes, and to link between actors of different regimes for translating integrated niche innovations." Swilling et al. present the vital role of intermediaries – or as they call them 'mediators'– in connecting visions and solutions to urban practice and policy across different domains. They highlight the importance of knowledge transfer, sharing of meanings and translation of meanings that the intermediaries are doing within the city as well as across city and national government. They remain reflective and criticize the ways that lack of intermediation as a process of transfer can inhibit successful implementation or take-up of sustainable solutions that can further catalyse sustainability transitions in cities.

Fourth, *social innovation and transformative civil society movements are richer and very diverse in cities*. Coming together with new hybrid organisations that take up intermediation between them and local governments, a new multileveled governance setting is created. Intermediaries together with urban grassroots create new institutional strata that have as a primary mission to put sustainability into everyday urban life and question existing symbols, meanings of places and roles. As such, these new institutional strata require new ways of experimenting, intervening and coordinating; a multi-valence and urban polycentric governance approach. Several chapters in the book implicitly address this point. Binz and Truffer demonstrate exactly this that actors at cities establish intermediating roles and processes by connecting situated innovation with out-of-the-city resources and developments. Wolfram addresses that urban grassroots and the coevolved intermediaries pose pressures to multiple regimes and across regimes due to the multiple services they put in place and multiple social relations that they reconfigure simultaneously.

Fifth, the ways urban sustainability transitions unfold *influence the diffusion of sustainability innovations* across single locations and single domain/ sectoral regimes. Swilling et al. point at the way cities can play a role in mediating for the uptake and diffusion of innovative solutions and visions that can influence transitions in the making. They specifically note that urban transitions can catalyse and leapfrog transformative change at global scale by showcasing what works and evidence gathered at city level. Kronenberg et al. also address collaborations between NGOs and city planners can allow for policy shifts and ecological modernization in cities that can move on across cities. Rohracher and Späth argue that urban sustainability transitions go "beyond the logics of regimes and niches". To conclude, it is important for examining and understanding urban sustainability transitions that one keep in mind that they develop as the result of the interactions and connections across scales (scalar networks) and across contexts (transnational processes of linking and transferring of experience and knowledge).

Sixth, there is explicitly *the link between cities and transnational exchanges and connections that can influence sustainability transitions at global scale*. Cities via their networks (like C40, ICLEI, Covenant of Mayors and Rockefeller's 100 Resilient Cities network) create channels for exchange of knowledge and experience, for quick diffusion of new ideas and new concepts that can benefit urban living, quality of life and livability conditions in cities. At the same time, cities allow for a fast testing on new environmental technologies, a breeding ground for social and governance innovations and lessons on how material flows can become more efficient, environmental responsible and circular. As such, they can assist as well as catalyse the connections for broadening and enriching transnational connections critical for scaling sustainability transitions.

Urban Transition Dynamics

The cases contained in this book illustrate the generative role that cities play as relational spaces in the formation of visions, the opening up of spaces of connection and the nurturing of diverse intermediary actors that can play a key role in the transition. Yet, this should not lead us to think that a snapshot of the diverse processes shaping the city at one given time will be sufficient to understand transitions to sustainability. Rather, transitions to sustainability are predicated on the advancement of pathways. In the urban context, looking at urban pathways to sustainability will entail examining the myriad of alternatives that may materialize in urban futures, as much as the areas of opportunities that are foreclosed by previous decisions (Rydin et al., 2012). This is not only a call to understand diversity and complexity in urban transformations. It is also an attempt to bring forward the urban transition dynamics, following the lessons of previous transition scholars.

From this first exploration of the distinct dynamics of urban sustainability transitions we propose a list of conceptual tenets that capture the characteristics of urban sustainability transition dynamics:

1 Urban sustainability issues allow for multiple meanings and practices to conflate and manifest in places that when addressed require integrative approaches to governance and planning beyond sectoral boundaries. As such, it resonates to relate urban services across sectoral systems and examine urban sustainability transitions across sectors and issues rather than as sector-based processes.

2 Urban sustainability transitions involve active local actors who seek solutions outside their city and effectively create connections and foster networks to translate and embed these new sustainable solutions to city's policy, practice and infrastructure.

3 Urban sustainability transitions are multi-scale processes. Cities can mediate between the local and national levels of governance to modernize and/or shift policy agendas in ways that enable sustainability transitions to occur across levels.

4 Local policy actions and new governance processes directly affect the conditions enabling transfer of knowledge and the opening up to new sustainable innovations (governance, technological and social innovations) that play an important role in initiating urban sustainability transitions.

5 Drivers of persistence for sustainability transitions in cities can be systemic as well as contextual and need to be considered when developing new narratives and innovative solutions for accelerating transitions.

6 Histories of and relations between urban agents of change are place-based determinants of the way sustainability transitions unfold. Urban agents of change have the ability to connect seemingly unconnected solutions and developments and mediate, accelerate and instigate transitions.

7 Drawing conclusions from historical and contemporary trends allows to properly addressing emerging social issues that can link up to sustainability transitions.

8 Governance of urban sustainability transitions has to consider conflict, contradiction and confluence between promising solutions and sustainability challenges in cities along with opportunities and visions.

9 Governance for urban sustainability transitions are multi-actor processes of relations, connectivity and proximity. Interfaces (such as transition management arenas and transition experiments) that enable and

foster interactions and connections between the multiple urban agents of transitions are essential for giving meaning and creating agendas to further and facilitate sustainability transitions in cities.

10   Governance for sustainability transitions is inherently experimental and aims at opening up governance space for new roles of urban actors, testing and localizing innovation as well as creating new social relations and agency configurations that will enable sustainability transitions to unfold.

References

Agnew, J. and Corbridge, S. (1995). *Mastering Space: Hegemony, territory and international political economy*. London: Routledge.

Bulkeley, H.A., Castán Broto, V. and Edwards, G.A. (2014). *An Urban Politics of Climate Change: Experimentation and the governing of socio-technical transitions*. London: Routledge.

Brenner, N. (2004). *New State Spaces: Urban governance and the rescaling of statehood*. New York: Oxford University Press.

Coenen, L., Benneworth, P. and Truffer, B. (2012). Toward a spatial perspective on sustainability transitions, *Research Policy* 41(6): 968–979.

de Haan, J. and Rotmans, J. (2012). Patterns in transitions: Understanding complex chains of change, *Technological Forecasting & Social Change*, 78, 90–102.

Droege, P. (2011). *Urban Energy Transition: From fossil fuels to renewable power*. Oxford, Amsterdam: Elsevier.

Frantzeskaki, N., Grin, J. and Thissen, W., (2016). Drifting between transitions: The case of the Greek environmental transition in relation to the river Acheloos Diversion project, *Technological Forecasting and Social Change*, 275–286, DOI information: 10.1016/j.techfore.2015.09.007

Frantzeskaki, N., Wittmayer, J. and Loorbach, D., (2014). The role of partnerships in 'realizing' urban sustainability in Rotterdam's City Ports Area, the Netherlands, *Journal of Cleaner Production*, 65, 406–417. (http://dx.doi.org/10.1016/j.jclepro.2013.09.023)

Grin, J. (2008). The multi-level perspective and the design of system innovations, in: J.C.J.M. van den Bergh and F. Bruinsma (eds. in association with R. Vreeker and A. Idenburg), *Managing the Transition to Renewable Energy: Theory and macro-regional practice* (pp. 47–80). Cheltenham, UK: Edward Elgar Publishing.

Grin, J., Rotmans, J. and Schot, J.W. (2010). *Transitions to sustainable development: new directions in the study of long term transformative change*. London: Routledge.

Hodson, M. and Marvin, S. (2009). Cities mediating technological transitions: understanding visions, intermediation and consequences, *Technology Analysis & Strategic Management*, 21:4, 515–534.

Hodson, M. and Marvin, S. (2010). Can cities shape socio-technical transitions and how would we know if they were?, *Research Policy* 39 (4), 477–485.

Hoffmann, M. (2013). Climate Change. In R. Wilkinson and T. Weiss (Eds.) *International Organization and Global Governance*. London, Routledge.

Monstadt, J. (2009). Conceptualizing the political ecology of urban infrastructures: insights from technology and urban studies. *Environment and Planning A* 41: 1924.

Rohracher, H. and Späth, P. (2014). The interplay of urban energy policy and socio-technical transitions: The eco-cities of Graz and Freiburg in retrospect, *Urban Studies*, 51(7), 1415–1431.

Rotmans, J., Kemp, R., and van Asselt, M. (2001). More evolution than revolution: transition management in public policy. *Foresight, 3*(1), 15-31.

Rydin, Y., Turcu, C., Chmutina, K., et al. (2012). Urban energy initiatives: the implications of new urban energy pathways for the UK. *Network Industries Quarterly* 14: 20–23.

Smith, A. and Raven, R. (2012). What is protective space? Reconsidering niches in transitions to sustainability, *Research Policy* 41(6): 1025–1036.

Wolfram, M. and Frantzeskaki, N. (2016). Cities and systemic change for sustainability: Prevailing epistemologies and an emerging research agenda, *Sustainability*, 8, DOI: 10.3390.

Index

For Product Safety Concerns and Information please contact our EU
representative GPSR@taylorandfrancis.com
Taylor & Francis Verlag GmbH, Kaufingerstraße 24, 80331 München, Germany